THE FREEZER COOKBOOK

THE *Freezer* COOKBOOK

Second Edition

****

Charlotte Erickson

CHILTON BOOK COMPANY

Radnor, Pennsylvania

Copyright © 1968, 1978 by Charlotte Erickson
Second Edition   All Rights Reserved
Published in Radnor, Pa., by Chilton Book Company
and simultaneously in Don Mills, Ontario, Canada,
by Thomas Nelson & Sons, Ltd.
Manufactured in the United States of America

Library of Congress Cataloging in Publication Data
Erickson, Charlotte Helen Zimmer.
   The freezer cookbook.
   Includes index.
   1. Cookery (Frozen foods)   I. Title.
TX828.E73   1978   641.5   77-15280
ISBN 0-8019-6665-5
ISBN 0-8019-6666-3 pbk.

567890   76543210

To my husband, Howard, my mother, Helen Zimmer, and my sons, Ken, Russ, and Dan, without whose help and understanding this book could never have been finished. I truly appreciate and value their comments and opinions regarding all the recipes and foods they've sampled.

In revising and updating this edition, we have taken into consideration new equipment often found in the modern kitchen. Symbols are used only to draw your attention to recipes for which you can utilize these time and energy-saving appliances. Be sure to check manufacturer's directions for specific instructions.

MICROWAVE OVEN

This symbol indicates that the recipe can be adapted to your microwave oven. The symbol appears alongside the recipe instructions where it would be used. Units vary, so refer to your manufacturer's instructions.

FOOD PROCESSOR

When you see this symbol, your food processor can be used to grate, shred, chop, grind, or perform other time-consuming operations.

SLOW COOKER

This symbol indicates that a recipe is easily adapted for a slow cooker. See your manufacturer's instructions for specifics.

Contents

****

Preface to the Second Edition

✳✳✳✳✳✳✳✳✳✳✳✳✳✳✳✳✳✳✳✳✳✳✳✳✳

The Freezer Cookbook has always emphasized saving time in the kitchen, so this newly revised edition has added many new timesaving features and ideas, along with energy-saving tips. The home freezer has been heralded as the great liberator, now joining ranks with the food processor, the slow cooker, and the microwave oven. These new appliances are revolutionizing our kitchens, changing our methods of cooking, the time we spend, and the type of recipes we select. This is why we indicated on our recipes which appliance will be useful in its preparation; you can tell at a glance by looking at the symbols in the margin. This doesn't mean you have to have these appliances to use these recipes, it'll just be quicker if you do. Dishes that were an afternoon project to prepare in quantity now can be assembled in a fraction of the time it formerly took.

Anyone having a freezer should seriously consider purchasing a microwave oven. These appliances complement each other perfectly. Fruits and vegetables from your freezer can be ready in a wink. Forgetting to take something out of the freezer in the morning or the night before is no longer a problem when you have this marvelous appliance. Those of you who already have microwave ovens will be happy to know that we have included complete instructions on how to blanch vegetables in your microwave oven. This puts an end to steamy kitchens and large pans of boiling water.

In recent years, much emphasis has been put on nutrition and we've all learned about fiber and whole-grain cereals, the benefits of fresh fruits and vegetables, about cholesterol and cutting down on fats in our diet.

Remember. frozen fruits and vegetables are almost identical in nutrition and calories to fresh fruits and vegetables. No additives nor preservatives are needed. Serve them often and in a variety of ways: try our many new and tempting recipes.

All these ideas have been incorporated in our recipes: polyunsaturated margarine is substituted for butter, fats reduced, unbleached flour can be used in all recipes, and I have successfully reduced the amount of sugar in many of the cake, cookie, and dessert recipes. We also give suggestions for the calorie watcher, including substituting yogurt for sour cream.

Preface to the First Edition

****

This book deals primarily with the time-saving aspects, rather than the economics, of owning and using a freezer. It would appear that this factor has been grossly overlooked or neglected so far.

With a little practice you'll spend less and less time preparing meals, yet your menus will be more diversified and interesting. This will allow more time for experimenting and trying new dishes. The recipes in this book are by no means all-inclusive, although they have all been tested, are easy to prepare and very tasty; they are here simply to guide you. Be sure to add your own favorites. Try new dishes on your own and add them to your file.

A kitchen should be run as efficiently, timewise, as a production line in a factory. To put these ideas into practice takes deliberate effort and thought, particularly at first. In a few weeks these efforts will pay off handsomely with leisure hours, and will automatically make for an effortless way of life. For example, the next time you are planning to cook spaghetti, you will automatically purchase 6 pounds of hamburger, make a triple recipe, serve your dinner, and freeze the remainder in dinner-sized quantities for time-free meals in the weeks to come. Just remember, it takes the same amount of time to clean up the kitchen when you are preparing a single recipe as when you are preparing a double or triple batch.

Acknowledgments

✳✳✳✳✳✳✳✳✳✳✳✳✳✳✳✳✳✳✳✳✳✳✳✳✳✳

To all the people, too numerous to mention, who so generously gave of their time and recipes. My special thanks to Gerry Fleer, who worked untiringly in typing the manuscript, advising and helping in many ways; to Marie Sievert, without whose encouragement this book would never have been started. The following companies and institutions shared their technical knowledge about freezing and other matters; their help was invaluable:

University of Illinois School of Agriculture
United States Department of Agriculture
Poultry and Egg National Board
University of Illinois Homemakers Service
National Livestock and Meat Board
National Dairy Council

THE FREEZER COOKBOOK

Introduction

✳✳✳✳✳✳✳✳✳✳✳✳✳✳✳✳✳✳✳✳✳✳✳✳✳✳

This book was written expressly for the busy urban and suburban homemaker, mother, and career woman who wants to organize more effectively the time she spends in the kitchen. By using the principles advocated in this book, you may save many hours each week, even though you're serving more delectable fare. It will take a little practice to buy automatically in large quantities and plan several meals at a time. You'll be glad you did, however, when, at some later date, things get a bit hectic and all you have to do is warm up a prepared meal from your freezer.

Your freezer is the result of modern man's effort to preserve food in its natural state without changing its texture, flavor, and color. Research has proven that freezing retains vitamins and minerals better than any other method of food preservation. The nutritive values of frozen foods are equal to those of fresh foods.

A freezer can be many things: an unpaid cook several nights a week; a treasure chest when unexpected guests arrive; a catering service when you are entertaining; a bartender's assistant when having a large party (mountains of ice cubes, frosted glasses, frozen daiquiris, bacardis, et cetera, can be plucked out of the freezer with the flick of a hand).

The most dramatic liberation of modern woman has taken place in the kitchen, where ancient drudgeries are now being consigned to modern appliances. Perhaps the most liberating of all is the freezer; once considered only a cold-storage bin, we now know it is capable of suspending food at almost any stage of preparation. However, only a small percentage of women who have this marvelous appliance, the freezer, use it to its fullest advantage. Some freezer owners have a very negative attitude about their freezers, and I should like very much to change this. I have heard it said, and I'm sure you have too, that Mrs. What's-Her-Name just doesn't like meat that has been frozen. I dare say that in a controlled test she couldn't tell the difference; that is, if the meat were properly packaged and frozen at zero degrees Fahrenheit or lower and defrosted and prepared in the proper manner. The same may be said for frosted cakes, casseroles, and many other items. After close questioning you'll find that either the wrong frosting was used or the cake wasn't wrapped properly. I can't stress this strongly enough, since improper wrapping is the main cause of food failure in freezing.

In this book I shall try to help everyone use a freezer properly and thereby gain more time for other interests. I should like to encourage you to use some of this extra time in trying new recipes and experimenting on your own, which is really creative cooking. I feel sure that even those who consider everyday cooking sheer drudgery will enjoy the creative aspect of cooking.

You will find after trying hundreds of main-dish recipes, as I have done, that most of them are actually variations of some old standby. In this book there are many old standbys used in our home. However, don't be afraid to add something here and make a change there.

Take chili con carne, for example. Some people like it really soupy; others like it meaty; some never serve it without adding macaroni (a dish known as chili-mac). I even know of one family that always adds noodles to it! So always adapt a recipe to the taste of your particular family. Some ethnic groups are very partial to certain spices and herbs. Don't hesitate to add these even if the recipe doesn't call for them.

CAUTION: It's a good idea when you are using a new recipe to try only one batch and taste it before making any changes.

Cooking can be a creative outlet for those who enjoy experimenting. I'm afraid most authorities in the field give the average cook a feeling that there are many mysteries involved, and that creative cooking is best left to the professionals. Nothing could be farther from the truth, and this is well illustrated by the many amateurs who win various cooking contests sponsored throughout the country every year.

Be creative; don't be afraid to experiment. When reading recipes in newspapers and magazines, check the ingredients of even a familiar recipe. Perhaps it has a new twist or new ingredient that you can try the next time you make your own version. You'll be amazed at some of the wonderful and exciting taste treats that are in store for you and your family. And what about an occasional flop? They usually aren't *that* bad! I tell my family that they share in my successes and they can suffer through my failures!

Actually, owning a freezer is as vital for the person living alone as it is for those with large families. Most people seem to think a freezer is only for those with large families or people living on a farm who have a lot of produce to freeze. This simply isn't true; anyone who has ever tried cooking for one or two people knows the problems involved. If you have a taste for baked ham, for example, you face the dilemma of eating ham for a week or not having it at all. A large family doesn't have this problem; neither does the person with a freezer. Have the butcher cut a steak from either the butt or shank end of a ham, wrap it, and freeze it for future broiling. After the first meal of baked ham, you can slice some of the meat for sandwiches, make a few small ham and scalloped potato casseroles, some delicious ham and potato soup from the bone, and so on. The possibilities are unlimited. The same may be said of many cuts of meat and poultry, especially turkey, and also pastries or even vegetable casseroles.

The recipes in this book are given in several different quantities so that they're adaptable to households of varying sizes. The person living alone will find the single quantities more suitable, while those with large families and larger freezers will find the multiple quantities more to their liking. However, if you have a very large family, you may want to double even the multiple quantities. Because space is limited, it isn't possible for one book to be all-inclusive; each reader must determine how these recipes can be used best. It should be a very simple matter, however, for any cook to increase any given recipe to a quantity suitable for her family's needs. When multiplying any recipe, it is best to take a minute first and write down the exact quantity of each ingredient (write on the recipe itself if there is sufficient space) to avoid error. A very common cause of failure in large quantity recipes is that somewhere along the line the cook was distracted and didn't add the right proportions of ingredients. This can easily be avoided by just jotting them down.

Last-minute entertaining and unexpected guests can now be welcomed graciously. You can be relaxed, knowing that your freezer will see you through with flying colors. Week-long visits from friends and relatives can now be enjoyed with never an hour spent in the kitchen. Just remember that everything that comes out of the freezer has to be put into it first. So why not start now, and plan to make a double or triple recipe the next meal you cook or the next time you bake?

Although the main theme of this book is saving time, let's talk briefly about saving a little money, too. For the most part, quick cooking is the most expensive type of cooking. By this I mean that store-frozen bakery goods cost a lot more than homemade goodies. While steaks and roasts are easier to prepare than spaghetti, needless to say, they're quite a bit more expensive. The same can also be said of most prepared frozen foods. I don't mean to downgrade these items; they're indispensable, but they *are* more expensive. By having all these prepared foods in your freezer, you will also cut the cost of your meals considerably, which is nothing to ignore these days, when the cost of living index is rising continuously. With a well-stocked freezer you'll find less and less need to run to the delicatessen for last-minute meals and will thereby save time, not to mention gas!

When entertaining or planning a large party, you can spread the cost over several weeks by shopping and preparing the food as you go along. You also can take advantage of special sales, day-old bread, etcetera.

ARRANGING YOUR KITCHEN

You've probably heard some man say, "If I ran my office (plant or factory) the way you run your house, I'd be out of business." We won't admit it, but it's undoubtedly true. Actually, a few simple changes can make the difference of an hour a week or more in time saved—and who wants to spend any more time in the kitchen than necessary? The time indicated for the various recipes should give you some idea whether or not your efficiency is up to par. These timings were made in the actual preparation of the recipe, with the cook working in a relaxed manner and with the normal amount of interruptions and distractions. However, I should like to remind you that most recipes will take a bit longer the first time they're prepared; this is only to be expected.

I think the main reason we don't strive for efficiency the way we should is because it's difficult to see the improvement. In other words, you don't simply end the week with nothing to do for an hour because you've saved an hour during the week. However, if you save only 3 minutes in the preparation of each meal, you'll be saving an hour a week.

Just remember, all our modern appliances will hinder rather than help if they're not placed properly and used effectively. This section will provide basic ideas for the most efficient setup.

The Telephone

If you're the kind of person who does a lot of socializing on the telephone, have your phone installed in the kitchen with the longest extension cord you can get. For an investment of a few dollars, buy a phone shoulder rest, the kind used in offices. They're available at most stationery stores. Now you're all set! When the phone rings, you can talk as you work, and have both hands free. The old saying that you can't do two things at once and do them well simply isn't true. You can peel potatoes and chop vegetables just as effectively while you are talking on the phone as you can when your entire attention is given to the job. Believe me, your family will never know the difference at dinner time.

Baking Supplies

If you're a baker, have all your baking supplies (items frequently used, such as sugar, flour, salt, vanilla, baking powder, baking soda) near your mixer. You'll be amazed at how quickly things go together when your supplies are handy. I keep my flour and sugar in a divided drawer made especially for these two items. They're large enough so that I can sift flour and measure sugar right in the container, eliminating a lot of spills and mess. In containers like these you can store your sifter, dry measuring cups, and scoops, and thus make it unnecessary to wash them every time they're used. Another idea is to keep all these items in a paper bag to eliminate flour dust in your cupboards. I have seen women keep their sugar and flour in narrow-necked apothecary jars. Although these are very decorative on the kitchen counter, I can't imagine anyone using them efficiently.

Electric Mixer Storage

It seems to me that a lot of women don't use their electric mixers as often as they might simply because they're stored way in the back of some bottom cupboard. I have mine in a cabinet made especially for the mixer. It swings out just like a typewriter shelf in an office desk. With the flick of one hand my mixer is ready and waiting, and it's used frequently, sometimes several times a day. Another solution is to keep the mixer on the kitchen countertop. Although this may give your kitchen a cluttered look, who cares as long as the mixer is convenient and used more frequently?

When we lived in a small apartment, with very limited kitchen space, I kept my mixer and all the rest of my electrical appliances on one of those moving carts especially designed for this purpose. The cart had three shelves and the mixer was kept on the top one, with the toaster and other appliances relegated to the lower shelves. Because the cart was mobile, it could be moved to any convenient location in just a few seconds, and then moved out of the way again.

I have given these examples simply as illustrations. Each kitchen presents its own challenge and problems. Think about your own kitchen arrangement and try to come up with a solution that will satisfy you. Be objective and willing to make changes.

Freezer Placement

Ideally, a freezer should be in the kitchen, where it's handy and convenient at all times. Those of us who have small kitchens and large freezers find this impossible. The next best thing is a separate freezing compartment in the refrigerator where everyday items may be kept. This is ideal for storing frozen juices, a small quantity of ice cream, frozen herbs, ice cubes, some rolls and bread, and a variety of frozen vegetables ordinarily used in everyday meal planning. Obviously, having such things handy will save many steps to the basement, garage, or wherever your larger freezer is located. Actually, the second most convenient spot for a freezer would be in your garage. When grocery shopping, help your clerk pack all your items for this freezer in separate bags. Unload these grocery items directly from your car into the freezer.

Never place a freezer near a stove, heater, register, or sunny window, since this will greatly interfere with the efficiency of the freezing unit.

For the small family or household many fine compact units are available—even under-the-counter freezers. These are particularly convenient in apartments where space is at a premium. They will usually fit into the little pantries, nooks, and so on, that apartment kitchens often provide.

A good guide in selecting a freezer is to allow 4 to 6 cubic feet of storage space per person in a household, depending on the use that the freezer will receive. However, for a person living alone, I feel that the minimum storage space should be 5 cubic feet.

Have a table or counter space adjacent to your freezer. It needn't be large; 2 square feet is usually sufficient. You'll find that you need this space when loading the freezer or removing articles from it.

Fresh Fruit and Vegetable Storage

I'm referring here to those fruits and vegetables not normally kept in the refrigerator. Store them near the sink (although preferably not *under* the sink, since the heat from hot-water pipes is not conducive to good storing practice) where you will wash, peel, and prepare them. The storage place should be cool, so be careful to avoid a spot near a heat register. Air circulation is also important to retard unwanted changes in the produce, such as potatoes sprouting.

Dishes and Flatware

Dishes, silverware, and serving pieces should be stored somewhere between the dishwasher (or sink) and the table, for very obvious reasons. The smaller the triangle between these three points, the better. The exception is when you have a portable dishwasher that can be moved readily. In this case, the dishes and silverware should be stored as close to the table as possible, rather than near the sink.

Pots, Pans, and Seasonings

Most people store their pots and pans near the stove. This is an obvious timesaver. However, cooking utensils, such as wooden spoons, wire whisks, colanders, are often scattered all over the kitchen. These too should be stored in an orderly fashion near the stove.

Instant soups, coffee, tea, and cocoa should also be in a nearby cabinet. Seasonings and condiments should be in a cabinet near the stove. Measuring cups and spoons, as well as sharp knives and cutting board, should be located somewhere between the stove and the sink. Potholders and hotplates should also be next to or near the stove.

Strainers, colanders, and what have you should be kept near the sink. If you do not have small childern you may wish to store your cleanser, detergent, and other cleaning supplies under the sink; otherwise, a shelf above the sink would be safer. Conveniences such as paper towels, plastic bags, and aluminum wrap should be stored near the sink.

Countertops are premium space in your kitchen. Never give permanent space to a small appliance that won't be used frequently. Keep your toaster near where your bread is stored, whether it is in the refrigerator, breadbox, or cabinet. Ideally, it should be close to the eating area. Electric canopeners are handy near the sink, which allows you to wash the tops of your cans before opening and to rinse the empty cans before disposal.

In today's supermarkets there's such a vast selection of herbs, spices, seasonings, and condiments that finding a place to store them is rapidly becoming a problem. A spice cabinet mounted on the wall, just under the top kitchen cabinets near the stove, is quite handy. I prefer that the spices be placed either to the right or left of the stove, rather than just above it, since they're less apt to be grease-spattered; your spices will keep better away from the heat of the stove. Another way to store all those little bottles and boxes conveniently is to mount a special holder for them (available at most department stores) on the inside of your cabinet doors. These holders are very nice, since they're out of sight and enclosed in your cabinet, which keeps them cleaner. However, there is one disadvantage: when your shelves get too full, you may not be able to close the doors. I speak from experience!

Cookbooks and Recipes

Don't store your cookbooks on a bookshelf in the living room or den. If you don't now have room in your kitchen, a simple shelf can be put up over the kitchen counter, under the top cabinets, with very little effort. This is the logical place for books intended for handy reference. Never keep them in a drawer, stacked one on top of another like so many sweaters. Incidentally, if you were trained from childhood that it's practically sacrilegious to write in any book, try to overcome this feeling. A good cookbook really isn't broken in until it's fairly well filled with your own notations. Any time you try a new recipe write some little note about it. Indicate any changes you made or would like to make the next time. If you didn't care for the recipe, note that too. (I hope there won't be many notations like that in this book!)

While we're on the subject of cookbooks, let's consider loose recipes that you've clipped from newspapers or magazines, or ones you've collected from friends. What do you do with them? If you're an avid clipper and saver, as many of us are, this can become quite a problem. After having tried many different systems, including the hunt-and-find method, I now use one that seems most effective, although it's by no means an answer to your every prayer.

As I clip the recipes, I file them in folders with captions: "cakes," "cookies," "vegetables," and so on. Then I have one folder marked "recipes to try soon." Only after a recipe has been approved by the family is it put in the "to type" or write-up folder. This avoids wasting time writing up a recipe that you won't like. Also, after you've finished tasting a new recipe, you'll find it very helpful to write a brief notation about your reaction to it and also any changes you might like to make the next time. Type or write your recipe on a 4 x 6-inch card. (The smaller file cards are inadequate for any but the most simple recipes.) File these cards in a metal file box, made especially for this purpose. You'll find them at every stationer's and at most variety stores. If you're going to use a recipe in larger quantities, write the ingredients and new proportions on a separate card. This is far more simple and foolproof than trying to figure it out while you're cooking.

From time to time go through your folders and weed out recipes that are no longer of interest or those that are very similar to ones you already have. Often there may be just an idea you like. Add it to the card already in your file. Using this method, you should be able to find almost any recipe you want quickly. Recipes that you've collected from a friend (assuming you've tasted them at her home or elsewhere) can, of course, be typed and filed without further testing.

EQUIPPING YOUR KITCHEN

Once your kitchen is conveniently arranged, the next step is to plan the proper equipment. A cabinetmaker cannot build a beautiful cabinet efficiently without the proper tools. Neither can a cook operate efficiently without the proper equipment. Just as no two craftsmen would probably agree on buying identical tools, every cook, I'm sure, has a different idea about what equipment is really essential. I shall try to list some of the things that I find helpful, as well as those that I find indispensable. You'll have to decide for yourself which utensils to add to your own kitchen.

Before you start to add any equipment, go over the accumulation of things already on hand. I think it's much easier to add to the equipment you already have than it is to get rid of old, never-used items. In fact, tossing out old take-up-space utensils that haven't been used in years can be a traumatic experience! Force yourself! Be firm! At least put those seldom-used things in a carton and pack them away in the basement or attic. This is the first step. Then, if you find you don't use any of them for another year or two, it will be much easier to take the final steps when the church or school has its annual rummage sale.

Dishwasher

Anyone cooking for three or more people should put a dishwasher at the head of the list of things to acquire. With the vast array of models now available—and there will be more to come—only those women with the tiniest of kitchens would have trouble finding a small niche for this most useful appliance. You're really not up on things if you still have the notion that dishes have to be rinsed almost clean before putting them into the dishwasher, that dishwashers are more trouble than washing by hand, and so on. I could easily write several paragraphs on the virtues of having a dishwasher and how different life has been since we got ours. Instead, I shall simply say that if I had it to do over again, I would have bought a portable dishwasher back in our apartment days and that, unless you absolutely adore washing and drying dishes, this marvelous appliance is indispensable.

Microwave Oven

The microwave oven has been around for a long time but is just now coming into its own. Because of increased demand, prices have come down. They are still by no means cheap but, considering the convenience, they are a fantastic asset for every cook. If you don't already have one, be sure to put this on your "want list." Microwave oven cooking lends itself perfectly to defrosting and heating frozen foods. Not all models have a defrost cycle on them, and it is certainly worthwhile to pay a bit more and have this on your microwave unit. Not only does the microwave oven cook and defrost frozen foods quicker than a conventional stove or oven, but it also uses considerably less energy.

All microwave ovens come with a book of instructions; read yours carefully from cover to cover. One of the reasons that many people don't use their microwave ovens frequently is they haven't familiarized themselves with techniques of using the unit properly. Often you will find courses offered in evening adult-education classes. Generally speaking, they are most worthwhile and I suggest that anyone who has a microwave unit attend such classes if they are available.

You will note that we indicate on our recipes where the microwave unit is applicable; however, this is a book about freezing and our space is limited. Please check your microwave instruction book for information on timing and other procedures.

Some of the advantages of microwave cooking are: potatoes may be baked in five minutes; leftovers stay moist and may be reheated right on the serving plate. Dish washing is cut down considerably, as food can be cooked right in its serving dish. Defrosting foods is never a problem. Puddings, custards, and gravies cook smooth and creamy in the microwave. You never have to worry about anything sticking to the bottom of the pan. You cannot burn anything in a microwave unit (although you can overcook it). These are just some of the advantages you'll find in using your microwave unit.

Blender

Remember to store everything in as convenient a place as possible or as near to where you'll be using it as you can. A blender kept down in a bottom cabinet won't be used so often as one that is out on the kitchen counter. What's that? You don't have a blender? Be sure to get your husband one for his birthday or for Christmas, whichever comes first. Never, never put a blender on *your* list. This is about the only item in the kitchen that the man of the house enjoys using for mixing malts, beverages, and cocktails. It may belong to him, but I'm sure he won't object to your giving it a good workout when you need it. This versatile little piece of machinery is one of the greatest timesavers for otherwise menial, time-consuming jobs. Be sure to read the manual. Try some of the recipes included with your new appliance and familiarize yourself with it in every aspect. This is the only way that you will get the full use out of it.

Food Processor

A relatively new kitchen appliance, the food processor is probably the greatest time-saver you can have. If I had to eliminate all my appliances excepting one (other than my dishwasher), the food processor is the one I would choose to keep.

The Cuisinart was the first such machine to have gained acceptance in the United States. It actually is a scaled-down version of a much larger food processor which has been used in the kitchens of French and other European restaurants for years.

As this book goes to press, I still feel the Cuisinart is the best machine available; however, several large American appliance manufacturers have recently come out with new models. Because this is not an inexpensive item to buy, I would recommend that you check with *Consumer's Guide*, *Consumer's Buying Guide*, or *Consumers' Research* at your local library, and see how they rate the various machines. Remember, you generally get what you pay for, and a $50 machine normally will not work as well as one costing over $200.

It is the type of machine that you want to have out on your counter so that you can use it several times a day. Actually, the food processor makes cooking so much more fun. Potato pancakes used to be a once-a-year treat (it would take that long for my knuckles to heal after grating all those potatoes). This dish can now be put together in a few seconds. A food processor will shred cabbage and cheeses; chop and/or slice vegetables for soups, stews, and casseroles; knead a piecrust in 30 second; puree fruit for jam; grind peanuts into fresh peanut butter; grate bread crumbs, cracker crumbs, and cookie crumbs; grind raw meat for steak tartare; whip up patés for spreads for hors d'oeuvres. Cheese balls are a snap, and you won't mind grating fresh horseradish, either.

Electric Mixer

A stationary *electric mixer* should be high on your list of things for your kitchen if you do a lot of baking. Portables are handy for some jobs, but they simply don't take the place of a regular mixer. If you have a food processor, perhaps a portable now is all that you need if you do only a very minimum amount of baking. While the Food Processor will do many things, it will not whip egg whites or cream butter and shortening until it's light and fluffy, as required in some recipes. You can mix yeast dough, but only in very small portions.

The stainless-steel electric mixers are slightly more expensive, but worth every additional cent. You'll never have to worry about chipping paint, and don't overlook the little-known fact that the stainless-steel bowls that come with these mixers have a much larger capacity than the glass bowls. The stainless-steel bowls of some models hold as much as 1 quart more than their glass counterparts. This makes an enormous difference when you are mixing large quantities of any recipe.

If you're thinking of buying a new mixer, it might be well to consider the larger, more expensive models that come with a bread hook. Kitchen Aide makes several models of this type, as do some of the other manufacturers. Making yeast dough is a dream with one of these hooks. It isn't necessary to knead your dough at all, and your mixing time is cut in half. Even if you've never done so before, you'll be tempted by owning one of these mixers to make breads and coffee cakes on a regular basis.

Broiler Toaster

Until our toaster suddenly "died" this past year, I never gave this handy appliance too much thought. Now that I have one, I'm sorry that our toaster didn't meet its ill fate years ago. Not only does this unit do what an ordinary toaster does, but it has the advantage of making toasted cheese sandwiches in an instant. You don't have to worry that the bagels are going to get stuck in the middle or that the thin-sliced rye is going to fall through the coils. Perfect for toasting almonds and sesame seeds without heating up your whole oven. It is also perfect for one or two lamb chops or heating a TV dinner. A broiler toaster would make a particularly perfect gift for anyone living alone.

OVENWARE. Invest in cookware that goes from freezer to oven and then to the table. A number of these in various sizes are available, and they're not very expensive. Incidentally, all Pyrex Ware, regardless of vintage, is freezer-to-oven-proof. So don't hesitate to use any of your Pyrex dishes for freezing—no need to thaw, just put the dish in a *preheated* oven and bake according to directions in recipe. *Do not put Pyrex Ware in a cold oven and then heat.* When food has burned or cooked onto glass or Pyrex Ware, soak in soda water.

Avoid harsh scouring powder or steel wool. Use of abrasives will break the surface tension and the glass will be more subject to breakage.

POT AND PANS. For quantity cooking, acquire proper-sized pots and pans. Be sure to start with a vessel of the right size; nothing is more disheartening than to have to change from one size to a larger one as the recipe is progressing. Not only is it messy and time-consuming, but it leaves the dishwasher with twice the work.

When buying kitchen equipment, look for quality and ease of cleaning. Extremely large enamelware pots and aluminum and stainless steel kettles of good quality are available for a fraction of their original cost at resale shops and rummage sales. One of these very large containers is indispensable for quantity cooking and mixing if you're cooking for an average-sized family or larger.

Here are some interesting facts, published by the University of Illinois College of Agriculture in a leaflet entitled "Materials for Your Pots and Pans": "Shiny, bright surfaces produce light-brown crusts; darkened surfaces and glass produce browner crusts. Foods baked in heavy pans (glass, pottery, cast metals, et cetera) will have thicker crusts than those baked in lighter-weight wares." So, when you're buying utensils, select the type that will best suit your needs.

The most enlightening remark in this little leaflet was, "Cooking utensils with a layer of copper on the bottom will absorb heat more readily if the bottom is left darkened than if it is kept polished." Now I can put my unpolished copper-bottomed pots away and still hold my head up!

Have enough muffin tins, cake pans, and cookie sheets on hand so that you can accommodate a large recipe. If storage space in the kitchen is a problem, perhaps you can find another place almost as convenient for these items.

Kitchen Gadgets and Utensils

MEASURING SPOONS AND CUPS. Keep on hand several sets of measuring spoons, the kind with a complete set on a ring. Having several sets saves washing them in the midst of a recipe, when you are measuring dry ingredients after having used the spoons for liquids.

An absolute "must" is a set of dry measuring cups. These cups come in different sizes, marked ¼ cup, ⅓ cup, ½ cup, and 1 cup. To measure an exact amount of sugar, say, you fill the proper cup and level it with a knife. These are more accurate and certainly much faster to use than the conventional measuring cups. A 2-cup size is more difficult to find, but worth the effort. When measuring 8 cups of flour, for instance, you're less likely to make an error in counting with the 2-cup size.

Besides a standard 1-cup liquid measuring cup, the larger 2-cup and 4-cup sizes are especially useful when you are making recipes in large quantities as well as heating and cooking in the microwave oven. These large measuring cups are also fine for pouring batter into muffin cups and pouring jelly into jars. They have dozens of other uses that you'll discover for yourself. Here, too, having several saves time spent in washing them in the midst of a recipe.

PEPPER MILLS. If you don't have a pepper mill, be sure to get one. A good pepper mill will last for years, and there's an incomparable difference in the flavor of fresh-ground pepper and preground pepper in cans or boxes. Once you start grinding your own pepper, chances are you'll never use preground pepper again.

WIRE WHISKS. No French cook would be caught without a wire whisk or whip, and this is easy to understand after you use one for a while. With just a few flicks of the wrist, all lumps disappear from your gravies and sauces as if by magic. They're excellent to use when you are folding two mixtures together. Here again, after you've used one, you'll wonder how you ever managed without it. The investment is very small.

ELECTRIC HEAT AND SEAL UNITS. These are particularly convenient for freezing many foods, especially anything with sauces or gravies; individual portions are best frozen in these plastic bags. Make certain that the plastic bags you are using are moisture-vapor-proof. Some of the bags are boilable, much like the commercial pouches you find at your grocer's. They are also great for warming or thawing directly in your microwave oven. Always poke a hole or two in the top of pouch before cooking or warming in your microwave, so that steam can escape—otherwise you could have an explosion.

PASTRY WHEELS. These utensils will make your baked goods more attractive whenever you cut rolled dough, whether for cookies, pies, tarts, or rolls. These wheels don't take much storage space and they're very inexpensive to add to your kitchen tools.

CHEESE SLICERS. Made of wire with a metal roller guide behind it, a cheese slicer is indispensable if you like nice, even slices of cheese. You can adjust the thickness of the slices somewhat by raising or lowering the angle of the handle when you are slicing.

KITCHEN TIMERS. If your stove doesn't have a timer, you should buy one. Unless you're an unusual person, you'll save the cost of this device in no time by eliminating scorched, overbaked, and overcooked foods.

ROLLING PINS AND PASTRY CLOTHS. Be sure you have a good rolling pin, with stocking cover, preferably one with roller-bearing handles for smooth action. You will also need a pastry cloth.

GARLIC PRESSES. A garlic press is a useful little gadget that presses the juice out of the garlic, but retains the pulp. According to some authorities, the juice gives the flavor of garlic, but the pulp is what causes the garlic breath. It certainly keeps your hands free from any garlicky smell.

FOLEY FOOD MILL. This comes in several sizes; buy the one suitable for your family's needs. Applesauce, purées, deviled eggs, egg salad, cookie crumbs that must be ground very fine—all are a snap with the Foley Food Mill.

TOMATO KNIVES. Imported from France, these knives have scalloped edges and are really the neatest tools to have in your kitchen. They are extremely sharp and make quick work of cutting almost any kind of vegetables, not only tomatoes. You can saw through the top of an artichoke in a wink.

RUBBER SPATULAS. These are fine for cleaning off the sides of your mixing bowl when you are using your electric mixer. Waste is held to a minimum, since every drop of batter, frosting, or what-have-you can be scraped easily from the bowl. When you are measuring liquids, you're assured of accurate measurement by scraping all the ingredients out of your measuring cups with a rubber spatula (I don't mean the plastic ones). Keep several handy at all times. They're excellent to use with Teflonware that would be damaged by hard utensils. They come in two sizes, 1 inch and 2 inches wide. The narrower width is less clumsy and more versatile; I always have three or more of these in the kitchen. The larger ones usually come with stronger handles and are useful when one is working with heavy batters and yeast doughs.

SPREADER SPATULAS. Advertised in catalogues and stores that specialize in cooking utensils, spreader spatulas are oval in shape and have serrated edges all around, with wooden handles. These spreaders save a tremendous amount of time when you are frosting cakes, making hors d'oeuvres, spreading sandwiches, buttering bread, and have numerous other uses. The serrated edge "grabs" the substance and spreads it easily. This allows you to spread the substance as thick or thin as you want to; the edges are just as easy to spread as centers.

APPLE PEELERS. An apple peeler, slicer, and corer is a little gadget just like those that were so popular years ago and they're still available in the catalog of one of the nation's largest mail-order houses for just over eleven dollars. A bargain, indeed! Now, with the modern convenience of a freezer, you'll want to freeze enough apples to last for the winter and it's easy with this old-fashioned timesaver. Just a few cranks and your apple is pared. Always start peeling apples when someone else is in the house. Once the children or your husband see your apple peeler they'll plead with you to let them use it. Then all you'll have to do is measure and pack the apples (see page 201).

THERMOMETERS. Several thermometers of good quality are a necessity, one to keep in your freezer at all times so that you're absolutely certain of the inside temperature. A roast meat and poultry thermometer is essential if you're to cook meat to the exact degree of doneness. I really wouldn't know how to cook a roast without one, so much do I depend on this little item. After having tried several that were inaccurate, I found the Roast Meat and Poultry Thermometer manufactured by Taylor to be very accurate and reliable. *Consumers' Research* bears me out. They report that many of the thermometers on the market today—even some very expensive models—are not at all reliable.

FREEZER ACCESSORIES. There are many freezer accessories available to help you organize the interior of your freezer, especially for the chest type. There are baskets that fit on the top of your freezer, baskets that hook one on top of another, mesh bags, stockinettes, and so on. Each person must judge his own needs, but remember that every time you spend five minutes hunting for some lost parcel, you're not only wasting time, but also electricity. The longer the freezer is open, the warmer the interior air becomes, and the freezer will have to run just that much longer.

Ordinary plastic dishpans are marvelous for storing small miscellaneous items and keeping them from getting lost in the far corners of your freezer. They come in an assortment of sizes which fit nicely in both the upright and chest-type freezers. Rubbermaid makes a variety of stackable bins and shelves that are equally useful for chest-type freezers. Not only are they invaluable for keeping little things together where they may be easily located, but they also give protection to delicate frozen pastries and pies.

SHARP KNIVES. Keeping knives sharp is essential to running a more efficient kitchen. You can spend the better part of an afternoon cutting up vegetables with a dull knife that would only take minutes with a sharp blade. Do all your cutting on a wooden cutting board. When cutting such things as celery, don't cut one piece at a time! Wash and trim five or six stalks (or whatever number you'll need) and line them all up together. One stroke with a sharp knife will cut six stalks in the same amount of time it takes to cut one.

KITCHEN SHEARS. Keep one pair of kitchen shears or scissors expressly for kitchen use. You can cut parsley, chives, and most herbs to any degree of fineness or coarseness in record time with a pair of scissors.

PLASTIC POP-OUT ICE CUBE TRAYS. If you don't have any, put these on your list too. You'll never go back to the old-fashioned metal ice cube trays that come with most refrigerators, once you start using these little plastic gems. The kind I use are made by the Dole Valve Company and are available in most department stores. No more running cold water over the trays to loosen the cubes from the sides! The ice cubes literally pop out when the tray is twisted slightly. The trays stack one on top of another. Fresh herbs, chicken broth, bouillon, and egg whites can easily be frozen in these. After they're frozen, you simply empty the cubes into a moisture-vapor-proof plastic bag, label it, and put them in the freezer. Since the trays don't have to be warmed with water to remove the cubes, these cubes won't stick together in the plastic bag, because they're dry and frozen solid.

FOOD BLANCHERS. Blanching food is a simple procedure if you have the proper equipment. Food blanchers, made especially for this process, are available from department stores and mail-order houses (see page 366). However, if you don't intend to do a lot of blanching, there are simple ways to improvise. A deep fryer, for example, is perfect for blanching. If you have a deep-well cooker on your stove, the screen insert or basket would work nicely also, as would some of the French wire baskets made for washing salad greens. Just be sure that the basket has a handle or some way for you to raise it without burning yourself.

MARKING PENS. Waterproof felt marking pens work best for labeling and dating everything before you put it into the freezer. If your freezer isn't in your kitchen, get two of these pens—one to keep beside the freezer and the other in the kitchen.

NUT MILLS. A nut mill takes the drudgery out of chopping nuts. It sells for about two dollars and is worth its weight in gold. It's a small gadget, so it won't take a lot of room on your shelves. It consists of a small jar with an apparatus that screws onto the neck of the jar. Some nut mills are so made that when you turn the handle one way, the nuts are coarsely chopped; turn it the other way and they're finely chopped. All of the nuts will be uniformly ground. Do a big batch at one time and store the chopped nuts in your freezer until you need them.

Sources of Supply

Because many of you do not live in a metropolitan area where all the latest in appliances, gadgets, and unusual food items are available, I am including a list of stores that put out a catalog of all their wares. They are fun to page through and certainly are an easy way to shop.

COOKING UTENSILS

Bazaar Français, 666–668 Sixth Ave. (between 20th & 21st St.), New York, NY 10010

The Complete Cook, 222 Waukegan Rd., Glenview, IL 60025

Hammacher Schlemmer, 147 East 57th Street, New York, NY 10022

FOODS, GIFTS, AND KITCHEN AND COOKING ACCESSORIES

Barth's Colonial Garden, 270 West Merrick Rd., Valley Stream, NY 11582

Garden Way Country Kitchen, 1300 Ethan Allen Ave., Winooski, VT 05404 (specializes in freezing and canning equipment)

Lekvar-by-the-barrel, 1577 First Ave. (corner 82nd St.), New York, NY 10028

Maid of Scandinavia, 3244 Raleigh Ave., Minneapolis, MN 55416

Paprikás Weiss Importer, 1546 Second Ave., New York, NY 10028

ENERGY-SAVING IDEAS

Refrigerator and Freezer

Rubber gaskets around refrigerator and freezer doors do wear out and need to be replaced from time to time. The gasket (the rubber insulation around the door) should be flexible. Stiff, cracked, or damaged insulation allows air leakage and will cost you a lot in the way of additional electricity. To check the tightness of the door seal, place a dollar bill between the gasket and the cabinet. Close the door with normal force. When you pull the dollar bill straight out, there should be a slight drag. Test all around the door, including the hinge side. If there are places where no drag occurs, have a serviceman check the gasket on the door for proper alignment.

If you have a manual-defrost freezer compartment in your refrigerator, defrost frequently. A frost buildup of ¼ inch or more actually serves as insulation against keeping foods frozen well, making the refrigerator work twice as hard. A full freezer operates more economically than one that is only partially filled. It will also stay cold longer in case of power failure.

Putting the refrigerator on dolly wheels will ease the job of moving it for cleaning the condenser coils on the back. Newer refrigerator models put the condenser coils beneath the unit; to clean, remove the front grill and vacuum. In summer homes or for very long vacations, turn off refrigerators and/or freezers, clean them, and leave them open.

Oven and Range Top

Slow cookers use less electricity than oven cooking; oven cooking is less expensive than top-of-the-range cooking. Surface units are on all the time you are cooking, while the oven is on for only part of each hour it is used. The rest of the time it coasts high, because its insulation holds the heat in. Self-cleaning ovens are better insulated and cost even less to use.

Baking two or three different dishes of food at one time in your oven will also save energy. If you have three dishes to be cooked at slightly variant temperatures, for example 325°, 350°, and 375° F, pick the mean temperature of 350° F to cook all three items, removing each as it is done. Naturally, if you are baking a cake at 325° F and want to make some popovers at 425° F, this would not work. However, baking the cake and then putting the popovers in the oven immediately after the cake is done will save electricity, since the oven has already been heated.

Avoid "oven-peeping"—it wastes heat. When baking in glass or ceramic utensils, lower oven by 25 degrees. These materials transfer heat better than metal.

Put lids on your pots and pans. Cooking with covered utensils will allow you to use a lower heat setting. Less heat escapes. The tighter the lid, the better. Also check all your utensils for flat bottoms which make firm contact with surface elements. Thermostatically controlled surface units also save energy. The heat sensor in the center provides a controlled heat and the on-and-off heat cycle saves energy. Check the manufacturer's instructions to be sure that you are using the correct sized pans on your controlled surface units.

Cooking with small amounts of water also saves energy, because small amounts of water heat faster. Use no more than one-third to one-half cup of water for cooking fresh vegetables.

If your tea kettle has lots of calcium deposits, soak with vinegar to remove. The calcium deposits act as an insulation and heating takes considerably more energy. Always turn your stove off after use.

Thaw frozen foods before cooking. Whether cooked in the oven, broiler, or on top of the range, frozen foods will use less energy if they are removed from the freezer and thawed in the refrigerator compartment first.

Small Appliances

Electric skillets, toasters, waffle irons, electric grills, popcorn poppers, and similar small appliances use less electricity than your range for specialized jobs. For example, it costs three times as much to toast bread in an oven as in a pop-up toaster. Make sure to turn your appliances off when you have finished using them; unplugging them when you are through is a good practice.

Dishwasher

The dishwasher conserves a lot of human energy in the kitchen. Without one, a person could spend the equivalent of 46 eight-hour days a year washing dishes. The following tips can help you get even more efficient use out of this appliance.

Only do full loads—your dishwasher works most economically at full capacity, since the same amount of water, detergent, and energy is used on a quarter, half, or full load. Accumulate the dishes in the dishwasher until it's full. Loading the dishwasher according to manufacturer's instructions will help insure operating efficiency. Use the correct amount of detergent with every load. Food caught in the dishwasher pump can hamper the machine's efficiency; scrape excess food from plates. Also clean filter screen over the drain regularly. You may wish to turn machine off before the drying cycle is completed, as the heat buildup from the hot water and initial drying cycle is sufficient to let the dishes "air dry." Open your dishwasher to allow better air circulation.

MANAGING YOUR FREEZER

Operating Cost

On page 21 are operating costs of freezers, refrigerators, and side-by-sides submitted by Commonwealth Edison, published in 1976 with a rate charge of .496 per KwH, but no state or municipal taxes.

Proper Temperature Setting

I keep my freezer at least 5° below zero, Fahrenheit, simply because some foods keep better at that temperature, and because it gives me a bit of a safety factor. Frozen foods deteriorate drastically at temperatures above 0° F. Their storage time is shortened; loss of vitamins, color, and flavor is very noticeable. A year of storage at 0° F is roughly equivalent to five months at 5° F; two months at 10° F; one month at 15° F; one week at 25° F, and only one day at 30° F. If your freezing compartment doesn't register 0° F, use the food quickly.

AVERAGE OPERATING COST

Appliance	Average Wattage	Operating Cost in cents per Day	Operating Cost in dollars per Month
Freezer 15 cu. ft.	340	14.1	4.08
Frost free, 15 cu. ft.	440	19.7	6.01
Refrigerator			
12 cu. ft.	240	8.6	2.48
Frost free, 12 cu. ft.	320	14.2	4.15
Refrigerator/Freezer			
14 cu. ft.	325	12.9	3.88
Frost free, 14 cu. ft.	615	20.6	6.24
Frost free, 19 cu. ft., side-by-side	800	27.3	8.19

When only a few packages are being frozen, there is no need to adjust the temperature control on your freezer. However, if you want to freeze a large quantity of food, say, a quarter of beef, be sure to set your control on its lowest setting a day before you expect to put the food in the freezer. After the food has been in the freezer for 24 hours, you may return the temperature control to its normal setting. Most butcher shops will do the freezing for you if requested.

Quick freezing is very important in order to maintain high standards in your frozen food. Do *not* put more than 35 pounds of unfrozen food in a 10-cubic-foot freezer on any one day. A 15-cubic-foot freezer can accommodate no more than 55 pounds, and a 20-cubic-foot freezer can handle no more than about 70 pounds. Leave space between packages so that air can circulate freely around them until they're frozen.

Always place the unfrozen food in your quick-freezing section until it's completely frozen (about 24 hours) before moving it to the desired location on another shelf. This is especially important with prepared foods; they should be cooled and frozen as quickly as possible. Freezing slows the action of yeasts, molds, bacteria, and enzymes that are responsible for food spoilage. Commercial freezing plants quick freeze their food at sub-zero temperatures that are not possible to attain in the home freezer. To maintain the same high quality in home-frozen foods, every precaution must be taken.

Recommended Food Storage Times

The following list gives the maximum storage time recommendations for fresh, cooked and processed meat, stored in freezer at 0° F, or lower.

RECOMMENDED STORAGE TIME FOR MEATS

Food	Months	Food	Months
Beef (fresh)	6 to 12	Sausage, fresh pork	2
Veal (fresh)	6 to 9	Frankfurters	1
Pork (fresh)	3 to 6	Bacon	1
Lamb (fresh)	6 to 9	Smoked ham, whole or slices	2
Ground beef, veal, and lamb	3 to 4	Beef, corned	2 weeks
Ground pork	1 to 3	Leftover cooked meat	2 to 3
Variety meats	3 to 4		
Luncheon meats	(freezing not recommended)		

You may defrost meat in or out of the refrigerator, though I recommend doing it in the refrigerator, especially during warm weather. For a large roast defrosted in the refrigerator, allow 4 to 7 hours per pound. For a small roast, allow 3 to 5 hours per pound. A 1-inch steak requires 12 to 14 hours to defrost in the refrigerator.

RECOMMENDED STORAGE TIME FOR HOME-PREPARED FOODS

Food	Months	Food	Months
APPETIZERS	1 to 2	Pie shells (baked and unbaked)	6
Canapes	1 to 2	QUICK BREADS	
CAKES		Boston brown (baked)	4
Angel food (baked)	4 to 6	Nut (baked)	2 to 4
Butter (baked)	9 to 12	Orange (baked)	4
Chocolate (baked)	4 to 6	STEAM PUDDINGS	2 to 4
Frosted	3 to 4	WAFFLES AND PANCAKES	2 to 4
Fruit (baked)	4	YEAST BREADS	
Plain (baked)	3	Bread	6 to 9
Sponge (baked)	4	Rolls (baked)	6 to 9
COOKIES		Swedish tea ring	4 to 6
Brownies (baked)	6 to 9	COMBINATION DISHES*	3 to 6
(unbaked)	2 to 3	CREAM PUFFS AND	
Chocolate chip (baked)	6 to 9	ECLAIRS	3
Filled (baked)	6 to 9	Filled with ice cream	1
Peanut butter (baked)	6 to 9	EGG WHITES	12
Refrigerator (baked)	6 to 9	EGG YOLKS	9
Sugar (baked)	6 to 9	FRUITS, HOME-PREPARED	9 to 12
PIES		MEATS, COOKED	**
Apple (baked and unbaked)	4	POULTRY, COOKED	**
Blueberry (baked and unbaked)	4	Chicken, fried	4
Chocolate chiffon	2	Poultry dishes	6
Lemon chiffon	2	Poultry sandwiches	1
Mincemeat (baked and unbaked)	2	Slices or pieces Covered with broth or gravy	6
Pumpkin (baked and unbaked)	2	Not covered with broth or gravy	1

Food	Months	Food	Months
POULTRY, UNCOOKED		SANDWICHES	3 to 4
Chicken and turkey	12		weeks
Duck and goose	6	VEGETABLES	
Giblets	3	all,	
Livers	1	*including home-prepared*	9 to 12

* Most prepared dishes can be kept for a period of 3 to 4 months without any flavor changes or loss of texture. However, if you haven't used them by the 4th month, don't throw them away, but be sure to use them before the 6th month. It's simply a good practice to rotate prepared combination dishes and use them in 3 or 4 months. In all combination dishes there's a gradual loss of flavor, aroma, and natural texture; so the sooner they're rotated, the better.

** Most meats are best cooked after thawing, the exception being prepared combination dishes. Cooked whole roasts, fried chicken, et cetera, lose some of their eye appeal and flavor if they are frozen after being cooked. So do this only in emergencies, and then freeze for only a short period of time.

Commercially frozen foods purchased at the store should be put in your home freezer as soon as possible. Otherwise, their keeping quality will be affected, as well as their flavor and appearance. When shopping, do other errands first, and leave the grocery shopping until last. A package of frozen vegetables will still feel very hard even though its temperature is 25° F.

If for some reason you can't get your food in the freezer as soon as you had planned (and this happens to all of us), mark the packages accordingly and plan to use them within the next few weeks.

The following list will give you the maximum freezer-storage time for commercially prepared foods. How long commercially frozen food can be stored at home and still retain its quality depends on several factors: the type of food; how long it was stored before you bought it; its temperature when you brought it home.

Always buy from reputable dealers; select packages that are clean and firm and from the bottom of the freezer chest. If the food has warmed enough to soften, you can be sure it has already lost quality. Frozen food that is exposed or poorly packaged will dry out quickly. Be sure to use any torn or crushed packages soon after purchase. Discolored packages indicate improper storage since processing and should not be purchased.

The following list suggests maximum home-freezer storage periods to maintain quality in commercially frozen and prepared foods. Recommended times are based on a freezer setting at 0° F.

RECOMMENDED STORAGE TIME FOR COMMERCIALLY FROZEN AND PREPARED FOODS

Food	Months	Food	Months
BAKED GOODS		Oysters, shucked	1
Breads and yeast rolls		Shrimp	4
White bread	3	*Cooked fish and shellfish*	
Cinnamon rolls	2	Fish with cheese sauce	3
Plain rolls	3	Fish with lemon	
Baking-powder biscuits	3	butter sauce	3
Muffins	6	Fried fish dinner	3
Cakes		Fried fish sticks,	
Angel food	2	scallops, or shrimp	3
Chiffon	2	Shrimp creole	3
Chocolate layer	4	Tuna pie	3
Fruit	12	FRUITS AND VEGETABLES	
Pound	6	*Fruits*	
Yellow	6	Cherries	12
Danish pastry	3	Peaches	12
Doughnuts		Raspberries	12
Cake type	3	Strawberries	12
Yeast raised	3	*Fruit juice concentrates*	
Pies (unbaked)		Apple	12
Apple	8	Grape	12
Boysenberry	8	Orange	12
Cherry	8	*Vegetables*	
Peach	8	Asparagus	8
DAIRY PRODUCTS		Beans	8
Butter	6 to 9*	Cauliflower	10
Natural cheese	6 weeks to	Corn	10
	2 months**	Peas	8
Pasteurized processed		Spinach	10
cheeses	4	MAIN AND SIDE DISHES	
DESSERTS (FROZEN)		(cooked)	
Ice cream	1***	Baked beans	6
Sherbet	1	Beef and veal stews	6
FISH AND SHELLFISH		Candied sweet potatoes	6
Fish		Cooked rice	6 to 8
Fillets:		Creamed dishes,	
Cod, flounder,		chicken à la king	12
haddock, halibut,		Fish dishes	3 to 5
pollack	4	French-fried potatoes	2
(in ice pack)	6	Meat loaf, meat balls, corned	
Mullet, ocean perch,		beef hash, Spanish rice	6
sea trout, striped		Roast meats and poultry	6
bass	3	MEATS	
Pacific ocean perch	2	*Beef*	
Salmon steaks	2	Hamburger or chipped	
Sea trout, dressed	3	(thin) steaks	3 to 4
Striped bass, dressed	3	Roasts	6 to 8
Whiting, drawn	4	Steaks	6 to 8
Shellfish		*Lamb*	
Clams, shucked	3	Patties	4
Crabmeat, King or		Roasts	6 to 12
Dungeness	2		

Food	Months			
Pork, cured	2	Livers	3	
Pork, fresh		Whole	12	
Roasts	3 to 8	Duck, whole	6	
Sausage	2	Goose, whole	6	
Veal		Turkey		
Cutlets and chops	3 to 6	Cut-up	6 to 12	
Roasts	3 to 8	Whole	6 to 12	
Meats, cooked		Poultry, cooked		
Meat dinners	3	Chicken or turkey dinners		
Meat pie	3	(sliced meat and gravy)	6	
Swiss steak	3	Chicken or turkey pies	12	
POULTRY		Fried chicken	3	
Chicken		Fried chicken dinners	3	
Cut-up	6			

* May be frozen in its original container for 1 month at 0° F. For longer storage, wrap in moisture-vapor-proof freezer packaging. For convenience, wrap in separate 1-pound portions.

** If unopened, in the original package (see page 35).

*** The short freezer life of ice cream and sherbet always comes as a surprise. However, I've found a way to increase the storage time in your freezer to at least four months, which should enable you to buy enough to last from one sale to the next. Be sure ice cream or sherbet is kept from melting or softening. Date your packages and seal them in moisture-vapor-proof plastic bags, each carton wrapped individually or several in one large plastic bag. Keep your freezer at least 5° below zero Fahrenheit. Commercial dairies store their ice cream at 30° below zero for six months or longer. They too keep their ice creams and sherbets in large plastic containers or other outer wraps. The cartons in which ice cream is packed simply aren't moisture-vapor-proof. Ice cream, ice milk, and sherbet that have softened or are partially melted and then refrozen, lose volume and become coarse in texture. If your ice cream and/or sherbet consumption is relatively small, it is best to purchase small quantities to avoid deterioration of quality and texture.

Quality Control

If you're in doubt about the quality of some of your purchased frozen foods, here are a few hints that will help you determine the quality.

Large amounts of frost on the inside of the package may indicate that the quality has been impaired. Also note the color of the food. Is it the natural bright color or are there definite color changes? Peaches and red cherries held at too high a temperature first darken and then turn brown. Berries lose some of their bright color to the syrup. Green snap beans darken to an olive green. Peas become grayish and then get a yellow cast. Poultry skin darkens. Look for any changes in texture too. When you taste the food, note the flavor; does it taste fresh or has it become tasteless or developed an off-flavor? Flavor changes usually develop more slowly than changes in color and texture.

Inventory Control

Freeze only the foods your family likes, and in quantities they'll eat within the recommended storage time. Don't overcrowd your freezer with seasonal foods simply because they seem to be "such a good buy." Budget your space. Make a list of things you want to freeze and the quantities, and make sure that you'll have enough room for all the family favorites. Keep a list of the amount of everything you put in the freezer, so that you can refer to it the following year. In other words, if you froze a crate of blueberries last year and you still have 10 pints left over, half a crate would be the proper quantity to freeze for your family. On the other hand, if you ran out of blueberries in December, I would suggest that you freeze a crate and a half.

Arrange the contents of your freezer in an orderly fashion; keep fruits or vegetables of one kind together, bakery goods in one section, meats in another. An orderly freezer holds more. To keep it in order, use baskets, shelves, dividers, and other accessories that either come with your freezer or can be purchased separately. See page 16, Freezer Accessories. Never, but *never*, put anything into the freezer without dating it. Two loaves of bread or two packages of frozen vegetables look exactly alike in the freezer; yet one may be six months old and the other fresh from last week's shopping. Even if you plan to use the item in a day or so, put a date on it. Circumstances may change your plans so that you won't use it as soon as you expected, but at least it's marked for future identification.

If you've been racking your brain to figure ways to cut meal costs, you may be wondering if you could save money by buying a side of beef.

The U. S. Department of Agriculture says the answer can be found only by making a careful comparison of costs among the alternatives available to you. USDA has a booklet to help you figure out which approach is best for you. For a copy of *How to Buy Meat For Your Freezer*, send 45 cents to Consumer Information Center, Dept. 4, Pueblo, Colorado 81109.

If you don't already have a running list of everything in your freezer, a good time to start is when you're defrosting it. List all the contents and their dates as you put the food back into the freezer. This list should be kept near the freezer in a convenient place so that additions and subtractions can be made easily. Your list can be arranged something like the following one.

This is only an example, of course, to give you some idea how it can be done. A card file is another good way of keeping track of your current food inventory. Use notebooks, charts, or whatever works and

FREEZER INVENTORY

Food	No. of Packages	Date Frozen or Added to Freezer	No. of Packages Removed
Blueberries	10 pints	7/29/66	𝍌𝍌
	4 quarts	7/29/66	//
Asparagus	15 1-pound packages	5/12/67	///
Chocolate Ice Cream	3 half gallons	3/2/67	/
Vanilla Ice Cream	3 half gallons	3/2/67	//

is convenient for you. Rather than indicating the date something is put into the freezer, some people prefer to mark it with the date it should be used. It's simply a matter of preference. When listing home-prepared foods, always be sure to list the amount or the number of servings, and perhaps the way it was made.

Vacation Preparations

Your freezer can be a big help when you are preparing to leave on vacation. There's always that last-minute job of cleaning out the refrigerator just before you go. Instead of running over to your neighbor with a bundle of perishables or, even worse, throwing them out, see how many things you can store in your freezer.

BACON. This doesn't keep well for any long period of time, so cut it up, bake it, and store it in a freezer carton to use as crumbled bacon in the future. (See page 41.)

BUTTER AND MARGARINE. These will keep for 6 months in the freezer.

CHEESE. Most hard and semihard cheeses can be frozen. Be sure to wrap them in moisture-vapor-proof containers or wrappings. Thaw in the refrigerator, and use promptly after thawing.

CHEESE SPREADS. These will keep in the refrigerator fairly well for a month. However, if you wish, put them in the freezer.

COTTAGE CHEESE. Dry cottage cheese can be frozen for 1 month. Thaw slowly in refrigerator while it is still in freezer carton. Cream-style cottage cheese will separate. However, you may freeze it and use it for cooking (cheese cake, lasagne) upon your return.

CREAM. Whipping and coffee creams can be frozen successfully for a month or so. Whipping cream can also be frozen whipped. If cream is frozen unwhipped, be sure to defrost it in the refrigerator before whipping. If you have trouble getting it to whip properly, add a few drops (no more) of lemon juice. It will not give you the volume that fresh cream does.

CREAM CHEESE. The texture may change after thawing. However, you may beat it when it has thawed to room temperature and use it for cooking, baking, or in cheese spreads.

CULTURED MILK, BUTTERMILK, YOGURT, AND SOUR CREAM. All can be frozen. Occasionally the smooth texture is affected. Simply put them into the blender, give them a twirl, and their texture should be revived.

EGGS. Do not freeze eggs in the shell. To freeze whole eggs, remove shells, mix yolks and whites with a beater, freeze in family-sized portions (i.e., the amount you would use for scrambled eggs), and add ¾ teaspoon of salt for every 8 eggs. However, if you want to use the eggs for baking, freeze in the quantity called for in your recipe and add 1 tablespoon of sugar for every 8 eggs.

CITRUS FRUITS. Grate the rind of lemons, limes, or oranges and freeze in small bags. Put whole citrus fruit in boiling water for 5 to 10 minutes, depending on size, squeeze, and freeze the juice in ice cube trays. (See page 17.) Boiled fruit yields about twice the volume of juice.

FRESH FRUIT. Fresh fruit can be frozen. See instructions in the chapter on fruits and desserts.

MEATS, POULTRY AND FISH. Most can be frozen if they are fresh. Cooked foods, such as casseroles, can also be frozen.

VEGETABLES. Fresh vegetables can be frozen. See instructions in the chapter on vegetables. Remember, lettuce, celery, radishes, and cucumbers do not freeze well.

Defrosting

A small freezer unit that is part of a refrigerator (unless it is frost-free) will require defrosting more frequently than larger freezer units. Just remember that the more frost on the unit, the more difficulty it has in operating efficiently and the more expensive it is to run. It will also affect the cabinet's ability to quick-freeze your unfrozen foods. (However, I must confess that the only time my small freezing unit got a good defrosting was when I discovered that the ice cube trays would no longer fit into their niches.) A good rule for larger units is to defrost once a year, need it or not. You'll be amazed at all the little goodies you'll find down in the dark corners. Defrosting also gives you an excellent opportunity to reorganize your space, put the items with the latest dates at the bottom (or the back, if you have an upright freezer), and put the older items on top or in the front where you'll see them.

February and March are good months for defrosting, because your freezer is generally at its emptiest. If you live in a cold climate, you can pick a cold day, put your food in boxes, and set these outside. Otherwise, put as many items as possible in your refrigerator, which has been turned to its coldest setting. Pack the remainder of your frozen food in cardboard cartons, which have been heavily lined with newspapers for insulation. Before closing the cartons, cover the food with a layer of newspapers. If you're a slow worker, or if it's a warm day, throw a blanket around the cartons. Actually, defrosting doesn't take very long, so a few simple precautions are all that are needed. Before you start all this, be sure to slip on a pair of rubber or heavy garden gloves! It's easy to get frostbite.

Turn off the current as soon as you start to empty your freezer. When all the food has been removed, use a plastic ice scraper to remove as much frost from the sides as will scrape off easily. *Never use salt* to melt the frost or ice, since this can do irreparable damage to your cabinet. *Never use a sharp instrument* or *pick* to scrape off the frost, either. It's simply too easy to damage your freezer permanently.

There are several ways you can now proceed. The easiest way will not, unfortunately, work for everyone. If you have an upright freezer or a chest type with a drain in the bottom, and your freezer is in the basement near a floor drain or in your garage, the very simplest way to defrost your freezer is to attach a garden hose to your hot water tap. Hose your appliance down with steaming water and it will defrost in just a few minutes. One way is simply to leave the doors open, let the warm air in, and wait until the cabinet is defrosted. Another method is to put pans of hot—not boiling—water in the box, close the doors, and wait until all the frost and ice loosen from the sides. The hose of a tank-type vacuum cleaner is also helpful. Put the hose on the exhaust end of the vacuum, so that air will blow out. The motor of the vacuum cleaner usually heats the air somewhat and this warm air really expedites defrosting. As the ice starts falling away from the sides, scoop it up and put it in a bucket or other suitable container. You don't have to wait for all the ice to melt and run out the drain. *Never use an abrasive cleaner* on your cabinet, either inside or out, since this will ruin the fine enamel finish. For cleaning the inside, use 4 tablespoons of baking soda mixed with 1 quart of warm water. When the cabinet is completely cleaned, dry it thoroughly with paper towels before turning the current on.

Wait until the inside temperature reaches zero before returning the food to the freezer. If you keep a running inventory of your frozen foods, now is a good time to bring it up to date. Check the dates on everything and put those items with the oldest dates where you'll use them soon. Put the newest packages at the bottom or back of your cabinet.

Power Failure

Don't open the door! If your freezer is full, it will be all right for a period of 36 to 48 hours. You should be prepared for such emergencies. Have the name, address, and telephone number of your nearest source of dry ice taped to the outside lid or the side of your freezer. In this way, even if you aren't home, whoever is looking after your dwelling will be able to take care of the matter easily. In the event that you do need dry ice, order 25 to 50 pounds, depending on the size of your freezer. Be sure to wear heavy gloves when handling dry ice. Fifty pounds of dry ice will keep a 20-cubic-foot filled freezer for about 4 days. If the freezer is only half full, it will keep for 2 or 3 days before needing more dry ice.

Devices can be installed that sound an alarm when the inside temperature rises to a danger point. These are nice to have, because occasionally a door will not be closed properly, which could cause food spoilage, or the plug may not be making a proper contact. If you have one of these alarms, be sure to check the batteries periodically.

If dry ice is not available and the power is expected to be off for several days, you may try to rent a commercial freezer-locker to house your food.

Emergency Guide

1. *If complete thawing has occurred:*
   Red meats should be cooked and then refrozen.
   Fruits may be used for jams, jellies, preserves, syrup, conserves, and sauces.
   Prepared food, meats in cream sauces, TV dinners, pies, and leftovers are best discarded.
   Fish that is completely thawed is also best thrown out.
   Poultry that is thawed, but still quite cold to the touch, may be cooked and refrozen. Any stuffed poultry should be discarded.
   Vegetables should be cooked and then refrozen. Make up large quantities of soups, stews, and casseroles.
2. *If food is partially thawed, but still has some ice crystals in it:*
   Vegetables that still show ice crystals may be refrozen, but should be used as soon as possible.
   Red meats that are still hard and have ice crystals may be refrozen.
   Variety meats, sausages, and hamburger, however, should be cooked and then refrozen. Sausage and hamburger meat is easiest cooked in spaghetti sauce, meat loaves, et cetera.
Remember that when you refreeze partially thawed fruits, vegetables, and meats, only the quality will be affected. They are not harmful.

Refreezing isn't hazardous in any way. If the food is safe to eat, it's safe to refreeze. However, there will be a loss of vitamins and flavor. Try to use all refrozen foods within two or three weeks. If, on the other hand, you detect any odor, throw the food out without further question.

WRAPPING AND PACKAGING

The importance of properly wrapping and packging foods for the freezer cannot be overemphasized. Regardless of the excellent quality of the food you put into the freezer, if it's not wrapped properly against the dry air in the freezer, the food will lose color, flavor, and vitamins.

Keep your wrapping and packaging materials handy. You'll need several different types of materials, depending on the kind of foods you will be freezing. The cost of these materials is very small compared with the price of the food they are protecting. Don't try to economize here. Never use anything but moisture-vapor-proof materials that are intended for freezing. *About 85 percent of all food failure in freezing is caused by inadequate packaging materials and methods.* Waxed cartons used for cottage cheese and other dairy products are not sufficiently moisture-vapor-resistant to use for freezing. Plastic freezer containers will crack and chip with use; especially the lids. Discard cracked containers promptly.

The food in a self-defrosting freezer needs more protection than that in an ordinary freezer, because of the constant circulation of air. Foods kept in these freezers for a long time tend to have freezer burn. The safest way to handle this problem is to use plastic bags as an outer wrap, after wrapping everything securely, and to shorten the storage time of all items. *Wrapping and freezing instructions in this book are for the conventional type of freezers.* If yours is a frost-free freezer, take extra precautions when wrapping and be sure to shorten the storage time.

If your supermarket doesn't carry a complete line of freezer supplies, most department stores and even some hardware stores do. New items are being introduced each year, and it's difficult for the uninitiated to know exactly what to buy. I shall comment on some of the more popular items and give you their advantages, as well as their shortcomings. Different kinds of food require different wrapping materials and containers, so you'll need a variety on hand.

ALUMINUM FOIL. Never use lightweight foil for the freezer; it simply isn't adequate. Heavy aluminum foil has many advantages. It's easy to use and takes the irregular shape of any parcel you're trying to wrap. It is also more expensive than some of the other wrapping materials available and has the disadvantage that, no matter how careful you are, tiny punctures or holes will develop. For this reason it's best to put an outer covering or wrap on foil packages or put them in plastic bags, so that when you move them around in the freezer you won't puncture them.

Unless your aluminum foil is plastic-coated, never put it in direct contact with cheeses of any sort. The acid of the cheese will attack the foil, leaving it corroded and full of little holes. When wrapping cheese-topped dishes or pizzas, always put a layer of waxed paper or cellophane over the cheese before wrapping in the foil. This is also true of fruit pies or anything containing fruit. The fruit should never be in direct contact with the foil.

PLIOFILM. This is heavier and sturdier than cellophane. It's derived from rubber and is excellent for wrapping irregular-shaped packages because it will stretch. If dipped momentarily in water that is about 180° F, it will shrink to the exact contours of your packages. However, Pliofilm does need some outer covering to protect it from breaking at low temperatures. This material is not readily found in local stores.

CELLOPHANE. This is also an effective moisture-vapor-proof material. It usually comes in sheets and is very similar to Pliofilm, except that it doesn't have the stretching qualities. It can be heat-sealed and it must have an outer wrap. Be sure to use only that cellophane meant for freezer use.

THERMOPLASTIC FILMS. These include both polyester film and polyethylene, which is available in sheet, tube, and bag form. They are inexpensive and easy to use, but be sure to buy a good freezer weight. There are a great variety of these films on the market, put out by any number of manufacturers. The bags vary in size from the small ones for leftovers to the very large ones that will hold a huge turkey. I find these little bags indispensable for leftovers. Because the material is transparent, you can see the contents at a glance. I use one of the really large-sized bags as an outer wrap for several smaller packages of the same kind. With reasonable care these outer wraps may be used over and over again. Simply wash them with sudsy water, rinse, and hang to dry. Before reusing, always fill the bag with water to see if there are any punctures. If you find holes, don't use the bag again, unless it can be mended with freezer tape.

HEAT-IN-THE-POUCH CONTAINERS. The newest convenience in home-freezer packaging is these pouches, made of polyester film. Not only is this material a marvelous wrapping agent for frozen foods, but it also withstands temperatures up to 240° F. The procedure is very simple: you fill the little pouches or bags with the prepared food, seal with a heat-sealing appliance, and freeze. When you are ready to serve the food, merely heat in the same bag. This method allows a vast variety of prepared foods to be frozen and served without so much as a dirty pan. These bags are doubly convenient if you have a microwave oven. Always poke a few holes in top of the pouch when cooking or thawing in microwave oven. See page 14, Heat and Seal Appliance.

I'd like to mention here that the term "moisture-vapor-proof" is not to be confused with "waterproof." Many wraps, such as giftwrapping cellophane and plastic bags, are waterproof, but *not* moisture-vapor-proof. Containers that are merely waterproof still permit the flow of moist air through their pores, and this in turn affects the quality of your food.

COATED AND LAMINATED WRAPPINGS. These come in many varieties, such as Pliofilm with aluminum foil, or glassine and cellophane laminated to heavy paper. Actually, these laminates are two sheets of different materials fused together to make a strong moisture-vapor-proof wrapping. They hold up well during long periods of storage. I prefer this type of wrap for all meats. Wrap meat with either the "drugstore wrap" or the "butcher's wrap," sealing ends securely with freezer tape. ("Drugstore wrap" simply means the method of wrapping packages used in most drugstores: placing the object lengthwise on the paper, bringing the matching ends together, and then folding them over at least once—or until all the excess is taken up—before sealing with tape. "Butcher's wrap" indicates the placement of the object crosswise on the sheet, and folding the ends in only once before taping. "Drugstore wrap" creates an airtight container because of the double-fold, while the single-fold of the "butcher's wrap" does not.) My preference is the "drugstore wrap" for irregular-sized packages.

Be sure to label packages properly with date, contents, number of servings or quantity. They all look alike once they're in the freezer.

WAXED PAPERS. These provide only moderate protection for frozen foods and are not recommended.

ALUMINUM CONTAINERS. Many commercially prepared foods and bakery products come wrapped in aluminum containers. They're also available in grocery and variety stores in a vast array of shapes and sizes. These containers are marvelous for pan-type cakes and bakery goods: bake right in container, cool, cover, and freeze. The deeper ones are also good for casseroles that you wish to bake right in the container. Thaw casseroles and prepared dishes in refrigerator; then bake and serve in the same container. They can be washed and reused several times.

SARAN WRAP. This transparent plastic film has tremendous clinging qualities, easily eliminating all air pockets. It's moisture-vapor-proof, resists tearing, and is very pliable.

PLASTIC CONTAINERS. Before you purchase a number of these containers, consider the needs of your family. Containers should be just large enough to accommodate one meal for a family. In other words, if there are only two of you, pint and ½-pint sizes will be used most frequently. If there is a large family, 1½-pint and quart sizes will usually be needed. Square containers waste the least amount of freezer space. Be sure that they stack easily when filled, as well as when they're empty. For this reason, I prefer the ones that taper a bit at the bottom. Also, the taper helps you to empty cartons filled with frozen food. Be sure to check the lids; they should fit securely and make a vacuum seal. These containers are far more expensive than any of the other materials mentioned; however, with reasonable care they should last indefinitely. I like these containers especially for liquids, such as soups, broths, sauces, and fresh fruits that have a lot of juice, like peaches and strawberries. These containers should be made of flexible plastic, some of which is opaque and some clear, and should have a fill-line marking to indicate how much head space to leave. This is very important, because as food freezes it expands, especially liquids. If not enough head room has been left, the container will split or the lid will be forced off, either of which could spoil your food. Discard any containers or lids that become cracked or chipped.

GLASS JARS. I am referring here to the glass jars especially designed for the freezer. They have wide mouths and tapered sides, so that food can be removed without thawing the entire contents.

DO'S AND DON'TS OF FREEZING

Don't freeze: cake batters; cream fillings, puddings and custards, unless they're made with Clearjel (see page 70); mayonnaise; milk; potato salad; salad greens, garnishes, crisp cabbage, other greens.

Don't freeze the whites of hard-cooked eggs; they become rubbery.

Skim as much excess fat as possible from chicken and meat stocks before freezing. The fat tends to become rancid.

Be sure to blend fat and flour thoroughly when preparing sauces for the freezer. The fat has a tendency to separate, but will recombine if stirred during heating. Using Clearjel instead of flour will eliminate this problem (see page 70).

Don't freeze more food in a container than you expect to serve at one time. If you're packaging a complete cooked dinner, do select food combinations that can be kept frozen for the same length of time.

Label everything! Put as much information as possible on your labels. Mark the amount or number of servings, ingredients, et cetera, and the date!

Don't try to quick-freeze large amounts of food at a time. Try to limit the food to be frozen to no more than 10 percent of freezer capacity.

Never use narrow-necked jars for freezing. You'll have to thaw the entire contents in order to empty the jar.

Don't use iron, copper, galvanized, or thinly tinned pots and pans when preparing food for the freezer. These metals can produce unpleasant flavors in your food.

Before preparing food for the freezer, be sure you have an adequate amount of the necessary supplies on hand.

Never refreeze foods. This does not apply to raw food that has been taken from the freezer, cooked, and then returned. Cooking food such as meat changes the enzymes so that you can safely refreeze it.

Vegetables, meats, and fruits may be refrozen as long as they contain ice crystals. However, plan to use them as quickly as possible.

Seafoods and fish should never be refrozen. If they have thawed, use them at once.

Shrimp and lobsters may be cooked and refrozen.

Bakery items may be refrozen with little change in quality and flavor.

Candies, both homemade and commercial, freeze well. Wrap the candies (box and all, if you wish) in moisture-vapor-proof material before freezing. Thaw package unopened to avoid moisture condensation on the candy.

Canned foods that have been accidentally frozen may have a slight breakdown of texture, but otherwise a single freezing and thawing doesn't affect them adversely. It's a good idea, however, when canned foods have been frozen, to use them as soon as possible.

Cheese is readily available in most areas the year round and the prices are reasonably stable. Cheese isn't a seasonal product, so there is really no need to freeze it. However, if necessary, you can freeze most natural cheese cut in small pieces that weigh no more than a pound. Wrap in moisture-vapor-proof freezer paper. Press paper tightly against cheese to force out all the air. Freeze immediately. Thaw in the refrigerator, *not at room temperature*, and use immediately. Varieties that can be successfully frozen are brick, Cheddar, Edam, Gouda, Muenster, Port du Salut, Swiss, provolone, mozzarella, Camembert, and Brie. Even these varieties, however, will sometimes undergo a change in body and texture, but their quality will still be good, according to dairy specialists. Neufchatel does not freeze well.

Don't wrap cheese in foil, unless it's foil with a plastic coating or other type of liner. The acids in the cheese will attack the foil, causing it to disintegrate.

Cottage cheese should not be frozen, since it separates with damage to texture and consistency. Some products similar to cottage cheese, such as baker's or farmer's cheese, may be frozen in waxed cartons or freezer containers for about a month.

Fresh cranberries can be frozen, but don't try to freeze them in the packages they come in, even though the label indicates that you may. The plastic bags used for cranberries are usually perforated to allow for ventilation. It's best to open the package, wash the cranberries, sort out any poor ones, and drain well. Then repackage in moisture-vapor-proof bags or cartons. If packaged in this way, cranberries may be kept from 6 to 9 months. Cranberries frozen in the original bag will lose weight and quality.

If cream must be frozen, thaw slowly in refrigerator, about 48 hours for a pint. Regular whipping cream frozen and thawed may be difficult to whip to desired volume and appearance. However, ultrapasteurized whipping cream may be frozen. Package for freezer storage if not to be used within a short time. Defrost before beating. See page 54.

When storing fruitcakes and fruit pies, *do not wrap in aluminum foil*. The combination of acid in fruits and a high degree of moisture causes the foil to pit. It's best to wrap them first in vinyl film or waxed paper and then cover them with foil. Commercial fruit pies are wrapped in lacquer-coated foil.

Honey that you intend to keep for a long time is best stored in the freezer. If kept on the kitchen shelf, it will become sugary and darker in color. Honey kept in the refrigerator will crystallize even sooner. None of this happens to honey kept in the freezer. Remove only enough of the frozen honey to last for several weeks. If the honey comes in glass jars, be sure to remove a little to allow for freezing expansion before storing the jar in the freezer.

Freezing milk is not recommended. When milk is frozen and thawed, a flaky protein deposit may show as fine flecks on the glass. This doesn't affect the nutritional value, however. If milk is frozen in waxed cartons, hold only for a short time unless covered with protective freezer-wrap. Thaw frozen milk slowly in the refrigerator (about 48 hours for a quart) or by immersing the carton in cold water for several hours.

Don't freeze salted nuts, since the salt may absorb moisture and become sticky.

Sour cream should not be frozen. Freezing will affect its smooth texture, causing it to separate as it thaws. However, prepared dishes made with dairy sour cream may be frozen successfully.

When freezer-wrapping in freezer bags, always be sure to squeeze out all air. There is a new item expressly made for this purpose, called the Freezer Vacuum Pump. With a quick twist of this pump, all the air is automatically eliminated from your plastic bag, leaving you with a nicely compressed package. It is inexpensive (under $2); if you cannot find it in your local store, you may order one by writing to: Poly-Commodity Corporation, 1350 Avenue of the Americas, New York, NY 10019.

Cooked foods should be packed in containers in which they can be reheated, if possible. Keep the transfer of food from one container to another to a minimum.

Seal, label, and freeze prepared foods as soon as possible. Always cool to room temperature before putting into freezer. Frost-free freezers quick-freeze food much more rapidly than the conventional type of freezers, so if you're fortunate enough to have both kinds, always quick-freeze in the frost-free freezer before transferring the food to your other freezer. It's the constant circulation of the air in the frost-free freezer that causes the food to freeze faster.

You will find some foods are best frozen *before* freezer-wrapping them, e.g., delicate hors d'oeuvres, whipped cream flowerettes, miniature and regular-sized muffins, and most individual pastries and sweet rolls. Because of their delicate shapes, they are best arranged on a large cookie sheet or tray and frozen until very hard. You can then drop them into freezer bags, date, label, seal, and return immediately to the freezer. *Do not* leave unwrapped foods in the freezer any longer than just overnight, or they will tend to pick up moisture and off-flavors. Usually just a few hours is all that is required to harden food sufficiently for packing.

Don't remove food from the freezer with wet hands. Removing food from a freezer is not without certain hazards. The Greater Detroit Safety Council reports that a homemaker reached into her freezer with wet hands, and three of fingers froze fast to the freezer wall. All attempts to release her failed. By the time the police had been summoned and had managed to extricate her from her awkward position, she was suffering from extensively frostbitten fingers. To be doubly safe in removing food from a freezer, *always wear gloves*.

If you have small children, it's a good policy to keep your freezer locked, especially if it's the chest type. There are many reasons for this precaution, from avoiding the disaster of a quick-frozen child to preventing a raid on your goodies!

If you don't have a microwave oven for quick thawing and you tend to forget to thaw meat ahead of time, you may wish to try this. Take a fresh package of ground beef in the size that you normally would use and lay it in a piece of waxed paper. Roll it out with a rolling pin into a thin layer. Cover with another thickness of waxed paper and cut in reasonable size squares and stack one square on top of the other one. Then wrap in moisture-vapor-proof wrapping, package, and label. These thin layers of hamburger rolled out between two sheets of waxed paper will separate easily and thaw much more quickly than the solid packages. Keep several of these in your freezer for emergency.

Don't use mayonnaise when making sandwiches for the freezer.

Don't put hot foods in waxed containers.

Don't put hot foods in your freezer.

When you're out of rubber bands and the regular wire ties, pipe cleaners make excellent fasteners to close freezer bags.

It's a good idea to keep a small bag of ice cubes in your freezer. If the temperature in your freezer temporarily rises, the ice cubes will partially melt and then freeze together, giving you a clue.

To help thaw meat faster, spinkle it with salt, being careful not to oversalt

Tips and Tricks

****

THINGS OTHER COOKBOOKS NEVER TAUGHT YOU

AIR BUBBLES IN CAKES. These can be eliminated if you pound or drop your pans on the kitchen table a few times before putting them into the oven. This is very important with rather stiff batters, such as angel food cakes, pound cakes, and so on.

ALMOND PASTE. Commercial almond paste may be purchased in 5-pound or larger cans at any bakery supply store. It's much cheaper than buying it in the small 8-ounce or 1-pound cans. Almond paste freezes well; I've kept it for over a year without any change in flavor or texture. When buying large quantities, divide paste into 1-pound pieces, wrap each piece in foil and put all the pieces in a moisture-vapor-proof plastic bag. This will give you convenient amounts and you won't have to thaw the large piece every time you want to use almond paste.

APPETIZERS. When you've arrived home later than you planned, after being out all day, and dinner isn't ready, but the head of the family is about to make an appearance, set the table first. Never mind that dinner isn't even started; just set the table as attractively as you can. This will give the appearance of being well organized and prepared. Take some appetizers out of the freezer, the kind that heat in the oven in a few minutes, and fix some sort of refreshment. Let your dinner thaw and cook while you and your dinner companions talk over the day's events. They'll never guess that you're simply stalling for time.

AVOCADO. Keep the stone in any unused portion of an avocado to prevent it from turning dark. A few drops of lemon or lime juice in an avocado salad or dip will also keep it a fresh green color.

BABY FOODS. Many young mothers are now preparing their own baby food, not only because it is less expensive but also because it is free of additives and seasonings. With all the new appliances, such as blenders and food processors, there is no need to make a big job out of this. A part of your own food before all seasonings are added can be processed and served fresh each day. However, there will be times when you will want to make up a quantity of these foods for those occasions when you are going out, or the food you are having does not lend itself to baby food.

Reasonable care should be used in preparing baby food, since babies are more sensitive to bacteria than are adults. Bacteria contamination of baby food can be minimized if you have clean hands, use clean, freshly washed utensils, and cook foods thoroughly. Great care should be taken with regard to storage of baby foods, whether commercial or homemade. It is best that you use raw or fresh food and cook it in the smallest amount of water possible. Any food that is not immediately used should be frozen in vapor-proof containers. Storage time should be kept to a minimum, with foods rotated frequently.

There are certain foods that should not be fed to very young infants nor sick infants, such as spinach, carrots, and beets, because these vegetables have a high nitrate content. A rare disease called aethenoglobinemia is related to nitrate content in foods. This disease is extremely rare, and mainly a problem for infants not old enough to eat solid foods. For this reason, most pediatricians agree it is best to avoid potential problems, no matter how small statistically, by avoiding the above-mentioned vegetables in very small or sick infants. For very small portions, freeze baby food in ice-cube trays; when frozen, remove immediately and pack in moisture-vapor-proof plastic bags. Thaw and warm just before serving time. Junior foods which are usually eaten in larger quantities lend themselves to freezing in larger containers. Small plastic bags, as well as very small rigid containers, are good for this. Tupperware makes a variety of very small rigid containers that are ideal for this type of freezing.

BACON. Anyone who has ever burned bacon will enjoy the easier method of frying it in the oven. Put bacon in a single layer on top of your broiling pan and insert into a 400° F preheated oven. Bake for 8 to 10 minutes, depending on how crisp you want it. (This timing is for thin-sliced bacon; thicker slices will take longer.) There's no need to turn the bacon; it stays flat and there seems to be much less shrinkage when bacon is cooked in this manner.

When draining grease from bacon on paper towels, use an extra towel to blot the top. This works well for anything greasy that you're trying to drain.

BACON, CRUMBLED. When a recipe calls for crumbled bacon, use your kitchen shears or a sharp knife to cut across the entire width of the package, making ¼-inch strips, until you have the desired amount. Put on top of your broiler pan and bake in a 400° F preheated oven for 20 minutes, stirring about twice. If your broiler pan is quite large, it will take less time, so watch it closely the first time. This is much faster than waiting for cooked bacon to cool so that you can crumble it properly. Also, the pieces tend to be more uniform.

Have you ever wanted a tablespoon or so of crumbled bacon, but really didn't have the time to prepare it or didn't want to dirty another pan? Well, make a whole pound of it at one time, put it into a container, and freeze. It'll be there when you need it. It's marvelous for deviled eggs, scrambled eggs, German potato salad, sandwich spreads, garnishes on top of soups. I can't tell you how much I use this frozen bacon. The only drawback is that I use twice as much bacon now as I formerly did! I can, however, buy in quantity when it's on sale.

BANANAS. After peeling bananas, dip or brush them with lemon juice to keep them from turning dark; especially nice for fruit salads, desserts, and garnishes.

BANANAS, OVERRIPE. These can be used in making banana cake or banana bread. Also try putting overripe bananas in your next waffle or pancake batter. See Banana Pancakes, page 124. They impart a delicious fruity flavor. These are especially good with black walnut pancake syrup. (See Pancake Syrup in this section.)

BEEF BONES. When ordering standing rib roast, boned (or any other cut of beef), roast the bones along with the meat. These roasted bones cooked with your beef stock will impart a wonderful flavor. Freeze stock in cubes for gravies or use it for soup, whichever you prefer.

BOUQUET GARNI. A metal tea ball holds whole spices like bay leaves, peppercorns, parsely sprigs, fresh or dried thyme, and sometimes garlic, and saves tying them in a cheesecloth bag as suggested in most recipes. Hang over the edge of the kettle to season food. Remove when done.

BOUILLON CUBES. These are fine to use as seasoning in gravies, soups, sauces. Try cooking noodles, rice or other pasta in bouillon or broth for an extra-rich flavor. They are also good for basting when you're roasting or barbecuing meat.

When making soups, sauces, and gravies, try salting with bouillon cubes. In other words, don't add any salt; just keep adding bouillon cubes until the sauce, soup, gravy is salted to taste. You'll be amazed at the full-bodied flavor.

BOUILLON GRANULES. The instant bouillon granules have the advantage of not drying out in a large, undissolvable chunk as the bouillon cubes tend to do. They dissolve more quickly and hence are easier to use. Substitute 1 teaspoon granules for 1 bouillon cube in any recipe.

BREAD. Leftover bread slices are easy to cube and grate for stuffing if they're frozen first. Use directly from the freezer.

French or Italian bread doesn't stay fresh very long; in fact, it should be eaten the first day to enjoy its fresh flavor. However, this isn't always possible; when you buy French or Italian bread, slice off the amount you think you'll use immediately and prepare the rest for the freezer. Slice and make garlic bread if you wish. Wrap sliced bread in aluminum foil and freeze. For longer storage, over-wrap with plastic moisture-vapor-proof bag. This allows you to take the bread out of the freezer a few slices at a time if you wish, or all the remainder can be heated at one time in the aluminum foil before serving it.

BREAD-CRUMB TOPPING. The next time a recipe calls for bread crumbs, either as a topping or as breading for meat, fish, and so on, try substituting crumbs made from the various flavored crackers that are now available.

BREADED PORK CHOPS OR CUTLETS. Try breading them with crumbs made from the seasoned prepared bread stuffing. The herbs in the stuffing mixture will give the chops or cutlets a deliciously different flavor.

BREADED VEAL. This will taste entirely different if it is breaded in flavored Italian bread crumbs. Just before serving it, you may wish to top each piece of meat with a slice of mozzarella cheese. Heat until the cheese starts to melt, and then serve immediately.

BREADING MEATS AND FISH. After breading meats, fish, or anything else that is going to be fried, be sure to let it stand for at least 15 minutes before frying. This little trick will set the breading and keep it from falling off while you are frying it. You'll be amazed at the difference this makes.

BROILING. When broiling steak or other meat, put ½ to 1 cup of water in the bottom of the broiler pan. This not only makes the pan much easier to clean, but the drippings make a delicious gravy.

BROWN SUGAR. After you've opened a package of brown sugar, always store the remainder in the refrigerator to keep it soft. Actually, keeping it in a vacuum-sealed plastic container is a very good way to store it; it will never dry out.

To soften brown sugar, place it in covered container in 300° F oven for about 15 minutes. Use immediately. Or place brown sugar in an airtight plastic container, top with a moistened paper napkin, and let it stand overnight.

When brown sugar is called for in a recipe, it should be packed when measured. This can be a rather time-consuming job. If the recipe specifies 2 cups of brown sugar, take a full 1-pound box and remove ¼ cup of the contents, packed measure, of course. The remainder in the box will measure 2 cups packed. Remember, each pound of brown sugar measures 2¼ cups. When measuring large quantities of brown sugar, this can be a real timesaver.

BUNS. When hurriedly heating frozen hot dog or hamburger buns, be sure to separate them first. This provides uniform heat and lets the insides warm up more quickly.

BUTTER. Prepare butter balls, butter curls, and butter molds at your leisure and store them in plastic cartons in the freezer for future use. When you are entertaining, they give your table that extra little touch, indicating a really special occasion.

BUTTERING A PAN. To butter a cooking dish quickly without any waste, simply use a stick of butter from the refrigerator, open only one end and rub it on the dish. No grease on your hand, either!

CAKE DECORATIONS. For festive occasions, gather rose leaves or some other leaves of about the same size. Wash them thoroughly, then dry gently with a towel. Paint one side with melted semisweet chocolate until the chocolate is about ⅛ inch thick. Place the painted leaves on a cookie sheet lined with waxed paper and refrigerate. Later, peel the leaves carefully from the underside and you'll have some lovely decorations. The chocolate leaves freeze well; so make a big batch. Store in a plastic carton to protect them from breakage. These are especially fine for unartistic souls like myself. They're most attractive when arranged on white, mocha, coffee, or carmel frostings. *Be sure you don't use poison ivy, laurel leaves, and so on!*

CALORIE COUNTERS. Try reducing the amount of sugar used in many of your cakes, cookies, and dessert recipes. When revising this book, I was able to reduce the sugar content in almost all these recipes. When you figure how many calories are in ¼ or ½ cup of sugar, a small amount of sugar eliminates a considerable number of calories from your recipes.

Gelatin molds and salads may be made with plain gelatin and colored and flavored with either a fruit juice or a package of unsweetened Kool-Aid. Use liquid sweetener or just several tablespoons of sugar, thereby omitting ½ cup of the sugar that is found in prepared boxes of gelatin. Remember, 1 tablespoon, or 1 envelope, of gelatin is equivalent to one 3-ounce package of flavored gelatin.

CANDIES. If you want to keep candy fresh, store it in the freezer. This is a fine idea for chocolate during the warmer months.

CARDBOARD. Save the heavy cardboard backing from your commercially prepared pizza pies. Not only are they nice to use when you are freezing your own pizzas, but they're an excellent protection for freezing flat piecrust (see page 309), unmolded frozen tortes, flans, some cakes, and so on. You'll find dozens of uses for them.

CHEESE. When recipes specify shredded cheese to put into a sauce and melt, use a wire cheese slicer and cut the slices very thin. It's much faster and easier than shredding, and the cheese melts almost as quickly.

Moldy cheese isn't spoiled. Remove mold and use promptly.

Freshly grated cheese keeps well in the freezer.

CHEESE IN FROZEN FOODS. The acids in some cheese products will attack aluminum foil; when wrapping things for the freezer, such as pizzas or casseroles with cheese topping, always put a layer of waxed paper or plastic wrap directly over the food before wrapping with aluminum foil.

CHICKEN BROTH. To have small amounts of frozen chicken broth handy for seasoning gravies and sauces, freeze your broth in ice cube trays. When it's frozen, store it in the freezer in moisture-vapor-proof containers or plastic bags. You can take out a few cubes whenever you need them. Do the same for meat stock.

CHOCOLATE CURLICUES. To make these, simply use your vegetable peeler. Depending on the size of your strokes, you can make either big or little shavings. Use squares of bitter or semisweet chocolate that have been warmed ever so slightly.

CITRUS FRUITS. Put whole citrus fruits in boiling water for 5 to 10 minutes, depending on size. Boiled fruit yields about twice the volume of juice.

Freeze lemon and orange juice in plastic ice cube trays (see page 17). Remove when frozen and store in plastic bags to be used as needed. You'll find these little juice cubes indispensable when you are making drinks, flavoring desserts, and cooking in general.

CITRUS RIND, GRATED. If you don't use the juice of a lemon or orange after you've grated off the rind, it will dry up in a few days unless you keep it in the vegetable crisper, and then it tends to mildew or rot very easily. I choose to let mine dry up and then, before using, I put them in boiling water for 5 minutes. The citrus becomes soft and easy to squeeze, and it's not a total loss.

A reverse procedure may also be used. After you've extracted the juice from a lemon or orange, put the rind in a plastic bag and freeze it. Then, when a recipe calls for grated rind, simply use the rinds from your freezer, and grate them while they're still frozen.

COCKTAILS, FROZEN. To make frozen daiquiris, bacardis, et cetera, without crushed ice, add 1 part of water to 2 parts of your favorite recipe, and store in your freezer. The cocktails become frothily iced, but never freeze solidly.

COCONUT. To toast coconut or nuts, bake at 375° F for 5 to 7 minutes, stirring occasionally until golden.

To tint coconut, combine 2 to 4 drops of food coloring with a small amount of water. Half fill a wide-mouth, screw-type jar with coconut, add coloring, and shake until all the coconut is evenly colored.

COOKED CEREALS. If you don't like cereals cooked in water, and cooking them in milk requires too much time at the stove, try this. Measure the usual amount of cereal you use, then add enough nonfat dry milk to reconstitute the water you're going to use. Now add boiling water from the tea kettle, measured to the proper amount. Set the heat low and, in 5 minutes, you'll have a perfect cereal every time. No watching, no stirring, and cheaper than whole milk.

COOKIES. When making cookies that have to be rolled into balls take a portion of the dough (either ½ or ¼ of the total) and roll it into a long thin roll about the diameter of the balls you want to make. Now cut this long roll into uniformed-sized pieces, and you'll have all your cookie balls made in a wink.

When slicing refrigerator cookies, use a wire cheese slicer for even slices. Works like a dream.

COOLING AND CHILLING. When a recipe calls for cooling items such as puddings, sauces, frostings, gelatin desserts, and some pastry doughs and batters, you can cut the cooling time in half by chilling them in the freezer. Food in metal bowls or containers will chill more quickly than food in glass or Pyrex Ware. Also, a frost-free freezer will chill the food more quickly than the conventional type. Remember, don't put hot foods into your freezer; always let them cool slightly. In an emergency, when you don't have time to wait, be sure that warm dishes are placed away from any frozen items in your freezer, or set them on a thick cloth towel for insulation.

CRANBERRY RELISH. When making cranberry relish or anything equally juicy and messy, freeze first, and then put through the food grinder while still frozen. End of mess!

CRANBERRY SAUCE. I thought everyone knew this little trick, but I found I was wrong, so . . . when you are opening a can of cranberry sauce, open one end completely, invert can on serving dish, and puncture the opposite end. The sauce will simply slide out.

CREAM CHEESE AND SOUR CREAM. Both will curdle if added to a substance that it too hot. It's the shock that causes this; the cold cream is broken up by the sudden contact with a hot material. Remove dish from heat before adding any cream cheese or sour cream, or stir a small amount of sauce into the cream and blend this mixture back into the sauce, stirring constantly. Once the cream is incorporated, keep the heat low so that the sauce doesn't bubble. Or bake at low oven temperature.

CREAMED FOODS, FROZEN. Some creamy foods may curdle or separate when thawed, although there is no flavor change. Heating may restore the original consistency. However, using Clearjel will eliminate this problem (see page 70). If you don't have Clearjel, try to use as little fat as possible in creamed dishes that are to be frozen. It's the fat that causes the curdling.

CREAMING. For easier creaming, allow cream cheese, butter, or margarine to warm up to room temperature. Always remove wrappings immediately after removing item from refrigerator and put into mixing bowl. Cheese, butter, and margarine will come out whole, and you won't have to scrape the wrapping paper—again saving time.

CREAMING BUTTER AND SUGAR. If you're in a hurry, rinse mixing bowl with hot water and slice butter in thin slices with either a cheese cutter or vegetable peeler. Your butter will cream in no time.

CRUSHED ICE. Always keep a bag of crushed ice in the freezer for entertaining. The bartender will love you for it.

For a spectacular effect at your next dinner or party, serve an arrangement of shrimp, vegetables, or fresh fruit on a bed of tinted or plain crushed ice. Cover a serving platter, bowl, or compote with the crushed ice, inserting a smaller bowl into the center. Freeze until ready to use. To prepare, fill the small bowl or cup with cocktail sauce (see page 190), dip, or fruit dressing (see page 221); arrange the shrimp, vegetables, or fruit on top of the crushed ice; garnish with parsley or mint leaves. Not only will the ice keep the food cold and fresh, it will add a professional look to your table.

CUPCAKES. When cupcake batter is fairly thin, pour all of it into a large measuring cup or pitcher. Now pour the batter from this into the muffin tins. It's very quick and easy, and barely a drop is spilled.

Cupcakes for a children's party may be baked in ice cream cones. Use the cones with flat bottoms and fill about ¾ full. When baked, they will look just like filled ice cream cones. Frost with your favorite frosting, simply dipping the cones into the frosting. Then, if you wish, you may dip the frosted cones into shredded or toasted coconut, chocolate shot, nuts, or whatever you like.

CUTTING. When cutting icebox cookies, jelly rolls, uncooked yeast dough (when making filled rolls, for instance), et cetera, use a piece of string instead of a knife. Put the string under the piece to be sliced or cut, and cross the ends over the top; now pull. Your dough will not be torn or squashed by the pressure of the knife, but will remain in exactly its original shape.

DATES. To cut dates, dip kitchen shears or knife into hot water or flour to prevent sticking.

DIETING. Freeze all leftover cakes and goodies that might tempt you. It's very difficult to nibble on frozen food! It also doesn't taste very good unless, of course, it's a frozen dessert.

Whenever you are making a low calorie, low cholesterol, or low sodium vegetable dish, soup, et cetera, make in quantity and freeze in individual-size portions. Of course, if everyone in your family is on the same diet, then freeze in family-size portions.

DIPS. Leftover dips can be frozen for a short period of time (2 to 3 weeks) and used in place of sour cream on baked potatoes. You'll be amazed at some of the interesting flavor combinations you'll discover. Because potatoes are fairly bland, they adapt themselves well to this type of "dressing up."

DOUBLE BOILER. If you're going to cook something in a double boiler that will take quite a bit of time, such as a custard or pudding, put a few marbles in the bottom with the water. If the water gets low, you'll know about it!

DRIED BEANS. Cook dried beans (any kind) in unsalted water for quicker cooking and more uniform texture. Add salt after they're cooked.

DUSTING CAKE PANS. Keep a powder puff in the flour bin for quick and easy dusting of cake pans.

EGGS. Separate eggs about 1 hour before using. They separate best when cold, but beat to a greater volume when at room temperature.

Always beat the whites before beating the yolks, and you won't have to wash your beaters.

EGG WHITES. Have you ever passed up a tempting recipe because it required several egg yolks and you didn't know what to do with the whites? No need to worry now. I keep a plastic moisture-vapor-proof carton handy in my kitchen freezer at all times, just for this purpose. As I use the yolks, I empty the whites into this carton. On the lid I have a strip of freezer tape on which I mark each egg white as it's added, like this: *H/ ///*. When I have enough for a specific recipe, I start a new carton. Homemade Chocolate Angel Food cake (see page 144) is a real taste treat; meringue shells (see page 239) are also easy to make and they're a nice treat too, especially when fresh fruit is in season. Topped with ice cream and fresh strawberries, who can conjure up a more delectable dessert?

When using egg whites collected in the manner mentioned above, be sure to let them stand at room temperature for an hour after defrosting. They whip up much more easily.

EGG WHITES, YOLKS IN. Beaten egg whites won't stiffen properly if they contain yolk or any other impurities. But when you inadvertently spill some yolk in the whites, don't panic. Freeze as usual. Yolks have a higher viscosity than the whites, especially when partly frozen. As the whites thaw and are in the icy stage, it's very simple to lift out the little particles of yolk which are in a solid state at this time. However, if you let them stand too long, it will be impossible to remove them. If the whites don't beat stiff, throw them out, because your cake or dessert won't be successful.

EGGS, HARD-COOKED. For recipes that call for chopped hard-boiled eggs, try poaching the eggs until they're firm. This method of cooking them is faster and eliminates the mess of removing the shells.

For perfect hard-cooked eggs, before cooking them poke a tiny hole through the shell with a sturdy darning or sewing needle, using a thimble so as not to hurt your hand. This keeps the shells from cracking and later the eggs will peel easily. These eggs may be dropped—gently—into boiling water without fear of having the shells crack. After adding the eggs, bring water just to a boil, lower heat, and simmer for 15 to 20 minutes. Remove from heat and immerse eggs in cold water immediately. Remove shells under running water.

If you're going to slice eggs to use as a garnish, stir them all the while they're cooking. The yolk will be centered, thus making the slices very attractive.

When cooking hard-boiled eggs for a picnic or for school lunches, peel the eggs while still slightly warm. Roll them in a mixture of salt and pepper. Cool thoroughly and wrap in aluminum foil, plastic wrap, or plastic bags.

Ever forget to mark your hard-cooked eggs? If you want to tell them from the uncooked ones, simply spin them on a flat surface. The cooked eggs will spin very fast, but the fresh eggs will not.

EGGS, SCRAMBLED. Are you in a rut? Do you prepare scrambled eggs the same way every time? Try these flavor variations: small chunks of cream cheese added when the eggs are half-cooked; instead of milk, add sour cream or sour half-and-half to the eggs; shred Cheddar cheese into the eggs immediately after putting them in the pan. Snipped parsley, green onions, and chives are other favorites to add, as well as a pinch of various herbs.

FINGER BOWLS. Here's a good substitute for finger bowls, when you are serving food such as barbecued spareribs, fried chicken, and other informal foods. Pass a plate or platter with a Wash 'n Dry napkin for each guest. These napkins should be removed from their wrappings and arranged attractively on the platter with lemon slices. Or, if you like, you may also scent them lightly with a citron-smelling toilet water or cologne.

FLOUR If a recipe calls for cake flour and you want to substitute all-purpose flour, subtract 1 tablespoon of flour for every cup used in the recipe.

FROSTING OR ICING (LEFTOVER). If you don't have enough frosting left to freeze and use on another occasion, add Rice Krispies or some other crunchy cereal and stir until well covered. (This is especially good with chocolate frostings.) Drop by teaspoonfuls on waxed paper and cool. This makes a nice little treat for children and grownups alike.

FRUIT. To keep fresh-cut fruit, such as apples, peaches, bananas, and avocados, from turning dark, sprinkle with lemon or orange juice or with ½ teaspoon of ascorbic acid crystals which have been dissolved in a tablespoon of water. If you have a large quantity of fresh fruit, such as a mixed fruit salad, double the amount of citrus juice or ascorbic acid.

FRUIT JUICE. Freeze fruit juice in cubes for refreshing summer drinks. Before freezing, put a sprig of mint, a twist of orange, lemon, or lime peel, or a maraschino cherry in each cube.

Use leftover frozen fruit juice instead of cold water when making gelatin salads and desserts.

FRYING IN BUTTER. To keep butter from burning and smoking at high temperatures, add about 1 part oil to 2 parts butter. You'll still have the flavor of butter, but the mixture won't burn or smoke at high temperatures the way pure butter will.

GARLIC. Always keep a cruet of olive oil in which a good-sized clove of garlic is soaking. (Slit the garlic in a few places.) This olive oil is perfect for making vinegar-and-oil salad dressings, sautéing foods to which you want to impart a bit of garlic flavor, et cetera. You'll be surprised how often you'll use this garlic-flavored olive oil, and it often saves cutting and rubbing a garlic clove in a pan or bowl. When the cruet has been emptied, remove garlic and put in a fresh piece before refilling.

GARLIC BUDS. To loosen the tight skin of a garlic bud, try pouring hot water over it. Or put it in your microwave oven for 5 seconds and the peel pops off.

GELATIN MOLDS. A foolproof way to unmold gelatin easily is to oil your mold generously with cooking oil and then put it in the refrigerator before you start mixing the gelatin. Have the gelatin fairly well cooled, remove the mold from the refrigerator, and blot up any excess oil with a paper towel. Pour your gelatin into the mold and refrigerate as usual. This method allows molds with intricate designs to be used without hesitation. It eliminates running a sharp knife around the edge of the mold, which usually ruins delicate designs.

Remove gelatin from the refrigerator about 20 minutes before you unmold it. Invert mold on your serving plate and the gelatin should slip right out. If it doesn't come out easily, leave it upside down on the serving plate for a few extra minutes, then simply lift the mold.

GRAVIES AND SAUCES. To thicken liquid mixtures, add 1½ tablespoons of flour mixed with 3 tablespoons of water for each cup of liquid. Cook, stirring, until thick.

Gravies and sauces can be ruined by too much fat. To avoid this, set sauce or gravy in the freezer for 15 to 20 minutes. Then skim off the fat that has risen to the top, and reheat the sauce. This method also works well with soups. The cold air in the freezer solidifies the fat floating on top.

Browned flour adds flavor and color to gravies. Make it by stirring flour, either dry or with drippings, over low heat until brown. If has only about half the thickening quality of unbrowned flour, so remember to double the amount used. Browned flour won't lump or thicken beyond control.

ICE BAG. When you need an ice bag, partially fill an ordinary hot water bottle with cold water, put into freezer for sufficient time to freeze water partially.

ICED COFFEE AND TEA. Pour surplus breakfast coffee into an ice cube tray and freeze. To serve iced coffee in the afternoon, simply pour warm or cold coffee over these cubes; no more watered-down iced coffee. The same may be done with iced tea, if you like your tea strong.

INSTANT OR FREEZE-DRIED COFFEE. These are ideal to use as a coffee flavoring in puddings, fillings, cakes, cookies, frostings, and desserts.

LIMES. When you have fresh limes, use their juice instead of lemon juice or vinegar in salad dressings, desserts, and so on. It gives a pleasant flavor change. Grated rind of the limes may also be substituted for either orange or lemon rind. Gives a pretty color too.

MARSHMALLOWS. These freeze well. They're easier to cut and much less sticky when partially frozen. Dip kitchen shears into hot water for a minute or two before cutting marshmallows. When dipping up marshmallow cream, put the spoon in hot water for a couple of minutes. Cream will slip off the spoon in a wink.

MEATBALLS. If you like "he-man-sized" meatballs, use your ice cream scoop. You can make them faster and they're uniform in size.

MILK, SOUR. To make sweet milk sour, add 1½ to 2 tablespoons of vinegar or lemon juice per cup of milk and let it stand for 5 minutes.

MUFFINS. When muffin batter is fairly thick, use your ice cream scoop to fill the muffin tins. You'll get just the right amount of batter every time.

MUSHROOMS. To freeze mushrooms, wash and slice or leave whole, whichever way you plan to use them. Freezer-wrap in the quantities you'll need. They may also be sautéed and frozen. Try them both ways; the texture of each is entirely different.

NUTS. Before shelling nuts, put them in boiling water for 5 minutes. The nutmeats will come out whole. Store nuts in your freezer; they keep very well.

Another method of shelling nuts is to freeze them first and then crack the shells while they are still frozen.

If whole walnuts are needed as a garnish, soak in the shell overnight in salted water.

To slice almonds or Brazil nuts, soak a few minutes in boiling water.

NUTS, BLANCHED. To blanch almonds, cover with boiling water, simmer 2 to 3 minutes, then drain and slip skins off with your fingers. Spread out on paper toweling to dry.

ONIONS. Chopped onions may be bought in 10-ounce packages already frozen. These are one of the most timesaving commodities on the frozen-food market. Simply shake out the amount needed, reclose the plastic bag, and return to the freezer. Once you try them, you'll never go back to the eye-watering task of chopping onions yourself.

ONIONS, GREEN. Green onions can be cut uniformly to almost any size quite simply with a pair of scissors. Don't discard the green ends; cut up fine and use in salads and casseroles. They also make a lovely garnish on the top of a bowl of potato soup, for example.

ORANGES. To remove white membrances easily, soak oranges in boiling water for 5 minutes before peeling them.

PANCAKES. When making pancakes from a mix, try using buttermilk instead of regular milk. You'll be amazed how much lighter and fluffier they'll be. If the recipe calls for an egg, and your eggs are small, try adding two instead of one.

PANCAKE SYRUP. Using either homemade syrup or the commercial variety, add a teaspoonful of black walnut flavoring. It will give just a hint of a rich nutty flavor that I'm sure you'll enjoy.

PARSLEY. The quickest way to mince or chop parsely is with a pair of kitchen scissors. Cut as fine or as coarse as desired.

Parsley will keep fresh and crisp in the refrigerator for about 2 weeks if it's washed and put into a closed glass jar while still damp. This is also a good way to perk up wilted parsley.

PARTY PARFAITS. For a really quick but festive-looking dessert, fill parfait glasses or goblets with layers of different-flavored ice cream and store in freezer until serving time. Top with syrup or fresh fruit and juice just before serving. If you're going to make these several days in advance, be sure to cover the top of each glass with Saran Wrap.

PASTA. When freezing noodle, spaghetti, or macroni dishes, cook the pasta about half as long as you normally would—only until it's just softened. A sauce with a low-fat content is best suited as a base. Too much sauce will make the pasta mushy when it's reheated. Thaw in refrigerator. Heat in a moderate oven without stirring.

Adding 1 tablespoon of olive oil to the water when you are cooking pastas will keep the water from boiling over.

POLISHING SILVER AND SILVERWARE. This can be a simple and easy job if you follow these directions. Line your kitchen sink with a large sheet of aluminum foil. Fill with very hot water and add ¼ to ½ cup (depending on the amount of water and silverware to be cleaned) of washing or sal soda (not to be confused with baking soda), or half that amount of trisodium phosphate. Swish the water to dissolve crystals, then add your silver, making sure that the silver is completely covered. It becomes tarnish-free virtually in seconds. You may need a sponge to wash very tarnished pieces gently. This method is disapproved of by jewelers because it gives the silver a "white" color and can eliminate oxidation usually found in trim and patterns. If the "white" color silver bothers you, a quick once-over with regular silver polish eliminates that. It is a quick way to get rid of heavy tarnish; however, I would not use it on any antique silver.

POTATO SALAD. When making American-style potato salad, always mix dressing with the potatoes while they're still hot. For moist potato salad, without too much mayonnaise, add a few tablespoons of boiling water. The water will disappear and the salad will become very moist. Taste, and add more water until you feel you have the right mixture.

PUDDINGS. If your family likes puddings, but you hate to stand at the stove stirring all the while they're coming to a boil, here's good news. When using prepared mixes, dissolve the pudding mix in ½ cup of milk and add ½ cup of instant nonfat dry milk. Stir in pan until completely dissolved. Now add 1½ cups of boiling water, stirring all the while. Continue cooking until thick or until it comes to a low boil as directed. This will reduce the cooking time to less than 5 minutes, even for double quantities. The same principle can be used for homemade puddings.

PUNCH. When preparing a large bowl of punch for a summer or hot-weather party, make a small batch of the punch recipe the day before and freeze it either in large cubes, in molds, or in ice cube trays. Use these in the punch bowl instead of ice cubes and your punch won't be watery.

Most punch recipes make up in quite large quantities. However, to serve in small amounts, you can mix the fruit base, freeze in cubes, and store in freezer bags. When ready to serve, put fruit-base cubes in glasses and add sparkling water, ginger ale, tea, wine, or whatever the recipe calls for. These drinks are usually very refreshing, particularly in warm weather. No need to save your best punch recipes for large-group entertaining.

For a festive-looking punch bowl, freeze fruits or holly in a ring or other mold with carbonated beverage or fruit juice. (Tint with food coloring if you wish, but go easy with the coloring. Faint pastel shades have the best eye appeal.) When it is frozen, unmold it and freezer-wrap in a plastic bag until ready to use. Your punch bowl will be very attractive with this ring or mold floating in it.

QUICK BREADS. In making quick breads, the quicker the mix, the lighter the batter. *Never* overmix the dough.

RAISINS. A quick way to chop raisins is to freeze them first and then twirl them for a few minutes in your blender. Frozen raisins will not gum up in the blender. However, do only half a cup at a time and remove from your blender immediately.

RICE. If you have just a small amount of rice left over and you're going to cook a little more for rice pudding or some other rice dish, never put the cooked and uncooked rice together before cooking the second batch. Cook the raw rice as usual; then add the leftover rice and heat. Otherwise, the soft, cooked rice will absorb all the liquid, leaving the uncooked rice hard, no matter how long you cook it.

SALAD DRESSING. Have your salad ready and chilled; wait until the last minute to add the dressing, or the salad will be soggy.

SALAD GREENS. Always tear salad greens, never cut them.

SANDWICHES. Make and freeze a week's supply of sandwiches at one time. Take what you need from the freezer each morning. The sandwiches are thawed and fresh-tasting by noon. Wrap them in individual bags and mark the type of sandwich on each. I keep all sandwiches in a plastic container for extra protection; they may be kept longer this way. When packing lunches, lettuce or tomato slices should be wrapped separately.

SHOPPING. When you finish the last of a staple or some item in the kitchen, never throw the container, box, or can away until you've added the item to your next week's shopping list. This will save you many a midweek shopping trip.

SOUP. To make better soup, cook gently and evenly. Remember the old adage, "Soup boiled is soup spoiled."

If you're freezing soups, gravies, and other liquids, and you're running short of freezer containers, pour into a metal bread pan and freeze. When it is frozen, remove food as you would from a metal ice cube tray. Put these blocks of frozen liquid into polyethylene bags and return to the freezer. Don't forget to measure the liquid before pouring it into the bread pans so that you can label the exact amount of food in the frozen blocks.

SPECIAL DIETS. If some member of the family is on a special diet, fix his food in quantity and freeze in individual serving portions.

SPRINKLED CLOTHES. Put dampened clothes in the freezer and you won't have to worry about mildew if you don't get around to ironing them right away.

STEW. When making stew, you don't have to thaw the meat first in order to brown it. Just put the meat under the broiler for 10 to 15 minutes, stirring occasionally. It should be nicely browned. Then proceed with your recipe as usual.

TOMATOES. If you like tomatoes peeled, put them in boiling water for 1 minutes, then plunge into cold water. The skin will slip off easily.

WHIPPING CREAM. If your frozen whipping cream doesn't whip easily when thawed, add either two or three drops of lemon juice or a bit of plain gelatin, dissolved, or both. However, the lemon juice will usually suffice. Cream that has been frozen will take longer to whip. Simply turn the electric beater on high and forget about it for a few minutes. Remember the old saying about the watched pot never boiling? The only time I decided to use gelatin, the cream finally whipped by the time I had the gelatin dissolved.

There's no doubt that cream will whip much faster in a blender than with a rotary beater. However, with a blender the volume is considerably less.

If you want to whip cream hours before serving, it's a good idea to stabilize it. To do this, dissolve 1 teaspoon of plain gelatin in 2 tablespoons of cold water (for each cup of cream used) in a Pyrex custard cup. Then set the cup in a pan with a few inches of water (or you can use a double boiler) and heat until all the gelatin is completely dissolved. While the gelatin is cooling, beat the cream until it's of medium consistency; then add sugar, vanilla, or any other flavorings you want, and the cooled gelatin. Continue beating until the cream clings to the bowl. The whipped cream won't become watery; simply keep it refrigerated. Stabilized whipped cream also freezes well.

Leftover whipped cream can be put into a cake decorator or cookie press. Line a cookie sheet or plate with waxed paper and make little swirls, rosettes, or whatever you like with the leftover whipped cream. Freeze these on the waxed paper. When they are frozen, remove and store in a plastic bag. These are lovely as cake decorations or floated in hot chocolate or coffee.

Whipping cream doesn't keep very long in the refrigerator and small quantities are difficult to thaw from the freezer. A good substitute is sour cream. Except as a garnish for desserts, sour cream may be used with confidence instead of whipping cream in such things as gelatin molds, soups, gravies, sauces, puddings, and dressings. Actually, it has been a successful substitute in absolutely everything I've tried. I do believe that the American Dairy Association made the faux pas of the century when they misnamed this product *sour* cream. Commercial sour cream has only the name, not the curdles or the taste, in common with the old type of sour cream. Use it frequently and you'll be surprised at the delicious flavor it imparts to many dishes.

All you calorie watchers may prefer to use sour half-and-half instead of sour cream, although the flavor is a little less rich. There are approximately 352 calories in a cup of commercial sour half-and-half compared to 480 calories in a cup of commercial sour cream. Plain yogurt may also be used as a substitute. It is even less rich in flavor and also in calories; about 180 calories per cup.

YEAST. The great advantage of dry yeast is that it keeps much longer than cake yeast. But did you know that dry yeast can be stored almost indefinitely in the refrigerator?

YOGURT. Before freezing fruit-flavored yogurt, stir to mix. Thaw in refrigerator and eat while still partially frozen. However, it won't have the same creamy consistency of your commercially frozen yogurts. Not a bad idea for brown-baggers.

Plain yogurt may be substituted for cream, sour cream, and sour half-and-half in most recipes if you're counting calories. Of course, the flavor will not be the same.

MEASUREMENTS, EQUIVALENTS, AND SUBSTITUTIONS

Suppose a recipe calls for some prepared ingredient in a specific amount—say, 4 cups of shredded cabbage. How big a head of cabbage do you need to buy? Many people find themselves in a quandary, since measurements of food change drastically when cooked, peeled, sliced, chopped, crumbled, or shredded. I have compiled the following table of the more common foods in their various forms to help you convert quantities with ease.

TABLE OF EQUIVALENT MEASUREMENTS

Apples, dried	2 cups = 5 cups cooked
Apples, fresh	1 pound = 3 medium apples or 3 cups sliced
Apricots, dried	1 pound = 3 cups uncooked or 5 cups cooked
Apricots, fresh	1 pound = 8 to 12
Asparagus	1 pound = 16 to 20 stalks
Avocado	¾ pound = 2 cups cubed (½ inch)

TABLE OF EQUIVALENT MEASURES (*Continued*)

Bacon	6 lean slices = Approximately ⅓ cup crisp, crumbled
Bacon	3 lean slices = Approximately 3 tablespoons crisp, crumbled
Bacon, lean, uncooked	1 pound = Approximately 24 slices
Bacon, lean, uncooked	1 pound = Approximately 1⅓ cups
Bananas	1 pound = 3 medium bananas
	2½ cups diced, sliced
	2 cups mashed
Beans, lima, dried	1 cup = 2½ cups cooked
Beans, large lima	1 cup = 2½ cups cooked
Beans, large lima in the pod	1 pound = ⅔ cups shelled
Beans, large lima shelled	1 pound = 2 cups
Beans, red, dried	1 cup = 2¾ cups cooked
Beans, snap, fresh	1 pound = 3 cups
Beans, white, dried	1 cup = 2½ cups cooked
Beets	1 pound = 2 cups diced
Berries	1 quart = 2½ cups
Berries, strawberries	1 pint = 1½ to 2 cups hulled
Bread crumbs, dry	1 pound = 2 cups
Bread crumbs, dry	1 slice dry = ⅓ cup
Bread crumbs, soft	1 pound, 1 ounce loaf = 11½ cups with crust
Bread cubes, dry	1 slice dry = ¾ cup
Bread cubes, soft	1 slice fresh, untrimmed = 1 cup
Bread stuffing, prepared	8-ounce bag = 3 cups (one bag makes enough stuffing for a 5-pound chicken; 2 bags for a 10-pound turkey)
Brussels sprouts	1 pound = 1 quart or less
Butter or margarine	¼ pound = ½ cup
Cabbage	1 pound = 4 cups shredded
Candied peels, mixed	1 pound = 2½ cups chopped
Carrots	1 pound = 5 medium or 2½ cups diced
Cauliflower	1 pound = 1½ cups
Celery	1 pound = 2 small bunches or 4 cups diced
Cheese, American	1 pound = 4 to 5 cups grated
Cheese, Cheddar	1 pound = 4 cups grated or shredded
Cheese, cottage	½ pound = 1 cup
Cheese, cream	3 ounces = 6 tablespoons
Cheese, cream	8 ounces = 1 cup
Cherries, red	1 pound = 2 cups pitted
Cherries, whole candied	6½ ounces = 1⅛ cups
Chicken	1 pound dressed = ½ pound or 1 cup boned
Chicken, boned	3 cups = 5 cups ground
Chicken breast	1 large = 1 cup boned
Chocolate, unsweetened	1 ounce = 1 square or ¼ cup grated
Citron	4 ounces = ½ cup chopped
Coconut, flaked	3½-ounce package = 1⅓ cups
Coconut, shredded	4-ounce package = 1½ cups
Coffee	1 pound = 80 tablespoons or 5 cups
Corn, ears	1 medium = 1 cup cut up
Corn flakes	18-ounce package = 16 to 20 cups
Cornmeal	1 pound = 3 cups uncooked
Cornmeal	1 cup = 4 cups cooked
Crackers, graham	9 coarsely crumbled = 1 cup

Crackers, graham	12 finely crushed = 1 cup fine crumbs
Crackers, soda	22 finely crushed = 1 cup fine crumbs
Crackers, soda	18 coarsely crushed = 1 cup fine crumbs
Cranberries	1 pound = 4 cups sauce
Cream, heavy	½ pint = 2 cups whipped
Cream, sour	½ pint = 1 cup
Currants	11-ounce package = 2 cups
Dates, pitted	8-ounce package = 1 cup whole or 1¼ cup cut up
Eggplant	1 pound = 2½ cups diced
Eggs, hard-cooked	12 = 3½ cups chopped
Egg whites	7 to 9 = 1 cup
Egg yolks	14 to 19 = 1 cup
Eggs, whole large	4 to 6 = 1 cup
Figs	1 pound = 2¼ cups or 4½ cups cooked
Flour, all-purpose	1 pound = 3½ cups sifted
Flour, cake	1 pound = 3¾ cups sifted
Flour, cake	1 cup = 1 cup minus 2 tablespoons all-purpose flour
Flour, rye	1 pound = 5 cups sifted
Flour, whole wheat or graham	1 pound = 3½ cups sifted
Fruit peels (candied)	4-ounce jar = ½ cup
Gelatin, unflavored	1 envelope = 1 ounce
Grapefruit	1 medium = ¾ cup juice or 1¼ cup cut-up segments
Grapes, Tokay, fresh	1 pound = 2¾ cups seeded
Lard	1 pound = 2 cups
Lemon	1 medium = 3 tablespoons juice
Lemon peel (candied)	4 ounces = ½ cup chopped
Lemon rind	1 medium = 1 teaspoon grated rind
Lobster	2½ pounds = about 2 cups cooked and cut into pieces
Macaroni	1¼ to 1½ cups = 2¼ cups cooked
Margarine or butter	¼ pound = ½ cup
Marshmallows	¼ pound = 16 marshmallows
Marshmallows, miniature	10 = 1 large marshmallow
Meat, ground raw	1 pound = 2 cups
Milk, evaporated	14½-ounce can = 1⅔ cups
Milk, evaporated	6-ounce can = ¾ cup
Milk, sweetened condensed	15-ounce can = 1⅓ cups
	14-ounce can = 1¼ cups
Mushrooms	1 pound = 15 to 20 with stems
Mushrooms	1 pound = 35 to 45 medium-sized with stems
Noodles	1½ to 2 cups = 2¼ cups cooked
Nuts in the shell:	
Almonds*	1 pound = 2 cups nut meats
Brazil nuts	1 pound = 1½ cups nut meats
Filberts	1 pound = 1½ cups nut meats
Peanuts	1 pound = 2 cups nut meats
Pecans	1 pound = 2 cups nut meats
Walnuts	1 pound = 2 cups nut meats
Nuts, shelled and chopped:	
Almonds*	4 ounces = 1 cup
Brazil nuts	1 pound = 3 cups
Filberts	4 ounces = 1 cup
Peanuts	7 ounces = 1½ cups
Pecans	3 ounces = 1 cup
Walnuts	4 ounces = 1 cup

TABLE OF EQUIVALENT MEASURES (*Continued*)

Oatmeal	1 cup = 1¾ cups cooked
Onions	1 medium = ½ cup chopped
Onions	1 pound = 3 large
Oranges	1 medium = ⅓ cup juice
Orange rind	1 medium = 1 tablespoon grated rind
Orange peel, candied	4 ounces = ½ cup chopped
Parsnips	1 pound = 4 medium
Peaches	1 pound = 3 medium or 2 cups peeled and sliced
Peaches, dried	1 pound = 3⅔ cups or 4½ cups cooked
Peanut butter	8-ounce jar = 1 cup
Pears	1 pound = 4 medium or 2½ cups, peeled and sliced
Pears, dried	1 pound = 2⅔ cups or 5⅓ cups cooked
Peas, in pod	1 pound = 1 cup shelled
Pineapple	2 pounds = 1 medium
Plums	1 pound = 8 to 20, depending on variety
Potatoes, sweet	1 pound = 3 medium or 3 cups sliced
Potatoes, white	1 pound = 3 medium or 2½ cups sliced
Prunes, pitted	1-pound package = 2¼ cups uncooked or 4 cups cooked
Raisins	15-ounce package = 3 cups not packed or 2 cups chopped or 4 cups cooked
Rhubarb	1 pound = 2 cups cut into ½-inch pieces
	3 cups cut = 2 cups cooked
Rice, brown	1 cup = 4 cups cooked
Rice, long-grain white	1 cup = 4 to 4½ cups cooked
Rice, precooked white	1 cup = 2 cups cooked
Rice, processed white	1 cup = 4 to 4½ cups cooked
Rice, wild	1 cup = 4 cups cooked
Rolled oats, quick-cooking	1 cup = 1¾ cups cooked
Rutabaga	1 pound = 2⅔ cups diced
Shortening, hydrogenated	1 pound = 2½ cups
Shrimp:	
Small size	1 pound = 60 or more
Average size	1 pound = 26 to 30 in shell
Jumbo size	1 pound = 15 to 18 in shell
Cooked and cleaned	1 cup = ¾ pound raw or 7 ounces frozen shelled
Spaghetti	1 to 1¼ cups = 2½ cups cooked
Suet	1 pound = 3¾ cups chopped
Sugar:	
Brown	1 pound = 2¼ cups firmly packed
Confectioners	1 pound = 4 cups sifted or 3½ cups unsifted
Granulated	1 pound = 2¼ cups
Granulated	1 cup = 1⅓ cups firmly packed brown sugar
Sugar, loaf	1 pound = 120 pieces
Superfine	1 pound = 2⅓ cups
Syrup:	
Corn syrup	1½ pounds = 2 cups or 1 pint
Honey	1 pound = 1½ cups
Maple-blended	12 ounces = 1½ cups
Molasses	1 pound = 1⅓ cups
Tomatoes	1 pound = 4 small

Turnips   1 pound = 3 medium
Vanilla wafers   30 small, finely crushed = 1 cup fine crumbs
         20 small, coarsely crushed = 1 cup
         1 pound = 4 cups finely crushed
Zwieback   12 slices = 1 cup fine crumbs
         9 slices = 1 cup coarse crumbs
 * 1 pound whole natural (unblanched) almonds = 3 cups
 1 pound sliced natural (unblanched) almonds = 5 cups
 1 pound slivered almonds = 3¾ cups
 1 pound hand chopped or roasted diced almonds = 3¾ cups
 1 pound whole almonds, ground in electric blender = 4 cups

GENERAL TABLE OF EQUIVALENTS
(To help you multiply your own recipes)

3 teaspoons = 1 tablespoon
4 tablespoons = ¼ cup
5⅓ tablespoons = ⅓ cup
8 tablespoons = ½ cup
10⅔ tablespoons = ⅔ cup
12 tablespoons = ¾ cup
16 tablespoons = 1 cup
2 tablespoons = 1 liquid ounce
1 cup = ½ pint
2 cups = 1 pint
4 cups = 1 quart
4 quarts = 1 gallon
8 quarts = 1 peck
4 pecks = 1 bushel

DIVIDED-RECIPE EQUIVALENTS

The following table will save you work in dividing recipe ingredients in halves and thirds. (NOTE: A *pinch* is as much as can be taken between tip of finger and thumb. A *dash* is about ⅛ teaspoon.)

⅓ of ¼ teaspoon = a pinch
⅓ of ½ teaspoon = a pinch
½ of ¼ teaspoon = ⅛ teaspoon
3 teaspoons = 1 tablespoon
⅓ of 1 tablespoon = 1 teaspoon
⅓ of 2 tablespoons = 2 teaspoons
⅓ of 5 tablespoons = 1 tablespoon plus 2 teaspoons
⅓ of 7 tablespoons = 2 tablespoons plus 1 teaspoon
½ of 1 tablespoon = 1½ teaspoons
½ of 5 tablespoons = 2 tablespoons plus 1½ teaspoons
½ of 7 tablespoons = 3 tablespoons plus 1½ teaspoons
2 tablespoons = ⅛ cup
4 tablespoons = ¼ cup
5 tablespoons plus 1 teaspoon = ⅓ cup
8 tablespoons = ½ cup
10 tablespoons plus 2 teaspoons = ⅔ cup

DIVIDED-RECIPE EQUIVALENTS *(Continued)*

12 tablespoons = ¾ cup
16 tablespoons = 1 cup
⅓ of ¼ cup = 1 tablespoon plus 1 teaspoon
⅓ of ⅓ cup = 1 tablespoon plus 2⅓ teaspoons
⅓ of ½ cup = 2 tablespoons plus 2 teaspoons
⅓ of ⅔ cup = 3 tablespoons plus 1⅔ teaspoons
⅓ of ¾ cup = ¼ cup
½ of ¼ cup = 2 tablespoons
½ of ⅓ cup = 2 tablespoons plus 2 teaspoons
½ of ½ cup = ¼ cup
½ of ⅔ cup = ⅓ cup
½ of ¾ cup = 6 tablespoons

TABLE OF SUBSTITUTIONS

1 teaspoon baking powder = ¼ teaspoon baking soda plus ½ teaspoon cream of tartar
1 square unsweetened chocolate = 3 tablespoons cocoa plus 1 tablespoon butter
1 tablespoon cornstarch = 2 tablespoons flour (for thickening)
1 cup 20% cream = 3 tablespoons butter and ⅞ cup milk
cream, whipping or half-and-half = commercial sour cream or sour half-and-half may be substituted, except as a decoration or topping. A little sugar may be added if necessary.
1 cup sifted all-purpose flour = 1 cup plus 2 tablespoons sifted cake flour
1 cup sifted cake flour = 1 cup minus 2 tablespoons sifted all-purpose flour
2 tablespoons flour = 1 tablespoon cornstarch (for thickening)
1 cup self-rising flour = 1 cup regular flour plus 1½ teaspoons baking powder plus ½ teaspoon salt
When making yeast dough, omit the salt.
When baking nonyeast dough, omit the baking powder and salt.
When recipe calls for baking soda, decrease by half the amount.
⅛ teaspoon garlic powder = 1 small clove of garlic
¼ teaspoon garlic salt = ⅛ teaspoon garlic powder plus ⅛ teaspoon salt
1 cup honey = 1 cup sugar plus ¼ cup liquid
1 cup bottle milk = ½ cup evaporated milk plus ½ cup water
1 cup sweet milk = 1 cup sour milk or buttermilk plus ½ teaspoon baking soda
¼ teaspoon onion salt = ⅛ teaspoon onion powder plus ⅛ teaspoon salt
Scallions = May be substituted for shallots in the same amount.
1 cup granulated sugar = 1 cup plus 2 tablespoons brown sugar
1 cup canned tomatoes = about 1⅓ cups cut-up fresh tomatoes, simmered 10 minutes
1 regular yeast cake = 1 package dry yeast
1-ounce yeast cake = 2 packages dry yeast
yogurt = sour cream in most recipes except baked goods. Yogurt is much lower in fat content.

SPICE AND HERB COOKERY

In recent years, many people have discovered that cooking with spices and herbs can be a fascinating pastime. A great variety of attractively priced and packaged herbs are now readily available in all grocery stores. You no longer have to go to gourmet or specialty stores looking for rare herbs.

When used with discretion, these pungent plants can add tantalizing aroma and flavor to the simplest foods. But, used with a heavy hand, they can turn any meal into a disaster. For general cooking purposes there's little difference between spices and herbs. An herb is described as a quiet, gentle, leafy plant; it imparts a delicate flavor. Actually, herbs are simply cultivated weeds and usually are very easy to grow.

Cultivating Herbs

You'll probably want to try growing a few herbs yourself. This is the easiest way of making sure that you'll have all the fresh herbs you want for freezing. To begin with, you may want to grow only those that are most familiar, such as parsley, marjoram, thyme, mint, rosemary, garlic, and the salad favorites, dill, basil, and tarragon.

Big seed companies now provide special seed kits of favorite herbs, with indoor-outdoor planting instructions. Warmth, sunshine, and fairly sweet, moderately enriched soil will produce the prettiest plants and tastiest herbs. A windowbox, as well as a spacious yard, can serve as an herb garden. When planting mint outdoors, be sure to contain this hardy plant in some way or you'll have mint growing like so many weeds. The easiest way to prevent mint from spreading is to plant it in a clay pot in the ground.

Herbs such as mint, chervil, wintergreen, and sweet woodruff thrive with moisture and some shade. Borage grows best in chalky, dry soil, and watercress is native to the brookside. Unlike watercress, upland cress is a hardy biennial that will thrive in ordinary garden soil.

During the winter months, herbs of the smaller variety may easily be grown in pots, even in the smallest kitchen. If you really want to make an impression on your friends, grow a pot or two of the lesser known herbs, such as burnet, germander, savory, sorrel, or borage. Then offhandedly mention, when asked what they are, that you simply couldn't cook without them. Your friends will immediately place you up with the great culinary experts; that is, unless your cooking for them disproves this theory!

The top leaves and tips of herbs can be picked any time during the growing season. When buds, flowers, or seed heads first appear, cut back to encourage new growth of tender leaves. The crucial time to gather most herb leaves for drying and freezing is just as the flower buds are ready to bloom. The leaves are then rich in the oils that carry their flavor.

Blending and Freezing

During the growing season, the refrigerator is the best place to keep fresh-picked or purchased herbs for daily use. The easiest way to preserve sprigs of herbs is to freeze them, but since the leaves turn limp and begin to darken soon after they have thawed, you must time their exit from the freezer carefully. To freeze, wash and pat dry. Spread out on freezer wrap and roll the wrap carefully so that there is only a single layer of leaves; then twist the ends tightly and seal with freezer tape. Make each package small, because leftover herbs can't be refrozen. *Don't forget to label each roll or package!*

I have found plastic molded ice cube trays ideal for freezing herbs (see page 17). Fill each cube indentation with herb leaves, either whole or cut up (the latter is my preference). Fill with just enough water to cover leaves, and freeze. These cubes don't have to be wrapped separately. Simply put them in a plastic bag (one type of herb to a bag), mark or label, and store in freezer.

Whole herbs frozen in ice cubes add decoration as well as flavor to cold tea or fruit drinks. Mint is the herb most commonly frozen in this way. Other herbs, such as rosemary, thyme, and basil, can be frozen in cubes to garnish cold consommé or broth. To make these, freeze a layer of water in the cube tray, place the herb in the middle, add more water, and refreeze.

This is quick and easy if you have a blender; be sure to try it. For each 2 cups of well-packed herb leaves, add 1 cup of water. Turn blender on low speed for coarse and high speed for finely chopped herbs; leave on just long enough for all the leaves to be chopped. Pour this liquid mass into ice cube trays (either plastic molded or regular trays) and freeze. Put cubes into plastic bags and label. Make sure the cubes are well frozen, so that they won't stick together after they've been unmolded. Because small bags have a way of getting lost in the dark corners of a freezer, I find it best to keep them all together, either in a large plastic bag or plastic bucket.

When using the herbs, simply pop your cubes of oregano, thyme, parsley, et cetera, into spaghetti sauce or whatever you're making. There is so little fluid in these cubes that it won't affect most recipes. However, if you don't want to add the water, simply set cubes in a small dish until they're thawed; then drain off the water.

The Uses of Spices and Herbs

Spices, which are generally more emphatic in flavor than herbs, are made from the fruit, bud, bark, or roots of aromatic tropical plants. Only a few spices lend themselves to the home garden; one of these is horseradish.

Although your own taste should be your guide when seasoning with spices and herbs, the beginner will find a few general rules helpful:

1. If a recipe doesn't specify an amount, use only a pinch of herb when experimenting. More can always be added later, after you've tasted it.

2. When fresh herbs are unavailable, don't hesitate to substitute the dried or powdered ones. The rule is: ½ teaspoon dried herbs or spices (¼ teaspoon of the powdered) is equal to 2 teaspoons of the fresh. Or the converse is true: 2 teaspoons of fresh herbs or spices are equal to ½ teaspoon of the dried or ¼ teaspoon of the powdered. Because most people don't have fresh or frozen herbs on hand, the recipes in this book will refer to powdered or dried, unless otherwise stated.

3. Buy herbs and spices in small amounts because they soon lose their pungency, unless, of course, you intend to use some fresh and freeze the rest. The defrosted leaves will be limp but still flavorful.

4. To achieve the fullest flavor from an herb, cut fresh ones with scissors before using; soak dried ones in liquid for a few minutes.

5. To taste the true flavor of an herb you've never tried before, use this simple method: Mix ½ teaspoon crushed herb with 1 tablespoon cream cheese or sweet butter. Let it stand for 10 to 15 minutes; then spread the mixture on a small piece of bread, and taste.

6. Spices react differently to freezing. Go light on cloves and garlic in dishes to be frozen. Their flavors often become much stronger. Onions lose strength in freezing. Little change occurs with cinnamon and nutmeg. The flavor of pepper and sage may increase during storage. However, unless you use very strong seasonings, you'll find most recipes acceptable without changing the ingredients. If herbs have lost some of their flavor with reheating, more can be added minutes before serving.

The following pages have been prepared to acquaint the novice with the seasoning possibilities of herbs and spices. As you become more daring, let your taste buds guide you in seasoning foods. Don't be afraid to experiment and try something new.

ALLSPICE. Usually found in ground form, the whole fruit is about the size of a currant and looks somewhat like a peppercorn. It's called allspice because it tastes and smells as if it were a combination of cloves, cinnamon, and nutmeg. It's used whole in pickling spices and for ham, stews, and pot roast. Ground, it's good in pumpkin and mincemeat pies, plum puddings, cookies, and cakes.

AMBROSIA. Difficult to purchase, but I understand that it's very easy to grow. This fragrant plant has dark-brown seeds which can be used along with its leaves.

ANGELICA. Called for occasionally in gourmet recipes, this usually refers to candied angelica, made from the stalks of the angelica plant, often used as a garnish.

ANISE. A licorice-flavored herb. The leaves of this plant can be used in salads and for garnishing. The seeds are used in flavoring cookies, candies, sweet pickles, and beverages, as well as some sweet rolls and coffeecakes.

BASIL. Rather peppery, yet sweetish in taste, basil has a cloverlike scent. Highly esteemed in American cooking. Excellent in green salads, tomato dishes, in soups and meat cookery; especially good with lamb. Fresh basil adds zest to new potatoes, green peas, and sauces.

BAY LEAF. Also called *laurel*, bay leaf is slightly bitter and overpowering unless used in moderation. *Use sparingly* for subtle flavoring. Best with meats like pot roast, stews and broth, poultry and game; also used in pickling. A pinch of crumbled dried bay leaf is good in stuffings, in wine sauces, and with tomatoes (soup, juice, and aspic).

BEE BALM/LEMON BALM. Both are of the mint family and, although different in flavor and aroma, are used in about the same way. Both make delicious teas. Also used as a garnish in chilled wine, punch, and fruit cups.

CAPERS. The unopened flower buds of the caper bush. They grow wild on the slopes bordering the Mediterranean Sea. They're mainly used in sauces, with seafoods and chicken, and also as a granish.

CARAWAY. A plant of the parsley family, with slightly sharp but pleasing flavor. Seeds are generally used in rye bread; also good in coffee cakes, sauerkraut, and sweet-sour beets. For a unique flavor lift, add a few seeds to cheese dips and when roasting pork. Also good in cottage cheese and with zucchini squash.

CARDAMOM. Related to the ginger family, cardamom has a highly aromatic, pungent flavor. The seeds harmonize in a flavorsome way with coffee; try adding a few seeds to your coffee grounds. It's especially good in demitasse. Scandinavian pastries, cookies, stewed fruits, fruit desserts, and puddings are frequently flavored with cardamom.

CAYENNE. Also called *capsicum*, it is of the pepper family and is called the most pungent of all spices. A very little goes a long way; always use with a light hand. It's excellent for getting just the right flavoring in sauces, gravies, and meat dishes. It's also used in seasoning pork sausage and curry dishes.

CELERY SEEDS. Quite versatile, most frequently used in pickling spices. They're also very good sprinkled over the top of bread, rolls or crackers in the same way poppy seeds are used. They add a distinctive flavor to fish and seafoods, as well as potato salad and seafood salads.

CHERVIL. This is delicate and looks like parsley. Akin to tarragon in flavor. Use fresh, frozen, or dried in salads, soups, fish, or eggs. The fresh leaves are particularly good in potato salad.

CHILI POWDER. A blend of chili pepper, cumin seed, oregano, and sometimes other spices. Keen, penetrating flavor. Used most often in Mexican-type dishes, such as chili con carne. Good too in scrambled eggs or omelets, cocktail and barbecue sauces, and in stews, meat loaf, and hamburger.

CHIVES. Delicately onion-flavored, used in cooking or with any food requiring a mild flavor of onion. Freeze well. Used in eggs, salads, sauces of butter, lemon, or sour cream, sprinkled on vegetables. Delicious in cream cheese, cottage cheese, and soft butter.

CINNAMON. One of the oldest spices known, Cassia cinnamon is used in this country. It's a reddish-brown bark in stick or ground form. Has an agreeable, pungently sweet taste. In Mexico, a whitish mild cinnamon is used called Cinnamon Zeylanicum. It's the most important baking spice. Also good in stewed and baked fruits (particularly apples) and in conjunction with chocolate. Ground, it's also good in custard and rice puddings, French toast, fruit pies, and desserts.

CLOVES. The dried buds of the evergreen clove tree. The flavor is strong and pungent. Commonly used to stud ham before baking, in pickling fruits, and in hot tea. Try a bit of ground cloves in chocolate pudding or hot chocolate, or when making gravy or stewing fruit.

CORIANDER. Often called *cilantro* in gourmet and foreign recipes, coriander is fragrant and pleasing, a cross between sage and lemon peel. Use ground or whole in meats, poultry, broth, and pickles. Also used in curry powder.

CUMIN. This spice has a keen flavor a little like caraway. Used commercially as a rule, but you'll like it in spaghetti, tamale pie, chili con carne, and pizza pie.

CURRY. A blend of several spices and herbs originating in India, mainly turmeric, cumin, and sage. It has an exotic, biting flavor greatly enjoyed by Americans in recent years. Unlimited flavoring possibilities; especially tasty in rice dishes, with chicken and shrimp, in creamed meat or fish dishes. A fleck of curry enhances French dressing and creamed soups. Curry also gives these dishes a lovely yellow coloring.

DILL. A fragrant herb with a pleasing tang. Dill weed is essential to pickles and dill sauces for lamb and fish. Seeds are excellent in potato salad, cole slaw, hamburger, macaroni, soups, and with marinated or creamed cucumbers, to name only a few uses. Dill butter is delicious over fish.

FENNEL. Often called *finochio*, fennel looks somewhat similar to celery. Italians use this in much the same way Americans use celery. The seeds are used in many Italian dishes, spaghetti, and lasagne; delicious sprinkled on pizza, and is used in most Italian sausages. Fennel is also used in flavoring some beverages and liquors.

GARLIC. A strong, clinging flavor; better to underseason than overseason with this delicious spice. Its uses are unlimited in meats, vegetables, and salad dressings. Puts zest into sauces and seafood, especially shrimp. The chivelike tops of this plant are delicious and milder in flavor than the root. Chop some in a salad, especially with vinegar and oil dressings. Garlic tops also freeze well.

GINGER. An ancient spice, in dried form this pungent, aromatic seasoner is strong. Dried ground ginger is an essential ingredient in some breads, and is also tasty stirred into melted butter for vegetables, in puddings, pumpkin pie, applesauce, and Brown Betty. Blend with salt and pepper and rub on steaks, chicken, or duck. Delicious in marinades for meats. Oriental cookery uses this spice frequently; also used in curry dishes.

HOREHOUND. Once a very popular herb, horehound has lost its popularity in recent decades. It's now mainly used in making candies and cough drops.

HORSERADISH. A root that is ground and made into the familiar commercial horseradish sauce. Used on meats, salads, and in fish sauces. A little goes a long way.

LEEK. Of the onion family, mild in flavor, it's used as a cooked vegetable. Delicious in soups and salads.

MARJORAM. A member of the mint family. It's aromatic with stinging undertones. Excellent on vegetables, particularly peas, green beans, and limas. Delicious on lamb and in poultry stuffings; also in cheese and egg dishes. Commercially, it's used in liverwurst, bologna, and headcheese.

MINT. Sweet, strong, and tangy. The dried leaves are spearmint and peppermint spices. Besides the obvious uses, such as in jelly, juleps, confections, and desserts, a bit of frozen or dried mint improves meat and fish sauces, particularly lamb. It also makes a lovely garnish for fresh fruit trays and fruit punch.

MUSTARD. Available in several varieties, its color varies from black or brown to yellow and white. The fresh leaves of the yellow mustard plant are wonderful in salads. The seeds from all these plants are ground and made into a prepared mustard. There are many varieties of prepared mustard, and if you've been using only one kind, you're missing a great taste treat. They store well in the refrigerator, so keep several varieties on hand. These prepared mustards are used for frankfurters, hamburgers, meat loaf, salad dressings, and sauces. The whole seeds are used in pickling spices, relishes, and potato salads. Ground, they're good in sauces, cheese and egg dishes, and seafood salads.

NUTMEG AND MACE. Two different spices, although they're both parts of the same fruit of an evergreen tree. Nutmeg is sweet and spicy; mace is softer and less pungent. Nutmeg is used as a flavoring for puddings, sweet sauces, eggnog, et cetera. It's a "must" for apple and pumpkin pies, as well as Swedish meatballs. Add a fleck to pastry for meat pies. Mace is good flavoring in cakes and a wonderful addition to cherry pies and chocolate dishes.

ONION. Found in four major types: Bermuda onions, Spanish red onions, and the smaller white and yellow onions. The Bermuda onion is the giant of the family; it has a sweet flavor and is best when you are serving onions raw. Its large round rings are marvelous for making onion rings, especially French fried and broiled. The Spanish red onion has eye appeal and a mild sweet flavor; it makes lovely garnishments, and is especially attractive in marinated salads. The yellow onion is probably the most popular of all and has the strongest flavor; it's a wonderful seasoning in stews, soups, boiled dinners, pot roasts, et cetera. It's the yellow onion that is usually used for the instant minced and frozen chopped onions. The little white onions have the mildest taste of all. The smallest ones are usually pickled; those a little larger are used in salads and served in a sauce with peas; the largest ones are often served whole, creamed or glazed.

OREGANO. The Spanish word for *marjoram* and the herb is often called *wild marjoram*. It's sharp and fragrant, somewhat stronger than sweet marjoram. Use fresh or dried leaves in dips, soups, and melted butter sauce. Marvelous in green salads, vegetables, potato salad, and in any tomato dish.

PAPRIKA. The same family as cayenne. There are many varieties, from mild to hot, and the color range is from dark green to yellow to dark red. The mild paprika is used for coloring as much as for flavor on the top of deviled eggs, baked potatoes, potato salads, and soups. The hot variety is used in many Hungarian recipes, such as goulashes and other meat dishes. Also excellent to season fried chicken.

PARSLEY. Probably the most widely used of all herbs. There are many varieties. The flat-leaf parsley has a more pungent flavor; the curly-leaf is more decorative. Use fresh as a garnish, and either fresh, frozen, or dried for flavoring. Good with fish, eggs, potatoes, in salads, soups, and vegetables. Freeze in large batches; chop fine by using scissors or blender.

PEPPER. The spice of all spices, found on tables throughout the world. It's second only to salt as a seasoning. There are many different kinds, mainly black, white, and red. The white and black peppercorns grow on the same vines. These vines are trained to grow like grape vines. The ripe berries from which we get our white pepper take about 7 years to mature. Hence the higher cost of white pepper. The black peppercorns are the unripened berries. They are picked, dried, and cured until their outer skins shrivel and become hard. The outer skin is removed from the white peppercorns, which gives them a more delicate taste. Pepper is indispensable as a seasoning, and every home should have a pepper grinder, since there's simply no comparison between freshly ground pepper and that which has been commercially ground.

PEPPER TABASCO. The hottest of all peppers. It grows in Mexico and is made into the commercially prepared Tabasco sauce. Use very sparingly in almost anything that needs a little *oomph!*

RED CHILI PEPPERS. Small and hot, they should be used with discretion. They're good in Mexican dishes, sauces, spaghetti, and beans; also with some pickling spices.

POPPY SEED. From the opium poppy, but free of any drug. It's widely used in pastries, rolls, breads, and cakes. Ground poppy seed is also commercially prepared as a filling for coffee cakes and puddings. It's interesting to note here that the opium and other narcotics are derived from the seed pod. In order to grow the opium poppy in the United States, it's necessary to obtain a permit from the Bureau of Narcotics, Treasury Department, Washington, D.C.

ROCAMBOLE. Used like garlic, but it has a much milder flavor. It too is of the onion family.

ROSEMARY. A distinctive, sweet, fresh flavor. Use restrained amounts in the water in which potatoes cook; sprinkle a little on beef before roasting, on fish, poultry, hot turnips, and cauliflower.

SAFFRON. The world's most expensive spice. A little goes a long way because of its intense flavor. Small amounts add a pleasing golden color and Oriental flavor to rice and chicken; good in yeast breads and curry dishes.

SAGE. A very popular American herb, strong and penetrating in flavor. Somewhat bitter unless used sparingly. Otherwise, it greatly improves many foods. Besides using it in stuffings, try the herb in cottage cheese, fish chowders, on pork roasts, chops and in meat loaf.

SAVORY. An agreeable fragrance and piquant taste; use dry or fresh. Try sprinkling savory in vegetable juices, cheese souffle, or water to cook vegetables (especially cabbage and peas), and when baking ham and in pot roasts.

SCALLIONS. Usually served raw, although they may be cooked. You'll often find them on relish trays, with carrot sticks and celery. When cutting them up for tossed salads, use entire onion, stem and all.

SESAME SEEDS. Mainly used in cookies, rolls, breads, cakes, and some candies. Try adding some to the flour mixture for coating chicken before frying. Also good with green beans and asparagus, or even tossed salad. Incidentally, health food stores carry sesame seeds by the pound at about one-fifth the price of small spice jars of the seeds.

SHALLOT. Also of the onion family, it looks much like garlic, in that it's a cluster of little buds. Use for mild onionlike flavor. The tops are good in salads.

SORREL. There are three different kinds: French sorrel, garden sorrel, and wood sorrel. As nearly as I can tell, they all taste about the same and can be used interchangeably. Sorrel imparts a lemonlike flavor and is used in fish, omelet, and egg dishes. It's also good with lamb and some vegetables.

SWEET CICELY. A member of the parsley family, most widely used in France. Its seeds are used in flavoring beverages; chartreuse, for example, gets its distinctive flavor from sweet cicely. It is said to enhance the flavor of any other herb with which it has been mixed.

SWEET WOODRUFF. A fragrant little plant used in making May wine, as well as other beverages. Make tea with it, and add it to punch and fruit cups.

TARRAGON. May taste like licorice, unless used in scant amounts. Adds a nice tang in small pinches. Perfect in salad dressings, vinegars, seafood cocktails, and in fresh or stewed fruits. Try it in eggs, with meats or fish, and in marinades.

THYME. A basic culinary herb, thyme has a strong, pleasing scent. Use a scant pinch in virtually any food you wish. Excellent in clam chowder, creamed dried beef, with fresh tomatoes, and in egg dishes.

TURMERIC. Used as a coloring agent in prepared mustards and as a substitute for saffron in some baking, except for curry turmeric (see *Curry*).

VANILLA BEAN. The seed pod of a rare orchid. Although expensive, it goes a long way. Keep several beans in a separate sugar container, and use this sugar exclusively for baking, making desserts, hot chocolate, or anything else that could use vanilla flavoring. Refill container, but leave some beans in it. This is what is commonly referred to as "vanilla sugar" in some recipes. Vanilla extract is used in most confections, icings, puddings, cakes, and cookies. It enhances the flavor of hot chocolate and chocolate desserts, as well as eggnogs, whipped cream, and ice cream, to mention only a few.

WATERCRESS. The lesser known *upland cress* and *garden cress* are quite similar in flavor to watercress and all are part of the mustard family. They have a rather peppery flavor much like strong radishes, and are great as a garnish, in salads and sandwiches.

WINTERGREEN. This plant grows in the acid soil of the woods. Its fresh leaves are good for making tea or used as a garnish, and its berries make attractive decorations.

CLEARJEL

I happened to learn about this wonderful product quite by chance. It has been in existence for a number of years and is widely used by commerical bakeries and companies that process a great variety of frozen food products. I can't understand why it isn't available for home use at grocery stores throughout the country (in some states, it is), because it's the magical ingredient for many frozen dishes.

Clearjel is a cornstarch derivative. You may use it as a substitute for cornstarch or flour in exactly the same proportions. Creamed sauces thickened with Clearjel, instead of flour or cornstarch, will not separate after freezing. Custards and puddings made with Clearjel can be frozen with never a worry that they will become soggy and watery when thawed.

Clearjel is bland, with essentially no cereal or starch taste. It's clear in color when cooked, has excellent stability, and remains smooth, with no tendency to jell. It prevents liquid separation and curdling after foods have been frozen. Commercial food processors have been using this product for years in both canned and frozen cream-style corn, pork and beans, soups, sauces and gravies, prepared dinners, and baby foods.

Instant Clearjel thickens on contact with liquids without cooking. Add Instant Clearjel to such things as pumpkin pie, and you can put your unbaked pie in the freezer without fear of sloshing the contents all over the freezer's interior. The pie filling will have a consistency somewhat similar to that of instant pudding. Instant Clearjel is also excellent to use when making fruit pies that have a lot of juice. Add it with sugar to the fruit juice, and you won't have to worry about soggy piecrusts. Sounds almost too good to be true, doesn't it? Fillings made with Instant Clearjel do not require cooking before baking or freezing, which can be a big timesaver in itself. *It must be cooked or baked before serving, however.*

To use Instant Clearjel, blend it with sugar before adding it to fruit, et cetera. The presence of sugar minimizes any tendency to lump and insures smoothness. Or mix Instant Clearjel with a small amount of liquid (as you do cornstarch) and blend until smooth. Fold fruit in last to insure whole-fruit appearance.

Since instant fillings are not cooked before baking, they should be either baked or frozen soon after preparation. When adapting your own recipes, use Instant Clearjel in the same proportions indicated for cornstarch, tapioca, or flour. If your fillings tend to "thin" during baking, increase the oven temperature and shorten the baking time. This thinning out during baking is called "oven boil out" and is usually caused by excessive baking at lower temperatures.

It seems strange that a product with all these marvelous characteristics should be hard to find at a time when most consumer products are so widely advertised and distributed. I'm hoping that Clearjel will soon be available at every grocery store but, in the meantime, you can buy it at any local bakery supply house, usually in 1-pound packages. (See the yellow pages of your telephone directory.) Or you can write to Maid of Scandinavia, 3244 Raleigh Avenue, Minneapolis, MN 55416 (612-927-7996), and ask for their general catalog, which lists "Clearjel." This is a good catalog to have because it contains so many items which are difficult to obtain, as well as cooking and baking supplies, cake decorations, unusual pans, cooking equipment, and also Magic-Cake Strips (see page 138). The Complete Cook, 222 Waukegan Road, Glenview, IL 60025 also carries Clearjel. Their telephone number is 312-729-7687. The catalog is free.

Note: Clearjel and Instant Clearjel are registered trademarks of the National Starch and Chemical Corporation.

Appetizers and Sandwich Spreads

✳✳✳✳✳✳✳✳✳✳✳✳✳✳✳✳✳✳✳✳✳✳✳✳✳✳✳

Appetizers play a very important role in American entertaining. Every cookbook and women's magazine will give you dozens of ideas and recipes. Try them! Your family and best friends (never experiment with anyone else) will enjoy being on your taste panel. You should have at least a dozen different appetizers that you're completely familiar with and enjoy serving. There are many that don't lend themselves well to freezing and I usually serve one or more of these (depending on the size of the group) besides my frozen standbys.

The beauty of having an assortment of hors d'oeuvres in the freezer is quite obvious; they're always on hand and ready for last-minute guests and entertaining. They can be made, at your convenience, days or weeks in advance of a large planned party or gathering, which will leave precious last minutes for more important duties, like taking a sick dog to the vet, or spending the afternoon rounding up a plumber because your kitchen sink refuses to drain.

Don't confine appetizers to "company only." Your family will enjoy them, too. They can make any ordinary meal seem a festive occasion.

As an aside, it's a good idea to keep a card file of what you've served your guests on previous occasions. List each course, starting with hors d'oeuvres and ending with the dessert. This is a good place to note any food allergies and the foods your guests don't like. I have one card on file that reads: "She won't eat anything with cheese (including cottage and cream), mushrooms, sour cream, fish, shrimp, or lobster. He doesn't care for creamed vegetables, asparagus, broccoli, or Brussels sprouts. They both like their meat *very* well done." Just think how very easy it would be to serve a completely elegant meal and not have one thing that either of these people liked!

Try to serve at least one new or different appetizer each time you entertain the same people. Also, make notations of things you thought they particularly liked and serve them from time to time. However, don't magnify a polite compliment!

BITE-SIZED PUFFS FOR HORS D'OEUVRES

These tiny puffs are invaluable to have in the freezer. As appetizers, all one kind may be served or with an assortment of fillings. Later on in the book, under "Desserts," you'll find all kinds of ideas for fillings that may be used to end a meal.

To make the batter for this recipe, whether single, double, or triple batch, takes only from 10 to 12 minutes. However, baking the larger quantity does require a bit more time. To make puffs rise properly, use an electric beater or food processor for incorporating the eggs and beat at least 1 minute for each egg.

SINGLE RECIPE
Yield: 4 dozen

¼ cup butter or margarine   dash salt
½ cup boiling water   2 eggs
½ cup sifted flour

DOUBLE RECIPE   TRIPLE RECIPE
Yield: 8 dozen   *Yield: 12 dozen*

½ cup butter or margarine   ¾ cup butter or margarine
1 cup boiling water   1½ cups boiling water
1 cup sifted flour   1½ cups sifted flour
⅛ teaspoon salt   ¼ teaspoon salt
4 eggs   6 eggs

Melt butter in boiling water. Add flour and salt all at one time, and stir vigorously. Cook, stirring constantly, until mixture forms a ball and leaves sides of pan. Remove from heat and cool slightly. Add eggs, one at a time, beating vigorously after each addition until mixture is smooth. Drop from tip of a teaspoon about 1½ inches apart onto a well-greased cookie sheet. Bake in a very hot oven (450° F) for 10 minutes. Then slow oven to 325° F for 10 minutes.

Puffs should be an even, delicate brown when done. Immediately remove with spatula and cool on rack. For crisper puffs, turn oven off immediately after removing the puffs, place them on cake racks, and wait about 10 minutes for oven to cool somewhat; then return them to oven for another 10 minutes.

TO FREEZE. Pack them immediately in a large suitable freezer-proof plastic container and freeze.

TO DEFROST. Take them out of the freezer (just the number you plan to use) and thaw at least half an hour before using them. After thawing, put in a 350° F oven for 3 minutes to freshen them up; cut off tops, fill, and serve.

FILLINGS. Filling for the Bite-Sized Puffs is limited only by the imagination. They're delicious filled with chicken salad (see page 352), shrimp salad, and even ham salad. Prepared ham salad from the local delicatessen is a real timesaver; with puffs from the freezer, it only takes a few minutes to prepare a lovely tray of looks-like-you've-slaved-all-day hors d'oeuvres. Below is a tasty tuna filling.

TUNA FILLING FOR BITE-SIZED PUFFS

SINGLE RECIPE
Yield: Filling for 2 dozen

One 6½- or 7-ounce can flaked tuna, drained
½ cup chopped celery
¼ cup chopped cucumber
3 tablespoons chopped sweet pickles
2 chopped or grated hard-cooked eggs
⅛ teaspoon salt
Dash pepper
2 tablespoons lemon juice
3 tablespoons mayonnaise or salad dressing
2 ounces toasted blanched almonds

DOUBLE RECIPE
Yield: Filling for 4 dozen

Two 6½- or 7-ounce cans flaked tuna, drained
1 cup chopped celery
½ cup chopped cucumber
⅓ cup chopped sweet pickles
4 chopped or grated hard-cooked eggs
¼ teaspoon salt
Dash pepper
4 tablespoons lemon juice
⅓ cup mayonnaise or salad dressing
4 ounces toasted blanched almonds

To toast blanched almonds, spread nuts in a shallow pan and put in 350° F oven for 5 to 7 minutes, or until nicely browned. Watch closely, since they burn easily.

 Combine tuna, celery, cucumber, pickles, eggs, salt, and pepper. Sprinkle with lemon juice. Moisten with mayonnaise. Chill. Fill tiny puffs just before serving. Garnish with toasted almonds.

LOBSTER TAILS AND DIP

This is a delicious appetizer that can be made in record time from frozen lobster tail out of your freezer. It can easily be made early in the day and kept in the refrigerator, or it can be made at the last minute and cooled quickly in the freezer for 30 minutes before serving.

SMALL SERVING
Yield: Approximately 12 pieces
1 frozen South African lobster tail
   (12 ounces or more)
Sauce:

3 tablespoons mayonnaise	1 egg yolk
1 tablespoon butter or margarine	Dash cayenne
2 tablespoons lemon juice	Pinch salt

LARGER SERVING
Yield: Approximately 24 pieces
2 frozen South African lobster tails
   (12 ounces each or more)
Sauce:
⅓ cup mayonnaise
2 tablespoons butter or margarine
¼ cup lemon juice
2 egg yolks
2 dashes cayenne
⅛ teaspoon salt

SERVING FOR A CROWD
Yield: Approximately 48 pieces
4 frozen South African lobster tails
   (at least 12 ounces each)
Sauce:
⅔ cup mayonnaise
4 tablespoons butter or margarine
½ cup lemon juice
4 egg yolks
Pinch cayenne
¼ teaspoon salt

Drop the frozen lobster tails into boiling salted water. When the water comes to a boil again, lower heat and simmer for 15 minutes (13 minutes if the tails have thawed). Remove tails from boiling water and immerse in cold water. Cut through the undershell with kitchen scissors; insert fingers between meat and shell and pull meat out. Chill meat thoroughly and then cut into cubes. Each lobster tail should yield at least 12 cubes. Reserve the shells if you wish. They make a colorful tray for serving the lobster tails.

SAUCE. See page 47 for suggestions on preparing yolks and whites. Over low direct heat combine mayonnaise, lemon juice, and butter or margarine. Stir until shortening is melted and mixture is blended. Add egg yolk immediately, stirring quickly to incorporate yolk into mayonnaise mixture. Continue cooking over low heat until mixture thickens (no more than 2 minutes). Add seasonings, stir, and serve.

TO SERVE. Place chilled lobster cubes into shells, inserting spears or toothpicks in each. Pour a little sauce over the lobster cubes and put the remainder in a small bowl for dipping.

APPETIZERS BY THE YARD

To make appetizers by the yard, purchase a large loaf of sandwich or butter-crust bread at your local bakery, and have it sliced the long way rather than the traditional way. Toast one side of these long bread slices under the oven broiler, watching closely so they don't burn. Now spread the untoasted side with any type of spread that tastes good broiled or baked. Freeze on cookie sheets for about 1 hour. Insert a double thickness of waxed paper between the slices of bread and stack. Wrap in foil or large freezer bags, label, date, and freeze. Wrap each type of filling in a separate package to avoid transfer of flavors.

TO SERVE WHEN FROZEN. Simply remove the number of slices you wish to use, being careful to rewrap the package securely before returning it to the freezer. Put long slices of bread on a cookie sheet and place under the broiler until topping is heated through and a bit bubbly. Now cut slices into triangles, squares, or strips and arrange on serving plate or platter.

Recipes that lend themselves to use in appetizers are: Cheese Spread (page 83), Hot Tuna Sandwich Filling (page 92), Hot Ham 'n Cheese Burgers (page 93), Barb's Shrimp Canapes (below), Hot Chicken Curry (page 89) Toby's Zesty Rye Rounds (page 83). Use Clearjel (page 70) in place of flour for the curry when you plan to freeze.

BARB'S SHRIMP CANAPES

I like to make this in large batches to keep on hand for emergencies. Freeze in small quantities, as a little goes a long way, and it must be completely thawed in order to spread properly. There are a number of small freezer-proof plastic containers sold that are just the right size for storing the spread in small quantities. Also, the little plastic containers in which you purchase frozen chives and different colored cake and cookie decorations are just perfect for storing small quantities of anything.

MEDIUM RECIPE
½ pound shredded sharp Cheddar
cheese
¼ pound soft butter
5 tablespoons grated onion
1 teaspoon Worcestershire sauce
2 tablespoons lemon juice
½ teaspoon dry mustard

LARGE RECIPE
1 pound shredded sharp Cheddar
cheese
½ pound soft butter
⅔ cup grated onion
2 teaspoons Worcestershire sauce
¼ cup lemon juice
1 teaspoon dry mustard

| ½ teaspoon paprika | 1 teaspoon paprika |
| 2 cups finely chopped cooked shrimp (either fresh or canned) | 4 cups finely chopped cooked shrimp (either fresh or canned) |

Mix all ingredients together. Spread on round crackers or rye rounds. Put under the broiler for about 2 or 3 minutes until golden brown and bubbly. Serve immediately. The mix freezes well for a period of 3 months. I've never managed to keep it around any longer than that.

GREEN-OLIVE-STUFFED PASTRIES

Stuffed pastries are always a hit with guests. You'll never have any leftovers! They may be filled with anything that strikes your fancy. Be daring; try something new! Making several different kinds of filling at one time does not take much longer than making all the filling the same. Here are two suggestions.

SINGLE RECIPE *Yield: 48 stuffed pastries*	DOUBLE RECIPE *Yield: 96 stuffed pastries*
2 cups finely shredded Cheddar cheese	4 cups finely shredded Cheddar cheese
½ cup softened butter	1 cup softened butter
1 cup flour	2 cups flour
1 teaspoon paprika	2 teaspoons paprika
48 large pimento-stuffed olives	96 large pimento-stuffed olives

Blend cheese with butter, mix flour and paprika, and stir into butter mixture until well mixed. Shape 1 teaspoonful of mixture around each olive, covering it completely. Bake at 400° F for 15 minutes or until golden brown. Serve warm, but wait about 5 minutes after taking them from the oven. (Or someone will have a scorched mouth. They cool on the outside and are steaming on the inside.)

TO FREEZE. Put these little balls on a tray or cookie sheet and freeze. When frozen solid, pack them in a moisture-vapor-proof freezing container. Bake about 17 or 18 minutes when frozen.

ANCHOVY-OLIVE-STUFFED PASTRIES

Buy the largest anchovy-stuffed olives you can find. Unfortunately, they'll still be considerably smaller than the large pimento-stuffed olives. Using the smaller olives is a bit more work but the yield will be greater; in a single batch you may have as many as 60 smaller pastries. However, I think that the added flavor is well worth the extra time and effort.

SHRIMP

Because fish and seafood are traditionally served as a first course in a multicourse dinner, they're usually included when appetizers are served. Of all the seafoods and fish, shrimp is probably the favorite appetizer. Because of their size and versatility, shrimp lend themselves well to being served as a finger food, which most appetizers are. Two suggestions follow. Also see Marinated Seafood in Cream Sauce, page 192.

When shrimp are to be served with toothpicks or spears and a cocktail sauce for dunking, take care to cook the shrimp in the right manner. *Never boil shrimp.* Put the cleaned and deveined shrimp into water that is already boiling and has been seasoned. (You may use commercially prepared seafood seasoning. Follow directions on package.) Now turn heat low and simmer gently just until the shrimp turn a bright pink—no longer. Overcooking toughens the shrimp.

Drain and rinse in clear, cold water; add ice to chill quickly. Drain well. Now toss shrimp with 1 or 2 teaspoons of olive oil until they're lightly oiled. This will keep them moist and tender until they're served. The olive oil may be mixed with any seasoning or herbs you like. Refrigerate until serving time. Serve with cocktail sauce (see page 190).

BROILED SHRIMP

This is a delicious variation from the usual shrimp and sauce served. They can be prepared ahead of time so that all you'll have to do is put them under the broiler for a few minutes before serving. This is a time when a heatproof serving tray or platter is really convenient. Garnish with a few sprigs of parsley and some stuffed mushrooms. You'll have a really impressive platter to set before your guests.

SINGLE RECIPE	DOUBLE RECIPE
1 pound cleaned shrimp	2 pounds cleaned shrimp
½ cup Italian seasoned bread crumbs	1 cup Italian seasoned bread crumbs
Olive oil flavored with garlic	Olive oil flavored with garlic

Place shrimp in boiling water containing your regular seafood seasoning. Turn heat low, simmer gently, just until the shrimp turn bright pink—no longer. Rinse in cold water and let drain on absorbent paper. Dip shrimp in garlic-flavored olive oil and then in the Italian seasoned bread crumbs. Place shrimp one layer deep in a shallow pan and put in 400° F oven for 5 minutes. Then put under the broiler for a few minutes (about 3 minutes; but watch them very closely) until nice and brown. Serve immediately with tartar sauce (see page 191) or seafood cocktail sauce (see page 190). They're also good served plain.

BARBECUED PETITE RIBS

These little barbecued spareribs are marvelous in that their texture and flavor is quite in contrast to most appetizers. Because these ribs are parboiled, they're never greasy. Be sure to have an ample supply of napkins when you are serving them, and you might pass a plate of Wash 'n Dri napkins afterward. (See page 48.)

Have your butcher prepare as many spareribs as you feel you can handle and broil at one time. Ask him to cut the rib bones in half the entire length of a slab of spareribs. Wash ribs; put into boiling water and simmer for 45 minutes. Remove from water and cut into individual ribs at this time. Now spread on broiling pan and broil or bake in oven until nicely browned on both sides.

You may refrigerate them until you're ready to serve. Then brush liberally with your favorite barbecue sauce (Because I so thoroughly enjoy the Open Pit barbecue sauce made by Good Seasons, I have never had the inclination to make my own sauce. However, if you have a favorite recipe, feel free to use it.) Place under the broiler for a few minutes, making sure they don't burn. When they're heated through thoroughly, serve.

If you only want to serve part of the ribs now, freeze the rest after they've been broiled or baked, but before the barbecue sauce has been added. It's best to use them within 6 weeks.

CHICKEN CRISPIES

Here's a quick make-ahead-of-time chicken appetizer. Either use canned, boned chicken or use the meat you have from making chicken stock. Chicken Crispies are crunchy on the outside, but soft inside.

SINGLE RECIPE	DOUBLE RECIPE
Yield: 4 dozen medium-sized appetizers or 5 dozen small appetizers	*Yield: 8 dozen medium-sized appetizers or 10 dozen small appetizers*
⅓ cup butter or margarine	⅔ cup butter or margarine
⅓ cup flour	⅔ cup flour
1 teaspoon salt	2 teaspoons salt
⅛ teaspoon pepper	¼ teaspoon pepper
1¼ cups milk	2½ cups milk
2½ cups ground cooked chicken	5 cups ground cooked chicken
1 teaspoon grated onion	2 teaspoons grated onion
2 tablespoons minced parsley	4 tablespoons minced parsley

 Melt butter and blend in flour. Add salt and pepper and gradually add milk, stirring constantly. Cook until sauce is thickened and smooth. Add ground chicken, onion, and parsley to sauce and chill this mixture for about 1 hour. Then shape into 40 medium-sized balls or 60 smaller-sized balls (for single recipe). Bake on greased tin at 475° F for 12 minutes. The smaller-sized balls will bake faster; so watch closely toward the end of baking time.

TO FREEZE. After they've been baked, freeze on cookie sheets. Then put into plastic bags, label, date, and freeze. Heat in 450° F oven for 3 minutes before serving.

CHEESE CHICKEN CRISPIES. For further flavor variation, add ½ cup shredded or ground sharp Cheddar cheese to half of a single recipe.

SAUSAGE BALLS

A real quickie appetizer. Make in advance and freeze. You'll always want some on hand.

Yield: About 100 appetizers

½ pound mild pork sausage	1 pound sharp Cheddar cheese, grated
½ pound hot pork sausage	3 cups biscuit mix

 In your mixing bowl, combine the uncooked pork sausage with the cheese until well blended. (The food processor mixes and blends this whole recipe in seconds. When using the food processor, divide ingredients in half and make two batches.) Add biscuit mix and mix thoroughly. Shape mixture into 1-inch balls and place on a cookie sheet. Bake in a preheated 375° F oven for 10 minutes or until nicely browned. Keep warm while serving on a hot tray.

TO FREEZE. Freeze balls before cooking. Place on large cookie sheet and freeze. When frozen remove from freezer, freezer-wrap, date, label and return to freezer.

TO SERVE WHEN FROZEN. Bake according to above instructions.

VARIATIONS. All hot sausage may be used, but the results will definitely be quite spicy. When using all mild sausage, add ¼ to ½ teaspoon of cayenne pepper; otherwise sausage balls will have a very bland flavor.

RITA'S SWEET-SOUR MEATBALLS

Marvelous as appetizers, these meatballs also make a tasty addition to any buffet dinner. They freeze well and are nice to have on hand.

SINGLE RECIPE	DOUBLE RECIPE
Preparation Time: 15 minutes	*Preparation Time: 20 minutes*
Yield: About 2 quarts	*Yield: About 4 quarts*
1½ cups water	3 cups water
1½ cups frozen chopped onions	3 cups frozen chopped onions
¾ cup sugar	1½ cups sugar
Juice 1 lemon or 3 tablespoons lemon juice	6 tablespoons lemon juice
2 pounds ground beef	4 pounds ground beef
1 egg	2 eggs
1 teaspoon salt	2 teaspoons salt
3 slices bread soaked in milk	6 slices bread soaked in milk
1 large can (1 pound) stewed tomatoes	Two 1-pound cans stewed tomatoes
One 8-ounce can seasoned tomato sauce	Two 8-ounce cans seasoned tomato sauce
6 gingersnaps	12 gingersnaps
2 chunks sour salt (or ¼ teaspoon granulated)	4 chunks sour salt (or ½ teaspoon granulated)

Combine water, onions, sugar, and lemon juice and simmer for ½ hour in a large covered pan. While sauce is cooking, mix meat with egg, salt, and bread that has been soaked in milk. (Sour salt is used in foreign cooking and in Jewish cooking. If your supermarket doesn't carry it, specialty stores will, or it may be ordered at your local drugstore. Without it the meat balls won't have the genuine sweet-sour taste.) Form into small meatballs. When you are using these for appetizers, they should be no larger than one inch in diameter. However, when you are using them as an entree, they may be just a little larger. After sauce has simmered for half hour, add meatballs and cook for another half hour. Meanwhile, in a small saucepan combine tomato sauce and gingersnaps, and cook until gingersnaps have dissolved. Add chunks of sour sàlt and pour mixture into pan with meatballs, adding stewed tomatoes. Continue cooking for another half hour.

TO FREEZE. Pour into freezing cartons in an amount that you're likely to use. Date, label, and freeze.

TO SERVE WHEN FROZEN. Partially thaw and heat thoroughly over moderate heat. A chafing dish is ideal for serving these meat balls.

CHOPPED CHICKEN LIVERS

Follow recipe on page 354. Mound chopped chicken livers in an oblong ball, placed on end, about the size of a pineapple. Cover the outside of this ball with rows of sliced stuffed olives. If possible, crown with the leafy top of a pineapple. Place in center of serving platter, surrounded with crackers and spreaders. Makes a very attractive plate.

HOT CHICKEN-LIVER STRUDEL

You'll have compliments galore on this one. Make in advance and have on hand.

Preparation Time: 21 minutes,
  using prepared Chopped
  Chicken Livers
Yield: 4 strudels

¼ pound butter
½ pint commercial sour cream
1 teaspoon salt
2 cups flour

1¾ to 2 pounds prepared chicken
  livers, or
Double recipe of Chopped Chicken
  Livers (page 354)

Cream butter and add sour cream. Beat well; sprinkle salt on top. Then add flour. When well blended, make a ball. Cover and refrigerate overnight.

Let stand at room temperature for about 1 hour before rolling out. Cut dough into 4 pieces. Roll out 1 part at a time on a floured board or pastry cloth, rolling as thin as possible in an oblong about the size of a jelly-roll pan, 15 x 18 inches. Divide chicken livers into fourths and spread a quarter of the filling on the edge of the longer side. Then roll up in jelly-roll fashion, being careful not to break dough. Tuck in sides and gently place on a greased cookie sheet or other large baking pan. Bake at 300° F for 1 hour.

TO FREEZE. Fill and prepare strudel and freeze (see page 37). When it is frozen solid, remove from freezer and freezer-wrap, date, label, and return to the freezer. This is best when used within 6 weeks.

TO SERVE WHEN FROZEN. Remove from freezer and bake for 1½ hours at 300° F. Serve immediately.

TOBY'S ZESTY RYE ROUNDS

Easy to make and marvelous to have in your freezer.

Yield: Approximately 4 to 5 dozen

1 pound lean ground beef	3 to 4 drops Tabasco sauce (optional)
1 pound pork sausage (hot or mild, or combination of both)	1 tablespoon oregano
	1 teaspoon garlic salt
1 pound Velveeta cheese	1 long package party rye bread

If you are using a mild pork sausage, add the Tabasco sauce. When using hot pork sausage or a combination of hot and mild, the Tabasco sauce may be eliminated.

Saute beef and pork sausage in a large skillet until brown. Drain off any excess grease. In mixing bowl slice cheese, add warm meat and seasoning; beat until well blended. Spread on party rye slices. (For crunchier texture, toast one side of rye under broiler. Then spread meat mixture on untoasted side.) Arrange on a cookie sheet and freeze until mixture is solid. Remove from cookie sheet and pack in freezer container. Freeze until ready to serve.

TO SERVE WHEN FROZEN. Preheat oven to 350° F. Bake for 10 minutes or until cheese and meat mixture is bubbly. Serve immediately.

CHEESE SPREAD

This versatile spread or topping lends itself very well to the method of making appetizers by the yard (see page 76). It also can be rolled into a long cheese roll, sliced, and arranged on rye rounds before being broiled.

SINGLE RECIPE

Time: 15 minutes to make and spread

Yield: 4 long sandwich-loaf slices

¼ pound sharp Cheddar cheese
¼ pound smoked Cheddar cheese
8 slices bacon, cooked and crumbled, or ½ cup cooked and crumbled bacon (see page 41)
2 green onions
½ teaspoon Worcestershire sauce
1 teaspoon dry mustard
2 teaspoons mayonnaise

DOUBLE RECIPE

Time: 22 minutes to make and spread

Yield: 8 long sandwich-loaf slices

½ pound sharp Cheddar cheese
½ pound smoked Cheddar cheese
16 slices bacon, cooked and crumbled, or 1 cup cooked and crumbled bacon (see page 41)
4 green onions
1 teaspoon Worcestershire sauce
2 teaspoons dry mustard
4 teaspoons mayonnaise

Put cheeses, bacon, and onion through food grinder. This can also be done in one step using a food processor with a metal blade. Soften to room temperature and add seasonings and mayonnaise. Mix well. Toast long bread slices on one side and spread cheese mixture on the other. Insert double thickness of waxed paper between slices, stacking them one on top of the other. Wrap with foil or other freezer wrap, label, date, and freeze.

TO SERVE WHEN FROZEN. Remove only the number of slices needed. Seal remainder securely in freezer-wrap and return to freezer. Place long slices of bread on cookie sheet and thaw. Put under preheated broiler just long enough for the cheese mixture to become bubbly. Watch closely because the cheese spread burns easily. Remove hot bread slices from oven and slice into strips or triangles. These may be served plain or garnished with sliced stuffed olives, small pieces of pimento that have been cut into various shapes with small aspic cutters, anchovy rounds, parsley, or even salted whole nuts.

CHEESE LOG

Make the cheese spread in the preceding recipe and shape into a long roll, no more than 1½ inches in diameter, and freeze. When you are ready to serve it, slice cheese with a wire cheese cutter and put rounds of cheese spread on little rye rounds that have been toasted on one side. Place under the broiler until cheese is bubbly, watching closely so that the cheese mixture does not burn. Serve plain or use garnishes suggested above.

DOLORES' CHEESE BALLS

Nice to serve before dinner with crackers. Makes two good-sized balls; use one and freeze the other for future use.

Time: 10 minutes
Yield: Two balls, about 2¼ cups
each

Two 3-ounce wedges of Roquefort cheese

Two 5-ounce jars processed Cheddar cheese spread

12 ounces cream cheese (one and one-half 8-ounce packages)

1 teaspoon instant minced onions
or
2 tablespoons ground or minced onions

1 teaspoon Worcestershire sauce

½ cup snipped parsley

1 cup ground pecans

Make this up at least the day before you intend to use it so that all the cheese flavors can mingle. Soften all cheese at room temperature. Combine cheeses, onions, Worcestershire sauce, and blend well, using mixer at low and then moderately fast speed. Or, using food processor, grate cheese with grating blade, then combine all ingredients and process with metal blade until blended. Stir in ¼ cup of parsley and half the pecans. Shape into two large balls or four smaller balls, whichever you prefer. Chill for an hour or so. Combine remaining nuts and parsley and roll balls in parsley-nut mixture. (You may need more chopped nuts and parsley to cover the four smaller-sized balls properly.) Return to the refrigerator or freezer-wrap, date, label and freeze for future use. For best flavor, cheese balls should be removed from the refrigerator about 1 hour before serving.

TO SERVE WHEN FROZEN. Let cheese ball thaw in refrigerator overnight or let stand at room temperature for 1 hour or so, and then refrigerate until about 1 hour before serving.

ITALIAN-STYLE APPETIZERS

These petite sandwiches are a little more hearty than the usual appetizers served just before a meal. However, they're fine to serve if you're having a cocktail party with a fairly substantial buffet. These are also perfect for the type of gathering that precedes a play, concert, et cetera, where a full dinner is not in order, but where something a little more substantial is needed.

SINGLE RECIPE

Preparation Time: After sausage has simmered, it takes only 10 minutes to prepare the remaining ingredients.

Yield: 1 yard of petite sandwiches

1 pound hamburger
1 pound Italian-style bulk sausage
1 teaspoon garlic powder
1 teaspoon salt
Dash pepper
1 can (8 ounces) tomato sauce
1 can (8 ounces) pizza sauce
1 teaspoon basil (sweet)
1 teaspoon fennel seeds
12 slices of mozzarella cheese
1 yard-long loaf of Italian bread

DOUBLE RECIPE

Preparation Time: After sausage has simmered, it takes only 15 minutes to prepare the remaining ingredients.

Yield: 2 yards of petite sandwiches

2 pounds hamburger
2 pounds Italian-style bulk sausage
2 teaspoons garlic powder
2 teaspoons salt
¼ teaspoon pepper
2 cans (8 ounces) tomato sauce
2 cans (8 ounces) pizza sauce
2 teaspoons basil (sweet)
2 teaspoons fennel seeds
24 slices of mozzarella cheese
2 yard-long loaves of Italian bread

Simmer sausage in water for 30 minutes; then throw water away. (This will remove most of the fat from the sausage.) Brown sausage and beef together in a large skillet. Add garlic powder, salt, and pepper; stir in both kinds of sauce. Add basil and fennel seeds and simmer uncovered for 1½ to 2 hours.

TO SERVE. At serving time, heat the bread, which has been cut in half, for 5 minutes at 375° F. Then slice bread lengthwise. Cover the inside of the top half with slices of cheese; sprinkle with paprika and put under the broiler until cheese melts and becomes bubbly. Spread meat-sauce mixture generously on bottom half of bread. Assemble sandwich on a long tray or platter, putting the cheese-covered top over the meat-covered bottom half of the sandwich. Now with a sharp knife cut these long sandwiches into slices 1 inch to 1¼ inches thick. Arrange Italian peppers, both mild and hot, together with olives and parsley, on either side of the bread and serve hot.

Depending on the size of the group you're entertaining, you may wish to serve both halves at once, or first serve one half and assemble the other later so that it too will be served hot. This meat sauce freezes well, so make more than you'll use and freeze the rest.

PREPARING LUNCHBOXES

Your mornings needn't be a hectic, dreaded time of the day, even though you have two or more lunches to pack every day. Simply make sandwiches once a week (at your leisure—ha!) on an assembly-line basis. Make several different varieties, enough of each to last a week. Once this system is in operation, you should have five or more varieties to choose from when packing lunches in the morning. Put all of one kind (each wrapped in its own bag) in a large freezer bag, label, and date. Now the lunch takers can pack their own lunches, and give you time to enjoy a leisurely breakfast with your family. Incidentally, frozen blueberries and other fruits in small plastic containers are also a nice addition to any lunch. The fruit will be thawed, but still cool for noon-time eating. (Too bad the freezer has no answer for lost books, mittens, scarves, gym shoes, and all the other emergencies. Just having sandwiches made, however, will help. Perhaps you can set the alarm a little later.) Actually, sandwiches that are packed frozen in the lunch boxes will be completely thawed by noon and will be fresher than those packed the conventional way. To avoid salmonella and other food poisoning, the FDA recommends that, in warm weather and warmer climates, sandwiches carried in sack lunches should be packed in their frozen state. This type of food poisoning is more common than most people realize.

All breads freeze well and, from a nutritional point of view, it is best to use or at least alternate whole-grain, enriched white, rye, raisin, egg, oatmeal, Boston brown, and nut breads. Use day-old bread for sandwiches that are to be frozen; it's better than fresh bread. (Bread can be thawed from the freezer, made into sandwiches, and refrozen. It is one of the few things that may be refrozen.)

Spread bread liberally with softened butter, margarine, dairy sour cream, or cream cheese to keep filling from soaking into bread. Do not use mayonnaise or salad dressing as a spread, because these products separate when frozen, soak into the bread, and make a very soggy sandwich. Use only a dab of mayonnaise or salad dressing when mixing salad-type spreads, e.g., chicken salad. If more of a binder is needed, try substituting dairy sour cream or softened cream cheese. Leaf lettuce should be added just before the sandwich goes into the lunch box, or it may be packed separately along with tomatoes and any other relishes you may want to include. Avoid putting carrots, celery, cucumbers, and tomatoes in any spreads that are to be frozen; they lose their crispness and change flavor when frozen. Avoid using cooked egg whites, since they become rubbery when frozen; however, chopped egg yolks are fine. Egg yolks may be poached until they're firm and then chopped for egg salad. (To freeze egg whites, see page 47.)

When making pork, beef, corned beef, ham, and lunch-meat sandwiches, slice the meat, or have it sliced, very thin. Several very thin slices in a sandwich will be easier to bite and seem to taste better.

Here are a few suggestions for sandwich spreads and fillings that freeze well. I'm sure you'll be able to think of many more. A dab of mayonnaise or salad dressing may be added if desired:

Roast pork (either sliced or chopped) combined with apple butter
Peanut butter, apple butter, and crisp crumbled bacon (see page 41)
Sliced turkey and cranberry relish or sauce
Chopped chicken, walnuts, and olives
Corned beef and mustard
Deviled ham, chopped pickle, and mustard
Chopped dates, chopped peanuts, and cream cheese
Cream cheese and jelly
Swiss cheese slices, deviled ham, and sweet pickles or relish
Salami or cold cuts spread with a mixture of 3 ounces cream cheese,
   2 teaspoons horseradish, ½ teaspoon dry mustard, and 1 teaspoon
   finely chopped onion
Chopped or diced chicken, pimento, and cream cheese
Canned salmon, chopped ripe olives, lemon juice, and cream cheese

  When using cream cheese in making spreads, be sure that the cheese has softened at room temperature; this makes mixing much easier.

CHICKEN SANDWICH SPREAD

Yield: 6 sandwiches

2 cups ground chicken	½ cup currant or crabapple jelly
1 tablespoon mayonnaise	12 slices bread
1 tablespoon sour cream	Butter

Mix chicken, mayonnaise, sour cream, and jelly. Spread on 6 slices of buttered bread; cover with remaining bread slices. Wrap, label, date, and freeze.

OLIVE AND BACON SPREAD

*Yield: Approximately 2 cups
   spread*

4 slices bacon, crisp cooked and crumbled	¼ cup milk
or	1 cup chopped ripe olives (one 2¼-can)
2 tablespoons crumbled cooked bacon (see page 41)	2 teaspoons grated onion
	1 teaspoon salt
Two 3-ounce packages softened cream cheese	1 teaspoon Worcestershire sauce
	Dash Tabasco sauce

Cream the cheese with milk; add bacon bits, ripe olives, and seasoning. Blend well.

HOT CHICKEN CURRY SANDWICHES

This is a fine way to use the frozen cooked chicken meat in your
freezer.

SINGLE RECIPE	DOUBLE RECIPE
Time: 6 minutes	*Time: 7 minutes*
Yield: 6 sandwiches	*Yield: 12 sandwiches*
3 tablespoons butter	6 tablespoons butter
3 tablespoons flour	6 tablespoons flour
¾ cup milk	1½ cups milk
½ teaspoon salt	¾ teaspoon salt
Dash pepper	Dash pepper
½ teaspoon curry	1 teaspoon curry
¾ cup coarsely chopped, cooked chicken	1½ cups coarsely chopped, cooked chicken
or	or
One 5-ounce can boned chicken	Two 5-ounce cans boned chicken
6 slices bread or English muffins	12 slices bread or English muffins
Parmesan cheese	Parmesan cheese

Over moderate heat, melt butter and add flour, making a paste.
Slowly add milk, stirring constantly. After mixture has thickened, add
chicken and seasonings and mix thoroughly. Simmer. Toast bread on
one side; spread chicken mixture on untoasted side. Sprinkle generously with Parmesan cheese. Broil 4 to 5 minutes or until bubbly and
golden brown. Serve immediately.

TO FREEZE. If you have used freshly cooked chicken or canned
chicken, simply freeze these sandwiches before broiling them; then
insert a double thickness of freezer paper between the sandwiches,
stack, wrap, date, label, and return to freezer. If you're using cooked
chicken that has been in your freezer, it's best simply to make enough
for one meal. However, if this isn't possible, be sure that every bit of
chicken in the sauce comes to a boiling temperature before spreading
on bread.

TO SERVE WHEN FROZEN. Lay open-faced Hot Chicken Curry
Sandwiches on a cookie sheet and bake in a preheated oven at 350° F
for 10 minutes; then put under the broiler until delicately browned and
bubbly.

VARIATION. This makes a good spread for Appetizers by the Yard
(see page 76). Substitute Clearjel (see page 70) for flour and freeze bread
slices before wrapping.

SLOPPY JOES

Thank goodness these taste better than the name implies. These are fine for impromptu company, for suppers, lunches, and late snacks, such as after an evening of bridge. An easy way to serve a crowd.

SINGLE RECIPE
Preparation Time: 10 minutes
Yield: 8 servings

1½ pounds ground beef or round steak
1 tablespoon olive oil or shortening
½ cup chopped onions
½ cup frozen chopped green peppers
1 cup Open Pit barbecue sauce

DOUBLE RECIPE
Preparation Time: 12 minutes
Yield: 16 servings

3 pounds ground beef or round steak
2 tablespoons olive oil or shortening
1 cup chopped onions
1 cup frozen chopped green peppers
2 cups Open Pit barbecue sauce

TRIPLE RECIPE
Preparation Time: 14 minutes
Yield: 24 servings

4½ pounds ground beef or round steak
2 tablespoons olive oil or shortening
1½ cups chopped onions
1½ cups frozen chopped green peppers
3 cups Open Pit barbecue sauce

QUADRUPLE RECIPE
Preparation Time: 16 minutes
Yield: 32 servings

6 pounds ground beef or round steak
2 tablespoons olive oil or shortening
2 cups chopped onions
2 cups frozen chopped green peppers
4 cups Open Pit barbecue sauce

Heat oil in skillet and add meat. (You do not need to increase the amount of shortening in proportion to the recipe.) Brown meat over fairly high heat, especially the larger quantities of meat, since it will go faster that way. Add chopped onions (I use the frozen chopped kind) and peppers; after onions have softened, add barbecue sauce. Simmer at least 10 minutes until ready to serve on hamburger buns or bread.

OLIVE SLOPPY JOES. For variety, serve 1 cup of sliced pimento-stuffed olives in a separate dish, about 1 cup for each recipe, or add the sliced olives to the meat sauce just before serving.

TO FREEZE. Freeze in meal-sized plastic containers. Thaw completely before heating. Heat thoroughly and serve.

SLOPPY JOES, ITALIAN STYLE

This is a hearty sandwich. It's the ideal fare to serve after a football game or out on the patio when you don't want to barbecue. If you like pizza, you'll love this.

SINGLE RECIPE

Preparation Time: After sausage has simmered, it takes only 10 minutes to assemble the remaining ingredients
Yield: Six 8-inch sandwiches

1 pound hamburger
1 pound Italian-style bulk sausage
1 teaspoon garlic powder
1 teaspoon salt
Dash pepper
One 8-ounce can tomato sauce

One 8-ounce can pizza sauce
1 teaspoon basil (sweet)
1 teaspoon fennel seeds
12 slices of mozzarella cheese
Six 8-inch torpedo rolls

DOUBLE RECIPE

Preparation Time: After sausage has simmered, it takes only 15 minutes to assemble the remaining ingredients
Yield: Twelve 8-inch sandwiches

2 pounds hamburger
2 pounds Italian-style bulk sausage
2 teaspoons garlic powder
2 teaspoons salt
¼ teaspoon pepper
Two 8-ounce cans tomato sauce
Two 8-ounce cans pizza sauce
2 teaspoons basil (sweet)
2 teaspoons fennel seeds
24 slices of mozzarella cheese
Twelve 8-inch torpedo rolls

TRIPLE RECIPE

Preparation Time: After sausage has simmered, it takes only 20 minutes to prepare the remaining ingredients.
Yield: Eighteen 8-inch sandwiches

3 pounds hamburger
3 pounds Italian-style bulk sausage
3 teaspoons garlic powder
3 teaspoons salt
⅓ teaspoon pepper
Three 8-ounce cans tomato sauce
Three 8-ounce cans pizza sauce
3 teaspoons basil (sweet)
3 teaspoons fennel seeds
36 slices of mozzarella cheese
Eighteen 8-inch torpedo rolls

Simmer sausage in water for 30 minutes; then discard water. (This will remove most of the fat from the sausage.) Brown sausage and beef together in a large skillet. Add garlic powder, salt, and pepper; stir in both kinds of sauce. Add basil and simmer uncovered for 1½ to 2 hours.

TO SERVE. At serving time heat rolls for 5 minutes at 375° F; then slice lengthwise. Cover the inside of the top half with 2 slices of cheese; sprinkle with paprika and put under the broiler until cheese melts and becomes bubbly. Spread meat sauce mixture generously on bottom half of roll. Close sandwich and serve hot with little Italian peppers (either mild or hot) and olives. If you're serving these for a meal, figure one sandwich per person. However, if you're serving them as a snack, cut the rolls into quarters and figure about one roll for two people.

TO FREEZE. Freeze any extra sauce in meal-sized serving portions. When serving, simply heat sauce thoroughly, warm buns, and follow above instructions.

VARIATION. Another way this can be served and made into elegant party fare is to buy the yard-long thin Italian bread. Cut loaf in half and then slice each loaf in half lengthwise. Put the cheese on the top half and broil; cover the bottom half with the meat mixture; assemble on a long platter or tray and cut the bread into slices 1 to 1½ inches thick. Arrange the peppers, olives, and some parsley on either side of the bread and serve. This is ideal for buffet serving or it can be used as an appetizer.

HOT TUNA SANDWICH FILLING

Marvelous for serving a crowd.

SINGLE RECIPE	DOUBLE RECIPE
Time: 8 minutes	*Time: 10 minutes*
Yield: Filling for 9 hamburger buns	*Yield: Filling for 18 hamburger buns*
¼ pound shredded or ground Cheddar cheese	½ pound shredded or ground Cheddar cheese
One 6½ to 7-ounce can tuna	Two 6½ to 7-ounce cans tuna
¼ cup mayonnaise	½ cup mayonnaise
¼ cup sour cream	½ cup sour cream
2¼-ounce can chopped ripe olives, drained	Two 2¼-ounce cans chopped ripe olives, drained
2 tablespoons chopped onions	¼ cup chopped onions
2 tablespoons chopped green pepper	¼ cup chopped green pepper
2 tablespoons sweet relish	¼ cup sweet relish

Combine all ingredients (you can use a food processor with a plastic mixing blade). Generously fill hamburger buns. Cover buns with aluminum foil and bake in a 250° F oven about 25 minutes.

TO FREEZE. When preparing this to serve a large crowd, put all the buns (in a single layer) in a large flat baking pan or cookie sheet; cover with foil and freeze. Buns may also be wrapped individually if desired.

TO SERVE WHEN FROZEN. Put frozen aluminum-foil-covered buns in 350° F oven for 35 minutes or until bubbly on the inside.

HOT HAM 'N CHEESE BURGERS

These Ham 'n Cheese Burgers are a nice change from the traditional hamburgers. Make and fill your buns in advance; simply put a panful or two in the oven and presto! your meal is ready. Ideal for teenage parties, late-night snacks, as well as weekend lunches and suppers. Great way to use leftover ham.

SINGLE RECIPE
Time: 10 minutes
Yield: 8 generously filled burgers

1 cup ground ham
1 cup ground or shredded Cheddar cheese
¼ cup sweet relish
¼ cup mayonnaise

DOUBLE RECIPE
Time: 15 minutes
Yield: 16 generously filled burgers

2 cups ground ham
2 cups ground or shredded Cheddar cheese
½ cup sweet relish
½ cup mayonnaise

Combine all the ingredients in a bowl. Generously fill hamburger buns. Preheat oven to 350° F. Put all the buns in a large pan or cookie sheet, cover with foil, and heat in the oven for 20 minutes. Burgers should be bubbly hot.

TO FREEZE. The easiest way to freeze these is to put the filled buns on a large platter or cookie sheet and freeze. Then wrap in meal-sized portions, using any freezer wrap you desire.

TO SERVE WHEN FROZEN. They may be baked in the oven while still completely frozen or partially thawed. Add an additional 10 to 15 minutes to the baking time, making sure that the centers are really hot.

GARLIC BREAD

While you're at it, it's just as easy to prepare several loaves of garlic bread at a time. You'll be glad you did. They're nice to serve with a salad on a hot summer evening, or when you serve spaghetti, chili, or soups.

SINGLE RECIPE
Preparation Time: 10 minutes
Yield: 1 long loaf

1 long thin loaf of French bread
¼ pound margarine or butter
½ package dry garlic-and-cheese salad dressing mix

DOUBLE RECIPE
Preparation Time: 15 minutes
Yield: 2 long loaves

2 long thin loaves of French bread
½ pound margarine or butter
1 package dry garlic-and-cheese salad dressing mix

Melt butter or margarine. (In this recipe margarine tastes every bit as good as butter.) Add salad dressing mix. Meanwhile, cut bread in diagonal slices, 1 to 1½ inches thick, making sure not to cut through the bottom crust, so that the loaf will remain intact. With a pastry brush, liberally brush butter-and-garlic mixture on sliced surfaces. Stir butter mixture continually with pastry brush, because the salad dressing mix tends to settle to the bottom. Divide bread into family-sized servings and wrap in foil (heavy freezer weight). Heat in a 350° F oven for 20 minutes and serve.

TO FREEZE. Wrap bread in the foil, date, label, and freeze.

TO SERVE WHEN FROZEN. Put frozen bread into 350° F oven for 30 to 35 minutes. If more crusty bread is desired, open foil on top and heat an additional 5 minutes.

RHODA's CHEESE SNACKS

Really a nifty appetizer made just like cookies. A real quickie you'll enjoy serving.

Yield: About 75 appetizers

1 cup butter or margarine (2 sticks)	2 cups flour
½ pound Cheddar cheese	2 cups Rice Krispies
1 teaspoon salt	

Preheat oven to 350° F. Cream butter. Shred cheese and add to butter, along with salt and flour. When well blended, gently fold in Rice Krispies. Roll mixture on waxed paper into a long rope about ¾ inch in diameter. Seal and refrigerate until baking time. Cut into ⅜-inch-thick slices. Place on ungreased cookie sheet. With a fork, flatten each piece of dough, making an indentation on each snack with the fork prongs. Bake at 350° F for 18 to 20 minutes. Watch carefully, as they will burn easily. Remove from oven when just nicely browned.

TO FREEZE. Freezer-wrap roll of unbaked dough, date, label, and freeze.

TO SERVE WHEN FROZEN. Remove dough from freezer and thaw at room temperature for about 30 minutes. Slice and bake according to above instructions.

Breads and Quick Breads

****

BAKING, MIXING, AND FREEZING BREADS AND DOUGHS

The person who can capture the smell of fresh-baked yeast dough and package it will surely make a fortune. Meanwhile, the only way to get that delectable aroma to permeate your home is to bake your own bread.

Many good cooks are afraid to try baking yeast bread. There's no real mystery about working with yeast, once you understand the fundamentals. Turning out a few loaves of bread or coffee cakes will give you a feeling of satisfaction and pride that no other form of cooking can quite duplicate.

You don't have time? Many people have the misconception that baking bread is an all-day affair or at least an all-morning one. This simply isn't true; the mixing time is relatively short. The first few times you bake yeast dough it will take longer than when you get the hang of it. But isn't that true of everything else? Working with yeast dough does take time, but then, you're not actually working all the time. You can do other chores or sit down and read while the dough is rising. Making bread takes less actual working time than mixing and frosting most cakes.

There are three basic types of yeast or bread doughs: water bread dough (French bread and rolls); milk bread dough (regular bread and rolls); and sweet bread dough (used for sweet rolls, coffee cakes, et cetera). There are many variations of these, but all can be made from one good basic dough with only a few changes.

If you're a novice at working with yeast dough, don't tackle the larger recipes until you feel more confident. It might overwhelm you and then you'd be too discouraged to try again. However, yeast breads freeze so easily and taste so good that I'm always sorry I didn't make a larger batch.

Yeast

Yeast comes in both dry and compressed forms that can be used interchangeably. The dry or granulated yeast is less perishable; in fact, if stored in the refrigerator it will keep almost indefinitely. To determine if your compressed yeast is still good, crumble it with your fingers. If it crumbles easily it is still good, or if you cover it with 2 tablespoons of sugar it should dissolve in 3 minutes.

The recipes on the following pages will call for granulated dry yeast, because of its excellent keeping quality. However, you may substitute compressed yeast if you wish. One regular-sized cake of compressed yeast (⅔ ounce) equals 1 package of dry yeast, and one 1-ounce cake of yeast about equals two packages of dry yeast. Be sure to note the weight when using compressed yeast: 2½ teaspoons of dry yeast = 1 package of dry yeast.

Both kinds of yeast may be dissolved in water (or other liquids, such as milk). The liquid should be warm; a temperature of 105° F to 115° F is ideal for granulated yeast, and 85° F to 100° F for compressed yeast. Use a thermometer if you aren't sure. When sprinkled on the inside of your arm, the liquid should feel warm, not hot. To keep the yeast at this temperature, use a bowl or container that has been rinsed with hot water. Actually, this is a very important step in yeast cookery. If the liquid is too hot, it will kill the live organisms and, if too cool, the yeast action will be too slow.

Liquids

Milk and water are the liquids usually called for in yeast dough. Milk adds nutrition to the bread, as well as a more velvety texture. Breads made with water are heavier and have a crisper crust, such as French breads.

 All liquids should be warmed before adding to yeast or yeast mixture: 105 degrees F to 115 degrees F for dissolving only the yeast, 120 degrees F to 130 degrees F for the rapid mix method. Hotter temperatures would kill the yeast. Unpasteurized milk should be scalded and cooled to the abovementioned temperatures.

Flour

Yeast doughs are made at least in part with all-purpose flour be-cause of its high gluten content. Gluten is the elastic or rubbery substance that is capable of surrounding and holding the carbon dioxide gas bubbles formed by the yeast. All recipes, even those made with rye, oat, bran, or cornmeal, should have a portion of all-purpose flour as a source of gluten. All recipes in this book work fine with unbleached all-purpose flour, a flour I prefer and use all the time.

Fats

Fats are usually added for flavor, but they also make the breads more tender. Liquid vegetable oils are very convenient. Butter and margarine are easily melted when added to warmed liquids; they should be soft but need not be completely melted.

Salt and Sugar

Salt and sugar are added mainly for flavoring, although since sugar is food for the yeast it's a good idea to add a tablespoon of sugar to the yeast mixture. The flavor of your yeast dough can be varied by substituting honey, molasses, brown sugar, and syrup in place of granulated sugar. However, when using the liquid sweeteners, decrease other liquids in the recipe by an equal amount. Remember, the more sugar, the browner the crust.

Eggs and Egg Yolks

Eggs and egg yolks make the dough tender, as well as richer and lighter. With eggs added, your breads will be more nutritious and will have a more golden color. Eggs should be at room temperature or else they will chill the dough.

Spices, Herbs, and Fruit

The addition of herbs and spices, as well as raisins, nuts, or dried and candied fruit, will give you flavor variations. Such additions generally don't require any adjusting of other ingredients.

Mixing the Dough

There are basically two types of yeast doughs, the no-knead dough, which is called a batter dough, and the regular dough that is kneaded. You'll find good examples of both kinds in the following pages. The batter dough is easier and quicker to make, but generally produces a bread that is less smooth, more coarse in texture.

 Unless you have a heavy-duty mixer with a large-capacity bowl, you'll be able to mix only the single recipes in your mixing bowls. Mix as much as you can with your mixer and, when the bowl is overflowing, pour into a very large container and work in the remaining flour with a large wooden spoon, or by hand. (Although this may not work with all makes of electric mixers that have two beaters, it worked very well on an old one I have. When the yeast dough becomes thick, the dough will start to creep up the mixers and make it impossible to use them. Simply remove one of the beaters—the innermost one—and continue mixing at a slow speed.)

Follow manufacturer's directions if you have a heavy-duty mixer designed for breadmaking. Kneading by hand may not be necessary when you are using this type of heavy-duty mixer.

When measuring large amounts of flour, it's sometimes difficult to keep count. It's best to measure all flour into a bowl before you start to mix. The new tall 1-pound coffee cans measure exactly 4½ cups. This is a quick way of measuring. When you're making a double recipe of Basic White Bread, simply fill the coffee can twice with sifted flour—which will give you a total of 9 cups. Add an additional cup or so of flour as needed. As you become more experienced in working with yeast dough, you won't need to measure your flour, but will be able to tell by "feel."

Kneading

Reserve about ¼ to ¾ cup flour (for single recipe) for the kneading. Sprinkle some of it on a pastry cloth or board. Place all the batter in the center of this and let it stand for about 10 minutes. Flour your hands well; roll dough over in order to cover all sides lightly with flour. Flatten dough slightly and shape into a round flat circle. Pick up the outer rim of dough at a point farthest from you and fold over on top toward you. Press down with the heel of your hands gently but firmly, pushing dough away from you. Give the dough a quarter turn and repeat the kneading process until the dough looks smooth and elastic. The dough should cease being sticky; you'll also note little bubbles just under the surface of the dough. Avoid adding too much flour because it will make your dough heavy. Sweet dough should be very light and adding too much flour will make it breadlike instead of light and flaky.

Rapid Mix Method

In this method, the dry granular yeast is mixed with the dry ingredients (this method eliminates the need to dissolve the yeast first in warm water and let it set for 5 minutes to dissolve). With this method, the dough rises faster because you add warmed liquid (120 ° F to 130° F); this warmed dough helps the yeast to work faster. All recipes can be adapted to this method.

Rising

Once the dough has been properly kneaded or mixed (as batter doughs), it's time for the dough to rise in a warm draft-free place. Your oven is ideal for this purpose. Simply turn the oven on for a minute, no more, until it's approximately 85° F. (Of course, in warm weather you won't have to worry about this.) Place dough in a well-greased bowl, turning dough to coat the entire surface with grease. This keeps the dough from drying out. Cover with waxed paper or a clean, warm, wet towel. Rising should not be done too quickly or too slowly. Best results are obtained at approximately 85° F.

Dough should rise until double in volume. A good test to see if it has risen enough is to press two fingers into the dough. If indentations remain, the dough has risen sufficiently. Punch down by pushing fist into the center of the dough; then fold edges toward the center. Some recipes require a second rising. Simply regrease bowl slightly and turn dough to coat. The second rising is much quicker—usually half an hour is all that is needed. (A second rising, although not required, will never hurt a dough.) Batter doughs are usually "punched down" with a wooden spoon and then spooned into their prepared baking pans.

Standard bread pans vary in size (I'm not referring to the miniature or demiloaf pans), but don't worry about this. In the smaller pans, usually about 8½ x 4½ x 2⅝, the bread will rise above the pan and a bit over the rim, forming a nice "head." In the larger pans, the bread will rise within the pan, rounding slightly above it.

Baking

The shaped dough should be allowed to rise again until almost double in volume before baking. Always bake in a preheated oven. When baking two loaves of bread, place pans on the center shelf with 2 inches between pans to allow good air circulation. For four loaves, stagger pans on both shelves, allowing ample space between pans for circulation of air.

When bread is done, it is well browned and shrinks away from sides of pan slightly. It will also sound hollow when tapped with the knuckles. Always make sure that your bread pans have been well greased all the way up the sides. Teflon pans are excellent for baking bread because the loaves simply fall out. When baking bread in glass pans, lower heat about 25° F to avoid burning the bottom edges.

Remove bread from pans immediately after taking them from the oven. Crusts will get soggy if the bread is left in the pans. For a soft-crust bread, brush loaves with soft butter or margarine. But this seems to me to defeat the whole purpose of baking your own bread; the crisp crust is the best part of it for me.

Timing

The mixing time, when given, usually includes dissolving the yeast, mixing, kneading, and shaping the loaves. It will take less time and be easier for those of you who have a large heavy-duty mixer designed for mixing yeast dough. If you don't have the heavy-duty mixer, simply mix as much flour into the batter as you can, removing the innermost beater (if possible) when the dough starts "climbing up." If your mixing bowl is overflowing, empty the contents into a very large container, such as the lid of a plastic cake taker; it's ideal for mixing large batters. Work in remaining flour, either with a wooden spoon or by hand, making sure not to add too much flour.

When you are working with sweet dough, the timing for rolling out, filling, et cetera, will vary greatly from person to person. The more often you make it, the more adept you become and the less time it will take. One lady at our church (the one who gave me the basic sweet dough recipe) often makes a quadruple or quintuple recipe at night when she comes home from work and thinks nothing of it! I'm simply not in her league. The largest amount I've ever tackled (and I do this frequently) is a triple recipe. From the very start to the end, it takes me about 5 hours (with time out while the dough is rising) and my yield has been 56 large caramel rolls, plus 16 small caramel rolls, 1 large Swedish tea ring, plus 2 small coffee cakes and 2 large pecan roll loaves, or 8 large coffee cakes, 27 large pecan rolls, plus 16 small ones. Not bad for one morning's work, and it's such fun. This is one time you'll wish you had a double oven. However, you can control the rising by keeping prepared cakes and rolls covered and out of a draft, but not too warm, until about 30 minutes before you're ready to bake them.

You'll enjoy the results for weeks or even months, and you'll be so glad you made a large quantity. You need to be in the right mood to work with yeast, and when you *are* in the mood, why not bake up a storm? You'll be happy you did, and so will your family.

Freezing

Breads freeze so well and easily that it's almost a sacrilege to make a single recipe. I've done it and I always regret it. Bread should be thoroughly cooled before wrapping for the freezer or the bread box. Bread will become soggy if you wrap it too soon. Sweet rolls and coffee cakes are best frozen on trays or cookie sheets and then wrapped for the freezer. Buy yourself a number of moisture-vapor-proof plastic bags large enough to hold a loaf of bread easily. You'll find these bags are just the right size for sweet rolls and coffee cakes too. They can be used repeatedly and will prove to be a good investment. Put completely cooled breads or frozen sweet rolls and coffee cakes into these bags, seal, date, and label. Remember to label the type of bread and the kind of fillings used in the coffee cakes. Flavors can transfer even while frozen, so pack only those of the same kind in each bag. You won't want your pecan rolls to taste almondy.

FROZEN DOUGH. If you cherish the aroma of fresh-baked bread, prepare yeast dough and let it rise once. Shape into loaves, rolls, coffee cakes, et cetera. Freeze; then freezer-wrap, date, and label. Allow to defrost and rise a second time. Then bake. *Unbaked bread dough should be kept for only 1 month.*

YEAST BREADS

BASIC WHITE BREAD: RAPID-MIX METHOD

With simple changes this basic white bread can be made into many things. Homemade bread never gets stale—it's always consumed too quickly. But that's one of the joys of baking bread.

SINGLE RECIPE
> *Time: Mixing, kneading—20*
> *minutes; shaping loaves—1*
> *minute each*
> *Yield: 2 loaves*

5½ cups sifted flour
2 tablespoons sugar
1 teaspoon salt
1 package dry yeast
¼ cup warm water (105° to 115° F)
1¾ cups milk
2 tablespoons margarine or butter
¼ cup flour

DOUBLE RECIPE
> *Time: 30 minutes total*
> *Yield: 4 loaves*

10½ to 11 cups sifted flour
¼ cup sugar
2 teaspoons salt
2 packages dry yeast
½ cup warm water (105° to 115° F)
3½ cups milk
¼ cup butter or margarine (½ stick)
½ cup flour

Combine flour, sugar, salt, and dry yeast in mixing bowl. Combine milk and shortening in a saucepan and heat over low heat until liquids are very warm (120 degrees to 130 degrees F). (Or heat in your micro-wave oven.) Add liquid to mixed dry ingredients and beat at medium speed of electric mixer for two minutes, scraping down bowl occasion-ally. Now beat at high speed for two minutes. Turn out yeast mixture onto lightly floured board, using reserved ¼ cup of flour. Let dough set for 10 minutes.

If at this stage your dough looks like a sticky glob, don't worry; that's how it's supposed to look. Roll dough into a ball and then fold dough over toward you with your fingers. Push dough back with the heel of your hand; give a quarter turn and repeat. Continue this until dough is no longer sticky. Add more flour if needed, but remember that using too much flour will make the dough heavy.

Place dough in a large, lightly greased bowl, turning dough so that all sides will be lightly coated. This keeps the dough from cracking and drying. Cover bowl and set in a warm place until doubled in bulk (about 1½ hours at 80° F). Now punch down dough and squeeze out all air bubbles. Divide dough in half, shaping each half into an oblong roll. Place in a greased bread pan, putting any seams on the underside. Cover and let rise in a warm place until almost doubled in volume. Have your oven preheated so that when the dough has risen to the proper height, you can simply put it into the oven. Bake at 375° F for 40 minutes or, if you use glass pans, bake in a 350° F oven for about the same length of time.

When bread is done, the top will be nicely browned and the dough just starting to pull away from the sides. Don't overbake or your bread will be dry. You may want to butter the top of the bread for a softer crust. However, that is one of the best things about homemade bread—the crunchy crust.

VARIATION. See following recipes for Sesame Braided Bread, Whole Wheat or Cracked Wheat, and Raisin-Cinnamon Bread.

SESAME BRAIDED BREAD

The nutlike flavor resulting from the addition of toasted sesame seeds is delicious. And the aroma, mmmmmm!

SINGLE RECIPE
  Yield: 2 loaves

½ cup sesame seeds
Dough from single recipe of Basic
  White Bread
1 slightly beaten egg white

DOUBLE RECIPE
  Yield: 4 loaves

1 cup sesame seeds
Dough from double recipe of Basic
  White Bread
1 slightly beaten egg white

Toast sesame seeds in a shallow pan at 425° F for about 4 to 5 minutes until seeds are golden brown. (Sesame seeds bought in the little 2-ounce spice and herb jars are quite expensive if you expect to use them in quantity. All health food stores carry them in 1-pound packages at one fifth the cost.) Prepare Basic White Bread according to instructions, using about ½ cup less flour (for a single recipe). Add toasted sesame seeds after adding about the first 2 or 3 cups of flour for a single recipe.

TO SHAPE. Divide a single recipe in half; then divide each half into 3 equal parts. Roll these out into long strands and braid the strands, tucking ends under. Place in loaf pans. Brush surface of bread with oil; let rise until double in bulk. Gently brush with beaten egg white and bake at 375° F for 40 minutes or 350° F if you're using glass pans. If you don't want to braid the dough, it's not absolutely necessary, but it does make an attractive loaf.

WHOLE WHEAT OR CRACKED WHEAT BREAD

Whole wheat or cracked wheat bread may be made by using 2½ cups of whole wheat or cracked wheat flour and an equal amount of all-purpose flour for a single recipe.

RAISIN-CINNAMON BREAD

This bread may be served plain or iced, whichever you prefer. Iced, it almost has a cakelike quality. Served plain or with peanut butter and jelly, it will disappear as if by magic when the youngsters spot it.

SINGLE RECIPE	DOUBLE RECIPE
Time: 20 minutes	*Time: 30 minutes*
Yield: 2 loaves	*Yield: 4 loaves*
1 cup dark seedless raisins	2 cups dark seedless raisins
1 tablespoon cinnamon	2 tablespoons cinnamon
¼ cup sugar	½ cup sugar
Dough from single recipe of Basic White Bread	Dough from double recipe of Basic White Bread

Follow the directions for Basic White Bread, adding raisins to milk. When dough is completely mixed and kneaded, roll dough for each loaf into a rectangle about 6 x 16 inches. Sprinkle sugar and cinnamon mixture over this area evenly and roll dough tightly, beginning at the narrow end. Seal ends and tuck in slightly. Place in greased bread pan and let rise. Continue baking directions for Basic White Bread.

ITALIAN OR FRENCH BREAD

Here is another simple variation of Basic White Bread. Water or potato water is substituted for milk, shortening is eliminated, and you have a lovely crusty bread; only 4 ingredients are needed.

SINGLE RECIPE	DOUBLE RECIPE
Time: Mixing and kneading— 20 minutes; shaping loaves—1 minute each	*Time: 30 minutes total*
Yield: 2 loaves	*Yield: 4 loaves*
1 package dry yeast	2 packages dry yeast
¼ cup warm water (105° to 115° F)	½ cup warm water (105° to 115° F)
1¾ cups warm water or potato water (105° to 115° F)	3½ cups warm water or potato water (105° to 115° F)
1 tablespoon salt	2 tablespoons salt
5 to 5½ cups sifted flour	10 to 11 cups sifted flour (approximately)

Dissolve yeast in warm water (110 degrees F), and let stand for about 10 minutes. Pour into mixing bowl with remaining warm water. Add salt and flour 1 cup at a time, mixing well. Reserve last ½ cup (1 full cup for a double recipe) of flour for kneading. Following kneading and raising directions on Basic White Bread.

TO SHAPE. When dough is ready to shape (after it has been punched down), divide in half and let it stand for about 10 minutes. Roll each ball of dough into a long loaf (about 14 inches) with your hands. Put on a greased cookie sheet. Cover loosely with a towel and set in a warm place until double in bulk.

TO BAKE. Preheat oven to 400° F. To increase crustiness, place a shallow pan of water in the oven. Bake for 40 to 45 minutes, or until golden brown.

COOL-RISE BASIC WHITE BREAD

Many homemakers prefer this way of making bread, since they can mix it one day and bake it the next. It's a boon to working people for that reason.

SINGLE RECIPE	DOUBLE RECIPE
Time: 20 minutes for mixing, kneading, and shaping loaves *Yield: 2 loaves*	*Time: 30 minutes for mixing, kneading, and shaping loaves* *Yield: 4 loaves*
2 packages dry yeast	4 packages dry yeast
½ cup warm water (105° to 115° F)	1 cup warm water (105° to 115° F)
2 tablespoons sugar	¼ cup sugar
1¾ cups warm milk (105° to 115° F)	3½ cups warm milk (105° to 115° F)
1 teaspoon salt	2 teaspoons salt
2 tablespoons butter or margarine	4 tablespoons butter or margarine
5½ to 6½ cups sifted flour	10½ to 11 cups sifted flour (approx.)

Dissolve yeast in warm water and add sugar. Meanwhile, warm milk to a little more than 115° F. Pour into mixing bowl and add salt and shortening. Now add yeast mixture. Add flour about 1 cup at a time, mixing well after each addition. After you've added about 3 or 4 cups, mix well for about 2 minutes. Then add remaining flour, reserving 1 cup for kneading. Turn out dough on a floured board or pastry cloth and let set for 10 minutes, then knead 5 to 10 minutes, or until smooth and elastic. Dough will no longer be sticky. Cover with greased plastic wrap and then a towel and let stand for 20 minutes.

Punch dough down and divide into two equal parts. Form into loaves and put into greased bread pans. Brush with oil and cover with plastic wrap. Place in the refrigerator for 2 to 24 hours. (Volume decreases slightly as refrigeration time increases beyond 24 hours; however, texture and quality remain acceptable up to 48 hours. So, in case of emergency, you can wait an extra day to bake your bread.)

To bake, remove from refrigerator and let stand uncovered for about 10 minutes while preheating the oven to 400° F (375° F if you're using glass bread pans). Puncture any surface bubbles that may have formed on dough during refrigeration, using greased toothpick. Bake at 400° F for 30 to 40 minutes, or until done. For best results, bake on lower oven racks. Remove from pans immediately and cool on racks. For soft crusts you may brush with butter or margarine.

VARIATIONS. You can make all the same variations with Cool-Rise Basic White Bread as you can with regular Basic White Bread.

ONION SPOON BREAD

Spoon breads are those mixed with a spoon or mixer; there's no kneading involved. If you're inexperienced and a bit leery of working with yeast dough and kneading, try making spoon bread first. Once you see how easy it is, you'll be ready to attempt other recipes.

SINGLE RECIPE	DOUBLE RECIPE
Time: 15 minutes	*Time: 20 minutes*
Yield: 2 loaves	*Yield: 4 loaves*
1 cup warm milk (120° to 130° F)	2 cups warm milk (120° to 130° F)
2 tablespoons sugar	¼ cup sugar
2 tablespoons butter or margarine	¼ cup butter or margarine (½ stick)
¾ cup warm water (105° to 115° F)	1½ cups warm water (105° to 115° F)
1 package dry yeast	2 packages dry yeast
1 envelope onion soup mix	2 envelopes onion soup mix
4 cups unsifted flour	8 cups unsifted flour

For a very mild onion flavor, use only ½ package of onion soup mix (about 3 level tablespoons) for a single recipe.

Heat milk and pour into mixing bowl, adding butter or margarine and soup mixture. Let stand. Meanwhile, dissolve yeast in warm water, add sugar, and let stand 5 minutes. When milk has cooled to 115° F, add yeast mixture; mixing at low speed, add flour 1 cup at a time. When all the flour has been incorporated, cover bowl and let dough rise in a warm place until double in bulk (about 45 minutes). Divide dough of single recipe in half, putting each half into a greased 1½-quart casserole. Knead the dough just a bit in the casserole to make sure that all the air bubbles are out. If the dough has absorbed the shortening from the bowl, regrease or oil and let dough rise until almost doubled in bulk. Preheat oven to 375° F Bake uncovered for 45 minutes. Bread should be a nice deep golden color. Loosen sides and cool on rack.

OATMEAL BREAD

This is a modern adaptation of an old recipe that comes from the owner of one of Chicago's leading restaurants. Katie Howell has made and sold this delicious bread in her restaurant for over 30 years. People come from far and near to buy her delicious Oatmeal Bread. Very quick and easy to make.

SINGLE RECIPE	DOUBLE RECIPE
Time: 10 minutes	*Time: 12 minutes*
Yield: 2 loaves	*Yield: 4 loaves*
2 cups warm milk	4 cups warm milk
1 cup steel-cut oatmeal	2 cups steel-cut oatmeal
or	or
regular rolled oatmeal	regular rolled oatmeal
2 tablespoons butter	¼ cup butter
2 teaspoons salt	1 tablespoon salt
½ cup warm water (105° to 115° F)	1 cup warm water (105° to 115° F)
1 tablespoon sugar	2 tablespoons sugar
2 packages dry yeast	4 packages dry yeast
1 egg	2 eggs
About 4½ cups flour	About 9 cups flour

Steel-cut oatmeal is available at some supermarkets and in all health food stores. Steel-cut oatmeal gives the bread more texture; definitely worth looking for. When you are using regular oatmeal, you will need about ½ cup more flour per single recipe.

Combine milk, oatmeal, butter, salt, water; warm in a saucepan or glass dish in your microwave oven to between 105° to 115° F. Soak one hour. Meanwhile, combine yeast in ½ cup warm water (for a single recipe), adding sugar. Cover and put in a warm place until double in size, usually about 1 to 1½ hours. (Be sure the container is large enough; the first time I made this bread I lost about half of my yeast mixture in the bottom of the oven.) Add egg to oatmeal mixture, beating well. Now add yeast mixture. Slowly add 2½ cups flour, beating very well; keep adding flour until the dough pulls away from the sides of the bowl. Knead dough for a few minutes and put into a greased bowl; set in warm place for 20 minutes. Punch down and divide single recipe into 2 well-greased loaf pans. Cover with greased waxed paper or Saran Wrap and refrigerate for 2 to 24 hours. When ready to bake, remove paper covering carefully and let set at room temperature for 10 minutes. Bake in a preheated oven at 400° F for 35 to 40 minutes.

REFRIGERATOR ROLLS

The recipe for these melt-in-your-mouth rolls has an added advantage. You may mix the dough any time you have a few minutes, put it in the refrigerator, and keep it until you're ready to roll out the dough and bake it.

SINGLE RECIPE	DOUBLE RECIPE
Time: 15 minutes	*Time: 20 minutes*
Yield: Approximately 4 dozen	*Yield: Approximately 8 dozen*
medium-sized dinner rolls	*medium-sized dinner rolls*
½ cup warm water (105° to 115° F)	1 cup warm water (105° to 115° F)
2 packages dry yeast	4 packages dry yeast
¾ cup sugar	1½ cups sugar
1 cup lard	2 cups lard
1½ cups hot water (120–130° F)	3 cups *hot* water (120°–130° F)
1 teaspoon salt	2 teaspoons salt
2 eggs	4 eggs
6 cups unsifted flour	12 cups unsifted flour

Dissolve yeast in warm water, add 1 to 2 tablespoons sugar (see page 97), and let set for at least 5 minutes. Meanwhile, cut lard in thin slices into a large mixing bowl (this is done very quickly with a wire cheese slicer). Add remaining sugar and pour hot water over the sugar and lard. Mix at low speed in your mixer to soften the lard. Add salt and eggs, and beat. When the lard and water mixture has cooled to between 105° and 115° F, add yeast. Add flour 1 cup at a time, mixing well after each addition.

You may now put the dough into a large covered container and store in the refrigerator until it's time to bake it, or you can set it in a warm draft-free place and let it rise until double in volume (about 1½ to 2 hours). This dough will keep in the refrigerator for about a week; however, you may have to punch it down occasionally. Be sure to keep it covered or it will dry out.

Remove dough from the refrigerator and let stand for 10 minutes. Divide dough from a single recipe into 4 equal parts. Take 1 part at a time and put it on a floured board or pastry cloth. Roll into a 14-inch circle. Cut circle into quarters and then divide each quarter into 3 pieces of equal size. This dough is so light and rich that it's best not to brush it with butter. Now start to roll from the wide end down to the point, pick it up gently, and lay it on well-greased cookie sheet or tray. Don't crowd the rolls, because they will rise. These rolls will seem quite small to you; however, they really puff up, once they're in the oven. Set rolls in a warm draft-free place and let rise until nice and light (about ½ hour). Preheat oven to 375° F, and bake until just tinged with a slight tan if you intend to freeze the rolls (about 8 to 10 minutes). Otherwise, continue baking until nice and brown (about 12 to 15 minutes).

TO FREEZE. You may freeze the rolls right on their baking pans after they have cooled. Then remove from pan and pack them in moisture-vapor-proof bags.

TO SERVE WHEN FROZEN. Treat these just like the brown-and-serve rolls available at grocery stores. Preheat oven to 375° F. Put rolls into the oven and bake until nicely browned. Serve immediately for that oven-fresh flavor.

VARIATIONS. Using small greased muffin tins, about 2 inches across the top, place a ball of dough sufficiently large to fill the tin ⅓ full. Let rise and follow the above instructions for baking, freezing, et cetera.

CARAWAY RYE ROLLS

These small caraway rye rolls are a marvelous addition to any meal, crusty on the outside and tender on the inside. Very simple to prepare, although it will take a little time. However, you can be doing other things while the dough is rising.

SINGLE RECIPE
Preparation Time: 10 minutes to mix; 12 minutes to shape
Yield: 3 dozen oval-shaped rolls

2 cups warm water
1 package yeast
4 tablespoons soft butter or margarine
1 tablespoon caraway seed
1 tablespoon salt
3 cups unsifted flour
3 cups rye flour
1 egg white
1 tablespoon salt

DOUBLE RECIPE
Preparation Time: 12 minutes to mix; 20 minutes to shape
Yield: 6 dozen oval-shaped rolls

4 cups warm water
2 packages yeast
½ cup (or 1 stick) soft butter or margarine
2 tablespoons caraway seed
2 tablespoons salt
6 cups unsifted flour
6 cups rye flour
2 egg whites
2 tablespoons salt

Soften yeast in warm water. Let stand for 5 minutes. Mix next 5 ingredients into yeast-water mixture. Knead bread until smooth and elastic. Put dough in a well-oiled bowl, cover, and let rise until double in bulk. Punch down and let rise again. Roll dough into approximately 36 oval-shaped rolls (for single recipe). Place them on greased cookie sheets. With scissors cut a lengthwise slit in the top of each roll. Let rise about 1 hour. Mix egg white and salt well. Brush over rolls and bake in 375° F oven for 25 to 30 minutes or until nicely browned. If you don't want to serve the rolls immediately, bake only 18 minutes, cool, put into plastic freezer bags, and freeze. Just before serving, heat in 375° F oven until browned.

ALVINA'S BASIC SWEET YEAST DOUGH

This recipe comes from an old German family, and has been handed down through the years. It's one of the lightest, most delicious doughs you can imagine, and very easy to make. I really became interested in yeast baking because of my great success the first time I tried this recipe. The goodies that can be made with this dough are almost as varied as your imagination will allow. A single recipe makes quite a large amount; if you're inexperienced at working with yeast dough, try only the single recipe the first time.

SINGLE RECIPE
Mixing Time: 17 minutes
Yield: See specific recipes

½ teaspoon salt
4 eggs plus 2 egg yolks
1½ cups milk or evaporated milk
½ cup sugar
½ cup butter or half butter and half margarine
2 packages dry yeast
7 cups sifted flour (approximately)

DOUBLE RECIPE
Mixing Time: 20 minutes
Yield: See specific recipes

1 teaspoon salt
8 eggs plus 4 egg yolks
3 cups milk or evaporated milk
1 cup sugar
1 cup butter or half butter and half margarine
4 packages dry yeast
14 cups sifted flour (approximately)

Have eggs at room temperature or they will cool the dough too much. If you're going to start baking early in the morning, leave the eggs at room temperature overnight. You won't need to do this with the yolks; remember, always separate your eggs while they're cold.

Heat milk to a warm temperature (105° to 115° F), adding salt, sugar, butter and yeast. Let set 5 minutes. Beat eggs and add. Add flour 1 cup at a time. When the dough starts pulling away from the sides of the bowl, roll into a ball. Put into a large container that has been liberally greased. Cover with waxed paper and let rise until double in volume. Punch down and form into any type of pastry you wish to make. Let rise again; divide dough and make into any one of the following recipes.

PECAN ROLLS

You'll find these the most delectable pecan rolls you've ever tasted.

Yield: 4 dozen large pecan rolls or
5½ dozen smaller pecan rolls

Single recipe of Alvina's Basic Sweet   Butter
     Yeast Dough   Pecans
1 pound brown sugar (approximately)   Honey glaze (see page 112)
1½ cups currants

Divide dough into thirds and roll into a 15 x 15-inch square. Brush dough with melted butter; then sprinkle with brown sugar and currants. Roll up jelly-roll fashion and cut into about ¾-inch slices. Butter muffin tins. Spread a rounded teaspoon of brown sugar in the bottom of each and then spoon ½ tablespoon of honey glaze into each muffin tin. Add chopped or whole pecans (I prefer the pecans coarsely chopped) and lay one slice of rolled dough, cut side down, in each muffin tin.

Let rise in a warm place for about 30 minutes or until light (not double in volume since they'll rise considerably in the oven). Brush with melted butter and bake in a preheated oven at 375° F for 15 to 20 minutes. Remove from oven and invert immediately on a cookie sheet or serving tray. With rubber spatula scoop up any syrup that may run down and spread it on the rolls. These rolls are best served warm.

TO SERVE WHEN FROZEN. See page 112.

PETITE PECAN ROLLS

Yield: About 5½ dozen petite pecan rolls

When serving the family, I always make the regular or large pecan rolls. However, the smaller ones are best for entertaining. Use the 2-inch muffin tins instead of the 3-inch ones. Divide the dough into 4 equal parts and roll into a rectangle about 12 x 18-inches. Brush dough with melted butter; then sprinkle with brown sugar and currants and roll into an 18-inch roll. Cut dough into ½-inch slices and place it in the prepared muffin tins, cut side down, using about 1 teaspoon honey glaze. Let rise until light and brush with melted butter. Bake at 375° F for 10 to 12 minutes or until nicely browned. Remove from oven and invert immediately on plates or trays.

PECAN ROLL CLUSTER CAKES OR LOAVES

Follow directions for regular Pecan Rolls. Butter 8- or 9-inch cake pans or bread pans, sprinkle with brown sugar, add honey glaze and nuts. Place cut dough in pans, cut side down, so that dough rolls are loosely touching. Let rise until light and bake in preheated oven at 375° F for about 20 minutes or until done. Remove from oven and invert immediately on plates or trays.

TO FREEZE. Let rolls or cluster cakes cool completely. Then place in freezer on trays or plates. When frozen, freezer-wrap, label, date, and return to freezer.

TO SERVE WHEN FROZEN. Put frozen rolls or cakes on cookie sheet, and warm in a preheated oven at 375° F for 5 to 10 minutes or until warm throughout. Cluster cakes or loaves will take about 15 minutes to heat.

 ## HONEY GLAZE

SINGLE RECIPE
⅓ cup honey
2 teaspoons water

½ cup brown sugar
¼ pound butter

DOUBLE RECIPE
⅔ cup honey
1 tablespoon plus 1 teaspoon water
1 cup brown sugar
½ pound butter

TRIPLE RECIPE
1 cup honey
2 tablespoons water
1½ cups brown sugar
¾ pound butter

 Combine honey, water, and brown sugar in pan; bring to boil and add butter. Cook on low heat until butter is just melted; stir as you use it. Do not continue cooking, but don't allow glaze to get cool. Triple recipe of Honey Glaze is just about the right amount for a single recipe of Basic Sweet Yeast Dough made into pecan rolls.

 ## CLUSTER COFFEE CAKE

Make this in a 10-inch tube pan or in two loaf pans, whichever you prefer.

*Yield: One 10-inch tube cake or 2
loaf-sized cakes*

½ of single recipe of Alvina's Basic
Sweet Yeast Dough
Grated rind from 2 oranges
¾ cup sugar

1 teaspoon cinnamon
¾ cup chopped pecans
About ¼ cup melted butter

Take one half of the prepared Basic Sweet Yeast Dough and then divide it again in half. Form each half into a long roll, using the palms of your hands, and cut into 24 uniform pieces. This will make a total of 48 pieces for a single 10-inch tube cake. Combine sugar, cinnamon, and orange rind in a shallow dish. Form the small pieces of dough into balls, dipping them into the melted butter, then into the chopped nuts, and then roll them in the sugar mixture. Place the coated balls in a greased tube or loaf pan, continuing until all the balls have been used. Let stand in a warm place about 40 minutes or until almost double in volume. Bake in a preheated oven at 350° F for 45 minutes for the 10-inch tube pan and about 40 minutes for the loaf pans. When done, remove from the oven and turn out on cake rack immediately to cool.

This is only one variation of the Cluster Coffee cake. You may eliminate the orange rind if you wish and add another teaspoon of cinnamon. Raisins or currants may also be added, but these should be worked into the dough while you're adding flour.

HOT CROSS BUNS

These delicious little rolls are traditionally served during Lent and at Easter time; however, they're good all year long.

Yield: About 5 dozen buns

Single recipe of Basic Sweet Yeast
  Dough
2 cups currants

1 teaspoon cinnamon
1 beaten egg white
1 cup confectioners sugar

Follow directions for Alvina's Basic Sweet Yeast Dough. After adding about 3 or 4 cups of sifted flour, add currants and cinnamon. Continue with recipe and let rise in a warm, draft-free place until double in volume. Punch down and turn out on a lightly floured surface. Cover and let stand for 10 minutes.

For uniform buns, roll dough out ⅜ to ½ inch thick. Cut dough with a 2½-inch biscuit cutter. Roll these circles of dough into round balls, using your hands. Place balls about 1 inch apart on a greased baking sheet. Cover and let rise. When rolls are light, brush lightly with beaten egg white; this gives them a shiny top. Bake in a preheated oven at 375° F for about 15 minutes or until lightly browned. (Those buns to be frozen should be just delicately browned.) Cool buns on a rack.

TO FROST. Use remaining egg white and 1 cup of confectioners sugar, sifted. Stir and add a little water, if needed, to make a thick frosting. While buns are still warm, pipe a cross on each with a pastry tube. If you wish, you may frost the entire surface, in which case you'll need a double recipe of frosting. Buns are best served warm.

TO FREEZE. After the buns have been frosted and cooled completely, put into freezer while still on racks or trays. After they're frozen, freezer-wrap, date, label, and return to the freezer.

TO SERVE WHEN FROZEN. Preheat oven to 350° F. Put frozen buns on cookie sheet or baking pans and bake for 5 to 10 minutes, or just until buns are warmed through. Serve immediately.

MINCEMEAT ROLLS

Yield: About 32 rolls

Divide dough from single recipe of Basic Sweet Yeast Dough in half. On lightly floured cloth or board, roll dough into a rectangle that measures approximately 8 x 16 inches. Brush with melted butter and spread half the contents of a 1 pound, 2 ounce jar of prepared mincemeat over the entire surface of buttered dough. (Sprinkle with ½ cup of currants if desired.) Roll up dough as you do for pecan rolls. You'll now have a 16-inch roll; cut into 1-inch slices. Place slices, cut side up, in buttered muffin pans. Allow to rise until almost double in volume. Bake in a preheated 350° F oven for approximately 18 to 20 minutes, or until done. Remove from muffin pans and cool on cake racks. Glaze with confectioners icing.

MINCEMEAT LOAF

Follow the instructions for Mincemeat Rolls, only don't slice the dough. Simply lift the roll gently onto a well-greased cookie sheet or large flat baking pan, making sure to seal all edges of the loaf. Bake at 350° F for about 30 minutes, or until done. Ice. To serve, simply slice with a sharp knife.

FRUITED SWEET ROLLS

Take one half of the prepared Basic Sweet Yeast Dough and roll out on a lightly floured cloth or board to about ¼ inch thick. Using a 2½-inch doughnut cutter, cut approximately 18 circles with a hole in the center and another 18 circles without the hole in the center. Place on a greased cookie sheet all the circles without a hole. With pastry brush, lightly brush with milk or cream; now top each with a doughnut-like piece. Set in a warm draft-free place to rise until almost double in volume. Fill holes with a rounded teaspoon of the fruit preserves or pastry filling of your choice (apricot, cherry, pineapple, peach, strawberry, raspberry, et cetera). Bake at 350° F for 18 to 20 minutes, or until done and lightly browned. While warm, frost with confectioners icing.

CHERRY COFFEE CAKES

Half a single recipe of the Basic Sweet Yeast Dough will make three Cherry Coffee cakes.

Yield: Three 9-inch coffee cakes

½ single recipe of Alvina's Basic
  Sweet Yeast Dough
½ cup sugar
2 tablespoons cornstarch or Clearjel
  (see page 70)

1-pound can tart cherries
½ cup flour
½ cup sugar
¼ cup butter

Divide half of a single recipe into three equal parts and press each into a 9-inch cake pan. Set in a warm place to rise until doubled in bulk. Drain cherries. Mix sugar and cornstarch or Clearjel with juice from cherries. Cook and stir until sauce is thickened and smooth. Add cherries and cook a little longer. Cool. With a pastry blender, mix flour, sugar, and butter that has been cut into small pieces until it resembles coarse meal. Spread cooled cherry filling on dough after it has risen. Sprinkle crumb mixture on top of cherry filling and bake at 350° F for about 35 minutes, or until done.

PLAIN STREUSEL-TOPPED COFFEE CAKES

Follow above directions and put dough into three 9-inch cake pans. Sprinkle with Streusel Topping and bake in a preheated oven at 350° F for 35 minutes, or until done.

STREUSEL TOPPING

*Yield: Topping for three 9-inch
  coffee cakes*

3 tablespoons cold butter
¼ cup flour
¼ cup chopped nuts

¼ cup sugar
½ teaspoon cinnamon

Combine sugar and cinnamon; add nuts and flour. Cut in cold butter with a pastry blender. Keep in refrigerator until just before baking. Sprinkle on top of coffee cakes just before putting into oven.

ALMOND-FILLED COFFEE CAKES

Yield: 4 coffee cakes

½ single recipe of Basic Sweet Yeast
Dough
½ cup (¼ pound) almond paste (see
page 39)
½ cup granulated sugar (or brown
sugar, packed)

1 slightly beaten egg
¾ cup cookie crumbs
2 tablespoons butter
½ cup finely chopped pecans
(optional)
About ¼ cup rich milk or cream

Cut almond paste in fine pieces and combine with sugar. Slowly add beaten egg. Beat with electric beater or blender until very smooth. Add cookie crumbs, melted butter, nuts, and enough milk or cream to make a mixture of a nice spreading consistency. This will give you enough filling for four coffee cakes.

Preheat oven to 350° F. Roll out half of the dough on a lightly floured cloth or board, making a rectangle about 12 x 18 inches. Cut down center of dough, making two pieces, each measuring about 6 x 18 inches. Pinch up the sides of dough, forming a little edge. Spread ¼ of the almond paste filling on each piece of dough. Carefully move filled pastry to a large greased cookie or baking sheet. Repeat with other half. Place filled dough in a warm place and let rise until light and fluffy—about 30 to 40 minutes. Bake at 350° F for about 30 minutes, or until done.

This almond filling is also delicious in Tartlets (see page 244).

SWEDISH TEA RING

Yield: 1 Swedish Tea Ring

½ single recipe of Basic Sweet Yeast
Dough
Melted butter

1 cup brown sugar
1 cup chopped nuts
1 cup raisins or currants

Using half of the dough from a single recipe of Basic Sweet Yeast Dough, punch down after the first rising. Place on floured surface and let stand for 10 minutes. Roll dough out into a rectangle about 15 x 22 inches. Brush liberally with melted butter; then sprinkle evenly with brown sugar, nuts, and raisins. Roll up jelly-roll fashion, making a

22-inch roll. Gently lift onto a well-greased cookie sheet or tray and shape roll into a circle, inserting one end into the other. With a sharp knife or scissors, cut ring halfway through at 1½-inch intervals, turning each section out to show filling. Let rise until light and then brush with melted butter. Bake in a preheated oven at 375° F for about 20 to 25 minutes, or until done. Remove from pan immediately. Glaze with icing given on page 120.

TO FREEZE. Cool completely; then freezer-wrap, date, label, and freeze. Tea Rings may be cut in half before freezing, if you wish.

TO SERVE WHEN FROZEN. Preheat oven to 350° F. Put Swedish Tea Ring on a cookie sheet or baking pan, and bake for about 10 to 15 minutes, or until it is warmed through.

VARIATIONS. Other fillings can be used; for instance, try mixed candied fruit.

DOUGHNUTS, BISMARCKS, AND CRULLERS

BASIC DOUGH

Nothing beats homemade doughnuts and bismarcks filled, not with only a drop of jam, but really filled-to-the-bursting with preserves or custard. Now, with a freezer, you can bake to your heart's content and enjoy all these goodies for weeks to come.

SINGLE RECIPE	DOUBLE RECIPE
Time: 10 minutes to mix	*Time: 15 minutes to mix*
15 minutes to roll out and cut	*30 minutes to roll out and cut*
Yield: 24 doughnuts	*Yield: 48 doughnuts*
1 cup milk	2 cups milk
½ cup butter or margarine	1 cup butter or margarine
½ cup sugar	1 cup sugar
1 teaspoon salt	2 teaspoons salt
2 eggs plus 1 egg yolk, well beaten	4 eggs plus 2 egg yolks, well beaten
2 packages dry yeast	4 packages dry yeast
About 4 cups sifted all-purpose flour	About 8 cups sifted all-purpose flour

Combine milk, butter, sugar, and salt. Heat milk mixture to a warm temperature (105° to 115° F).

Add eggs and yeast and let stand for about 5 minutes. Add sifted flour a little at a time to form a soft dough. When dough is fairly thick and smooth, turn out on heavily floured pastry cloth. (Dough will be quite soft.) Knead gently by flipping cloth up first on one side and then the other for about 10 times. Flour your hands and gently knead dough for about 2 minutes. Add flour, if needed. Put dough in a greased bowl and let rise until double in volume. Punch down dough and divide in half.

DEEP-FAT FRYING. While the shaped doughnuts, bismarcks, et cetera, are rising, heat vegetable oil to 375° F in an electric skillet or deep fryer. You may also use an ordinary heavy kettle with a candy thermometer clipped to the side. Allow oil to heat slowly. If you are using a skillet or shallow pan, make sure that it's amply deep to hold 1½ to 2 inches of oil and still have enough head room so that the oil won't bubble over.

Anyone attempting to make a triple batch should have an electric skillet or some other utensil with a very large capacity for frying; the smaller deep fryers will accommodate only 2 or 3 doughnuts at a time, which is insufficient. Your doughnuts will be overraised by the time you get around to deep-frying the last of them.

Don't use butter or margarine, drippings, lard, or any other shortening that will smoke at low temperatures. A good-grade vegetable oil is really best for deep frying. This oil may be reused repeatedly. After you have completed frying, cut a potato and fry it in the oil to remove any unpleasant flavors that may have developed. After the potato is browned, remove and let oil cool slightly. Pour oil into storage container through a very fine tea strainer. Do not attempt to drain the silt in the bottom; just throw it away. Always add some new oil the next time you deep-fry. It is better not to keep for reuse oil that has been heated beyond the smoking point.

DOUGHNUTS

Roll out Basic Dough about ½ inch thick and cut with a doughnut cutter. You may want to fry the doughnut "holes," or you can press all the scraps into a ball and roll out again. Dip cutter into flour occasionally to keep it from sticking. Cut or tear waxed paper into 3-inch squares and place on cookie sheets or trays. Place 1 doughnut on each square. Set in warm place to rise, about ½ hour or until light. Pick up doughnuts and waxed paper from tray with a spatula. Hold waxed paper with thumb and flip doughnut into hot oil and fry until golden brown on both sides, turning only *once*. With a slotted spoon or wire basket, lift doughnuts from oil, holding over pan for a few seconds to drip, and then place them on paper towels to drain. Cool on cake racks. Uncooked doughnuts should be handled gently, or they will fall; that is why it's advisable to put them on squares of waxed paper. Glaze with confectioners icing (see page 120), Chocolate glaze (see page 159), or roll in granulated sugar while still warm.

BISMARCKS

Roll dough to about ¼ to ⅜ inch thick. Cut out with a 2½- or 3-inch biscuit cutter. Line cookie sheets or trays with 3-inch squares of waxed paper. Lift bismarcks onto these little squares; press remaining dough into ball, reroll, and cut. Place dough in a warm draft-free place (you may cover with a towel if you wish) and let rise until double in volume. Prepare oil for frying. Follow instructions as given above. Handle uncooked bismarcks very lightly so that they won't fall while you are putting them into the deep fat. Gently pick up bismarcks and waxed paper from tray with spatula. Hold waxed paper with your thumb and flip bismarck into hot oil. Fry until golden brown on both sides, turning only *once*. With a slotted spoon or wire basket, lift bismarcks from oil, holding them over pan for a few seconds to drip and then place them on absorbent paper to drain. Roll in granulated sugar and cool on cake racks. Using a plain pastry tube or a special bismarck filling attachment, fill with jelly, preserves, or custard. (Some cookie presses also have a tube attachment that can be used for filling bismarcks.) French Cream Filling on page 237 is very good and freezes well too. My other favorite is the prepared Bohemian raspberry pastry filling.

TWISTS OR CRULLERS

Roll half of a single recipe into a rectangle 8 x 12 inches. With a sharp knife, cut into twelve 1-inch strips. Fold each strip in half, pinching ends together. Twist twice and place twist on little squares of waxed paper about 3 x 4 inches. Place dough in a warm place, free from drafts, and let rise until double in volume. Prepare oil for frying and follow directions as given above. Handle uncooked twists or crullers very carefully so they won't fall while you are putting them into the deep fat. Gently pick up twists and waxed paper from tray with spatula. Hold waxed paper with your thumb and flip twists into hot oil. Fry until golden brown on both sides, turning twists only *once*. With a slotted spoon or wire basket, lift twists from oil, hold them over pan for a few seconds to drip, and then place them on absorbent paper to drain. Roll in granulated sugar and cool on cake racks. Or you may wish to glaze them after they have cooled. (For glaze, see page 120.)

CINNAMON SWIRLS

Yield: 24 swirls for single recipe

Roll half a single recipe of Basic Dough into a rectangle about 10 x 12 inches. Combine ½ cup instant sugar with 1 teaspoon cinnamon. Sprinkle half of this mixture over rolled dough. Roll rectangle up to form a 12-inch roll. With a sharp knife, cut into twelve 1-inch pieces. Lay these pieces, cut side up, on 3-inch squares of torn or cut waxed paper. Press down to flatten and seal the edges firmly so they won't come apart when frying. Set in a warm, draft-free place and let rise until double in volume. Prepare oil for frying; follow instructions as given above. Handle uncooked cinnamon swirls very gently so they won't fall while putting them into the deep fat. Gently lift cinnamon swirls and waxed paper from tray with spatula. Hold waxed paper with your thumb and flip cinnamon swirls into hot oil. Fry until golden brown on both sides, turning swirls only *once*. With a slotted spoon or wire basket, lift swirls from oil, holding over pan for a few seconds to drip. Place on absorbent paper to drain. Cool on cake racks. When cool enough to handle, dip into confectioners sugar glaze that has been mixed with 1 teaspoon of cinnamon.

CONFECTIONERS SUGAR GLAZE

1 cup confectioners sugar   3 tablespoons water

Measure sugar and then sift into a small mixing bowl. Add water. With a wire whisk, stir until blended. Dip swirls into this mixture and then allow glazed swirls to dry.

VARIATION. Add 1 teaspoon cinnamon or grated lemon peel (1 lemon) and substitute 1 tablespoon lemon juice for water.

SPECIALTY BREADS

CHEESE WAFERS

These little cheese wafers are delicious served with either soup or salad; also good for munching with appetizers. They're wonderful to have on hand.

SINGLE RECIPE
> *Preparation Time: 12 minutes*
> *Yield: Approximately 80 wafers*

DOUBLE RECIPE
> *Preparation Time: 21 minutes*
> *Yield: Approximately 160 wafers*
> *(this may seem a great many,*
> *but they go fast)*

½ pound grated or shredded sharp cheddar cheese
2½ cups flour
¼ teaspoon salt
¼ teaspoon cayenne pepper
½ pound butter (2 sticks)

1 pound grated or shredded sharp cheddar cheese
5 cups flour
½ teaspoon salt
½ teaspoon cayenne pepper
1 pound butter

Preheat oven to 375° F. Chill cheese. Mix flour, salt, and cayenne together. Cut cold butter into flour mixture, using a pastry blender until mixture is crumbly. Add cheese and work in until it's evenly distributed. Divide dough in half for a single recipe—into quarters for a double recipe—putting half the dough into the refrigerator. Meanwhile, roll out the remaining dough on a lightly floured cloth. Shape into a rectangle about 20 inches long and 5 inches wide. With a pastry wheel, cut down the center; then cut crosswise at 1-inch intervals. Separate and transfer the wafers to a baking sheet. Bake for about 10 minutes or until lightly golden. Meanwhile, repeat with remaining dough. Cool wafers on paper towels.

TO FREEZE. Simply place the cooled wafers on top of one another in a protected freezer-proof plastic container.

TO SERVE WHEN FROZEN. Let wafers thaw and serve at room temperature, or you may prefer to heat them in the oven at 375° F for 2 or 3 minutes and serve them warm.

BOSTON BROWN BREAD

Imagine ten loaves in 20 minutes! This delicious bread can be made with several variations, all of them mouth-watering. When they are spread with cream cheese, my children consider this a real treat in their lunch boxes. Start saving empty 1-pound vegetable cans (No. 303 size cans) now, so that you'll have them on hand for this recipe. Of course, Boston Brown Bread can also be baked in conventional bread pans, but it is traditionally round.

SINGLE RECIPE
Preparation Time: 15 minutes
Yield: 5 round loaves

1 cup raisins
2 cups boiling water
2 cups firmly packed brown sugar
½ teaspoon salt
2 tablespoons vegetable oil
2 eggs
2 teaspoons baking soda
4 cups flour
½ cup chopped nuts

DOUBLE RECIPE
Preparation Time: 20 minutes
Yield: 10 round loaves

2 cups raisins
4 cups boiling water
4 cups firmly packed brown sugar
1 teaspoon salt
4 tablespoons vegetable oil
4 eggs
4 teaspoons baking soda
8 cups flour
1 cup chopped nuts

Early in the day, pour boiling water over raisins and let cool. When the raisins are plump and the liquid is sufficiently cool, put sugar, salt, shortening, and eggs in mixing bowl and cream well. Add baking soda to raisin mixture; stir and pour this into creamed batter. Mix well and add flour to this soupy mixture. After flour has been completely incorporated, add nuts and stir again. Liberally oil the empty tin cans. Now pour your batter into each, filling about ⅔ to ¾ full. Bake 1 hour at 350° F, or until a toothpick inserted in the center comes out clean. If you're making a double batch, divide the bread tins on two shelves in your oven. Be sure to lower the top shelf, or the bread may rise too much and burn. Cool bread completely. With a sharp, narrow bladed knife, loosen bread around the sides; now gently pull bread out of can. To freeze, wrap the loaves in Saran Wrap or other appropriate moisture-vapor-proof wrapping, date, label, and freeze.

VARIATIONS. For those of you who don't care for raisins or nuts, either of these ingredients may be eliminated. Increase nuts to 1 cup per single recipe if you're going to eliminate the raisins.

DATE NUT BREAD. Substitute 2 cups chopped dates for raisins (approximately 8 ounces), and bake in two 9 x 5 x 3-inch loaf pans for 55 minutes in preheated 350° F oven.

MOLASSES-FLAVORED BROWN BREAD. For each single recipe, decrease water by ¼ cup and substitute ¼ cup of molasses.

ORANGE BROWN BREAD

SINGLE RECIPE
Preparation Time: 15 minutes
Yield: 5 round loaves

1 cup raisins
1¼ cups boiling water

DOUBLE RECIPE
Preparation Time: 20 minutes
Yield: 10 round loaves

2 cups raisins
2½ cups boiling water

One 6-ounce can thawed orange juice concentrate	Two 6-ounce cans thawed orange juice concentrate
2 cups firmly packed brown sugar	4 cups firmly packed brown sugar
½ teaspoon salt	1 teaspoon salt
2 tablespoons vegetable oil	¼ cup vegetable oil
2 eggs	4 eggs
2 teaspoons baking soda	1 tablespoon baking soda
4 cups flour	8 cups flour
½ cup chopped nuts	1 cup chopped nuts

Follow the instructions for Boston Brown Bread; add frozen juice concentrate directly to the creamed sugar and egg mixture.

AUNT HAZEL'S NUT BREAD

This is a very nutty bread. When it's cold, you can slice it wafer-thin and a loaf goes a long way. Baked in small loaf pans, this nut bread makes ideal little gifts.

SINGLE RECIPE	DOUBLE RECIPE
Time: 7 minutes	*Time: 10 minutes*
Yield: 1 loaf	*Yield: 2 loaves*
2 cups flour	4 cups flour
2 teaspoons baking powder	1 tablespoon plus 1 teaspoon baking powder
1 teaspoon salt	2 teaspoons salt
1 egg	2 eggs
¾ cup packed brown sugar	1½ cups packed brown sugar
⅔ cup milk	1⅓ cups milk
1 cup chopped pecans	2 cups chopped pecans

Cream eggs with brown sugar; add milk, baking powder, and salt. Add flour and mix well. Fold in chopped nuts. Pour into a small greased bread pan. Bake at 325° F for 1 hour, or until done. No, I haven't forgotten—there *isn't* any shortening in this bread.

PANCAKES, WAFFLES, AND CREPES

Pancakes freeze surprisingly well and are easy to heat in your toaster. In prefreezer days, pancakes and waffles were strictly for the leisurely breakfasts that are possible only on weekends. Now, however, I make an extra-large batch on the weekend and freeze half of it for a midweek treat. What a pleasure it is to pop them in the toaster, with no further fussing, on a busy weekday morning! The toaster method is especially convenient for families that eat breakfast in shifts. For the larger family, it might be more expedient to put pancakes on a cookie sheet and heat them in the oven.

In most of the following pancake recipes, biscuit mix has been recommended as an ingredient. If you don't have this, try pancake mix—but only as a substitute in case of emergency.

PANCAKES

SINGLE RECIPE
Yield: About 18 medium-sized pancakes

2 cups bicsuit mix   2 cups buttermilk
1 egg

DOUBLE RECIPE   TRIPLE RECIPE
Yield: About 36 medium-sized pancakes   *Yield: About 54 medium-sized pancakes*

4 cups biscuit mix   6 cups biscuit mix
2 eggs   3 eggs
1 quart buttermilk   1½ quarts buttermilk

 Mix all the ingredients together, but don't overmix. The mixture should be a little lumpy. Let it stand for 5 minutes before cooking. Griddle should be good and hot and slightly greased. Don't turn pancakes until bubbles have formed on top.

This basic recipe takes only minutes to prepare and yet it's light and delectable. Using buttermilk rather than regular milk seems to make any pancake mix turn out lighter. Buttermilk is easy to keep on hand. When used for baking, it may be kept in the refrigerator for several weeks without spoiling.

BLUEBERRY PANCAKES. For a single recipe, simply shake 1 cup of frozen or fresh blueberries into batter and mix gently with a wooden spoon (see page 208).

BANANA PANCAKES. Quarter and slice 2 or 3 well-ripened bananas into the batter and mix with a wooden spoon (see page 205).

OTHER VARIATIONS. Nuts and crumbled bacon may also be used, as well as crushed pineapple, et cetera.

If you're going to make pancakes fairly regularly, a griddle is indispensable. Not only is it easier to use, but pancakes taste better and brown more evenly on a temperature-controlled griddle. Because most griddles have a special finish, very little grease is necessary, which thereby eliminates any heavy greasy taste.

TO FREEZE. When making pancakes that are going to be frozen, be sure to make them large enough so they won't get lost in your toaster. Cut or tear freezer paper in squares and put a double thickness between the pancakes. Make several stacks and wrap these either in foil or freezer wrap.

WAFFLES

SINGLE RECIPE
  Yield: Three 9-inch

2 cups biscuit mix	1 egg
2 tablespoons vegetable oil	2 cups buttermilk

DOUBLE RECIPE
  Yield: Six 9-inch

TRIPLE RECIPE
  Yield: Nine 9-inch

4 cups biscuit mix
¼ cup vegetable oil
2 eggs
1 quart buttermilk

6 cups biscuit mix
¼ cup plus 2 tablespoons vegetable oil
3 eggs
1 quart plus 2 cups buttermilk

Mix all the ingredients together, but don't overmix. The mixture should be slightly lumpy. Let it stand for 5 minutes before cooking. Waffle iron should be good and hot before using.

VARIATIONS. Most of the variations that can be used for pancakes are also good for waffles; the one exception is blueberries. The waffle iron tends to squash the berries, making them run into the batter. Chopped pecans are particularly good in waffles.

TO FREEZE. Waffles are best frozen first on a cookie sheet or some other flat container, and then wrapped after they're frozen. If you stack them before freezing, they tend to become flat and the waffle effect is somewhat distorted.

MARIE'S RICE PANCAKES

These are very delicious and can easily be mixed the night before. Their texture is different and a delightful change from traditional pancakes.

SINGLE RECIPE
Yield: About 18, medium sized

1 cup cooked rice	1 cup buttermilk
1 egg	2 tablespoons vegetable oil
1 cup biscuit mix	

DOUBLE RECIPE
Yield: About 36, medium sized

2 cups cooked rice
2 eggs
2 cups biscuit mix
2 cups buttermilk
¼ cup vegetable oil

TRIPLE RECIPE
Yield: About 54, medium sized

3 cups cooked rice
3 eggs
3 cups biscuit mix
3 cups buttermilk
⅓ cup vegetable oil

    Combine all ingredients and let stand at least 10 minutes. If you make the batter the evening before, you may want to add a little more buttermilk to the mixture. Prepare and cook as for Basic Pancakes.

TO FREEZE. Follow the same steps as given for Pancakes.

SOUR CREAM PANCAKES

These sour cream pancakes are quite thin and rather crisp, but light and tender. Especially good with Blueberry Sauce (page 211) or Apple Topping (page 203).

SINGLE RECIPE
Yield: 30 medium-sized pancakes

1⅓ cups milk
1 cup commercial sour cream
2 eggs
2 tablespoons vegetable oil or melted butter
2 cups pancake or biscuit mix

DOUBLE RECIPE
Yield: 60 medium-sized pancakes

2⅔ cups milk
2 cups commercial sour cream (1 pint)
4 eggs
4 tablespoons vegetable oil or melted butter
4 cups pancake or biscuit mix

Combine milk, sour cream, eggs, and shortening in a bowl and mix thoroughly. Add pancake mix and mix lightly, making sure not to overmix. Pour onto hot, lightly greased griddle and turn when underside is nicely browned.

MARION'S MAPLE SYRUP

This recipe comes from a mother of five who says her family uses syrup as though it came out of a tap—which prompted her to find a good and easy homemade recipe. Not only is it delicious and easy to make, but it costs only a fraction of the price of the commercially prepared variety.

SINGLE RECIPE
Yield: 2½ cups

2 cups sugar	½ cup light corn syrup
½ cup water	½ teaspoon maple flavoring
1½ cups boiling water	¼ teaspoon vanilla

DOUBLE RECIPE
Yield: 5 cups

TRIPLE RECIPE
Yield: 7½ cups

4 cups sugar	6 cups sugar
1 cup water	1½ cups water
3 cups boiling water	4½ cups boiling water
1 cup light corn syrup	1½ cups light corn syrup
1 teaspoon maple flavoring	1½ teaspoons maple flavoring
½ teaspoon vanilla	¾ teaspoon vanilla

Combine sugar and ½ cup of water (for a single recipe); mix well. Cook without stirring until light caramel color (338° F). Very gradually stir in boiling water and corn syrup. Boil 2 to 3 minutes, stirring constantly. Add flavorings.

I always make the large recipe and freeze 1 quart or more of the syrup. The rest I keep stored in the refrigerator. The syrup won't freeze solidly, so you can pour it out of the container at any time, warm it, and serve it.

VARIATION. For a nutty flavor, add ½ teaspoon black walnut flavoring to the single recipe. For a real buttery syrup, add 2 to 4 tablespoons butter (for a single recipe) when adding flavors. Stir until melted. With butter added, syrup is best served with a ladle as butter tends to float on top.

BASIC CREPES

Not only are crepes fun to make and serve, they can be made in advance. Almost any low-sided pan with a 6 to 8-inch-diameter cooking surface should produce good crepes. Stores and catalogues are filled with a variety of pans, both electric and surface cooking units. Most of them work very well; pick one that you think will suit your needs and cook up a storm.

The two recipes are nice to have on hand in your freezer, as they can be used for almost any type filling (the basic crepe for all entrée or vegetable fillings, and the dessert crepe for all types of sweet or dessert fillings). If you want to get into the intricacies of crepe cooking, whole books have been written about it.

*Yield: 12 to 14 crepes, 6 to 6½
 inches*

1 cup all-purpose flour
¼ teaspoon salt
3 eggs

1½ cups milk
1 tablespoon melted butter or oil

Combine ingredients and beat until smooth or twirl for a few seconds in your electric blender. Let batter stand for an hour. (This is to eliminate air bubbles). Dip upside-down crepe pan into batter. (When using upside-down crepe pan, it is best to pour batter into an 8 or 9-inch pie pan.) Or pour batter onto hot greased griddle or brush a 6 to 7-inch omelet pan with butter and pour in just enough batter to coat the bottom (about 1½ tablespoons). Cook on both sides until brown. Make ahead and reheat with filling if you wish.

MAKING CREPES AHEAD. Once you are all set up for making crepes, you may decide to make enough for several meals at one time. When covered properly, crepes may be stored in the refrigerator for 2 or 3 days satisfactorily. Make sure that they are properly wrapped (a plastic bag is fine for this), so that they do not dry out. Crepes may be stored in the freezer up to 4 months if properly wrapped. Pack your cooled crepes with a double thickness of waxed paper between each one. Wrap securely in foil and then in a freezer bag. You may wish to tape another covering of paper plates around the crepes to protect the edges from breaking, as they are very fragile when frozen. Let crepes thaw at room temperature before separating them.

FREEZING FILLED CREPES. Although it is possible to do this, often the crepes become soggy and the entire taste experience isn't as good as if they were made fresh. I find it best to make the crepes separately and freeze them ahead of time, and also the filling, if it is a meat or vegetable type of filling. Dessert crepes are usually best when assembled just before serving, unless they have a frozen filling.

Fill crepes and arrange on cookie sheet and freeze. When completely frozen, carefully wrap for freezer storage in moisture-vapor-proof material.

SUGGESTED FILLINGS FOR BASIC CREPES. Beef Stroganoff (page 288); Shrimp Supreme (page 186); Chicken à la Briar (page 348); Chicken à la King (page 352); Chicken Cacciatore (page 354) filling with Cacciatore Sauce (page 354) topping; Asparagus and Ham filling with cheese sauce (page 372) topping; Vegetable Medley (page 397), topped with grated cheese; Chicken Croquettes (page 349), (using only half the bread crumbs), and topped with Mushroom Sauce (page 385).

DESSERT CREPES

Follow instructions for basic crepes, adding 1 tablespoon of sugar to batter. Here are suggestions for filling dessert crepes: Lemon Tart Filling (page 244); Chocolate Cream Filling (page 242); Choco-scotch Filling (page 241).

Velvet Cream Cheese Filling (page 238) is great when topped with fresh fruit, such as strawberries, peaches, or raspberries, as is the French Cream Filling (page 323).

Fill crepes with fresh fruit and top with Sunshine Sauce (page 230) or fill with coffee ice cream and top with Dino's Cup (page 228).

For frozen crepes, fill with frozen grasshopper or frozen eggnog filling (page 238). Freeze and serve frozen, topped with whipped cream or chocolate sauce.

Cherry Cream Freeze is another good possibility, topped with cherry liqueur.

Dream Puff Filling (page 238) topped with Kahlua sauce is another excellent choice for dessert crepe filling.

DELUXE FRENCH TOAST

This elegant dish can be enjoyed all year round, thanks to frozen strawberries. It may be served for breakfast, brunch, lunch, or late-night snacks. Be sure to make enough, because second and third helpings are the rule rather than the exception.

SINGLE RECIPE *Yield: About 10 slices*	DOUBLE RECIPE *Yield: About 20 slices*
1 cup evaporated milk	2 cups evaporated milk
3 tablespoons water	6 tablespoons water
1 egg	2 eggs
1 teaspoon vanilla	2 teaspoons vanilla
1 tablespoon sugar	2 tablespoons sugar
½ teaspoon salt	1 teaspoon salt
¼ teaspoon cinnamon	½ teaspoon cinnamon
10 slices day-old bread	20 slices day-old bread
Corn flake crumbs	Corn flake crumbs
Butter	Butter
One 10-ounce package thawed frozen strawberries	Two 10-ounce packages thawed frozen strawberries
1 cup commercial sour cream	1 pint commercial sour cream
½ teaspoon cinnamon	1 teaspoon cinnamon
Dash nutmeg	¼ teaspoon nutmeg

Mix milk, water, egg, vanilla, sugar, and spices in a shallow bowl. Mix well with wire whisk or fork. Dip bread into this mixture and then in corn flake crumbs. Grease griddle lightly with butter and brown toast on both sides. Combine sour cream, cinnamon, and nutmeg. Fold this mixture into thawed strawberries. Spoon strawberry mixture over hot toast and serve immediately.

When serving a large group, I find it easier to make French toast in the oven. The results are not the same, but it's quicker and more convenient. Butter a large Teflon cookie sheet and put the bread, which has been dipped in egg mixture and crumbs, on the cookie sheet. Preheat oven. Turn on the broiler and put cooky sheet under broiler. Watch closely and remove when the toast is golden brown. The toast will usually not need to be turned, since the bottom side bakes itself. However, if the bottom is not sufficiently browned, turn bread and put under broiler briefly. It's amazing how quickly you can make a huge batch of French toast by using this method, and it certainly beats standing over a hot stove for what seems an eternity.

MUFFINS AND CORNBREADS

BLUEBERRY MUFFINS OR COFFEE CAKE

Baking blueberry muffins is usually relegated to Saturday mornings at our house and, while I'm at it, I like to make an extra-large quantity so that I won't have to bother with it again for some time.

SINGLE RECIPE
Preparation Time: 12 minutes
Yield: 14 large muffins or one
8 x 8-inch cake

1⅓ cups biscuit mix
½ cup sugar
3 tablespoons liquid shortening
1 egg
1 teaspoon vanilla
¾ cup buttermilk or sour milk
½ to ⅔ cup frozen or fresh
  blueberries

DOUBLE RECIPE
Preparation Time: 16 minutes
Yield: 28 large muffins

2⅔ cups biscuit mix
1 cup sugar
¼ cup plus 2 tablespoons liquid
  shortening
2 eggs
2 teaspoons vanilla
1½ cups buttermilk or sour milk
1 to 1⅓ cups frozen or fresh
  blueberries

TRIPLE RECIPE
Preparation Time: 20 minutes
Yield: 28 large plus 40 miniature
  muffins

4 cups biscuit mix
1½ cups sugar

QUINTUPLE RECIPE
Preparation Time: 24 minutes
Yield: 28 large plus 40 miniatures
  plus one 9 x 13-inch cake

6⅔ cups biscuit mix
2½ cups sugar

½ cup plus 1 tablespoon liquid
  shortening
3 eggs
3 teaspoons vanilla
2¼ cups buttermilk or sour milk
1½ to 2 cups frozen or fresh
  blueberries

1 cup less 1 tablespoon liquid
  shortening
5 eggs
1 tablespoon plus 1 teaspoon vanilla
3¾ cups buttermilk or sour milk
2½ to 3 cups frozen or fresh
  blueberries

Preheat oven to 350° F. Add all the ingredients except the blueberries and beat lightly. Batter should be just a trifle lumpy. Add blueberries and stir gently with a wooden spoon until they're equally distributed in the batter. Put paper liners in muffin cups or grease baking dish, if you want to bake it as a cake. For muffins, use a large 2- or 4-cup pitcher to pour batter into muffin tins. Bake muffins about 20 minutes and blueberry cake about 30 to 35 minutes. Don't overcrowd your oven; for the larger recipes you'll have to bake in shifts. It doesn't hurt the batter to stand for a short time before it is baked.

TO FREEZE. Set muffins on cookie sheet and freeze. When firm, you can toss them into a moisture-vapor-proof bag. Cakes can be frozen in the pan. Simply cool, wrap, label, and freeze.

TO SERVE WHEN FROZEN. Muffins and cakes may be thawed and served cold or you may prefer to put frozen muffins in the oven at 350° F for about 10 minutes until heated through. Serve with butter if you wish.

CORNBREAD

There's nothing quite so appealing as hot cornbread and honey for breakfast on a cold wintry morning. A double recipe takes less than 10 minutes to prepare; so make a large batch and freeze the rest.

SINGLE RECIPE
  Preparation Time: 6 minutes
  Yield: One 9 x 13-inch pan

DOUBLE RECIPE
  Preparation Time: 9 minutes
  Yield: Two 9 x 13-inch pans or
    equivalent

¾ cup yellow cornmeal
1 cup unsifted flour
¼ cup liquid shortening
1 cup buttermilk
2 large eggs
¼ cup sugar
1 tablespoon double-acting baking
  powder
1 teaspoon salt

1½ cups yellow cornmeal
2 cups unsifted flour
½ cup liquid shortening
2 cups buttermilk
4 large eggs
½ cup sugar
2 tablespoons double-acting baking
  powder
2 teaspoons salt

If you're planning to make cornbread for breakfast, you can measure cornmeal, flour, sugar, baking powder, and salt in your mixing bowl the night before. In the morning turn your oven on to 475° F; it'll take about 10 minutes to preheat to this high temperature. Now add eggs, shortening, and buttermilk all at once to the premeasured dry ingredients, and stir until they're well blended; don't overmix. Pour batter into a greased 9 x 13-inch pan and bake for about 15 minutes or until golden brown on top. We like our cornbread rather crispy, and that's why I use this large-sized pan. For a more fluffy, thicker cornbread, use a 9 x 9-inch pan.

TO FREEZE. Remove cornbread from oven as soon as it's done, before it's browned. Otherwise it will be dried out when you reheat it. Cool, wrap, label, date, and put into freezer.

TO SERVE WHEN FROZEN. Preheat oven to 400° F. Warm cornbread in hot oven for 10 minutes or until it's heated through and slightly brown.

CORNBREAD WITH BACON

Follow the preceding recipe, substituting bacon drippings for some of the shortening and adding 2 slices of crisp cooked bacon, crumbled (for single recipe). This is when some of that crumbled bacon in your freezer comes in handy (see page 41).

CORNMEAL MUFFINS

Follow either of the preceding recipes. Fill well-greased muffin pans ⅔ full and bake at 475° F for 10 to 12 minutes, or until slightly browned on top.

APPLE PANLETS

A combination omelet and pancake, panlets are good served for breakfast, brunch, or lunch, and also for late-evening snacks. Although easy to prepare, they must be served directly from the oven, preferably on warmed plates. They may be served year-round. When apples are out of season, use sliced apples from your freezer. Because this dish is such a family favorite, freezing enough in the fall to last the remaining year is a must.

SINGLE RECIPE
> *Preparation Time: 5 minutes*
> *(with blender)*
> *Yield: 2 servings*

2 tablespoons butter
2 eggs
½ teaspoon salt
2 tablespoons sugar
½ cup sifted flour
⅔ cup milk
1 apple, cored and quartered

½ teaspoon grated lemon peel (fresh or prepared)
1 tablespoon lemon juice
Topping:
¼ to ½ cup commercial sour cream
Powdered sugar

DOUBLE RECIPE
> *Preparation Time 6 minutes*
> *(with blender)*
> *Yield: 4 servings*

4 tablespoons butter
4 eggs
1 teaspoon salt
¼ cup sugar
1 cup sifted flour
1⅓ cups milk
2 apples, cored and quartered
1 teaspoon grated lemon peel (fresh or prepared)
2 tablespoons lemon juice
Topping:
½ to 1 cup commercial sour cream
Powdered sugar

TRIPLE RECIPE
> *Preparation Time: 7 minutes*
> *(with blender)*
> *Yield: 6 servings*

6 tablespoons butter
6 eggs
1½ teaspoons salt
6 tablespoons sugar (¼ cup + 2 tablespoons)
1½ cups sifted flour
2 cups milk
3 apples, cored and quartered
1½ teaspoons grated lemon peel (fresh or prepared)
3 tablespoons lemon juice
Topping:
1 to 1½ cups commercial sour cream
Powdered sugar

Preheat oven to 450° F. For single recipe, place 1 tablespoon of butter in each of two 9-inch glass pie plates (or Teflon-coated ovenproof pans) and place in 450° F oven for a few minutes while the butter melts. Be sure the butter doesn't burn. Now place all the ingredients, including the quartered apple, into the blender and turn on several times for just a second. (Apples should remain somewhat coarse.) If a blender or food processor is not available, use a grater or shredder, or chop the apples with a sharp knife. Mix all ingredients until batter is blended. If you don't have a blender, add ½ cup coarsely chopped or shredded unpeeled apple, or an equal quantity of cored and peeled apples from the freezer (see page 201). Actually, for a more fruity flavor you can double the amount of apples. When apples are frozen, they can be chopped very easily. Divide batter, pouring half into each pie plate containing the melted butter. If necessary tilt pan to spread batter over bottom and sides of pan. Return to oven and bake 12 minutes at 450° F, or until panlet is puffy and delicately browned. Remove from oven. Panlet may be served in baking dish or transferred onto serving plate. Spread with sour cream and dust with powdered sugar.

TO SERVE. When making a double recipe, you may use two pie plates and one 9 x 13-inch glass baking dish. The large panlet may be cut into squares and served. When making the triple recipe or more, I use two 9 x 13-inch pans. When cooked, cut panlets into serving-sized pieces and transfer to a heated platter. Now butter pan again and put remaining panlet batter into dish and bake. By the time everyone has finished eating the first batch, the second will be ready.

Cakes and Frostings

****

BAKING AND FREEZING CAKES

First, I want to assure you that there's nothing mysterious about baking cakes successfully. Anyone who claims that there is undoubtedly wants either to impress you with her unique abilities or else wants an excuse for not baking.

I'm sure that many home economists will disagree with me, but the one big timesaver I use in baking is *not to sift flour with salt, baking soda, or baking powder*. After you've creamed the sugar and shortening and added the eggs, milk, or whatever, simply sprinkle your salt and soda or baking powder (or both) on top of the batter, and mix well. Then add the flour and remaining dry ingredients. This method works very well and it saves the many precious minutes needed for sifting all the dry ingredients together.

For those of you who haven't used anything but "box cakes" in recent years, I strongly urge you to try some of these simple recipes. You'll find that they really don't take any longer; they're cheaper and a real taste treat. I recommend the Easy Chocolate Cake as a starter.

NOTE. I do not suggest baking the cakes in this section in your microwave oven. Use recipes especially formulated for microwave baking.

The Small Household

In preparing this book, I have been concerned with the needs of the person who is cooking for one or two people, as well as those cooking for large families. When baking any of the following recipes for a small household, the trick is to bake a lot of little cakes and freeze them individually. This will mean that you won't have to eat the same kind of cake for dessert all week long. Many times I've heard someone say, "I just can't bake any more because I'm all alone now." This simply isn't true; get out your favorite recipes and start baking! Then, if guests arrive, you'll be able to serve an impressive assortment of small cakes.

There are many different sizes of small loaf and cake pans on the market today; buy a number of them in sizes to suit your personal needs. Because space is limited, it's impossible to give the baking time for each and every size cake. As a general rule, smaller cakes take less time to bake; so watch them carefully (they tend to dry out when overbaked). For future reference, make a note of the pan size you used and the baking time required. Also record the yield, that is to say, how many cakes the recipe made in whatever pan size you used. You'll find such notations very helpful the next time you use the recipe.

Larger cakes can be baked and cut into individual serving portions, each wrapped and frozen individually; however, this is usually more time-consuming than baking in smaller pans. For pan-type cakes, bake, frost, and freeze them right in their pans. The small aluminum pans used for commercially baked and prepared frozen foods are marvelous for small cakes. These pans can be used over and over again; so once you've collected a good assortment, they'll last you for some time.

Figuring Yield

It's impractical to list all the various cake sizes possible from multiple-quantity recipes. Simply multiply the yield of a single recipe by the quantity of the recipe that you intend to make. This will give you some idea about how many cakes you will bake. Here are some rules to follow:

One angel food cake pan will approximately equal two standard loaf pans (9 x 4 x 3 inches).

You can substitute a 9 x 9-inch pan for an 8 x 8-inch pan, the latter resulting in a slightly higher cake; the converse is also true.

The batter for three 9 x 9-inch or 8 x 8-inch cakes will yield two 13 x 9-inch cakes.

Most frosted pan-type cake recipes can be made as cupcakes. The exceptions are upside-down cakes and self-frosted or fruit-topped cakes.

A single recipe that calls for a 9 x 9-inch or 8 x 8-inch pan will generally yield a dozen cupcakes. A single recipe that calls for a 13 x 9-

inch pan will usually yield a dozen and a half cupcakes. There may be some variation from recipe to recipe, but this general rule will help to guide you.

As a rule, never fill a cake pan more than two thirds full in order to leave room for the cake to rise. This will prevent messy spills in your oven.

When making smaller cakes from a recipe designed for one large cake, remember that cupcakes and smaller cakes take less time to bake. Watch them closely, since overbaking will produce dried-out cakes, not to mention scorched ones. Make a note of the size of cake you baked and the number of minutes it took, so you'll be able to refer to this information the next time you use the same recipe.

Preparation Time

The preparation time given in the following cake recipes includes all preparation from the time you start the cake until it's safely in the oven. Since you can go on to other things, once the cakes are in the oven, I haven't included baking time in figuring the preparation time. With a few of the cakes, the time saved in making double recipes isn't so great as with others; in fact, there may not be any time saving at all. However, remember that the clean-up time is the same whether you're baking one cake or a dozen. Also, even though you can be doing other things while the cakes are in the oven, they still need to be watched occasionally, and it doesn't take any longer to watch one cake than a dozen.

Testing for Doneness

Different materials used in baking pans may vary the baking time for cakes; glass, for instance, bakes cake much faster, and cakes should be baked in glass at a lower temperature to avoid burning them on the outside edges. Oven thermometers may vary several degrees; so it is best to set the timer 5 minutes before the recipe indicates the cake should be through baking. Check the cake then and keep testing it every 2 minutes until you are satisfied it is done. Never rely solely on the baking time indicated in a recipe; it is only a guide. Overbaking will ruin a good cake, making it dry; and an underbaked cake may fall if removed from the oven prematurely.

My favorite way of testing a cake for doneness is the old-fashioned "toothpick" test. Take a toothpick, a cake tester, or a clean straw from a broom and insert it into the cake. It should come out clean. For very deep cakes, such as those baked in the large round tube pans, it is best to have a "tester" long enough to reach the center of the cake.

When a cake is done, it will look as though it is loosening at the sides a bit. Press on the top very lightly with your fingertip and test for springiness. If the cake bounces back, it is completely baked.

Be sure to let your cakes cool in the pan for about 5 minutes before removing them, unless otherwise instructed. A hot cake is very delicate and might break, crack, or crumble if it's handled immediately after removal from the oven.

Common Causes of Cake Failures

A cake will fall because: it has too much sugar; it has too much shortening; too little baking time; too much leavening; too slow an oven.

A cake will have an uneven surface because: oven grate or oven is not level; oven heat is not even; this may be caused by too many pans and poor circulation of heat.

A cake will be dry because: it is baked too long; not enough shortening; too much flour; oven temperature is too low.

A cake will be coarse-grained because: it is not creamed enough; it has too much leavening.

A moist, sticky crust will result from too much sugar.

A cake will split on top because: it is baked in too hot an oven; it has too much flour.

A cake will have a heavy layer on the bottom because it is not creamed sufficiently.

A cake will have a heavy crust because: it doesn't have enough sugar or shortening; it has too much flour; it has been baked too long; it has been baked in too hot an oven.

Your batter is running over the pan because: your pan is too small; the cake has too much leavening; the oven is too slow; the cake has too much sugar or shortening.

When baking layer cakes, you'll find that the top of the cakes sort of "balloon" out in the center a bit, making it difficult to place one layer on top of another one. For years I've been trying to even them out by adding more frosting around the edges. This is no longer necessary. Buy a set of Magi-Cake Strips. They will end high-rise centers, uneven layers, cracked tops, and browned crisp edges. Wrap a moistened strip of this aluminized quilted liner around each pan; this maintains an even temperature, allowing the outer edges of your cake to bake at the same time the center does. This will give you moist cakes that are even, and without cracks. Not only does it make frosting and decorating layer cakes much easier, your cakes are so much more attractive. Complete instructions on using these strips come with the package and are available from Maid of Scandinavia, #340-53 in their winter catalog (for address, see page 71).

To eliminate large bubbles or air holes in your cakes, be sure to pound the pan firmly on your kitchen sink or table before baking. If batter is exceptionally thick, it may be necessary to insert a knife around the edges and center, and then drop or pound the pan on the sink again.

One of the most common causes of cake failure is overbaking. It only takes 2 or 3 minutes to turn a delectably moist cake into a dried, rubbery mess. Baking time can vary, depending on the accuracy of your oven control, the type of pan you use, and the size of your cake. I always set the timer about 5 minutes ahead of the designated time, check the cake, and continue accordingly.

You may wish to apply the principles of this book to your own favorite recipes; multiply the ingredients carefully and write them down. When baking larger quantities, most recipe failures can be attributed to the incorrect quantity of one or more of the ingredients.

Wrapping Cakes for the Freezer

Preparing cakes for the freezer is very simple and uncomplicated. Here's a good rule to remember: If the cake is frosted, freeze it first and then wrap. Plain cakes may be wrapped and then frozen. Pan-type cakes may be frosted and frozen in the pan; then seal pan and all in a moisture-vapor-proof wrap, date, and label. Frosted cakes should be put into a sturdy container or box for protection. However, you may wrap the cake in a moisture-vapor-proof wrap either before or after you put the cake into its protective container. Here again, for large fancy and decorated cakes, I like to use a large freezer-proof plastic cake taker.

Cupcakes and small cakes are best frozen first and then wrapped. Cupcakes that are in paper liners can then simply be put into moisture-vapor-proof plastic bags. Small cakes should be wrapped individually and then you can put them into bags so that you'll have all of one kind together.

Cut slices of a cake and wrap in individual plastic bags for lunches. Keep these in some kind of protective container so that they don't get mashed or broken. When packing lunches, take them directly from the freezer and they'll be thawed by lunchtime.

Be sure that your cakes are completely cooled before you freeze them.

Thawing Cakes

Frosted cakes should be unwrapped while frozen and then thawed. Unfrosted cakes or pan cakes may be thawed, wrapped, in the refrigerator or at room temperature (unless recipe indicates otherwise). They may also be reheated (to serve warm), unwrapped, in a very slow oven, 275° F.

SHEET, LAYER, AND LOAF CAKES

EASY CHOCOLATE CAKE

This recipe is a favorite standby in our household. It takes only a few minutes to make, and you'll have a freezerful handy for lunches, picnics, bake sales, et cetera. Besides being easy to prepare, it requires very basic and inexpensive ingredients you're apt to have in the house and no eggs or butter are needed. I must admit that if I hadn't eaten a piece of this cake first, I would never have tried the recipe. So don't worry about the ingredients. I'm sure you'll agree that it's the moistest, best-tasting chocolate cake you've ever eaten.

SINGLE RECIPE
Mixing Time: 8 minutes

1½ cups sifted flour
1 cup sugar
2 tablespoons cocoa
1 teaspoon soda
⅓ teaspoon salt

1 tablespoon vinegar
1 teaspoon vanilla
⅓ cup vegetable oil
1 cup strong coffee*

DOUBLE RECIPE
Mixing Time: 9 minutes

3 cups sifted flour
2 cups sugar
¼ cup cocoa
2 teaspoons soda
⅔ teaspoon salt
2 tablespoons vinegar
2 teaspoons vanilla
⅔ cup of vegetable oil
2 cups strong coffee*

TRIPLE RECIPE
Mixing Time: 10 minutes

4½ cups sifted flour
3 cups sugar
⅓ cup cocoa
1 tablespoon soda
1 teaspoon salt
3 tablespoons vinegar
1 tablespoon vanilla
1 cup vegetable oil
3 cups strong coffee*

* If you don't have the strong coffee on hand, use 1 heaping tablespoon of instant coffee to 1 cup of water.

QUADRUPLE RECIPE
Mixing Time: 12 minutes
6 cups sifted flour
4 cups sugar
½ cup cocoa
1 tablespoon plus 1 teaspoon soda
1⅓ teaspoons salt
¼ cup vinegar
1 tablespoon plus 1 teaspoon vanilla
1⅓ cups vegetable oil
4 cups strong coffee*

QUINTUPLE RECIPE
Mixing Time: 14 minutes
7½ cups sifted flour
5 cups sugar
⅔ cup cocoa
1 tablespoon plus 2 teaspoons soda
1⅔ teaspoons salt
5 tablespoons vinegar
1 tablespoon plus 2 teaspoons vanilla
1⅔ cups vegetable oil
5 cups strong coffee*

Preheat oven to 350° F.

For a single recipe, you may put all the ingredients in an 8 × 8-inch or 9 x 9-inch baking pan. With a fork, mix well and bake at 350° F for 35 minutes, or until done. The pans do *not* need to be greased.

For larger recipes use your mixing bowls. You will need a 4½-quart mixing bowl for the quintuple recipe. Put all ingredients into bowl; then stir until well mixed. That's it! Simply pour the batter into the size of baking containers you've chosen *without* greasing them and bake in a 350° F oven for 35 minutes, or until cakes test done.

A single recipe will make either an 8 x 8 or 9 x 9-inch pan cake, 12 to 15 regular-sized cupcakes, or two 8-inch round layers for a layer cake.

A double recipe will make one 13 x 9 x 2-inch pan cake plus 8 large cupcakes.

A triple recipe will make 36 cupcakes plus one 8-inch round layer cake.

A quadruple recipe will make four 8 x 8 or 9 x 9-inch pan cakes or 48 to 60 cupcakes.

A quintuple recipe will make approximately 65 cupcakes.

Cupcake batter should be poured into paper-lined muffin pans and baked at 350° F for about 18 to 22 minutes. Watch them carefully so they don't bake too long and dry out.

SUGGESTED FROSTINGS. Caramel Frosting or Chocolate Icing on pages 158–159.

TROPICAL CHOCOLATE-CHIP PAN CAKE

Self-frosted pan cakes are my favorites for many things, such as church socials, potluck, picnics. This is an easy yet different type of pan cake, and I'm sure it will make a hit in your home too.

SINGLE RECIPE
> *Time: 8 minutes*
> *Yield: One 9 x 13-inch cake or 32 cupcakes*

1 cup soft margarine
¾ cup sugar
¾ cup firmly packed brown sugar
2 eggs
1 teaspoon vanilla
1 teaspoon baking soda
1 teaspoon salt
2¼ cups sifted flour
> *topping:*
> *Time: 8 minutes*

1 cup firmly packed brown sugar
2 eggs
¼ teaspoon salt
1 teaspoon vanilla
2 cups semisweet chocolate chips or one 12-ounce package
1 cup chopped nuts (peanuts, pecans, walnuts, et cetera, are all good, each giving the cake a different flavor)
1 cup shredded coconut

DOUBLE RECIPE
> *Time: 10 minutes*
> *Yield: Two 9 x 13-inch cakes or 64 cupcakes*

2 cups soft margarine
1½ cups sugar
1½ cups firmly packed brown sugar
4 eggs
2 teaspoons vanilla
2 teaspoons baking soda
2 teaspoons salt
4½ cups sifted flour
> *topping:*
> *Time: 8 minutes*

2 cups firmly packed brown sugar
4 eggs
½ teaspoon salt
2 teaspoons vanilla
4 cups semisweet chocolate chips or two 12-ounce packages
2 cups chopped walnuts (peanuts, pecans, walnuts, et cetera, are all good, each giving the cake a different flavor)
2 cups shredded coconut

Preheat oven to 375° F. Combine the margarine, sugar, and vanilla and beat until light and creamy. Add eggs one at a time and beat well after each. Add salt and baking soda. Now add flour and beat until well blended. Spread batter into a well-greased 9 x 13-inch baking pan (or 32 paper-lined muffin tins, using about 1 rounded tablespoon of dough for each cupcake). Bake cake for 20 minutes (10 to 12 minutes for cupcakes) and remove from oven. Immediately spread with topping and return to oven. Continue baking for an additional 25 minutes (15 minutes for cupcakes).

TOPPING. While cake is baking in the oven, combine brown sugar and eggs, along with salt and vanilla; beat until light in color and thick—about 5 minutes. Add remaining ingredients. Spoon over the top of cake as evenly as possible. Return to oven and bake an additional 25 minutes. For cupcakes, spoon about 1 tablespoonful of topping over each and return to oven for another 15 minutes.

ANGEL FOOD CAKE

This plain Angel Food Cake is marvelous with all those frozen fruits you have in your freezer. Use Fresh or Frozen Strawberry Sauce (page 218) or Blueberry Sauce (page 211). Wonderful year-round dessert.

Mixing Time: 10 minutes

1½ cups (11 to 13) egg whites (see page 47)
2 teaspoons cream of tartar
¼ teaspoon salt
1 cup sugar
1½ teaspoons vanilla
2 tablespoons water
½ cup sugar
1½ cups sifted flour

Preheat oven to 375° F. Have egg whites at room temperature. Beat egg whites until frothy; sprinkle cream of tartar over top and continue beating until whites are stiff enough to form peaks but are not dry. Gradually add water and vanilla. Beat in 1 cup of sugar, sifting in 2 tablespoons at a time over the surface of beaten egg whites. Sift flour with salt and remaining ½ cup of sugar. With wire whisk or spatula carefully fold sifted dry ingredients into first mixture, about ¼ cup at a time. Turn into *ungreased* tube pan; bake at 375° F for 45 minutes or until cake is done when tested. Invert pan until cake is cool—about 1 hour. If you don't have a regular angel food cake pan, invert your tube pan on a thin-necked bottle, such as a catsup bottle.

APRICOT ANGEL CAKE

This Apricot Angel Cake is more moist and tangy than most angel food cakes, and even the texture is different. The fruit flavor is quite strong, almost as though you were eating a fruit-filled coffee cake.

Mixing Time: 10 to 12 minutes

1½ cups (11 to 13) egg whites (see page 47)
2 teaspoons cream tartar
¼ teaspoon salt
1 teaspoon almond extract
1 teaspoon vanilla
2 tablespoons water
¾ cup sugar
1 cup apricot preserves
1½ cups of sifted flour
½ cup sugar

Preheat oven to 375° F. Have egg whites at room temperature. Beat egg whites until frothy; sprinkle cream of tartar and salt over top and continue beating until whites are stiff enough to form peaks but are not dry. Gradually add water and flavorings. Beat in ¾ cup of sugar, sifting in 2 tablespoons at a time over the surface of beaten egg whites. In a separate bowl beat apricot preserves until they're frothy and liquefied. Fold this mixture into egg whites gently with a spatula or wire whisk. Combine remaining sugar and sifted flour; fold into egg-white mixture about ¼ cup at a time until well blended. Turn into *ungreased* tube pan and bake at 375° F for 40 to 45 minutes, on bottom rack of your oven. Watch cake carefully because the top will scorch very easily. Remove from oven when cake is done. Invert pan until cake is cool—about 1 hour or more. If you don't have a regular angel food cake pan, invert your tube pan on a thin-necked bottle, such as a catsup bottle. Loosen sides with a sharp-bladed knife and invert on a cake plate.

Frost or glaze with apricot frosting or glaze (pages 160–161).

PINEAPPLE ANGEL FOOD CAKE

Follow directions for Apricot Angel Cake, but substitute one 8-ounce can of crushed pineapple, well drained, for the apricot preserves, and use vanilla flavoring instead of almond flavoring. Also use pineapple juice instead of water.

This is very good frosted with whipped cream to which crushed pineapple and a bit of sugar have been added. Stabilize whipped cream according to directions on page 54.

CHOCOLATE PECAN ANGEL FOOD CAKE

This is a wonderful recipe for using up your frozen egg whites. Guests will comment on how different it is from the usual box angel food cakes so often served these days. It takes no longer to make than a boxed angel food cake. For special parties I bake it in advance and then freeze it in a freezer-proof plastic cake taker. Remove from freezer about 2 hours before serving. Take lid off cake taker and let it thaw. Make it once and I'm sure you'll make it often.

Mixing Time: 11 minutes

1½ cups (11 to 13) egg whites (see page 47)
2 teaspoons cream of tartar
2 tablespoons water
1 teaspoon vanilla
1 teaspoon almond extract

¾ cup sugar
1 cup sifted flour
¼ teaspoon salt
½ cup cocoa
¾ cup sugar
1 cup chopped pecans

Preheat oven to 375° F. Beat egg whites until frothy; sprinkle cream of tartar over top and continue beating until whites are stiff enough to form peaks but are not dry. Gradually add water and flavorings. Beat in ¾ cup of sugar, sifting in 2 tablespoons at a time. With a wire whisk, carefully fold into first mixture the sifted dry ingredients combined with remaining ¾ cup of sugar, about ¼ cup at a time. Then fold in pecans. Turn into an *ungreased* tube pan, bake at 375° F for 45 minutes or until cake tests done. Watch closely for the last 5 minutes because the top will scorch easily. Invert pan until cake is cool—about 1 hour. Remove from pan and frost.

We loved Mocha Frosting (page 158) on this cake. The light texture of the cake blends well with the almost fudgelike frosting. Garnish with pecan halves, if you wish, for a more festive appearance.

Home mixers will not accommodate more than one angel food cake, which makes it impractical to mix a double recipe.

ANY FLAVOR ANGEL FOOD CAKE

With this formula, the variations of flavor combinations with cakes, fillings, and frostings are unlimited.

Here are a few ideas: lemon cake with Chocolate Icing (page 159); butterscotch cake with Caramel Frosting (page 158).

Mixing Time: 10 minutes

1½ cups (11 to 13) egg whites (see page 47)	¼ teaspoon salt
	1 cup sugar
2 teaspoons cream of tartar	1 package pudding-pie filling (any
2 tablespoons water	flavor)
1 teaspoon vanilla	1 cup sifted flour

Preheat oven at 375° F.

Beat egg whites until frothy; sprinkle cream of tartar over top and continue beating until whites are stiff enough to form peaks but are not dry. Gradually add water and flavoring. Beat in sugar, sifting in 2 tablespoons at a time over the surface of the whites. Sift pudding filling with flour and salt. With a wire whisk carefully fold sifted dry ingredients into first mixture, about ¼ cup at a time. Turn into an *ungreased* tube pan; bake at 375° F for 45 minutes or until it tests done. Invert pan until cake is cool, about 1 hour.

For lemon-flavored pudding-pie filling, substitute lemon juice for water. You may also add lemon rind for added flavor. You cannot use the lemon-flavored pudding and pie fillings that have a flavor capsule in the package.

POUND CAKE

When you're in a hurry and don't have time to fuss, this is a marvelous standby. It only takes 15 minutes for a single recipe and there's no frosting, either; simply use powdered sugar. For a fancier look, bake in a bundt pan. This cake is made with margarine instead of butter, but it really has a buttery flavor. I have tried using butter instead of margarine; the flavor may be a trifle improved, but the texture is more crumbly and I had trouble getting the cake out of the pan.

SINGLE RECIPE
> *Mixing Time: 15 minutes*
> *Yield: One 10-inch tube cake or 2*
> *loaf pans*

1 pound margarine
1 pound superfine sugar
6 unbeaten eggs
1 teaspoon vanilla
Grated rind of 1 lemon
1 tablespoon lemon juice
3 cups sifted flour
1 cup raisins or chopped nuts
(optional)

DOUBLE RECIPE
> *Mixing Time: 25 minutes*
> *Yield: One 10-inch tube cake plus*
> *2 loaf pans, or 4 loaf pans*

2 pounds margarine
2 pounds superfine sugar
1 dozen unbeaten eggs
2 teaspoons vanilla
Grated rind of 2 lemons
2 tablespoons lemon juice
6 cups sifted flour
2 cups raisins or chopped nuts
(optional)

Preheat oven to 300° F. Cream butter until light and fluffy, add sugar, and blend well. Add eggs, one at a time, beating 1 minute after each addition. Add vanilla, lemon juice, and lemon rind. Mix well; then add flour. Add raisins or chopped nuts, if desired. Pour batter into lightly greased 10-inch tube pan. Bake at 300° F for 1 hour and 20 minutes for tube cake and about 5 minutes less for loaf cakes. Cool in pan 5 minutes. Then remove from pan and cool.

CHOCOLATE POUND CAKE

Because of the long baking time this isn't the type of cake to start late in the afternoon, if you intend to use the oven for your dinner. This cake has an unusual texture and flavor—very fudgy and smooth. It's an interesting change from the usual chocolate cakes, and I guarantee that you'll get many comments and compliments when you serve it.

SINGLE RECIPE
> *Mixing Time: 25 minutes*
> *Yield: 2 loaf-sized cakes*

2 packages (¼ pound each) sweet
cooking chocolate

DOUBLE RECIPE
> *Mixing Time: 35 minutes*
> *Yield: 4 loaf-sized cakes or 2*
> *loaves and one 10-inch tube*

4 packages (1 pound) sweet cooking
chocolate

1 cup butter or margarine	2 cups butter or margarine
¼ cup vegetable oil	½ cup vegetable oil
2½ cups sugar	5 cups sugar
5 unbeaten eggs	10 unbeaten eggs
1 teaspoon vanilla	2 teaspoons vanilla
1 teaspoon baking powder	2 teaspoons baking powder
½ teaspoon salt	1 teaspoon salt
1⅓ cups milk	2⅔ cups milk
3½ cups sifted flour	7 cups sifted flour

A double recipe won't fit into a 14-cup mixing bowl. Cream shortening and sugar; add eggs and chocolate in mixing bowl. Then transfer batter to a very large, shallow mixing bowl, about 20-cup capacity or more. (I use the top of my Tupperware Cake Taker, which is fine for this type of mixing; because it's so pliable and lightweight, it's easy to pour the batter from it.) Add your flour and milk to the batter in this larger vessel; use your electric mixer or a heavy wire whisk, whichever you prefer, and mix until smooth. If this sounds like a lot of bother, it really isn't when you consider the results.

Preheat oven to 300° F. Heat chocolate over hot water until partially melted. Remove from hot water and stir rapidly until chocolate is entirely melted. Cool. Cream butter and shortening until softened, gradually add sugar, and mix until light and fluffy. (This takes about 13 minutes with an electric mixer at high speed.) This step is very important because your cake will be heavy at the bottom if you don't mix it properly. Add eggs, one at a time, beating well after each is added. Stir in cooled chocolate, vanilla, baking powder, and salt. Beat well. Alternately add flour and milk, beating after each addition until batter is smooth.

For single recipe, divide batter between two 9 x 5 x 3-inch loaf pans, which have been greased and lined with waxed paper on the bottom. Bake at 300° F for 1 hour and 30 minutes. Cool cake in pans for 15 minutes; then loosen sides with a knife. Remove to cake racks and cool. Frost, glaze, or sprinkle with powdered sugar as desired. To store, wrap tightly in moisture-vapor-proof wrap or container. Keeps for about a week without refrigeration.

CRUNCH CAKE

This Crunch Cake is rather like an upside-down pound cake in that, turned out of the pan, it's covered with its own crunchy-nut topping on all sides. It's good served at any meal, including breakfast.

SINGLE RECIPE
   Mixing Time: 25 minutes
   Yield: 2 loaf-sized cakes

Topping:
½ cup butter or margarine
⅓ cup sugar
1 cup chopped pecans
1½-cups crushed vanilla wafers

Batter:
1 cup butter or margarine
2 cups sugar
4 unbeaten eggs
1 cup milk
1½ teaspoons vanilla
1½ teaspoons baking powder
½ teaspoon salt
2⅔ cups sifted flour

DOUBLE RECIPE
   Mixing Time: 40 minutes
   Yield: 4 loaf-sized cakes

Topping:
1 cup butter or margarine
⅔ cup sugar
2 cups chopped pecans
3 cups crushed vanilla wafers

Batter:
2 cups butter or margarine
4 cups sugar
8 unbeaten eggs
2 cups milk
3 teaspoons vanilla
3 teaspoons baking powder
1 teaspoon salt
5⅓ cups sifted flour

Preheat oven to 350° F.

TOPPING. Melt shortening. Mix sugar, pecans, and crushed vanilla wafers; add melted shortening and mix well. Press on bottom and sides of greased loaf pans that measure 9 x 5 x 3 inches (2 for single recipe; 4 for double). Because the crumb crust burns easily, make certain pans are not near a heating element. Double recipe should be baked in double or large-sized oven.

BATTER. Cream butter and sugar until light and fluffy. (It may take 10 minutes.) This step is very important and it's almost impossible to overbeat at this stage. Add eggs and beat well. Mix milk, vanilla, baking powder, and salt; add alternately with flour, starting and ending with flour. Pour into loaf pans and bake at 350° F for 1 to 1¼ hours. Turn out on cake rack to cool. To judge if the cake is done, use a cake tester or a toothpick if you like, but if the cake has shrunk away from the sides of the pan and if the surface springs back when you press it with your forefinger, the cake should be done.

Cool and serve, if you wish, or freeze. I find it better to freeze these on a cake rack or platter and then wrap them after they're frozen.

GOLDEN SPONGE SHORTCAKE

There seems to be a divergence of opinion about shortcakes. Some people strongly favor baking-powder biscuit shortcake, and others prefer the sponge-type shortcake. I favor the latter, and here's a family favorite for your approval. Serve with fresh or frozen fruit at any time of the year.

SINGLE RECIPE
Mixing Time: 16 minutes

1 cup superfine sugar
6 eggs
½ teaspoon almond or vanilla flavoring
½ teaspoon baking powder
¼ teaspoon salt
1 cup sifted flour

DOUBLE RECIPE
Mixing Time: 22 minutes

2 cups superfine sugar
1 dozen eggs
1 teaspoon almond or vanilla flavoring
1 teaspoon baking powder
½ teaspoon salt
2 cups sifted flour

Preheat oven to 350° F. Separate eggs. Gradually beat sugar into egg yolks until light in color. Add flavoring, baking powder, and salt. Beat whites stiff; fold lightly into sugar mixture. Now add sifted flour gradually. When this is well blended, turn batter into two greased 7 x 11-inch pans with bottoms lined with waxed paper. Bake in 350° F oven 16 to 18 minutes, or until cake springs back when lightly touched. Turn out on cooling racks. If you don't have any 7 x 11-inch pans, use a jelly-roll pan and cut cake in half.

TO SERVE. Spread bottom layer with fresh or frozen fruit. See Fruits, pages 198–223. Add second layer; then add more fruit and top with whipped cream. Serve immediately.

TO FREEZE. Make sponge cake in advance. Set cooling racks in freezer. When sponge cake is frozen, remove. Take a piece of cardboard cut to the size of one layer of sponge cake and cover with waxed paper. Set first layer of sponge cake on this. Then add a double thickness of waxed paper and set the next layer on top. Now wrap in moisture-vapor-proof wrapping, date, label, and freeze.

TO SERVE WHEN FROZEN. All you have to do is thaw at room temperature for half an hour, separating the layers. Have fruit ready and cream whipped before serving time. Then simply assemble and serve.

One recipe will also make three 8-inch layers if you prefer a high, round shortcake.

DREAMY BANANA CAKE

This versatile cake can be baked as a pan cake, in bread pans when served as a banana bread, or in layers for a layer cake. The rolled oats and citrus rind give it a really fruity-nut flavor. This type of cake is very easy to make in large quantities and freeze. You may even wish to use part of the batter for cupcakes.

SINGLE RECIPE
Mixing Time: 20 minutes

½ cup butter or margarine
1 cup firmly packed brown sugar
½ cup granulated sugar
2 eggs
1 teaspoon grated lemon or orange rind
¾ teaspoon baking soda

½ teaspoon baking powder
½ teaspoon salt
⅓ cup buttermilk or sour milk
1¼ cups sifted flour
¾ cup oatmeal
1 cup mashed bananas (see page 205)

DOUBLE RECIPE
Mixing Time: 25 minutes

1 cup butter or margarine
2 cups firmly packed brown sugar
1 cup granulated sugar
4 eggs
2 teaspoons grated lemon or orange rind
1½ teaspoons baking soda
1 teaspoon baking powder
1 teaspoon salt
⅔ cup buttermilk or sour milk
2½ cups sifted flour
1½ cups oatmeal
2 cups mashed bananas (see page 205)

TRIPLE RECIPE
Mixing Time: 30 minutes

1½ cups butter or margarine
3 cups firmly packed brown sugar
1½ cups granulated sugar
6 eggs
3 teaspoons grated lemon or orange rind
2¼ teaspoons baking soda
1½ teaspoons baking powder
1½ teaspoons salt
1 cup buttermilk or sour milk
3¾ cups sifted flour
2¼ cups oatmeal
3 cups mashed bananas (see page 205)

To make a triple recipe you need a 4½-quart mixing bowl. Check the capacity of your large mixing bowl before attempting a triple recipe.

Preheat oven to 350° F. Cream butter and sugars thoroughly. Add eggs and citrus rind; beat well. Stir soda, baking powder, and salt into buttermilk. Alternately add buttermilk mixture and flour, mixing well after each addition. Blend in oatmeal and bananas. Pour into greased and floured pans.

A single recipe will make two 8 x 1½-inch round layers or a 12 x 8-inch pan cake. Bake in a 350° F oven for 40 to 45 minutes or until cake tests done. Frost and fill as desired. My own preference is a chocolate frosting or grated citrus-rind icing. See page 159.

UPSIDE-DOWN CAKE

Instead of the usual pineapple rings on your upside-down cake, try peaches or apricots for a real taste treat. Frozen peaches and apricots are especially good. If you like upside-down cake with a sticky and caramelized top, you'll love the following recipe. If you prefer a drier cake, decrease margarine by 2 tablespoons and brown sugar by ¼ cup.

SINGLE RECIPE
> *Mixing Time: 11 minutes*
> *Yield: One 8 x 8-inch cake*

½ cup margarine
¾ cup well-packed brown sugar
1½ pints fresh frozen fruit or 1 large
   (No. 2½) can peaches or apricots
1⅓ cups biscuit mix
½ cup sugar
1 egg
¾ cup buttermilk
½ teaspoon vanilla
½ teaspoon almond extract

DOUBLE RECIPE
> *Mixing Time: 15 minutes*
> *Yield: Two 8 x 8-inch cakes*

1 cup margarine
1½ cups well-packed brown sugar
3 pints fresh frozen fruit or 2 large
   (No. 2½) cans peaches or apricots
2⅔ cups biscuit mix
1 cup sugar
2 eggs
1½ cups buttermilk
1 teaspoon vanilla
1 teaspoon almond extract

TRIPLE RECIPE
> *Mixing Time: 18 minutes*
> *Yield: Two 13 × 9-inch cakes*

1½ cups margarine
2¼ cups well-packed brown sugar
4½ pints fresh frozen fruit or 3 large
   (No. 2½) cans peaches or apricots
4 cups biscuit mix
1½ cups sugar
3 eggs
2¼ cups buttermilk
1½ teaspoons vanilla
1½ teaspoons almond extract

QUADRUPLE RECIPE
> *Mixing Time: 21 minutes*
> *Yield: Four 8 x 8-inch cakes*

2 cups margarine
3 cups well-packed brown sugar
6 pints fresh frozen fruit or 4 large
   (No. 2½) cans peaches or apricots
5⅓ cups biscuit mix
2 cups sugar
4 eggs
3 cups buttermilk
2 teaspoons vanilla
2 teaspoons almond extract

Defrost and/or drain fruit. Preheat oven to 350° F. Melt margarine either in the baking pan in the oven or in separate pan on top of the stove. While the shortening is melting, measure biscuit mix, granulated sugar, eggs, milk, and flavoring into mixing bowl. Remove 3 table-spoons of the margarine for each recipe you're making (6 tablespoons for double recipe, et cetera) and add to ingredients in mixing bowl. Sprinkle brown sugar over the remaining shortening in baking dish. Now arrange well-drained fruit in an attractive manner over the brown sugar and melted shortening. Dribble 1 tablespoon of fruit syrup (per recipe) over the top of the fruit. Mix all ingredients in mixing bowl lightly and pour gently over the top of the arranged fruit in baking dish or pans. If some of the shortening or fruit syrup comes to the top, don't worry; it will all go to the bottom during the baking. Bake at 350° F for about 40 minutes.

Cakes should be turned upside down as soon as they're removed from the oven. For cakes that are going to be frozen, line plates or cookie sheets with heavy-duty foil. Invert cakes on the foil-lined plates or cookie sheets. When they're cool, put into freezer until frozen. Now you can wrap them in a moisture-vapor-proof wrap of your choice. Large cakes can be cut into smaller ones when they're partially frozen. Then wrap them individually.

MOCHA TORTE

If you want to impress someone with your culinary skills, this torte will do the trick. It isn't too difficult to make; although assembling it will take a little time, it's well worth the effort.

SINGLE RECIPE
*Mixing Time: 10 minutes to mix
and line pans*
Yield: 1 torte

¾ cup sifted flour
2½ squares unsweetened chocolate
5 unbeaten eggs
¾ cup sugar
½ teaspoon salt
½ teaspoon baking powder
¼ cup cold water
¼ teaspoon soda
2 tablespoons sugar

DOUBLE RECIPE
*Mixing Time: 12 minutes to mix
and line pans*
Yield: 2 tortes or 1 giant torte

1½ cups sifted flour
5 squares unsweetened chocolate
10 unbeaten eggs
1½ cups sugar
1 teaspoon salt
1 teaspoon baking powder
½ cup cold water
½ teaspoon soda
¼ cup sugar

Preheat oven to 350° F. Measure sifted flour and set aside. Melt chocolate over hot water. Beat eggs in a large mixing bowl until thick and light in color. Add sugar (¾ cup) gradually, 1 tablespoon at a time, beating after each addition. Add baking powder and salt, and mix well. Now add flour all at once and blend in with a wire whip, wooden spoon, or spatula. Remove chocolate from hot water and immediately add cold water, soda, and sugar. Stir until thick and smooth; then quickly add to batter. Pour into a 15½ x 10½ x 1-inch jelly-roll pan that has been greased and lined on the bottom with waxed paper and again greased, making sure to spread batter evenly to outer corners. Otherwise, the corners will be crisp and brittle before the center is done. Bake at 350° F for 18 to 20 minutes, being careful not to overbake. Meanwhile, sprinkle confectioners sugar on a clean towel. When cake is baked, turn it immediately upside down on sugared towel. Remove waxed paper and cool. Then cut cake into 4 parts and split each quarter crosswise, making 8 layers. Spread 3 tablespoons of Fluffy Coffee Frosting (see page 161) on each layer of cake. Cover sides with frosting, and cool.

When you make a double recipe, you may assemble the cake in the same way you do a single recipe: it will yield 2 cakes the same size. Or you can divide each cake in half the long way and then split the halves crosswise; this will make 1 large, long torte. This is especially nice for a very large crowd. Your finished cake will measure about 16 x 5 inches. Be sure you have a plate, platter, or tray large enough for serving it.

PLUM CAKE (OLD-FASHIONED ZWECHGEN KUCHEN)

Unfortunately, this cake can be made only when the Italian prune plums are in season, unless you freeze your own plums or are fortunate enough to find a place where you can secure them frozen. I haven't been able to find them commercially, so I freeze my own each year. The fresh plums are available for at least 3 months out of the year, at which time I make the sixfold recipe several times and fill my freezer with these cakes, to be enjoyed throughout the winter months. Be sure to buy freestone plums (see page 215). Because this is a pan cake, all kinds of aluminum pans from commercially frozen foods can be used for baking.

SINGLE RECIPE
    Mixing Time: 20 minutes
    Yield: One 9 x 9-inch cake
1⅓ cups Bisquick
1 egg
3 tablespoons vegetable oil
½ cup cream
¾ cup sugar
1 teaspoon vanilla
⅓ cup white raisins (optional)
Approximately 16 pitted Italian prune
    plums
Topping:
¼ cup sugar
¼ cup flour
¼ teaspoon cinnamon
⅛ teaspoon nutmeg
4 tablespoons cold butter or
    margarine

DOUBLE RECIPE
    Mixing Time: 25 minutes
    Yield: Two 9 x 9-inch cakes
2⅔ cups Bisquick
2 eggs
6 tablespoons vegetable oil
1 cup cream
1½ cups sugar
2 teaspoons vanilla
⅔ cup white raisins (optional)
Approximately 32 pitted Italian prune
    plums
Topping:
½ cup sugar
½ cup flour
½ teaspoon cinnamon
¼ teaspoon nutmeg
¼ pound cold butter or margarine

QUADRUPLE RECIPE	SIXFOLD RECIPE
Mixing Time: 35 minutes	*Mixing Time: 45 minutes*
Yield: Four 9 x 9-inch cakes	*Yield: Six 9 x 9-inch cakes*

5⅓ cups Bisquick	8 cups Bisquick
4 eggs	6 eggs
¾ cup vegetable oil	1 cup plus 2 tablespoons vegetable oil
2 cups cream	3 cups cream
3 cups sugar	4½ cups sugar
4 teaspoons vanilla	6 teaspoons vanilla (or 1 tablespoon
1 cup white raisins (optional)	plus 2 teaspoons)
Approximately 60 pitted Italian prune	2 cups white raisins (optional)
plums	Approximately 90 pitted Italian prune
Topping:	plums
1 cup sugar	*Topping:*
1 cup flour	1½ cups sugar
1 teaspoon cinnamon	1½ cups flour
½ teaspoon nutmeg	1½ teaspoons cinnamon
½ pound cold butter or margarine	¾ teaspoon nutmeg
	¾ pound cold butter or margarine

You'll need a 4½-quart mixing bowl for the sixfold recipe.

Preheat oven to 350° F. Mix Bisquick, eggs, and shortening with half the amount of cream. Add sugar and vanilla. Then add remaining cream and mix until smooth. Place in greased pan or dish. Batter should measure ⅜ to ½ inches in depth, no more. Sprinkle with raisins and cover with sliced plums, cut side up, arranged in a neat pattern, as close together as possible.

TOPPING. Mix sugar, flour, cinnamon, and nutmeg. Cut in butter or margarine with pastry blender until the crumbly consistency of coarse meal. Sprinkle on top of plums. Bake 35 to 40 minutes in a 350° F oven. The baking time depends on the size of cake you're baking. The pans used for commercially prepared individual potpies are marvelous for small individual plum cakes. These, of course, will require a shorter baking time.

SPONGE BABA

This delicious light dessert can be served during the summer with luscious fresh fruit or during the winter with fresh-frozen fruit from your freezer. (See Fruits, pages 198 to 222.) May also be served plain.

SINGLE RECIPE
Mixing Time: 11 minutes
Yield: 1 baba

½ cup melted butter
¾ cup lukewarm milk
6 eggs
¾ cup sugar
2 tablespoons baking powder
2 cups sifted flour

DOUBLE RECIPE
Mixing Time: 15 minutes
Yield: 2 baba

1 cup melted butter
1½ cups lukewarm milk
1 dozen eggs
1½ cups sugar
¼ cup baking powder (or 4
tablespoons)
4 cups sifted flour

Preheat oven to 325° F. Melt butter in the warm milk; meanwhile, beat eggs with sugar until very light in color (about 6 minutes). Add baking powder and blend. Now add sifted flour and blend thoroughly. Add butter and milk and beat well. Bake in a greased and floured 9-cup bundt pan for 30 to 35 minutes or until cake tests done. Cool for 10 minutes and then unmold.

SYRUP FOR BABA

SINGLE RECIPE
Mixing Time: 6 minutes
*Yield: 1 cup when you use extract;
about 1½ cups when you use
rum*

½ cup sugar
½ cup water
½ cup white rum or 2 teaspoons rum
extract

DOUBLE RECIPE
Mixing Time: 7 minutes
*Yield: 2 cups when you use
extract; about 3 cups when you
use rum*

1 cup sugar
1 cup water
1 cup white rum or 1 tablespoon plus 1
teaspoon rum extract

When you use the rum extract, make a double recipe of the syrup for a single Baba.

While cake is baking, cook the syrup. Combine sugar and water and boil for 5 minutes until a thin syrup is formed. Remove from heat and add rum or rum extract. After you've unmolded the cake, spoon hot syrup over hot cake until all the syrup has been absorbed. Single-recipe cake will serve 16. Sponge Baba is especially good with fresh or frozen strawberries (see page 217). Each serving may be garnished with whipped cream or ice cream, if you wish.

These cakes are best frozen without the syrup. After they're thawed, add warm syrup just before serving them. Or let each person help himself to the warm syrup. However, for self-service, you'd better make a double batch of the syrup. (Leftover syrup may be poured over any fruit for another dessert on another day.)

SPICE COFFEE CAKE

This is a good pan cake that needs no frosting, since the topping is baked with the cake. Delicious, and especially suited for breakfasts and brunch. Make a big batch to have on hand in your freezer for impromptu entertaining.

SINGLE RECIPE
Mixing Time: 11 minutes
Yield: One 9 x 13-inch cake

2 cups dark brown sugar (see page 42)
2 cups sifted flour
½ cup margarine
1 unbeaten egg
1 cup buttermilk
1 teaspoon baking soda

1 teaspoon vanilla
1 teaspoon lemon juice
1 teaspoon cinnamon
¼ teaspoon nutmeg
½ teaspoon salt
¼ cup chopped nuts

DOUBLE RECIPE
Mixing Time: 15 minutes
Yield: Two 9 x 13-inch cakes

4 cups dark brown sugar (see page 42)
4 cups sifted flour
1 cup margarine
2 unbeaten eggs
2 cups buttermilk
2 teaspoons baking soda
2 teaspoons vanilla
2 teaspoons lemon juice
2 teaspoons cinnamon
½ teaspoon nutmeg
1 teaspoon salt
½ cup chopped nuts

TRIPLE RECIPE
Mixing Time: 19 minutes
Yield: Three 9 x 13-inch cakes

6 cups dark brown sugar (see page 42)
6 cups sifted flour
1½ cups margarine
3 unbeaten eggs
3 cups buttermilk
1 tablespoon baking soda
1 tablespoon vanilla
1 tablespoon lemon juice
1 tablespoon cinnamon
¾ teaspoon nutmeg
1½ teaspoons salt
¾ cup chopped nuts

Preheat oven to 350° F. Mix together brown sugar and flour; then cut in shortening with a knife or pastry blender until crumbly. Set aside 1 cup of this crumbly mixture for the topping. For double recipe, set aside 2 cups of crumbly mixture for topping; for triple recipe, set aside 3 cups. To the remainder add eggs, and beat until well blended; then add the buttermilk which has been combined with the next 6 ingredients. Mix together thoroughly.

Spread batter into a greased and floured 9 x 13 x 2-inch pan for a single recipe. Add nuts to the crumbly mixture and sprinkle over the top. Bake in a 350° F oven for 25 to 30 minutes, or until cake tests done.

FROSTINGS AND ICINGS

Frostings made with confectioners sugar, butter, or cream cheese are best for freezing. Boiled frostings may be frozen; however, they do not freeze solidly and are, therefore, hard to handle and wrap. Frostings and icings made with egg whites should not be frozen. If you want to use this type of frosting, freeze the cake plain and frost it after you've removed it from freezer. Also, cream fillings should not be frozen. They will make your cake soggy. Here again, freeze cake plain and make filling just before serving.

The following recipes for frostings and icings have been carefully selected and tested to withstand freezing very well, unless otherwise indicated. Be sure to freeze frosted or iced cakes before wrapping them (see page 139).

The following table will give you an idea how much frosting you'll need for the various multiple recipes. It will also help you adapt your own favorite recipes. Since icings and frostings differ greatly in texture and spreadability, this table is intended only as a guide. Also, the grain or texture of a cake will make a difference.

BUTTER FROSTINGS

Cake Size	Center	Top	Sides	Total
8-inch layers (2)	½ cup	¾ cup	1 cup	2¼ cups
9-inch layers (2)	⅔ cup	¾ cup	1¼ cups	2⅔ cups
8-inch square (1)		⅔ cup	⅔ cup	1⅓ cups
9-inch square (1)		1 cup	1 cup	2 cups
13 × 9 × 2-inch (1)		1⅓ cups	1 cup	2⅓ cups
13 × 9 × 2-inch, cut into two 9 × 6½-inch layers	⅔ cup	⅔ cup	1⅔ cups	3 cups
9- or 10-inch tube		½ to ¾ cup	2 to 2¼ cups	2½ to 3 cups
24 cupcakes		2¼ cups		2¼ cups

FLUFFY FROSTINGS

Cake Size	Center	Top	Sides	Total
8-inch layers (2)	1 cup	1¼ cups	1½ cups	3¾ cups
9-inch layers (2)	1 cup	1½ cups	1¾ cups	4¼ cups
8-inch square (1)		1⅓ cups	1⅔ cups	3 cups
9-inch square (1)		1⅔ cups	2 cups	3⅔ cups
13 × 9 × 2-inch (1)		2 cups	2¼ cups	4¼ cups
13 × 9 × 2-inch, cut into two 9 × 6½-inch layers	1 cup	1 cup	2½ cups	4½ cups
9- or 10-inch tube		1½ cups	2 cups	3½ cups
24 cupcakes		2 cups	3½ cups	5½ cups

MOCHA FROSTING

This is a very smooth, rich frosting, not too sweet, but very creamy. If you cool this frosting and roll it into balls, it makes a delicious confection.

SINGLE RECIPE
Time: 10 minutes
Yield: 1⅔ cups

4 squares (4 ounces) unsweetened chocolate
¼ cup strong hot coffee
2¼ cups unsifted powdered sugar
2 egg yolks
6 tablespoons butter

DOUBLE RECIPE
Time: 12 minutes
Yield: 3⅓ cups

8 squares (8 ounces) unsweetened chocolate
½ cup strong hot coffee
4½ cups unsifted powdered sugar
4 egg yolks
¾ cup butter

Melt unsweetened chocolate; remove from heat. Mix in sugar and hot coffee. For a stronger mocha flavor, add 1 tablespoon of instant coffee to coffee called for. With electric mixer beat in egg yolks. Then blend in butter, 1 tablespoon at a time, beating well after each addition. Any unused frosting will keep well in the refrigerator for weeks.

CARAMEL FROSTING

This frosting has a distinctive caramel-like flavor. It's quick and easy to make and freezes well. It tastes especially good on spice cakes, caramel or butterscotch cakes, and chocolate cakes or cupcakes.

SINGLE RECIPE
Time: 9 minutes
Yield: 1 scant cup

¼ cup butter
½ cup brown sugar
2 tablespoons milk
1¼ cups sifted confectioners sugar
¼ teaspoon vanilla

DOUBLE RECIPE
Time: 11 minutes
Yield: 1¾ cups

½ cup butter
1 cup brown sugar
¼ cup milk
2½ cups sifted confectioners sugar
½ teaspoon vanilla

Melt butter over low heat; add brown sugar. Cook for 2 minutes. Add milk; stir until it boils. Remove from heat and add confectioners sugar and vanilla.

CHOCOLATE GLAZE

This is a nice, light and shiny glaze that is good on anything from doughnuts to the Chocolate Pound Cake on page 146.

SINGLE RECIPE
Time: 10 minutes
Yield: ¾ cup

one 4-ounce package sweet cooking chocolate
or
⅔ cup semisweet chocolate morsels
1½ tablespoons butter
3 tablespoons water
1 cup sifted confectioners sugar
Pinch salt
½ teaspoon vanilla

DOUBLE RECIPE
Time: 12 minutes
Yield: 1½ cups

two 4-ounce package sweet cooking chocolate
or
1⅓ cups semisweet chocolate morsels
3 tablespoons butter
⅓ cup water
2 cups sifted confectioners sugar
2 pinches salt
1 teaspoon vanilla

Melt chocolate and butter in water, over moderate heat or in microwave oven. Remove from heat. Add salt and stir until combined. Sift sugar into the chocolate mixture, mixing well after each addition. When well blended, add vanilla and mix well. Glaze sets up rapidly, so work quickly.

CHOCOLATE ICING

This is a good icing, not too soft and liquid, but nice and shiny as an icing should be. It will remain equally nice and shiny after freezing too, which all icings won't do.

SINGLE RECIPE
Yield: About 5 ounces

2 tablespoons melted butter
¾ cup sifted confectioners sugar
1 tablespoon milk
1 tablespoon corn syrup
½ teaspoon vanilla flavoring
1 square melted unsweetened chocolate

DOUBLE RECIPE
Yield: About 1¼ cups

4 tablespoons melted butter
1½ cups sifted confectioners sugar
2 tablespoons milk
2 tablespoons corn syrup
1 teaspoon vanilla flavoring
2 squares melted unsweetened chocolate

Combine butter, sugar, milk, corn syrup, and vanilla. Add melted chocolate and blend until smooth. Spread icing.

With this type of icing, a quick way to ice cupcakes is to dip them into the icing. Of course, the cupcakes must have risen slightly above the paper liner for this method to work. Try it!

A single recipe will ice approximately 48 miniature brownies (see page 165).

APRICOT GLAZE

Not only is this good on the Apricot Angle Food Cake (page 143), but it's delicious on any plain cake, e.g., pound cake, sponge cake.

SINGLE RECIPE
1 cup apricot preserves
½ cup water
2 tablespoons cornstarch
¼ cup sugar
2 tablespoons butter

DOUBLE RECIPE
2 cups apricot preserves
1 cup water
¼ cup cornstarch
½ cup sugar
¼ cup butter (half a stick)

Beat apricot preserves well, either in mixing bowl or in blender. Mix cornstarch and sugar, and add water. Combine with apricot preserves and heat, stirring constantly. Remove from heat when thick and bubbling. Add butter. Stir until butter is completely melted and cool. Spread when glaze has cooled to the right consistency.

A single recipe should be enough for one angel food cake.

VARIATION. Peach, Orange Marmalade, or Pineapple Glaze can easily be made by substituting orange marmalade or peach or pineapple preserves for the apricot preserves.

WHIPPED FILLING AND FROSTING

Because the usual custard fillings don't freeze well, try substituting this basic whipped filling and frosting for baked goods that are freezer bound. It has a nice creamy texture and yet it isn't too sweet or rich.

The way this frosting is made is rather unusual, but you'd never guess from tasting it. The recipe makes quite a bit and can be used for many things.

SINGLE RECIPE
Time: 15 minutes
Yield: About 2½ cups
5 tablespoons flour
1 cup milk

DOUBLE RECIPE
Time: 20 minutes
Yield: About 5 cups
½ cup plus 2 tablespoons flour
2 cups milk

1 cup butter or margarine	2 cups butter or margarine
1 cup granulated sugar	2 cups granulated sugar
1 teaspoon vanilla	2 teaspoons vanilla

Stir flour and milk over heat until thick. (Stir continuously or it will get lumpy.) Cool to body temperature. Cream butter and sugar; add vanilla. Beat at high speed until it is very light and fluffy. Now beat cooled milk mixture into creamed mixture at high speed, until it resembles whipped cream. Add drained crushed pineapple and mix well. If the topping is a trifle thin for spreading, put it in the refrigerator for 15 to 30 minutes. Use for filling as well as frosting. Freeze any unused portion to use another time. Simply thaw at room temperature. If a more creamy texture is desired, you may want to rebeat it.

PINEAPPLE FROSTING. Add one 8-ounce can of well-drained, crushed pineapple to a single recipe.

CHOCOLATE MALT FILLING AND FROSTING. Use 1 cup of instant chocolate malted milk instead of 1 cup of sugar.

BURNT SUGAR FROSTING. Melt ¼ cup of sugar in a heavy skillet, stirring constantly. When the sugar is completely melted (it should be a caramel-colored syrup) remove from heat and slowly add ½ cup of boiling milk. Cool. Meanwhile, heat remaining ½ cup of milk to which the flour has been added. When this mixture has thickened, add to the sugar and milk mixture. Continue according to the above instructions.

PEPPERMINT FROSTING. This can be made by adding 1 cup of crushed peppermint candy. To give it a pale pink glow, add a drop or two of red food coloring to the cooled flour and milk mixture. A teaspoon of peppermint flavoring may also be desirable.

COFFEE-FLAVORED FROSTING. Add 2 tablespoons instant coffee to a single recipe.

MOCHA-FLAVORED FROSTING. Add 1 tablespoon each of instant coffee and cocoa to a single recipe.

FRUITED FLAVORS. Add 1 cup of either peach or apricot preserves, 1 cup of toasted shredded coconut, and so on. The combinations are unlimited.

FRUITED FILLING. For a truly fruity filling, remove one cup of Whipped Filling and Frosting, and combine with one 8-ounce can of well-drained, crushed pineapple, or apricot or peach preserve, coconut, et cetera. Fill cake and frost sides and top with remaining Whipped Frosting.

WHIPPED CREAM FROSTING

Remember that whipped cream freezes very well and can be kept at least 4 weeks. It's a simple and easy frosting for almost any type of cake and can be varied considerably by adding a few extra ingredients. After cream has been whipped, add marmalade (if marmalade is really thick and heavy, beat or blend it before adding to the whipped cream in your mixer, blender or food processor), honey, maple syrup, drained crushed pineapple, instant chocolate drink mix, cocoa and sugar, rum and vanilla flavoring, as well as any other flavorings; even add food coloring, if you want a special effect. Be even more adventurous. Try adding Crème de Cacao, Crème de Menthe, or any other liqueur.

To stabilize your whipped cream, follow directions on page 54.

Cookies and Confections

✳✳✳✳✳✳✳✳✳✳✳✳✳✳✳✳✳✳✳✳✳✳✳✳✳✳✳

FREEZING COOKIES AND COOKIE DOUGHS

As a general rule, all cookies freeze well, usually up to 6 months. However, cookies that are crunchy and crisp should have the extra protection of a moisture-vapor-proof material plus a container for protection, especially if they're to be kept for a long period. It's also best to thaw them uncovered, rather than in a container.

Most cookies keep quite well in a cookie jar—that is, if you hide the cookie jar—so there are only a few occasions that call for freezing them. Christmas is one occasion. With a freezer, Christmas cookies may be baked at your leisure on the first cool days of September, tucked away in the freezer, and all but forgotten until the holidays. You'll be very grateful for your foresight. This is especially true when you make any of the traditional Christmas cookies that are very time-consuming to prepare. If you like, save the no-bake kind for last-minute making, simply to get in the Christmas spirit.

If you're making a very large batch of oatmeal or chocolate-chip cookies, say, it's nice to freeze half of them so that the children won't have the same kind of cookies in their school lunches for days on end. Also, if you're making extra-fancy cookies for some special occasion, make them ahead at your leisure and freeze them. If you lock your freezer, at least you'll be assured that your cookies won't have mysteriously disappeared by the Big Day! Husbands who are supposed to be hard at work in the basement have been known to sample a few frozen wares!

Although there's nothing new about refrigerator cookies, they're perfect for freezer use. Make the dough in large quantities and freeze it.

When you're ready to bake, simply thaw your cookie rolls, slice and bake. You'll be glad to have a variety on hand in your freezer at all times. All refrigerator cookies may be frozen unbaked for periods of about 3 months. A number of recipes for refrigerator cookies are included in this chapter. However, refrigerator-cookie recipes are easy to find. So why not add to the ones in this book and start your own collection?

I haven't given preparation time for any of these cookies, since it will differ greatly with each individual. The time for baking cookies in quantity will naturally depend on whether you have two ovens or one, and the size of each. Mixing the cookie batter shouldn't take more than a few minutes, and the rest is up to you and your equipment.

In general, the following recipes are of two types: fancy cookies for special occasions and a few favorites to make in large quantities.

Coffee cans, 2 and 3-pound sizes, make excellent containers in which to freeze cookies. After cleaning and drying them thoroughly, you may coat them with a very thin coat of vegetable oil to insure that they will not rust. Line with plastic wrap. Very small cookies could even be packed in 1-pound cans. For long-term storage, you might wish to tape the lid on to make sure that this moisture-proof barrier is intact.

Freezing cookies is a very simple procedure. Soft or shaped cookies are best frozen first and then packaged; drop cookies, balls, or other fairly firm cookies can easily be packaged and then frozen. Pack only the same kinds of cookies in one container. However, several plastic bags, each holding a different variety, may be placed in the same protective outside container. (Remember that metal canisters will rust.) Be sure that each bag is sealed properly so that the flavors of one kind won't mingle with those of another.

When properly wrapped and stored, these cookies will keep for 9 to 12 months without any adverse effect on their quality or flavor.

COOKIES, BROWNIES, AND SQUARES

PECAN TASSIES

It's sheer nonsense to make only a single batch of these unless you're on a diet or simply don't like sweets.

PASTRY:

SINGLE RECIPE
   Yield: 36 Tassies

One 3-ounce package cream cheese   1 cup sifted flour
½ cup margarine or butter

DOUBLE RECIPE   TRIPLE RECIPE
   Yield: 72 Tassies   *Yield: 108 Tassies*

Two 3-ounce packages cream cheese   Three 3-ounce packages cream
1 cup margarine or butter   cheese
2 cups sifted flour   1½ cups margarine or butter
                                     3 cups sifted flour

Cream butter and cheese; stir in flour. Chill about 1 hour. Then shape into 36 balls per batch. The balls should be about ¾ inch in diameter. Place in ungreased 1-inch muffin cups and press against bottom and sides with a flat-bottomed shot glass dipped in flour. Fill with pecan filling. When working with more than a single recipe, be sure to put unused dough back into refrigerator until needed.

PECAN FILLING

SINGLE RECIPE
1 egg   1 teaspoon vanilla
¾ cup brown sugar   Dash salt
1 tablespoon butter   ⅔ cup chopped pecans

DOUBLE RECIPE   TRIPLE RECIPE
2 eggs   3 eggs
1½ cups brown sugar   2¼ cups (1 pound) brown sugar
2 tablespoons butter   3 tablespoons butter
2 teaspoons vanilla   3 teaspoons vanilla
⅛ teaspoon salt   Scant ¼ teaspoon salt
1⅓ cups chopped pecans   2 cups chopped pecans

Beat eggs, sugar, butter, vanilla, and salt until smooth. Add nuts. Fill muffin cups with mixture. Bake at 325° F for 25 minutes or until set. Cool and remove from pans. In order to make a triple recipe efficiently you should have at least three pans with twelve 1-inch cups.

FUDGY BROWNIES

Brownies freeze best uncut in the pan, as they will crumble if frozen when cut. If you can't spare a pan for this purpose, simply eat them as you bake them. Or try making miniature brownies in small muffin tins, lined with paper liners, for freezing. A single recipe makes about 4 dozen miniature brownies. They may be frosted or not as you wish, and these freeze very well. Always separate the layers of brownies with waxed paper to avoid sticking. These miniatures have a lovely appearance and may be served on the most elegant occasions.

SINGLE RECIPE	DOUBLE RECIPE
Mixing Time: 7 minutes, if baked in pan	*Mixing Time: 10 minutes, if baked in pan*
½ cup margarine or salad oil	1 cup margarine or salad oil
2 cups sugar	4 cups sugar
4 eggs	8 eggs
4 squares melted unsweetened chocolate	8 squares melted unsweetened chocolate
1 teaspoon vanilla	2 teaspoons vanilla
1⅓ cups sifted flour	2⅔ cups sifted flour
¼ teaspoon salt	½ teaspoon salt
1 cup chopped nuts	2 cups chopped nuts
1 cup raisins (optional)	2 cups raisins (optional)

Preheat oven to 350° F. If using margarine, beat well, add sugar to shortening, beat, then add eggs and beat until light and smooth. Stir in vanilla and melted chocolate, mixing thoroughly. Add salt. Gradually beat in flour. Add nuts and raisins, if desired. Turn batter into a greased shallow pan, about 10 x 15 inches, or a jelly-roll pan will do nicely too. If making a double recipe, pour half the dough into this pan. Use the remainder in small muffin tins. Fill paper cups ⅔ full. Bake miniatures at 350° F for 18 to 20 minutes and large pan of brownies for 25 minutes, or until it tests done. Watch closely, since they become dry when overbaked. Yields 4 dozen miniatures per single recipe.

For a more festive look, use Chocolate Icing (page 159) to finish the brownies.

MINCEMEAT SQUARES

Anyone who likes mincemeat will love these. They seem especially tasty in the fall and early winter. They freeze well. I freeze them in a flat oblong freezer-proof plastic container, and put waxed paper in between the layers. If not frozen, they must be refrigerated.

SINGLE RECIPE	DOUBLE RECIPE
Yield: 3 dozen	*Yield: 6 dozen*
2 cups rolled oats	4 cups rolled oats
1¾ cups sifted flour	3½ cups sifted flour

½ teaspoon soda	1 teaspoon soda
1 cup brown sugar	2 cups brown sugar
1 cup butter or margarine (or ½ cup each)	2 cups butter or margarine (or 1 cup each)
3 cups mincemeat	6 cups mincemeat
2 large cooking apples, cored, peeled, and chopped	4 large cooking apples, cored, peeled, and chopped
1 teaspoon brandy flavoring or 1 tablespoon brandy	2 teaspoons brandy flavoring or 2 tablespoons brandy

Preheat oven to 350° F. Put rolled oats through coarse food chopper to measure 2 cups. Add flour, soda, and sugar. Mix thoroughly. Cut in shortening until mixture is crumbly. Divide into 2 parts. Press one half firmly into bottom of an oiled baking pan about 10 x 15 inches, or a jelly-roll pan will do. Combine chopped apples with mincemeat and add brandy or brandy flavoring. Mix well. Spread this mixture over the dough. Sprinkle rest of dough on top; pat with hand or spoon. Bake at 350° F for 40 minutes. Cool thoroughly and cut into bars.

LITTLE SWEDISH TEA CAKES

These take a little time to make, but they're well worth the effort. This elegant dessert freezes well. While you're at it, you might just as well make a double recipe, using half the dough for Raspberry Filled Tea Cakes.

SINGLE RECIPE	DOUBLE RECIPE
Yield: 32	*Yield: 64*
1 cup butter or margarine (or ½ cup each)	2 cups butter or margarine (or 1 cup each)
½ cup sugar	1 cup sugar
1 egg	2 eggs
1 teaspoon vanilla	2 teaspoons vanilla
2 cups sifted flour	4 cups sifted flour
¼ teaspoon salt	½ teaspoon salt
Filling:	*Filling:*
2 well-beaten eggs	4 well-beaten eggs
½ cup sugar	1 cup sugar
¼ teaspoon salt	½ teaspoon salt
½ pound finely ground almonds or almond paste (see page 39)	1 pound finely ground almonds or almond paste (see page 39)

Cream butter and sugar until light and fluffy. Add egg and vanilla; continue beating. Add salt, then flour, and mix well. Chill dough for about 1 hour. Place about 1 teaspoonful of batter in very small muffin pans (about 1 inch in diameter and 1 inch deep). Press batter up sides and over bottom with a flat-bottomed shot glass dipped in flour. Combine ingredients for filling and place about 1 teaspoonful in each cup. Bake at 350° F for 30 minutes. A blender or food processor is marvelous for mixing the filling, especially when you are using almond paste. Cool 10 minutes before removing from pan.

RASPBERRY-FILLED TEA CAKES. Make dough as in Little Swedish Tea Cakes, then fill with prepared raspberry filling—the kind used to fill bismarcks (see page 119). Cool and remove from pans. Sprinkle with powdered sugar.

SPRITZ COOKIES

These cookies are wonderful because of their versatility and because they're so easy to freeze. Put them in bags or any moisture-vapor-proof container. If you are storing them in bags, put the bags in some kind of box to protect cookies from breakage.

SINGLE RECIPE	DOUBLE RECIPE
Yield: About 6 dozen cookies	*Yield: About 12 dozen cookies*
1 cup butter	2 cups butter
½ cup sugar	1 cup sugar
1 egg	2 eggs
¼ teaspoon salt	½ teaspoon salt
2½ cups sifted flour	5 cups sifted flour

Cream butter and sugar with an electric mixer until light and fluffy. Add egg and salt, and beat well. Add flour and blend until smooth. (If dough is too soft, chill in refrigerator for half an hour before putting in cookie press or pastry bag.) Force dough through cookie press or pastry bag into desired shape. Place on ungreased cookie sheets and bake in a 350° F oven for about 10 minutes, or until very delicately browned.

VARIATIONS. For chocolate spritz, add ¼ cup cocoa to a single recipe, or make a double recipe and add the cocoa to half the dough. A very pretty cookie that is fun to make is the finger spritz. On your cookie press or pastry bag, use a tip that resembles a star, no bigger than about ½ inch across. Press dough in 2-inch strips on your cookie sheet. They can be placed very close to one another, since they spread very little. When they are baked, dip one end of the cookie into melted semisweet chocolate and then into chocolate shot. Other variations can be made by topping the cookies with pieces of candied cherries, pecans, or colored sugar before baking.

PECAN BUTTER COOKIES

A quick, simple butter cookie that keeps very well in the freezer. They may be shaped into balls or crescents, then dipped into powdered sugar. They have a crunchy texture and buttery flavor.

SINGLE RECIPE
Yield: About 3 dozen

½ pound butter
½ cup confectioners sugar
1 teaspoon vanilla flavoring

2 cups sifted flour
1 cup chopped pecans

DOUBLE RECIPE
Yield: About 6 dozen

1 pound butter
1 cup confectioners sugar
2 teaspoons vanilla flavoring
4 cups sifted flour
2 cups chopped pecans

TRIPLE RECIPE
Yield: About 9 dozen

1½ pounds butter
1½ cups confectioners sugar
3 teaspoons vanilla flavoring
6 cups sifted flour
3 cups chopped pecans

Cream butter with mixer, add sugar, and beat until well blended. Add vanilla, nuts, and flour. Place in refrigerator for 1 hour. Shape small pieces of dough into crescents or balls and place on ungreased cookie sheet. Bake at 350° F for about 15 minutes. As soon as crescents are removed from oven (while still warm), roll them in powdered sugar.

CHOCOLATE CRISP BRAN COOKIES

These are good "packin' cookies"—for lunches or picnics. Oatmeal Flakes or some other cereal may be substituted for the bran; each will give a subtle flavor variation.

SINGLE RECIPE
Yield: About 6½ dozen

1 cup soft butter or margarine
1½ cups sugar
2 eggs
1 teaspoon vanilla
½ teaspoon baking soda
½ teaspoon salt
2 cups sifted flour
2 cups Kellogg's 40% Bran Flakes
1 cup (6 ounces) chocolate morsels

DOUBLE RECIPE
Yield: About 13 dozen

2 cups soft butter or margarine
3 cups sugar
4 eggs
2 teaspoons vanilla
1 teaspoon baking soda
1 teaspoon salt
4 cups sifted flour
4 cups Kellogg's 40% Bran Flakes
2 cups (12 ounces) chocolate morsels

Preheat oven to 375° F. Blend butter and sugar, beating until light and fluffy. Add egg, vanilla, baking soda, and salt; beat well. Add sifted flour and mix until smooth. Now stir in bran flakes and chocolate morsels. Drop by teaspoonfuls onto ungreased baking sheets. Bake for about 12 minutes at 375° F.

EDITH'S SUGAR COOKIES

An easy all-purpose sugar cookie. It too can be varied with the addition of chopped nuts or of cocoa for chocolate-flavored cookies. I usually make a double batch, take out half the dough, and then add cocoa to the other half, making two different kinds of cookies at one time.

SINGLE RECIPE	DOUBLE RECIPE
Yield: 6½ dozen	Yield: 13 dozen
½ cup butter	1 cup butter
½ cup margarine	1 cup margarine
½ cup granulated sugar	1 cup granulated sugar
½ cup well-packed brown sugar	1 cup well-packed brown sugar
1 egg	2 eggs
1 teaspoon vanilla	2 teaspoons vanilla
½ teaspoon salt	1 teaspoon salt
2 teaspoons cream of tartar	1 tablespoon plus 1 teaspoon cream of tartar
1 teaspoon baking soda	2 teaspoons baking soda
2¼ cups sifted flour	4½ cups of sifted flour

Preheat oven to 375° F. Cream butter and sugar; add egg, vanilla, salt, cream of tartar, and baking soda. Mix well. Add flour. Refrigerate for ½ hour or more. Shape in small balls, roll in granulated sugar, and place on greased cookie sheet. Press balls flat, using the bottom of a smooth glass or jar. Rub bottom of glass or jar with shortening; then dip in sugar and press cookies gently. These cookies spread, so don't put them too close together on the cookie sheet. Bake in a preheated 375° F oven for 10 to 12 minutes.

For further flavor variation, add ½ cup of chocolate morsels to ¼ of a single recipe.

FRIEDA'S TURNOVERS

This is a good basic dough that can be used for many things. It makes delicious kolacky, as well as turnovers.

SINGLE RECIPE
Yield: 30 to 36

1 cup butter
1 cup cottage cheese

2 cups flour

DOUBLE RECIPE
Yield: 60 to 72

2 cups butter
2 cups cottage cheese
4 cups flour

TRIPLE RECIPE
Yield: 90 to 108

3 cups butter
3 cups cottage cheese
6 cups flour

Cream butter very well, add cottage cheese, and beat until fluffy.
Then add flour. Mix well. Chill one hour. Roll out on floured cloth and
make turnovers or kolackys as desired. If you're making a large amount
and don't want to use all the dough at one time, it will keep well in the
refrigerator for a few days or you can freeze the unused portion for a
week or two.

For turnovers, take a workable amount of dough and roll out to
about ⅛-inch thickness. Using a pastry wheel, cut dough into 3- or
4-inch squares. Use pie filling for the centers in any flavor you like—
apple, cherry, blueberry, mincemeat, et cetera. Either commercial fillings or the homemade variety that you might have in your freezer are
suitable. A heaping tablespoonful on the 4-inch squares is just about
right. Put filling in center of square. Then fold over one corner of the
dough to the corner opposite it, making a triangle, pinching to seal. If
you have trouble sealing the edges, moisten with cream and reseal.
Bake at 350° F for 12 minutes. When cool, turnovers may be iced with a
plain powdered-sugar icing made with cream or lemon juice and powdered sugar. The icing should be fairly soft and liquid and brushed on
with a pastry brush, or you may wish to simply dust with powdered
sugar.

TO FREEZE. Freeze turnovers on cookie sheets. When frozen, put
them into moisture-vapor-proof containers, inserting a sheet of waxed
paper between layers. They may be heated for serving, or simply
thawed and served cold.

They may also be frozen unbaked. However, I found it much more
satisfactory to bake them first.

KOLACKY

1 batch of Frieda's Turnover dough
1 can (12 ounces) cake and pastry

filling (almond, poppy seed, or fruit
flavored)

Make dough as for turnovers or use remaining dough from a large
recipe. On lightly floured board or pastry cloth, roll dough to about

⅛-inch thickness. Cut into 2-inch squares with a pastry wheel or knife. Place 1 tea-spoonful of filling on each square. Overlap two opposite corners of each square, pinching to seal. If you have trouble sealing the edges, use cream to moisten edges; then pinch together.

For a fancier kolacky, make a cut about ¾-inch long from each corner toward the center, using a pastry wheel, as shown in the diagram. Then turn in every other spoke over the filling.

Place filled dough on cookie sheets about 1 inch apart. Bake at 350° F for 12 minutes, or until golden brown. When slightly cool, dust with powdered sugar.

ORANGE REFRIGERATOR COOKIES

A triple batch isn't too much. You'll be delighted to have these cookies in your freezer.

SINGLE RECIPE
Yield: About 10 dozen small cookies

1 cup butter
½ cup granulated sugar
½ cup firmly packed brown sugar
1 egg
2 tablespoons orange juice

Grated rind of 1 orange
1 teaspoon baking soda
¼ teaspoon salt
2½ cups sifted flour
¾ cup chopped pecans or walnuts

DOUBLE RECIPE
Yield: About 20 dozen small cookies

2 cups butter
1 cup granulated sugar
1 cup firmly packed brown sugar
2 eggs
¼ cup orange juice
Grated rind of 2 oranges
2 teaspoons baking soda
½ teaspoon salt
5 cups sifted flour
1½ cups chopped pecans or walnuts

TRIPLE RECIPE
Yield: About 30 dozen small cookies

3 cups butter
1½ cups granulated sugar
1½ cups firmly packed brown sugar
3 eggs
⅓ cup orange juice
Grated rind of 3 oranges
3 teaspoons baking soda
¾ teaspoon salt
7½ cups sifted flour
2¼ cups chopped pecans or walnuts

Cream butter and sugar until light and fluffy. Add egg, juice and rind, salt, and soda, mixing well. Add sifted flour and mix thoroughly.

Stir in nuts. Set in the refrigerator for about 1 hour to chill dough so that you can form it into rolls. On waxed paper, form dough into rolls about 1 to 1¼ inches in diameter (they will spread and rise when baking). Freezer-wrap uncooked or bake as desired. For thin slices, use a wire cheese cutter or a serrated knife. Slice and lay on an ungreased cookie sheet. Bake in a preheated 350° F oven for 10 to 12 minutes, or until delicately browned.

BUTTERSCOTCH PECAN REFRIGERATOR COOKIES

These cookies have a sandy texture and an appealing flavor.

SINGLE RECIPE *Yield: About 10 dozen 1-inch cookies*	DOUBLE RECIPE *Yield: About 20 dozen 1-inch cookies*
1 cup butter or margarine	2 cups butter or margarine
2 cups firmly packed brown sugar	4 cups firmly packed brown sugar
2 eggs	4 eggs
1 teaspoon vanilla flavoring	2 teaspoons vanilla flavoring
½ teaspoon salt	1 teaspoon salt
1 teaspoon cream of tartar	2 teaspoons cream of tartar
1 teaspoon soda	2 teaspoons soda
4 cups sifted flour	8 cups sifted flour
1 cup chopped pecans	2 cups chopped pecans

Cream butter and add sugar (see p. 42), mixing at moderately fast speed, until light and fluffy. Add eggs, one at a time. Add vanilla, salt, cream of tartar, and soda, mixing very well. Add flour, one cup at a time. When well mixed, add nuts. Shape dough into rolls, wrap in waxed paper, and chill overnight or until very firm. Or freezer-wrap, date, label, and freeze for future use.

TO BAKE. Preheat oven to 400° F. Slice dough into ⅛-inch slices and bake on an ungreased cookie sheet for 8 to 10 minutes, or until lightly browned.

TO BAKE AFTER FREEZING. Thaw dough until it's soft enough to slice without crumbling. Use a serrated knife or wire cheese slicer for cutting cookies. Follow above baking instructions.

MARIE'S LEMON REFRIGERATOR COOKIES

These are almost white, crispy-crunchy cookies with a nice hint of lemon.

SINGLE RECIPE
Yield: 10 dozen 1-inch cookies

1 cup soft butter
1 cup sifted confectioners sugar
1 teaspoon lemon flavoring
¼ teaspoon salt
2½ cups sifted flour

DOUBLE RECIPE
Yield: 20 dozen 1-inch cookies

2 cups soft butter
2 cups sifted confectioners sugar
2 teaspoons lemon flavoring
½ teaspoon salt
5 cups sifted flour

Cream butter and sugar until light in color and fluffy. (Measure sugar unsifted; then sift into the butter and mix.) Add flavoring and salt, mixing well. Then add flour and mix well.

Shape into rolls, 1 to 1½ inches in diameter, and wrap in waxed paper. Refrigerate until very firm. Or freezer-wrap, date, label, and freeze for future use.

TO BAKE. Preheat oven to 350° F. If frozen, thaw until soft enough to slice without crumbling. Using a serrated knife or wire cheese slicer, cut into ⅛-inch slices. Lay cookies on an ungreased cookie sheet and bake at 350° F for 8 to 10 minutes, or until delicately browned.

VARIATION. In place of lemon extract, substitute orange extract, almond, or black walnut flavoring.

STOVE-TOP SWEETS

TRUFFLES

These mouth-watering little delicacies could almost be called a confection. They virtually melt in your mouth, but because they're so rich (loaded with calories), a few will go a long way. They keep well and take up little room in the freezer.

SINGLE RECIPE
Yield: 3 dozen

½ pound semisweet chocolate
¼ cup butter
2 egg yolks

2 tablespoons cocoa
1 teaspoon rum flavoring
Chocolate shot

DOUBLE RECIPE
Yield: 6 dozen

1 pound semisweet chocolate
½ cup butter
4 egg yolks
¼ cup cocoa
2 teaspoons rum flavoring
Chocolate shot

TRIPLE RECIPE
Yield: 9 dozen

1½ pounds semisweet chocolate
¾ cup butter
6 egg yolks
6 tablespoons cocoa
3 teaspoons rum flavoring
Chocolate shot

Melt semisweet chocolate over hot water, add butter, and stir until butter is melted. Remove from heat and add egg yolks, cocoa, and flavoring. Place in refrigerator and watch closely. When mixture begins to set and is cool, remove and shape into small balls about ¾ inch in diameter. Roll balls in chocolate shot. Place on waxed paper and chill again until very firm. I put these in little paper candy cups, so that they're very easily removed from any container when they're frozen. They make an attractive and delectable addition to any dessert platter.

MINT MELTAWAYS

Follow Truffles recipe, but omit rum flavoring and add 1 teaspoon mint flavoring per single recipe. If you plan to make both kinds of truffles, you may want to add a little green-colored sugar to the chocolate shot, so that you'll be able to tell the difference when serving both kinds. The colored sugar tends to settle to the bottom; so stir it occasionally when rolling balls in it.

BALLS OF GOOD CHEER

Christmas just wouldn't be Christmas without a large quantity of these delightful little cookies. Men are especially fond of them. They keep almost indefinitely if stored in an airtight container. If your freezer is crowded, just store them in a cool place.

SINGLE RECIPE	DOUBLE RECIPE
Yield: 6 dozen	*Yield: 12 dozen*
2 cups dark raisins	4 cups dark raisins
2 cups chopped pecans	4 cups chopped pecans
1 pound vanilla wafers or 4 cups of wafer crumbs	2 pounds vanilla wafers or 8 cups of wafer crumbs
½ pound powdered sugar	1 pound powdered sugar
2 tablespoons cocoa	4 tablespoons cocoa
¼ to ⅓ cup light corn syrup	½ to ⅔ cup light corn syrup
6 ounces bourbon	1½ cups bourbon
½ cup powdered sugar	1 cup powdered sugar
1 teaspoon instant coffee	2 teaspoons instant coffee

Chop raisins and pecans fine, using food processor with a metal blade or blender for raisins and nut chopper for pecans. Crush vanilla wafers. Combine the first seven ingredients, adding the larger amount of corn syrup if wafers are very dry. Mix well and let mixture set for 45

minutes. Then, with hands, shape into 1-inch balls, and roll in mixture of powdered sugar and instant coffee.

CHINESE NESTS

These luscious cookies can be made any time you have 5 minutes to spare. It's a good recipe for children to use, since even a 6 or 7-year-old can make these cookies with a little supervision.

SINGLE RECIPE
Yield: 4 dozen

One 3-ounce can chow-mein noodles
One 6-ounce package chocolate
  morsels

One 6-ounce package butterscotch
  morsels

DOUBLE RECIPE
Yield: 8 dozen

Two 3-ounce cans chow-mein
  noodles
One 12-ounce package chocolate
  morsels
Two 6-ounce packages butterscotch
  morsels

TRIPLE RECIPE
Yield: 12 dozen

Three 3-ounce cans chow-mein
  noodles
One 12-ounce plus one 6-ounce
  package chocolate morsels
Three 6-ounce packages butterscotch
  morsels

 Over very low heat or in a double boiler melt chocolate and butterscotch, stirring frequently. It's best to remove the mixture from the heat before all the chocolate has melted and stir until the mixture is smooth. Add noodles and stir until all are covered with chocolate mixture. Drop from end of teaspoon onto sheets of waxed paper. Let stand until hard.

VARIATION. Add 1 cup salted peanuts to a single recipe.

PEANUT BUTTER COOKIES

These are popular with young and old alike. A large batch can be whipped up in no time, which is especially appealing when a church group or the PTA asks you to bake something and you don't have a minute to spare.

SINGLE RECIPE
Yield: Approximately 30

½ cup sugar
½ cup light corn syrup

1 cup peanut butter
2 cups corn flakes or Rice Krispies

DOUBLE RECIPE
Yield: Approximately 60

1 cup sugar
1 cup light corn syrup
2 cups peanut butter
4 cups corn flakes or Rice Krispies

TRIPLE RECIPE
Yield: Approximately 90

1½ cups sugar
1½ cups light corn syrup
3 cups peanut butter
6 cups corn flakes or Rice Krispies

Put sugar and corn syrup in a saucepan on low heat; stir until dissolved. (If you are making a triple batch, use a very large pan.) Remove from heat and stir in peanut butter; mix well. Then add corn flakes or Rice Krispies and mix thoroughly again. Drop from end of teaspoon onto waxed paper and let cool.

EASY CHOCOLATE FUDGE

Sometimes a few confections are a nice addition to a tray of assorted cookies. Here's a very simple, never-fail recipe for chocolate fudge. This fudge also makes handsome gifts, especially at holiday time. For gifts, pour fudge into small aluminum pans and wrap with plastic wrap. For family eating and nibbling, simply make a large quantity and freeze any you don't intend to use immediately. It stays fresh in your freezer.

SINGLE RECIPE
Preparation Time: 30 minutes
Yield: One 9 x 9-inch pan of fudge

3 cups sugar
¼ teaspoon salt
3 squares unsweetened chocolate
1 cup milk
2 tablespoons light corn syrup

4 tablespoons butter or margarine
1 teaspoon vanilla extract
1 cup coarsely chopped walnuts or
  pecans

DOUBLE RECIPE
Preparation Time: 40 minutes
Yield: Two 9 x 9-inch pans of
  fudge

6 cups sugar
½ teaspoon salt
6 squares unsweetened chocolate
2 cups milk
¼ cup light corn syrup
¼ pound butter or margarine
2 teaspoons vanilla extract
2 cups coarsely chopped walnuts or
  pecans

TRIPLE RECIPE
Preparation Time: 50 minutes
Yield: Two 9 x 13 pans or
  equivalent

9 cups sugar
¾ teaspoon salt
9 squares unsweetened chocolate
3 cups milk
¼ cup plus 2 tablespoons light corn
  syrup
1½ sticks (12 ounces) butter or
  margarine
1 tablespoon vanilla extract
3 cups chopped nuts

Lightly butter your pans, either one 8 x 8-inch or one 9 x 9-inch pan per recipe, or several for the large recipes. Combine the first six ingredients in a heavy saucepan (at least a 3-quart size for a single recipe, because the liquid will bubble as it cooks). Cook, stirring, over medium-high heat until the sugar is dissolved. Insert candy thermometer and continue cooking until the syrup reaches 234° F (or until it reaches the soft-ball stage, when a little is dropped in cold water). Stir only occasionally. Remove from heat. Add the butter now, but do not stir. Let cool to 105° F on your candy thermometer (or until the outside of pan feels lukewarm). Add vanilla and, with wooden spoon, beat fudge until it ceases to be glossy. Immediately stir in nuts (or raisins, if desired) and pour into prepared pans. This last step should be done quickly, because the fudge tends to solidify rather quickly. Spread fudge smooth, cover, and refrigerate until firm. With a sharp knife, cut into squares.

You may have heard the old saying that fudge should be made only on a clear day. On a rainy or humid day, the syrup sometimes absorbs moisture from the air. On such damp days, cook the syrup to a temperature 2 degrees higher than usual.

VARIATION. Raisins may be substituted for nuts or a cup of raisins may be added with the nuts for a really fruity fudge.

ENGLISH TOFFEE

This is a confection that is so good and easy to make. Make up in large batches to have on hand for serving and gift giving. Freezer storage is particularly recommended in warm climates or during the warm-weather season.

SINGLE RECIPE
Time: 15 minutes
Yield: One 9 x 13-inch pan or
about 4 dozen pieces

1 cup sugar
1 cup butter
3 tablespoons water
1 cup chocolate morsels
¾ cup finely chopped pecans

DOUBLE RECIPE
Time: 20 minutes
Yield: Two 9 x 13-inch pans or
about 8 dozen pieces

2 cups sugar
2 cups butter
6 tablespoons water
2 cups chocolate morsels
1½ cups finely chopped pecans

Combine sugar, butter, and water in heavy saucepan. Cook over moderately high heat to the hard-crack stage, or 300° F on your candy thermometer. Watch closely and give an occasional stir, particularly toward the end of cooking time, to prevent burning. When liquid reaches 300° F, remove from heat and pour into generously buttered 9 x 13-inch pans. Sprinkle chocolate over hot mixture immediately and spread as soon as the chocolate has melted. Sprinkle with chopped nuts. If you wish, you may score the candy now into 1- or 1½-inch pieces. Let cool. Break into pieces.

Fish and Shellfish

✳✳✳✳✳✳✳✳✳✳✳✳✳✳✳✳✳✳✳✳✳✳✳✳✳✳✳✳

The frozen-seafood industry has come a long way since its infancy. Highly sophisticated cleaning and freezing equipment is carried right on today's modern fishing fleets. This insures the highest degree of quality and freshness possible, as well as a vast assortment of seafood from around the world. Available, too, are prepared fish and seafood dishes, some even with their own sauces. To add variety to your menu, serve fish or shellfish once a week.

Fish is quick and easy to prepare. Unlike meats, fish is best cooked at high temperature, but for short periods of time. Don't overcook or your fish will be dry. If it's flaky, it's done. Remember that in the Orient fish is served raw, so don't worry about undercooking. The recipes in this chapter are simple to prepare, yet tasty enough so that they may be served on any occasion.

BUYING FRESH AND FROZEN SEAFOOD

Fish

Here are a few basic rules to remember when you are buying fish:

Buy only very fresh fish. To tell if a fish is fresh, note the eyes: they should be clear and bulging, never sunken.

Never buy a fish that has an objectionable odor. Fresh fish have a nice clean smell, not a strong fishy odor.

Gills should be reddish-pink; as quality slips, the gills begin to darken. The flesh should be firm, not spongy, and should adhere to the bones. If a fish has been dressed, turn it over and look at the intestinal cavity, which should be pink and have a fresh, clean appearance.

Scales should look fresh and shiny and be free of slime.

The flesh should be firm, not spongy, and should adhere to the bones.

Buy only in the amounts that you can prepare or freeze quickly.

Frozen fish may be water-glazed (see page 182) to protect the fish from dehydration. As long as the glaze remains intact and the fish remains frozen, it will keep well. If the glaze has melted or is chipped, the unprotected fish may turn a cottony white. This is called freezer burn and, even though the fish is still frozen, the exposed flesh is beginning to suffer a cellular breakdown and should be rejected.

Avoid damaged packages. Fish is packed in moisture-vapor-proof materials that prevent dehydration and contamination. If the package is damaged, it could mean quality loss. Also, don't buy packages that are stacked above the freezing line in the store freezer. Take your package from the bottom of the freezer container.

Any fresh cut of fish should have firm flesh which will spring back when gently pressed with your finger.

Whole fish must be scaled and dressed before it is cooked. You will probably lose about 40 percent of the fish weight before it is ready to be cooked. (This includes the intestinal tract, tails, fins, and scales.) It's something that should be considered when figuring the price of fresh fish. Dressed fish, i.e., the heads, tails, fins, and scales have already been removed, has approximately a 20 percent loss with the skin and bones.

FISH FILLETS. There is no waste in this cut of fish, which consists of slices of fish cut away from the backbone and ready to cook.

Shellfish

SHRIMP. Fresh shrimp is called "green" shrimp, meaning raw and in the shells, and can be purchased with or without the heads.

Frozen shrimp are sold according to color and count size. The smaller the size of the shrimp, the less expensive it is per pound. Count size means number of shrimp per pound and should be listed somewhere on the package. If a package says 16 to 20 count size, that means there will be 16 to 20 shrimp per pound.

CRABS AND LOBSTERS. When they are fresh, look for movement of the legs. If there is no movement, they are probably dead; do not buy.

CLAMS AND OYSTERS. They should be alive when bought in the shell. If the shells are closed, the shellfish are alive. If the shell is open, tap it gently and see if the shell closes. If it doesn't, the fish is probably dead and should be rejected.

SHUCKED OYSTERS. Check them for plumpness and to see if they have a natural creamy color, and are in a clear liquid. They should smell fresh.

BREADED SEAFOODS. Check the label of the breaded product. If the label says "regular breading," it contains 50 percent fish. If the label says "lightly breaded," it must contain at least 65 percent fish.

FISH COOKERY

SERVING QUANTITIES

Cut of Fish	Two Servings	Four Servings
Whole	About 1½ pounds	About 3 pounds
Steaks	About 1 pound	About 2 pounds
Fillets	About ¾ pound	About 1½ pounds

Freezing Fresh Fish

Consider yourself fortunate if you happen to have a fisherman in the house or if you live in the coastal areas where fresh fish abound. You'll want to freeze some fish for future meals and here are some pointers. Fresh fish is one of the most perishable foods and must be handled with care and caution. Remember that the warmer the weather, the more quickly fish will spoil.

Fish should be cleaned and scaled immediately. Small fish may be frozen whole; otherwise, remove fins, tail, and head, and, if your fisherman is very clever, he can bone the fish at the same time. Fish should be packed in ice if it will be more than an hour before you can get them into your freezer, especially in warm weather.

WATER-GLAZE METHOD. For longer freezer storage, it's best to freeze fish in a water glaze. Dip cleaned fish in ice water and lay on a sheet of freezer paper; return to the freezer until water is frozen solid. Repeat this procedure several times or until fish is well coated with ice.

Wrapping and Packaging

Freezer-wrap much as you would meat (see page 33), label, date, and return to the freezer. Fish frozen with an ice glaze can generally be kept for 6 months. For shorter storage, simply freezer-wrap cleaned fish, label, date, and freeze.

For easier handling when defrosting fish, separate steaks, fillets, et cetera, with a double thickness of freezer wrap or waxed paper. Fish is best thawed in the refrigerator; it should be at least partially thawed before cooking. The one exception is fish steaks, which may be broiled frozen. Remember to allow more cooking time for frozen or partially frozen fish.

SHELLFISH COOKERY

Freezing Shellfish

Shrimp, oysters, and clams are best frozen raw. They tend to toughen during freezing if frozen after they're cooked. Crab and lobster may be frozen fresh or cooked. Whole lobsters are best cooked and the meat removed from the shell before freezing.

Cooking Shrimp

Shrimp are usually purchased fresh frozen, either in the shell or cleaned and shelled. Most recipes require that these shrimp be cooked before using and *they must be cooked properly or they will toughen.*

To clean fresh frozen shrimp, partially thaw so that you can separate the shrimp, then remove shell with fingers. Shells slip off easily. With a shrimp deveiner, one motion is all that is required to clean the shrimp. If you don't have a shrimp deveiner, you may use a knife and cut a slit down the back of the shrimp, lift up, and remove the little vein. Shrimp may be deveined before or after cooking. However, it's much quicker to devein them before cooking. After cooking, the vein isn't likely to come out in one piece as it does before cooking.

Place deveined and shelled shrimp in rapidly boiling water. (The addition of seafood seasoning to the boiling water enhances the flavor of shrimp. Follow manufacturer's directions for the amount needed.) Turn heat low and simmer gently just until the shrimp turn bright pink—no longer!

If you wish to serve the shrimp in a salad or as a first course, toss cooked shrimp gently with 1 tablespoon of olive oil and any desired seasoning until all the shrimp are very lightly covered. This keeps them moist and tender.

LOBSTER TAILS

Cook lobster tails in boiling, salted water. Allow 2 minutes per ounce if they're frozen and 1 minute if they're fresh or thawed. However, it's best simply to put the frozen lobster into boiling water. Keep heat high until water almost returns to boiling; then lower and simmer until done. Serve with Lemon Hollandaise Sauce.

LEMON HOLLANDAISE SAUCE

This sauce blends well with most fish and shellfish. It can turn a plain meal into an extraordinary one.

Yield: About ½ cup sauce
Time: 5 minutes

4 tablespoons mayonnaise
2 tablespoons lemon juice
3 tablespoons butter

1 egg yolk (see page 47)
Dash or 2 of cayenne pepper
Dash of salt

Over low direct heat, combine mayonnaise, lemon juice, and butter. Stir until shortening is melted and mixture is blended. Add egg yolk immediately, stirring quickly to incorporate yolk into mayonnaise mixture. Continue cooking over low heat until mixture thickens (no more than two minutes). Add seasonings, stir, and serve.

This sauce may be served in small individual dishes for dunking the lobster tail. You may wish to serve a plate of lemon wedges with it, as well as some melted butter to which some lemon juice and a bit of salt has been added.

LOBSTER POINSETTIAS

This makes a very nice luncheon or hot-weather supper. Very easy to prepare.

Yield: 4 servings

2 cups cooked frozen lobster
½ cup diced celery
1 finely snipped green onion
½ cup mayonnaise
2 tablespoons capers

1 tablespoon lemon juice
1 teaspoon salt
½ teaspoon Tabasco sauce
4 large tomatoes

Dice the cooked lobster. Add to celery. In a small bowl combine mayonnaise, capers, lemon juice, salt and Tabasco sauce. Toss ⅔ of this mixture lightly with the diced lobster. Cut tomatoes in sixths, almost but not quite through to the bottom, to form poinsettias. Fill center of each tomato with ¼ of lobster mixture. Place on salad greens and serve with remaining sauce poured over the top. Deviled eggs, ripe and green olives, and potato chips make a nice accompaniment.

CHICKEN POINSETTIAS. Using the recipe above and substituting cooked chicken for the lobster, substitute 1 teaspoon dry mustard for the Tabasco sauce and add one 2-ounce jar of chopped pimentos.

LOBSTER AND SHRIMP CANTONESE

Not exactly what you'd call a budget stretcher, but a little shrimp and lobster go a long way in this recipe.

Time: About 20 minutes
Yield: 6 servings

¼ cup butter
1 clove garlic
¼ pound sliced mushrooms
3 cups chicken broth
3 tablespoons soy sauce
3 teaspoons beef bouillon granules
1 teaspoon sugar
¼ cup cornstarch
¼ cup water

One 6-ounce can drained and sliced water chestnuts
1 cup celery, sliced diagonally
1 cooked and diced lobster tail (12 to 16 ounces)
2 cups peeled and deveined shrimp
One 7-ounce package frozen pea pods
⅓ cup cashew nuts

First prepare your fresh or frozen lobster tails and shrimp. Frozen lobster tails will take longer to cook than the shrimp; so cook them separately in seasoned water. (See pages 183 and 184 for instructions on cooking shrimp and lobster.)

Melt butter in a large skillet and add garlic clove that has been cut into slivers. Sauté garlic over moderate heat (so the butter won't burn) for about 3 minutes; then remove garlic. Add mushrooms and sauté for another 3 minutes. Add chicken broth, soy sauce, bouillon granules, and sugar. Cook until the bouillon granules are completely dissolved. Mix cornstarch with water and add to the chicken-broth-mushroom mixture. Continue cooking and stirring until the liquid begins to thicken and is clear. Lower heat and simmer for 15 minutes or longer.

About 5 minutes before serving, add chestnuts, celery, shrimp, lobster, and frozen pea pods. Bring to a low boil and simmer until vegetables are just crisply tender. Add nuts and simmer for 1 more minute. Remove from heat and serve over hot fluffy rice. More soy sauce may be added to individual servings.

BAKED ALASKA KING CRAB LEGS

A very simple dish that is rarely made at home. No need to eat out to enjoy this delicacy.

Time: 15 minutes
Yield: Approximately 6 servings

6 pounds frozen Alaska King crab legs	2 teaspoons paprika
1 cup melted butter or margarine	3 lemons, cut into wedges

Preheat oven to 375° F. Defrost crab legs thoroughly, then slit them with a sharp knife to expose the meat. Using a pastry brush, generously brush melted butter or margarine in the slits of the crab legs. Arrange crab legs in a baking pan, cover with aluminum foil and bake for 15 minutes. Serve hot with additional melted butter and lemon wedges.

DOTTIE'S SHRIMP MOLD

This shrimp mold is an elegant addition to any buffet or smorgasbord meal. It's especially attractive when made in a fish-shaped mold. For very large groups the recipe can easily be doubled.

Time: 20 minutes
Yield: One 4-cup mold

One 10-ounce can tomato soup	1 cup mayonnaise
Three 3-ounce packages cream cheese, warmed to room temperature	½ cup chopped celery
	½ cup frozen chopped onion
	3 chopped hard-boiled eggs
½ cup cold water	1 pound cleaned, cooked, and cut up
1 package plain gelatin	fresh frozen shrimp

Heat soup to boiling. Add cream cheese and beat until smooth. (This can be done in a few seconds in your blender or food processor with metal blade.) Soak gelatin in water for 5 minutes. Add to soup mixture. Add vegetables, chopped eggs, mayonnaise, and shrimp. Pour shrimp mixture into an oiled 4-cup mold. Refrigerate for several hours before serving.

SHRIMP SUPREME

A delicious casserole that may be made in quantity for future meals, as well as for serving a large crowd. It's so good that it disappears quickly, so be sure you have enough.

SINGLE RECIPE
Time: 15 minutes
Yield: 6 servings

¼ cup butter
1 cup chopped celery
½ cup coarsely chopped green pepper
1 teaspoon minced instant onion
3 tablespoons flour
¾ teaspoon salt
⅛ teaspoon curry powder
2 dashes cayenne
Dash Tabasco sauce
2 teaspoons Worcestershire sauce
1 can (1⅔ cup) evaporated milk
4 cups cooked, cleaned shrimp
¼ cup grated Parmesan cheese

DOUBLE RECIPE
Time: 23 minutes
Yield: 12 servings

½ cup butter
2 cups chopped celery
1 cup coarsely chopped green pepper
2 teaspoons minced instant onion
¼ cup plus 2 tablespoons flour
1½ teaspoons salt
¼ teaspoon curry powder
4 dashes cayenne
2 dashes Tabasco sauce
1 tablespoon plus 1 teaspoon
  Worcestershire sauce
2 cans (1⅔ cup each) evaporated milk
8 cups cooked, cleaned shrimp
½ cup grated Parmesan cheese

Melt butter in saucepan. Sauté celery, green pepper, and onion in butter for about 5 minutes. Add flour, salt, curry powder, cayenne, Worcestershire sauce, and Tabasco, mixing well. Add evaporated milk and cook, stirring constantly, until smooth and thick. Remove from heat and add shrimp. Pour into a buttered 1½-quart casserole. Top with grated Parmesan cheese and bake in a preheated 425° F oven for 20 to 25 minutes. Serve with fluffy buttered rice.

TO FREEZE. If you want to freeze this casserole, it should be made with freshly cooked shrimp. Follow all the above instructions and pour into buttered casserole dish. Freezer-wrap, date, label, and freeze.

TO SERVE WHEN FROZEN. Bake uncovered casserole in a preheated 425° F oven for about 50 minutes, depending on size of casserole, or until dish is nice and bubbly all the way through.

SHRIMP BAKE

Here's another shrimp dish that may be made in quantity for the freezer. A company meal.

SINGLE RECIPE	DOUBLE RECIPE
Time: 15 minutes	*Time: 20 minutes*
Yield: 6 to 8 servings or 2 quarts	*Yield: 14 to 16 servings or 4 quarts*
1 pound fresh mushrooms, sliced	2 pounds fresh mushrooms, sliced
¼ cup butter	½ cup butter
2 cups cooked and deveined shrimp	4 cups cooked and deveined shrimp
2 cups cooked rice	4 cups cooked rice
1 cup chopped green pepper	2 cups chopped green pepper
1 cup chopped frozen onions	2 cups chopped frozen onions
½ cup chopped celery	1 cup chopped celery
One 4-ounce jar chopped pimento	Two 4-ounce jars chopped pimento
1 No. 2 can (2½ cups) tomatoes	2 No. 2 cans (5 cups) tomatoes
1 teaspoon salt	2 teaspoons salt
½ teaspoon chili powder	1 teaspoon chili powder
½ cup mealted butter	1 cup melted butter

Sauté mushrooms in butter until just tender. Combine with shrimp, rice, vegetables, and seasonings. Pour into greased casserole dishes in meal-sized portions. Pour melted butter over the top and bake in preheated 325° F oven for 45 to 50 minutes. Garnish with snipped parsley and sliced olives.

TO FREEZE. If you're going to make this to freeze, use only freshly cooked shrimp, not cooked and frozen shrimp. Combine all the ingredients as in the above instructions. Pour into baking dishes, and pour melted butter over the tops. Freezer-wrap, date, label, and freeze.

TO SERVE WHEN FROZEN. Put uncovered frozen casserole in 325° F oven and bake for 1 hour and 15 to 20 minutes. Casserole should be bubbly all the way through.

SKILLET SHRIMP

Shrimp in a tomato sauce with a touch of garlic, served over rice.

SINGLE RECIPE	DOUBLE RECIPE
Time: 15 minutes	*Time: 20 minutes*
Yield: About 5 servings	*Yield: About 10 servings*
½ cup frozen chopped onions	1 cup frozen chopped onions
2 snipped green onions	4 snipped green onions
3 or 4 pressed cloves garlic	6 or 8 pressed cloves garlic
¼ cup finely chopped celery	½ cup finely chopped celery
½ cup butter	1 cup butter
2 tablespoons flour	¼ cup flour
2½ cups water or fish stock	5 cups water or fish stock
One 10½-ounce can tomato purée	Two 10½-ounce cans tomato purée

2 bay leaves	4 bay leaves
1 tablespoon Worcestershire sauce	2 tablespoons Worcestershire sauce
4 drops Tabasco sauce	8 drops Tabasco sauce
1 teaspoon salt	2 teaspoons salt
½ teaspoon sugar	1 teaspoon sugar
½ teaspoon crushed thyme	1 teaspoon crushed thyme
⅛ teaspoon pepper	¼ teaspoon pepper
3 cups thawed, cleaned raw shrimp	6 cups thawed, cleaned raw shrimp

In a large skillet, sauté onions, green onions, garlic, and celery in butter for about 4 minutes. Add flour and stir until lightly browned, making a smooth paste. Add water and tomato purée, stirring constantly, until sauce is thickened and smooth. Add bay leaves, Worcestershire sauce, Tabasco, and seasonings. Simmer uncovered for about 20 to 25 minutes over low heat, stirring occasionally.

Add shrimp and continue cooking for an additional 15 minutes. Serve over parsleyed rice. Shrimp may be cut into quarters or left whole, whichever you prefer.

FRENCH FRIED SHRIMP

Served with a variety of sauces, this can be made into a very elegant meal.

Batter

1 cup sifted flour	1 teaspoon baking powder
1 egg	1½ teaspoons salt
1 cup milk	
	Cleaned raw shrimp with tails intact

Combine the first 5 ingredients in a small bowl and mix with electric mixer until smooth. Let stand for at least 15 minutes before using. For a thicker coating on the shrimp, add another ¼ cup of flour.

Thaw shrimp enough to separate them. With shrimp deveiner or sharp knife, shell and devein shrimp, leaving tails intact. Rinse under cold water.

Heat oil to 375° F. Hold shrimp by the tail and dip into batter, making sure not to cover tails with batter. Deep fry several at a time until golden brown and crisp. Serve with the sauces given below.

VARIATION. This batter may be used for any kind of fish fillets that you wish to deep fry.

SEAFOOD COCKTAIL SAUCE

This sauce is especially good with shrimp served plain as a first course.

Yield: ⅓ cup

1 tablespoon lemon juice
2 tablespoons catsup
1 tablespoon chili sauce

2 teaspoons hot barbecue sauce
1 teaspoon Worcestershire sauce
¼ teaspoon garlic salt

Use 3 teaspoons of barbecue sauce for a hotter sauce, or use regular barbecue sauce and add Tabasco to taste.

Mix all ingredients well. Serve separately or pour over the shrimp. Lemon wedges may also be served.

SWEET-SOUR SAUCE

This is like the sweet-sour sauce served in the Cantonese restaurants. It's delicious with French Fried Shrimp.

Yield: About ⅔ cup

½ cup apricot preserves
1 tablespoon vinegar

1 tablespoon soy sauce

Combine the above ingredients in a small dish, mixing well. The amount of vinegar might have to be adjusted a bit, depending on how sweet the apricot preserves are. If the preserves are very thick, you may prefer to make the sauce in the blender.

MUSTARD SAUCE

This is a mild and creamy sauce, quick and easy to prepare, and is delicious served with ham and corned beef, as well as French fried shrimp.

Yield: About ½ cup

½ cup mayonnaise
1 teaspoon dry mustard

1 tablespoon prepared mustard
1 teaspoon lemon juice

Mix the above ingredients, adding more lemon juice to thin the sauce, if necessary.

For those who like a *hot* sauce, add 1 to 2 additional teaspoons dry mustard.

PIQUANT TARTAR SAUCE

If you use a blender or food processor, this sauce only takes seconds to make.

Yield: About 3 cups

1 clove garlic	2 hard-cooked eggs
3 green onions	2 cups mayonnaise
¼ cup parsley	3 drops Tabasco sauce
½ teaspoon capers	3 tablespoons lemon juice
1 small dill pickle	

Put all the ingredients in your blender and give it a whirl until they are completely blended. Serve this sauce cold on hot fish. Keep the unused portion in a covered jar in your refrigerator.

LEMON BUTTER SAUCE FOR BAKED FISH

Can be used for whole or filleted fish. The grated lemon rind gives this sauce its unique flavor.

SINGLE RECIPE

¼ cup melted butter or margarine	juice of 1 lemon (3 tablespoons)
1 teaspoon seasoned salt	1 tablespoon chopped onion
grated rind of 1 lemon	1 tablespoon chopped parsley

All the ingredients can be blended in a blender or food processor or mixed by hand. Pour sauce over fish, cover with foil, and bake in 400° F oven for 30 minutes. Remove foil and continue baking for another 10 minutes if fish is not done. Continue basting with sauce.

QUICK TARTAR SAUCE

This is very good served with Crisp Oven-Fried Fish, and can be made in seconds.

Yield: About ⅓ cup

¼ cup mayonnaise	1 tablespoon chili sauce
2 tablespoons relish	½ to 1 teaspoon horse-radish

Simply combine the above ingredients and mix well. Serve.

SOUR CREAM CUCUMBER SAUCE

A nice light sauce for your fish dinners.

Yield: 1½ cups

1 cup commercial sour cream
1 teaspoon dried dill weed
2 teaspoon snipped parsley

½ cup grated cucumber
1 tablespoon anchovy paste
Salt and pepper to taste

Blend together in food processor or blender all the above ingredients. Chill.

MARINATED SEAFOOD IN CREAM SAUCE

Quick and easy, and oh, so good! Use shrimp, crab, or lobster or a combination of all three. Serve as a cold entrée or appetizer.

1½ pounds cooked cleaned shrimp,
  lobster, and/or crab
2 cups mayonnaise
¼ cup lemon juice

1 very large Spanish or Bermuda
  onion
1½ teaspoons sugar
Salt and pepper to taste

Combine all the above ingredients, mixing well. Marinate overnight in refrigerator.

TOPPING FOR BROILED FISH

Mix 2 tablespoons of commerical sour cream to 1 tablespoon of mayonnaise. Add a pinch of curry, dill, snipped parsley, minced onion, or any other herb, and mix well. Or, instead of an herb, add a liberal amount of anchovy paste. About 3 minutes before the fish is done, spread sauce liberally over fish. Return to broiler and continue cooking until done. Serve immediately with lemon wedges.

SCALLOPS IN RAMEKINS

This is a quick and easy way to fix scallops. In smaller portions this will make a lovely fish course if you plan to serve a multicourse dinner. May be prepared early in the day and refrigerated until serving time.

Yield: 6 servings
Time: 17 minutes

1½ pounds thawed scallops
Flour, salt, and pepper
6 tablespoons butter
3 tablespoons flour
1 cup milk
½ cup cream
½ teaspoon salt
½ teaspoon Worcestershire sauce
½ teaspoon lemon juice
1 tablespoon dry sherry
1 egg yolk
1 cup shredded or coarsely grated
   provolone cheese
Butter
Paprika and parsley (optional)

Wash scallops; if they're large, cut in ½- to ¾-inch pieces. Drain on absorbent paper and dredge very lightly with seasoned flour. Melt 4 tablespoons butter in a large skillet; add scallops, a single layer at a time. Sauté scallops very quickly, browning them lightly on all sides. Repeat until all scallops have been browned. Remove from skillet and set aside.

Add remaining butter and blend in the flour. Add the milk and cream a little at a time, stirring constantly until mixture is thick and smooth. Add salt, Worcestershire sauce, lemon juice, and sherry. Beat the egg yolk in a cup with a fork; add a few tablespoons of the hot sauce to the egg yolk, mixing well. Then pour egg mixture into skillet. Stir until completely incorporated in sauce. Add scallops. Turn mixture into individual ramekins or shells, top with cheese, and dot with butter. Bake at 400° F for 15 to 20 minutes or until cheese is golden brown and scallop mixture is bubbling. Garnish with snipped parsley and paprika. Serve immediately. Increase baking time if ramekins are refrigerated.

CRISP OVEN-FRIED FISH

This is much easier, quicker, and less fattening than the old stove-top method. If you're cooking for a large group, such as for a fish fry, you may prepare several pans at once in your oven.

SINGLE RECIPE
  Time: 10 minutes
  Yield: 6 servings
2 pounds thawed fish fillets, steaks, or
  small whole fish
¼ cup milk
1 beaten egg
1 cup cornmeal, crushed corn flakes,
  or crushed potato chips
¼ teaspoon thyme
¼ cup Parmesan cheese (optional)
⅓ cup melted butter
Parsley and lemon

DOUBLE RECIPE
  Time: 15 minutes
  Yield: 12 servings
4 pounds thawed fish fillets, steaks, or
  small whole fish
½ cup milk
2 beaten eggs
2 cups cornmeal, crushed corn flakes,
  or crushed potato chips
½ teaspoon thyme
½ cup Parmesan cheese (optional)
⅔ cup melted butter
Parsley and lemon

Preheat oven to 500° F. Combine milk and egg. Dip fish in milk mixture and then into seasoned crumbs. Let stand for about 15 minutes. Place a single layer of fish in a buttered baking dish. Sprinkle with any remaining crumb mixture and drizzle with melted butter. (Parmesan cheese may be mixed with crumbs or sprinkled on top.) Bake for 12 to 15 minutes, or until fish is tender and flaky. No need to turn fish. Don't overbake or the fish will become dry. Garnish with parsley and lemon wedges. Serve with tartar sauce (page 191).

DEEP FRIED HALIBUT

Halibut is a lean, firm-fleshed fish with a certain delicacy in flavor. It takes well to deep-fat or pan frying. Serve with Sour Cream Cucumber Sauce.

Time: 20 minutes
Yield: 6 servings

2 pounds halibut, frozen and thawed, or fresh	2 eggs
	3 tablespoons water or milk
Salt and pepper	Fine dry bread crumbs

Beat eggs and add water or milk. Sprinkle steaks with salt and pepper and cut into serving-sized pieces. Dip halibut into egg mixture and then into crumbs. Let stand on baking sheet for 15 to 20 minutes to dry coating slightly. This makes the crumb coating stick more firmly to the fish.

Heat vegetable oil in deep-fat fryer to 375° F. Lower halibut steaks in wire basket into hot oil and fry, a few pieces at a time. Remove when golden brown—about 3 to 6 minutes. Drain on absorbent paper and sprinkle with more salt. Keep fish in a 200° F oven until ready to serve. Serve with lemon wedges and Sour Cream Cucumber Sauce (page 192).

SAUTÉED HALIBUT

Halibut steaks may also be sautéed with fine results. Select halibut that is 1 to 1½ inches thick. Dip fish into bread crumbs, following the above instructions. Sauté gently in butter mixed with a little olive oil (page 49), turning only once. It should take no longer than 8 to 10 minutes. Serve with lemon wedges and Sour Cream Cucumber Sauce (page 192).

RED SNAPPER ÉLÉGANT

This recipe may be used with any kind of fish steaks or fillets, fresh or frozen. If you have a batch of fresh fish, you can prepare them in the foil and then freeze. They're then ready to bake.

Time: 10 minutes
Yield: 6 servings

2 pounds fresh or frozen red snapper
  fillets, fish fillets, or fish steaks
1 teaspoon salt
Dash freshly ground pepper
½ cup melted butter
2 tablespoons chopped parsely

1 tablespoon lemon juice
½ teaspoon dry dill weed
6 thin slices onion
1½ cups thinly sliced carrots
One 8-ounce package sliced Swiss
  cheese

Thaw frozen fillets and cut into 6 serving-sized portions. Sprinkle fish on both sides with salt and pepper. Combine butter, parsley, lemon juice, salt, and dill weed. Cut six 12-inch squares of freezer-weight aluminum foil. Grease lightly. Place 1 teaspoon of the parsley butter on half of each square of foil. Place fish in butter. Separate onion slices into rings and place on fish. Top with ¼ cup carrot slices. Pour remaining parsley butter over carrots, dividing evenly among the 6 packages. Top each serving with a cheese slice. Fold foil over cheese and fish (using drugstore wrap; see page 33), sealing securely. Place packages on a baking pan. Bake in a preheated 400° F oven for 35 minutes or until fish flakes easily when tested with a fork and the vegetables are tender.

TO SERVE. Cut around edges of each package and fold the foil back.

TO FREEZE. If you're using fresh fish, follow the above directions except for baking. Freeze foil packages after they have been properly dated and labeled. It's best to put all the foil packages together in a freezer bag so that you won't have trouble finding them later.

TO SERVE WHEN FROZEN. Put frozen foil packages on baking pan and bake in a preheated 400° F oven for 65 to 75 minutes. Open a package and test it after 65 minutes of baking.

HOT SEAFOOD SALAD

This versatile salad may be made with shrimp, crab, or lobster, or a combination of these. Makes a nice quick meal at any time.

Time: 8 minutes
Yield: 5 servings

1 cup diced, thawed and cooked
   shrimp, crab, or lobster
⅓ cup mayonnaise
1 can cream of mushroom soup
1 tablespoon lemon juice
¼ cup sherry (optional)

¼ cup toasted slivered almonds
¼ teaspoon salt
½ cup chopped celery
1 snipped green onion
1 jar (4½ ounces) sliced mushrooms
1 cup cooked rice

Combine mayonnaise, undiluted soup, lemon juice, and sherry and mix thoroughly. Fold in remaining ingredients. Pour into a 1½-quart buttered casserole. Keep refrigerated until 15 minutes before serving. Preheat oven 400° F and bake for 15 minutes or just until the casserole is heated through, leaving the celery and onions crisp.

CURRIED SEAFOOD SALAD

This one may sound weird, but it's really delicious. It may be made with any kind of seafood but, budgetwise, I find the following combination best.

SINGLE RECIPE
   Time: 13 minutes
   Yield: 4 to 5 servings

One 7-ounce can chunk-style tuna
1 cup cut-up cooked shrimp
½ cup chopped celery
¼ cup ripe or stuffed olives, sliced
½ cup mayonnaise
2 tablespoons lemon juice
1 teaspoon curry powder (or more if
   desired)
3 cups cold cooked rice
2 to 3 tablespoons French dressing
½ cup snipped parsley

DOUBLE RECIPE
   Time: 15 minutes
   Yield: 8 to 10 servings

Two 7-ounce cans chunk-style tuna
2 cups cut-up cooked shrimp
1 cup chopped celery
½ cup ripe or stuffed olives, sliced
1 cup mayonnaise
¼ cup lemon juice
2 teaspoons curry powder (or more if
   desired)
6 cups cold cooked rice
4 to 6 tablespoons French dressing
1 cup snipped parsley

Combine tuna and shrimp and refrigerate. Just before serving add celery and olives. Add mayonnaise blended with lemon juice and curry powder. Toss.

In a separate bowl toss rice, French dressing, and parsley. Spoon onto serving platter. Top with tuna-shrimp mixture. Serve

TUNA NOODLE CASSEROLE

A budget stretcher that's really good. Make a double or triple batch for easy future meals.

SINGLE RECIPE
Time: 13 minutes
Yield: 6 servings

6 ounces noodles (about 3½ cups uncooked)
1 can tuna (6½ to 9¼ ounces)
½ cup mayonnaise
1 cup sliced celery
⅓ cup chopped frozen onions
¼ cup diced green pepper
One 4-ounce jar chopped pimentos
1 teaspoon salt
1 can undiluted cream of celery soup
½ cup milk
1 cup shredded or thinly sliced sharp Cheddar cheese (see page 44)
½ cup slivered blanched, toasted almonds

DOUBLE RECIPE
Time: 16 minutes
Yield: 12 servings

12 ounces noodles (about 7 cups uncooked)
2 cans tuna (6½ to 9¼ ounces)
1 cup mayonnaise
2 cups sliced celery
⅔ cup chopped frozen onions
½ cup diced green pepper
Two 4-ounce jars chopped pimentos
2 teaspoons salt
2 cans undiluted cream of celery soup
1 cup milk
2 cups shredded or thinly sliced sharp Cheddar cheese (see page 44)
1 cup slivered blanched, toasted almonds

Cook noodles in boiling salted water until tender; drain. Combine noodles, drained tuna, mayonnaise, vegetables, and salt. In a small saucepan blend soup with milk and heat through. Add cheese and continue cooking, stirring until cheese melts. Add to noodle mixture. Turn into a greased 1½-quart casserole for a single recipe. Top with almonds. Bake in 425° F preheated oven for about 20 minutes. Serve immediately.

TO FREEZE. Freezer-wrap uncooked casserole, date, label, and freeze.

TO SERVE WHEN FROZEN. Bake frozen casserole in a preheated 425° F oven for about 35 minutes or until nice and bubbly. Serve.

Fruits, Fruit Salads, and Desserts

✳✳✳✳✳✳✳✳✳✳✳✳✳✳✳✳✳✳✳✳✳✳✳✳✳✳✳✳✳

PREPARING AND FREEZING FRUITS

APPROXIMATE YIELD OF FROZEN FRUITS FROM FRESH

Fruit	Fresh, as Purchased or Picked	Frozen
Apples	1 bushel (48 pounds)	32 to 40 pints
	1 box (44 pounds)	29 to 35 pints
	1¼ to 1½ pounds	1 pint
Apricots	1 bushel (48 pounds)	60 to 72 pints
	1 crate (22 pounds)	28 to 33 pints
	⅔ to ⁴/₅ pound	1 pint
Berries*	1 crate (24 quarts)	32 to 36 pints
	1⅓ to 1½ pints	1 pint
Blueberries	11 pounds	12 pints
Cantaloupes	1 dozen (28 pounds)	22 pints
	1 to 1¼ pounds	1 pint
Cherries, sweet or sour	1 bushel (56 pounds)	36 to 44 pints
	1¼ to 1½ pounds	1 pint
Cranberries	1 box (25 pounds)	50 pints
	1 peck (8 pounds)	16 pints
	½ pound	1 pint
Currants	2 quarts (3 pounds)	4 pints
	¾ pound	1 pint
Peaches	1 bushel (48 pounds)	32 to 48 pints
	1 lug box (20 pounds)	13 to 20 pints
	1 to 1½ pounds	1 pint
Pears	1 bushel (50 pounds)	40 to 50 pints
	1 western box (46 pounds)	37 to 46 pints
	1 to 1¼ pounds	1 pint

* Includes blackberries, boysenberries, dewberries, elderberries, gooseberries, huckleberries, loganberries, and youngberries.

Fruit	Fresh, as Purchased or Picked	Frozen
Pineapple	5 pounds	4 pints
Plums and prunes	1 bushel (56 pounds)	38 to 56 pints
	1 crate (20 pounds)	13 to 20 pints
	1 to 1½ pounds	1 pint
Raspberries	1 crate (24 pints)	24 pints
	1 pint	1 pint
Rhubarb	15 pounds	15 to 22 pints
	⅔ to 1 pound	1 pint
Strawberries	1 crate (24 quarts)	38 pints
	⅔ quart	1 pint

Most frozen fruit keeps as well without a syrup pack. However, most freezer books and pamphlets still recommend that all fruits be frozen in a sugar syrup. Not only does it take more time to prepare the fruit in this manner, but the defrosted syrup-packed fruit is far less versatile than the dry-packed fruit.

A larger selection of frozen fruit is now available and in the dry pack, which I prefer. These dry-pack frozen fruits can be substituted for fresh in most of your recipes, adjusting the amount of sugar used.

This is not to say that *no* fruit should be packed in syrup; syrup-packed fruit is ideal when one wants to serve plain fruit for breakfast or for a light dessert. When using a syrup pack, make the syrup in advance. Bring water and sugar to a full boil. Chill thoroughly before using. If you're going to add ascorbic-acid crystals to the syrup, add them after the syrup has cooled.

Preparation

Freezing fruit is a very simple procedure. The fruit doesn't need to be blanched, as do vegetables. Fresh fruits should be prepared for freezing as quickly after harvest as possible. They should be fully ripe and at their peak of perfection for the ultimate in taste when defrosted. Always select top-quality fruit of uniform ripeness and free from spoilage, especially when freezing whole or sliced. Slightly bruised or over-ripe fruit is best used in preserves, conserves, jams, jellies, purées, or crushed fruit, to be used in cooking.

Ascorbic acid he'ps prevent browning. Fruits, such as peaches and apricots, brown less readily if ascorbic acid is added to the sugar or syrup with which the fruit is packed for freezing. Ascorbic acid is a vitamin C preparation and is sold under different trade names in all drugstores and some grocery stores, especially during the fruit season. Read the manufacturer's instructions carefully. Crystals of ascorbic acid are easier to use than the tablet form. Insist on the crystals.

When freezing fruit that darkens quickly, work with small quantities at a time. Prepare and freeze one batch before starting the next. Several hands working together make peeling and slicing large amounts of fruit go very quickly. You'll be surprised what a big help even little hands can be.

Packaging

Most fruits are best packaged in rigid freezer containers. However, fruit such as blueberries, rhubarb, and plums that are to be frozen without sugar may be packaged in moisture-vapor-proof freezer bags. Apples freeze well in freezer bags. When packing fruits in bags, press air out of unfilled portion and seal at once.

When packing in rigid containers, make sure that the fruit is packed tightly to avoid air pockets. When you are using a syrup pack, some of the fruit may float to the top. Insert a small piece of crushed waxed or freezer paper before sealing with the lid. This will keep the fruit down in the syrup. Remember to allow sufficient head space in cartons for expansion during freezing. Keep sealing edges clean and free of fruit and syrup. Always package fruit in meal-sized portions. Leftover fruit loses its flavor and spoils quickly. Syrup-packed fruit is at its best when there are still a few ice crystals remaining.

Labeling

Not only is the date important, but also notes about how much sugar was used, the type of fruit (e.g., what kind of apples or from whose tree, et cetera), how much ascorbic acid, type of syrup, and so on. I must confess that at times I have omitted such information only to regret it at a later date. It's also a good idea to keep a record on file, perhaps in your recipe box, listing the quantity of fruit that was frozen, and the month and year. When fruits are in season the following year, you'll know whether to freeze more or less than the previous year. Remember that all properly frozen fruit, stored at 0° F, will keep for twelve months.

Pie Fillings

TO FREEZE. Having a freezer enables you to put together a delicious homemade pie in a matter of minutes. When fresh fruit is in season, make and freeze fruit pie fillings according to your favorite recipes (or see Pies, pages 308 to 329). Prepare these pie fillings in quantity—

triple or quadruple recipes at least. With heavy-duty freezer-weight plastic wrap, line the proper number of pie tins, letting the wrap extend about 5 inches beyond the rim. Divide pie filling among the wrap-lined pans. Fold the wrap over loosely and freeze until firm. Then cover filling tightly, making sure to seal all the edges properly. Remove from pie tin, date, label, and return to the freezer. For long-term storage, it's best to store several of these pie fillings in large freezer bags for extra protection and easy identification.

TO BAKE. Remove filling from plastic wrap. Do not thaw. Place in pastry-lined pie tin (the same size used for freezing filling) and bake at about 425° F for approximately 1 hour, or until pie syrup boils with heavy bubbles. The time may vary, depending on the size of the pie. (See Frozen Pie Crust on page 310.) For a double-crusted pie, add top crust, seal, and flute edge. Cut slits in top crust and bake as directed above.

Try using Instant Clearjel as a thickener for pies that are very juicy, and you'll be amazed how crisp your crust will remain. (See Clearjel on page 70.)

FRUIT JAMS, GLAZES, AND SAUCES

APPLES

When freezing apples, always use a good cooking apple. There are many varieties. I prefer tart green apples or winesaps.

Although apples may be frozen in a syrup, I prefer to freeze them dry, sprinkled with ascorbic acid or ascorbic acid and sugar. They may be used just as you would use fresh apples, allowing for the sugar if you've used any in freezing. Wash, peel, and core; cut medium apples into twelfths and larger apples into sixteenths. Because apples tend to darken, work quickly and in small quantities (see Apple Peeler, page 15).

1. For 2 quarts of apples, peeled, quartered, cored, and sliced, sprinkle with 2 teaspoons of ascorbic acid crystals. Shake well to assure even distribution of ascorbic acid. Put into freezer bags, date, label, and freeze immediately.

2. For 2 quarts of apples, peeled, quartered, cored, and sliced, sprinkle with ½ cup of sugar that has been well mixed with 2 teaspoons of ascorbic acid crystals. Put into freezer bags and shake well to assure even distribution of sugar mixture. Don't forget to date and label before freezing.

3. For those of you who prefer a syrup pack, use 1 cup of sugar to 1¼ cups of water. Bring to a boil or heat, making sure that all the sugar is completely dissolved. Cool before adding to apples. A teaspoon of ascorbic acid crystals may be added after syrup has cooled.

See Apple Panlets, page 132; Apple Filling for Quick and Easy Strudel, page 247; Apple Topping for Sour Cream Pancakes, page 203.

APPLESAUCE

Wash apples, cut into quarters, and core. Simmer with a bit of water until soft in a covered pan or kettle. Put apples through your food mill or sieve. Leaving the peelings on not only saves time, but adds a lot of flavor to the sauce. Add sugar to taste; cinnamon and spices are best added just before serving, since they tend to get stronger with time. Pour sauce into freezing containers, leaving sufficient head room, and cool before freezing, making sure to date and label.

SHERRIED APPLES

These are especially good served with any kind of pork or duck. If you can't buy frozen apples in your local store, you'll just have to put up your own and then enjoy this regal repast all winter long.

*Time: Just a little watching now
and then*
*Yield: 4 servings, if you aren't
greedy*

1 quart frozen apples (cored, peeled, and cut into eighths or sixteenths, depending on size of apples)

3 tablespoons butter
2 tablespoons sugar
¼ cup sherry

The trick in cooking Sherried Apples is cooking frozen apples over a high temperature quickly. If apples are cooked at a lower temperature, a large quantity of juices will collect in the bottom of the pan and instead of sautéing the apples, you will end up with applesauce. Take frozen apples directly from freezer and put into skillet, separating the apples into sections if you can. Over high heat, sauté apples and turn them from time to time until they are completely separated and defrosted. Lower heat and continue sautéing until apples seem tender. Don't overcook. Sprinkle with sugar and add wine just before serving; continue cooking over fairly high heat until the sugar and wine make a syruplike glaze over the apples. Serve immediately.

APPLE TOPPING FOR PANCAKES, OMELETS, CREPES, BLINTZES

Made with frozen or fresh apples, this sauce is a tasty topping that can be served all year round if you put some sliced apples in the freezer during the fall season. Remember, frozen apples are almost impossible to buy on the commercial market.

Yield: 2½ cups topping

1 pint frozen apple slices   ¼ teaspoon cinnamon
⅓ cup butter   Dash nutmeg
⅓ cup sugar

Cook partially thawed apple slices in butter for 10 to 15 minutes. (If you use fresh apples, peel, core, and cut into 8 or 12 pieces, depending on the size of apples.) Combine sugar with cinnamon and nutmeg; add to apples and cook over low heat for 5 minutes or until the apples are crisply tender. Remove from heat and serve. This topping may also be served at room temperature. See Sour Cream Pancakes, page 126, and Spicy Meringue Shells, page 240.

APPLE SLICES

Especially good for serving a crowd or you may want to make a large batch, cut it into individual portions, and freeze in family-sized quantities.

SINGLE RECIPE
Yield: One 13 x 9-inch pan
(approximately 24 pieces)

Crust:
2 cups flour
½ teaspoon salt
½ teaspoon baking powder
¾ cup lard
1 teaspoon lemon juice
2 beaten egg yolks
½ cup water

DOUBLE RECIPE
Yield: One 12 x 18-inch pan
(approximately 48 pieces)

Crust:
4 cups flour
1 teaspoon salt
1 teaspoon baking powder
1½ cups lard
2 teaspoons lemon juice
4 beaten egg yolks
1 cup water

Sift together flour, salt, and baking powder. Cut in the lard with a pastry blender or your hands, mixing until crumbly. Add mixture of lemon juice, egg yolks, and water by sprinkling it over the flour mixture. Blend in lightly. Divide pastry into 2 parts and roll to fit the pan.

SINGLE RECIPE
Filling:
5 to 6 peeled, cored, and sliced tart
  cooking apples (approximately 5 to
  6 cups sliced, frozen apples)
1 cup sugar
2 tablespoons flour or 1 tablespoon
  flour plus 1 tablespoon Clearjel (see
  page 70)
½ teaspoon cinnamon
1 cup confectioners sugar
2 tablespoons butter
½ teaspoon vanilla
2 tablespoons milk

DOUBLE RECIPE
Filling:
10 to 12 peeled, cored, and sliced tart
  cooking apples (approximately 3
  quarts sliced, frozen apples)
2 cups sugar
4 tablespoons flour or 2 tablespoons
  flour plus 2 tablespoons Clearjel
  (see page 70)
1 teaspoon cinnamon
2 cups confectioners sugar
4 tablespoons butter
1 teaspoon vanilla
4 tablespoons milk

Preheat oven to 400° F. Arrange sliced apples in crust-lined pan;
then sprinkle apples with mixture of sugar, flour and/or Clearjel, and
cinnamon. Roll remaining dough to fit top of pan. Arrange over filling
and seal edges. Cut steam vents in top crust and bake at 400° F for 30 to
40 minutes. While still warm, frost top with mixture of remaining
ingredients.

TO FREEZE. When made with Clearjel, these apple slices may be
frozen before or after baking, whichever you prefer. Freezer-wrap the
entire pan, uncooked, label, and date. Or, if you want to bake first,
slice into serving-sized pieces and then wrap in meal-sized portions.

TO SERVE WHEN FROZEN. Baked apple slices are simply thawed
and served. Unbaked apple slices may be baked in a preheated 400° F
oven for 45 to 50 minutes, or until apples seem tender and the crust is
golden brown. The nice part about having the unbaked apple slices in
the freezer is that they can be put into the oven just before you want to
serve them. They're very good served slightly warm.

APPLE CRISP

Served warm with ice cream, whipped cream, or plain cream, this
makes an elegant dessert.

Time: 10 minutes
Yield: 6 generous servings

6 cups sliced and cored apples, either
  fresh or frozen

1 tablespoon sugar
1 cup crushed wheat flakes

2 tablespoons lemon juice (if apples have been frozen with ascorbic acid, use only 1 tablespoon lemon juice.)
½ teaspoon cinnamon
¼ teaspoon nutmeg
½ to ⅔ cup brown sugar, depending on taste
½ cup flour
5 tablespoons cold butter or margarine

Arrange sliced apples in a buttered 8 x 8 or 9 x 9-inch baking dish. Sprinkle with lemon juice. Combine nutmeg, cinnamon, and 1 tablespoon of sugar, mixing well. Sprinkle over the apples and then toss to cover the apples evenly with cinnamon and nutmeg mixture.

Combine crushed cereal, brown sugar, and flour, mixing well. Cut in butter with a pastry blender or knives. Sprinkle evenly on top of apples and bake in a preheated 375° F oven for 30 to 35 minutes, or until nicely browned and bubbly.

APRICOTS

Although I love apricots, they're such a delicacy in most parts of the country that I have never purchased them in sufficient quantities to freeze. I remember, during my childhood in California, spending weeks (I'm sure it just seemed that long!) washing, pitting, and packing apricots for the cold-water pack my mother used in canning. Preserving fruit was really a chore in the days before freezers.

Apricots are usually frozen in syrup. However, I chanced upon a recipe for a semidry pack, and here it is:

Wash, halve, and pit apricots.

1. Dissolve ¼ teaspoon of ascorbic acid in ¼ cup cold water and pour over 1 quart of prepared apricots. Add ½ cup of sugar, mixing well but gently. Pack in freezer cartons leaving ½ inch of head space. Label, date, and freeze.

2. Prepare apricots and cover with a syrup made of 1 cup of sugar to 1¼ cups water. Heat syrup until all the sugar is dissolved; then cool. Add ½ teaspoon ascorbic acid, mixing well before pouring over apricots.

Frozen apricots may be used interchangeably with peaches (see pages 150, 213–214).

BANANAS

Ripe mashed bananas may be frozen and used at a later date for cooking in such things as banana breads and cakes, waffles, pancakes, et cetera (see pages 41, 124, and 125). This is a particularly good and economical way of using bananas that are getting overripe. Mash and add ¼ teaspoon of ascorbic acid to every cup of mashed bananas. Freeze in quantities called for in your recipes.

CHOCOLATE-COVERED BANANAS

A neat treat to have in the freezer. Make when bananas are on sale.

SINGLE RECIPE
Yield: 6 servings

6 small ripe, but firm, bananas   ½ cup chopped nuts
1 cup chocolate chips

Melt chocolate chips in a shallow skillet over low heat. Pour chocolate into a tall, narrow glass. Dip freshly peeled bananas into melted chocolate. Roll in finely chopped nuts. Lay on a cookie sheet that has been covered with waxed paper. Freeze for several hours or until frozen solid. Then freezer-wrap and return to freezer. To be eaten while still frozen. You may wish to insert wooden skewers into the bottom end of bananas before serving.

VARIATION.   ¾ cup peanut butter
            ½ cup butterscotch chips
            2 tablespoons butter or margarine
            2 cups of your favorite cereal, crushed, or coconut

Follow the above instructions. Combine peanut butter, butterscotch pieces, and margarine in saucepan on low heat, stirring frequently. Cool slightly, dip fresh bananas into above mixture, and roll in the crushed cereal or coconut.

FROZEN BANANA SPLIT

A really super dessert to have on hand in your freezer. Make ahead when bananas are on sale.

SINGLE RECIPE
Yield: 24 servings

½ gallon Neapolitan ice cream   ½ cup chopped nuts (pecans,
1 cup graham cracker crumbs   walnuts, or mixed)
5 ounces butter or margarine, melted   1 cup chocolate chips
4 ripe, but firm, bananas   ½ cup butter or margarine

2 cups powdered sugar
1½ cups evaporated milk

1 teaspoon vanilla
1 pint whipping cream

This recipe fits nicely into an 11 x 15-inch pan; however, this is not a standard size pan, and if you do not have a baking or broiling pan that equals approximately 165 square inches, you can make this up in two 8 x 8 or 9 x 9-inch pans or one 9 x 13-inch pan. If using a 9 x 13-inch pan, by the time you put the chocolate sauce on, it will be filled to the very brim. Handle it carefully until frozen. Freeze the whipping cream as per instructions and wrap carefully. Or you may want to add the whipping cream at serving time or slice the ice cream a bit thinner.

Remove Neapolitan ice cream from freezer to soften. Put graham cracker crumbs in the bottom of pan. Add melted shortening. Mix well and press evenly in the bottom of the pan. Slice bananas crosswise to cover graham cracker crust, about ½ inch thick. Slice ice cream into ½-inch slices until all of the bananas are covered. Sprinkle with nuts and freeze until firm. Meanwhile, melt chocolate chips in butter or margarine. Add sugar and evaporated milk. Cook, stirring constantly, until thick and smooth. Remove from heat. Add vanilla and cool. (If mixture is not sufficiently cool, it will melt your ice cream.) When mixture is cool, pour over ice cream layer and freeze until firm. Whip cream and spread on top. Return to freezer. When frozen solid, wrap with a layer of plastic wrap and then with heavy-duty foil.

TO SERVE WHEN FROZEN. Let dish stand out at room temperature for about one hour to soften; this will enable you to slice it into serving-sized portions more readily. Naturally, if it is a 90-degree day and you do not have air-conditioning, 15 or 20 minutes would probably be sufficient.

BERRIES
(BLACKBERRIES, DEWBERRIES, BOYSENBERRIES, LOGANBERRIES, RASPBERRIES AND YOUNGBERRIES)

Wash thoroughly, removing all sand and soil. Remove stems and leaves. Sort out all bruised or overripe berries. Drain well.

1. For each quart of berries, add ¾ cup sugar. Toss berries gently until all the sugar is dissolved. Pack into freezer containers, leaving ½ inch of head space. Seal, date, label, and freeze.

2. For a syrup pack, prepare berries as directed above. Pack into freezer cartons and cover with a syrup made with 1 cup of sugar to 1¼ cups water. Seal, date, label, and freeze.

BLUEBERRIES

Although blueberries may be frozen with a syrup pack, my preference is freezing them plain. This allows you to shake them out of the freezer container in the desired quantity and use them just as you would fresh blueberries.

Wash, stem, and sort blueberries. Drain well.

1. Pour prepared blueberries into freezer containers. Seal, date, label, and freeze. This method makes blueberries one of the easiest fruits to freeze. A whole case of blueberries may be frozen in less than an hour, which will give you a supply that will last all winter long.

2. For a syrup pack, prepare blueberries as directed above. Pack into freezer cartons and cover with a syrup made with 1 cup of sugar to 1¼ cups of water. Seal, date, label, and freeze.

For additional recipes using blueberries, see Blueberry Muffins (page 130), Blueberry Pancakes (page 124), and Winter Fruit Salad (page 220).

BERRY SYRUP (BLUEBERRY, STRAWBERRY, BOYSENBERRY, BLACKBERRY, AND RASPBERRY)

If you live where blueberries are abundant—as I do, in Illinois—try making blueberry syrup. It's delicious served over hot buttered pancakes, waffles, puddings, ice cream, plain cakes, et cetera. This syrup bears no relation to commercial berry syrups that are made mainly with artificial flavorings.

Wash berries and put into a large pot or kettle. For every pint of berries, add 1 tablespoon of lemon juice. Crush fruit with a potato masher and bring to a boil, stirring constantly. Lower heat, and continue cooking for just a minute or two until berries become soft. Don't overcook or you'll lose that fresh-fruit flavor.

Pour cooked berries into a jelly bag and let juice drain. When cool enough to handle, squeeze bag, extracting all the juice. Throw out pulp. Measure juice and add an equal amount of sugar. Bring to a boil, being careful to watch, since it will easily boil over and make an awful mess to clean up. Cool syrup slightly and pour into freezing cartons, leaving ½ inch of head space. Seal, date, label, and freeze.

TO SERVE WHEN FROZEN. Because of the high sugar content, the syrup will remain semiliquid in its frozen state. So, when you're ready to use it, simply pour out the amount you need and return the remainder to the freezer. You may let the syrup warm to room temperature or you may wish to warm it, depending on how you plan to use it. Over pancakes and waffles, the syrup is good heated.

BLUEBERRY CREAM CHEESE TORTE

This elegant and tasty dessert can be made the year round with frozen blueberries from your freezer. Made in a spring-form pan, it's transformed into a regal dessert fit for any occasion. A double batch takes only 10 extra minutes; so why make only one?

SINGLE RECIPE
Yield: One 9x9-inch pan or one 9-inch round spring-form torte

1⅓ cups fine vanilla wafer crumbs
¼ cup sugar
⅓ cup melted butter or margarine
One 8-ounce package cream cheese
½ cup sugar
2 eggs
1 teaspoon vanilla

DOUBLE RECIPE
Yield: Two 9 x 9-inch pans or two 9-inch round spring-form tortes

2⅔ cups fine vanilla wafer crumbs
½ cup sugar
⅔ cup melted butter or margarine
Two 8-ounce packages cream cheese
1 cup sugar
4 eggs
2 teaspoons vanilla

Preheat oven to 350° F. Warm cheese to room temperature. Combine vanilla wafer crumbs, sugar, and melted butter or margarine. Press firmly onto sides and bottom of pan. Cream the cream cheese (warmed to room temperature); add sugar gradually and cream well. Add eggs one at a time and beat well after each addition. Add vanilla. Pour into crumb-lined pan. Bake at 350° F for 25 to 30 minutes, or until knife inserted in center comes out clean. Bake in center of oven so that the vanilla-wafer crust will not scorch. Cool completely. Then spoon blueberry topping over the cheese layer.

BLUEBERRY TOPPING

SINGLE RECIPE
1 pint frozen or fresh blueberries
¼ cup sugar
¼ cup cornstarch
2 tablespoons lemon juice
1⅔ cups boiling water
Drop of blue food coloring

DOUBLE RECIPE
2 pints frozen or fresh blueberries
½ cup sugar
½ cup cornstarch
4 tablespoons lemon juice
3⅓ cups boiling water
2 drops of blue food coloring

Combine sugar and cornstarch, add lemon juice, and stir until all the cornstarch is dissolved. Slowly add boiling water, stirring constantly. Cook until thick and clear, continuing to stir. Add blueberries and bring mixture to a boil. Stir very gently in order not to break the berries. Boil hard for 2 minutes. To give juice more color, add a drop or two of food coloring for a nice dark syrup. Cool. While still slightly warm, pour over cheese layer. Chill or freeze as desired. A few swirls of whipped cream may be added as decoration.

BLUEBERRY FILLING

Here's a simple recipe that takes only minutes to make, even in large quantities. When blueberries are in season, you may want to make up a batch to put in your freezer. Besides using it as a pie filling, you can use it to fill the strudel on page 246, the little tarts on page 244, and even to top the cream cheese torte on page 209. You'll find many uses for this versatile filling.

SINGLE RECIPE

3 cups (1 pint) blueberries	2 tablespoons quick-cooking tapioca
½ cup water	1½ tablespoons cornstarch
¾ cup sugar	1 tablespoon lemon juice

DOUBLE RECIPE	QUADRUPLE RECIPE
6 cups (2 pints) blueberries	12 cups (4 pints) blueberries
1 cup water	2 cups water
1½ cups sugar	3 cups sugar
¼ cup quick-cooking tapioca	½ cup quick-cooking tapioca
3 tablespoons cornstarch	6 tablespoons cornstarch
2 tablespoons lemon juice	4 tablespoons lemon juice

You may use either frozen or fresh blueberries. If frozen, thaw berries until most of ice has disappeared. Drain off juice, measure, and add water to make the amount called for in recipe. Stir into a mixture of sugar, tapioca, and cornstarch in saucepan. Heat rapidly until thickening is complete. Boiling is not necessary. Set aside to cool. Then add lemon juice and blueberries. Pour filling into pie pan lined with pastry. Add top crust, seal, and flute rim. Cut slits in top crust. Bake in 425° F oven for 30 minutes or until nicely browned. For a browner crust, bake on lowest shelf. If you use commercially frozen blueberries in syrup pack, they should not be sugared.

BLUEBERRY SAUCE

This simple yet delicious sauce can be made from frozen as well as fresh blueberries. It's a very versatile sauce that can be served over ice cream, pancakes, crepes, pound cake, and shortcake, just to give you a few ideas. It takes only 5 minutes to make and may be stored in the refrigerator for several days.

1 pint frozen or fresh blueberries	1 tablespoon water
¼ cup sugar	Grated rind from 1 lemon
1 tablespoon fresh lemon juice	1 tablespoon kirsch

If berries are fresh, wash and drain thoroughly. Combine sugar, lemon juice, and water in a saucepan; add the berries and bring to a full boil. Stir gently and watch closely. Boil for 2 minutes and remove from heat. Add lemon rind. Let sauce cool and then add the kirsch.

CHERRIES

SOUR CHERRIES. Unfortunately, sour cherries are available only if you live in "cherry country" or if you happen to have a cherry tree in your yard. These fresh frozen cherries are definitely superior in flavor to the canned variety for pies and other desserts.

Select bright-red, tree-ripened cherries. Stem, sort, and wash them thoroughly. Then pit them, making sure to catch any of the juice that might drip while you're doing this. You may want to make pie filling from some of them.

Measure cherries, and for every quart add ¾ cup of sugar. Toss gently so that the sugar will dissolve. Pack into freezer containers, seal, date, label, and freeze.

SWEET CHERRIES. These may be prepared in the same manner as the sour cherries, or you may prefer to freeze them in a syrup pack, depending on how you wish to use them later. Sweet cherries are apt to be expensive; I suggest freezing them in small freezer containers and using them combined with other fruit.

1. Measure cherries and for every quart add ¾ cup of sugar. Toss gently so that the sugar will dissolve. Pack into freezer containers, seal, date, label, and freeze. Work quickly to avoid any color changes. Dark-red varieties are best.

2. For syrup pack, pack cherries into freezer containers and cover with a sugar syrup made with 1 cup of sugar to 1¼ cups of water.

CRANBERRIES

If you like fresh cranberries, there's no reason why you shouldn't enjoy them year round. Cranberries must be repacked in your own freezer bags to eliminate shrivelling. (See page 36.) Wash and discard any that might be spoiled, drain well, and then blot on a towel. Pour into bags, seal, label, date, and freeze. If time is short, you may simply repack and freeze them, but remember to wash and sort them when you take them from the freezer. Do *not* thaw. Berries are easier to chop and grind while still frozen. When running several pounds of frozen cranberries through an automatic food chopper, the mechanism may freeze up and lock. Simply wait a few minutes and it will warm up again. (Also see Cranberry Apple Pie, page 322.)

WHOLE CRANBERRY SAUCE

Yield: Approximately 1 quart

4 cups (1 pound) fresh or frozen
  cranberries

2 cups sugar
1 cup to 1½ cups water

Combine cranberries, sugar, and water in saucepan. The amount of water you use depends on how thick you like your cranberry sauce. Heat to boiling, stirring until sugar dissolves. Boil rapidly until berries pop open—about 5 to 10 minutes.

CRANBERRY-ORANGE RELISH

Yield: Approximately 4½ cups

This can be made fresh and kept frozen, or it can be made from frozen cranberries. However, when making it from fresh cranberries to serve immediately, I freeze the berries for a short period—several hours or overnight; freezing the berries makes the relish deep red in color.

4 cups (1 pound) fresh or frozen
  cranberries

1 large or 2 small oranges
2 cups sugar

Wash and cut oranges into quarters or eighths, removing seeds. Wash and drain cranberries. Put both the oranges (skin and all) and the cranberries through a food chopper. Add sugar, stir well, and serve. Keeps well for several days in the refrigerator.

MELONS (CANTALOUPE, HONEYDEW, WATERMELON)

Before freezing melons of any kind, make sure that they're fully ripe and at the peak of their flavor for best flavor after thawing. Cut in half and remove the seeds. Ball, slice, or cube, whichever you prefer. For slicing and cubing, it's faster if you also peel the melons first. Pack into freezer cartons and cover with a syrup made with 1 cup of sugar to 2 cups of water. Leave ½ inch of head room, seal, label, date, and freeze.

Remember, when thawing melons, serve them before they thaw completely. For best results they should be soft but just icy when served.

PEACHES

Peaches frozen with only sugar and ascorbic acid on them may be used just as you would use freshly peeled peaches. Thaw, and use them in any of your favorite peach recipes—pies, cobblers, and so on. If, when thawed, you find that there's a bit too much juice, simply dissolve a teaspoon (or more, if needed) of Instant Clearjel in the juice for instant thickening (see Clearjel, page 70.)

Use only firm, ripe fruit. Peel and slice enough for one carton at a time, covering with sugar and ascorbic acid mixture or syrup immediately to prevent discoloring. Dip peaches into boiling water for easier peeling.

1. For every 3 cups of peaches, add ½ cup of sugar that has been well mixed with 1 teaspoon ascorbic acid crystals. Toss fruit gently until all the sugar has been dissolved. Pack into cartons, leaving head room. Seal, date, label, and freeze.

2. For a syrup pack, use 1 cup of sugar to 1¼ cups of water, adding ⅛ teaspoon of ascorbic acid crystals after it has cooled. Pour over packed and sliced peaches, leaving ½ inch of head space. Seal, date, label, and freeze. See Peach Upside-Down Cake, page 150; Winter Fruit Salad, page 220; Fruit-Filled Tartlets, page 245.

JIFFY PEACH COBBLER

This is one of the quickest and easiest desserts to prepare. It tastes better the second day, which is an advantage when you're entertaining and want to cook ahead of time.

Time: 5 minutes
Yield: One 8 x 8-inch cobbler

2½ cups thawed frozen peaches	⅛ teaspoon nutmeg
¼ cup sugar	1 tablespoon lemon juice
1 tablespoon plus 2 teaspoons Clearjel (see page 70)	One 9-ounce package jiffy cake mix
¼ teaspoon cinnamon	¼ pound melted butter
	¼ cup chopped nuts (optional)

Preheat oven to 325° F. Combine sugar, Clearjel, cinnamon, and nutmeg. Stir into thawed peaches. Add lemon juice. Pour into a well-buttered 8 x 8-inch pan. Sprinkle yellow cake mix over the top and then drizzle with melted butter. Add nuts, if you wish. Bake for one hour at 325° F. Cool slightly before serving. This is quite rich and small portions are in order. Very good served with ice cream.

VARIATION. Use 1 can of frozen cherries (20 ounces). Increase sugar to ½ cup and substitute almond and vanilla flavorings for the cinnamon and nutmeg. Food coloring is optional.

PEACHY TREAT

This dessert is put together in an unusual way, with rather unusual results. Try it; I think you'll like it.

Time: 5 minutes
Yield: One 8 x 8-inch pan, or 6 to
8 servings

1½ pints thawed frozen peaches	1 egg
1 cup sugar	1 cup sweet milk
1 cup biscuit mix	¼ pound butter
½ teaspoon cinnamon	

Preheat oven to 350°F. To thaw peaches quickly, you may put them in a pan and warm over moderate heat until all the ice has disappeared. Drain and reserve juice. In mixing bowl combine sugar, biscuit mix, cinnamon, egg, and milk into a thin batter. Put butter into an 8 × 8-inch baking dish and put in heated oven until butter is melted. Pour the batter slowly into the melted butter. Do not stir. Place the drained peaches on top of the batter. Bake in a 350° F oven for 35 minutes. Serve warm with ice cream or whipped-cream topping. See page 162. Heat reserved peach juice, add a bit of sugar, and bring to a boil. Spoon peach syrup over the top of dessert.

PLUMS AND PRUNES

The easiest way to freeze plums and prunes is whole, unsweetened, simply washed and pitted. If they're very large, you may prefer to quarter them. Pack them into freezer bags or cartons, seal, date, label, and freeze. That's all! Be sure to buy freestone plums. Not only will they save you time in pitting, but they also make a more attractive fruit.

For those of you who want a syrup pack, use the following:

Make syrup with 1 cup of sugar to 1¼ cups of water. Wash, pit, and pack plums or prunes into freezer cartons and pour syrup over fruit. Seal, date, label, and freeze.

See Plum Pie, page 326, and Plum Cake, page 153.

PLUM BREAD PUDDING

Time: 10 minutes
Yield: About 8 servings

3 cups thawed frozen Italian plums	½ teaspoon cinnamon
2¼ cups milk	1 tablespoon lemon juice
2½ cups bread, cut into 1-inch cubes	Pinch nutmeg
2 tablespoons butter or margarine	¼ to ½ cup sweet port (optional)
3 eggs	1 tablespoon lemon juice
1 cup sugar	Dash salt

If you wish to omit the wine, add another ¼ cup of milk to the milk mixture, making the total amount 2½ cups.

Preheat oven to 350° F. Grease a 9 x 13-inch baking pan. Drain juice from thawed plums. Heat milk until a film forms on top; then toss in bread cubes and butter and let stand while you combine the remaining ingredients.

Put eggs, sugar, spices, lemon juice, wine, and fruit juice all in a blender or food processor and give them a twirl for a second. (If you don't have a blender or food processor, beat slightly with beater or mixer.) Combine with milk and bread mixture, mixing well. Pour into buttered baking dish and add plums, stirring to distribute the plums evenly. Bake about 60 minutes. Pudding should be semifirm when removed from the oven, but it will solidify as it cools.

RASPBERRY SAUCE

This sauce has many uses: mixed with ice cream to make a lovely parfait, for fruit-filled tarts (see page 245), as a topping for pudding and pudding-filled pies. Just let your imagination run wild and you'll think of another dozen uses.

One 10-ounce package defrosted
   frozen raspberries
2 tablespoons sugar

2 tablespoons cornstarch
1 tablespoon lemon juice

Drain thawed raspberries. Combine sugar and cornstarch in a saucepan; add raspberry juice and lemon juice and cook over moderate heat, stirring constantly. Bring to a boil and continue cooking for another minute or two. Fold in drained raspberries. Chill.

RHUBARB

Simply wash tender young rhubarb. Cut off leaves and trim root ends; then cut into 1-inch pieces and drain thoroughly. Do not peel. Pack into freezer bags or cartons and seal, date, label, and freeze. Shake out the amount you wish to use, as needed.

STEWED RHUBARB

As with applesauce, rhubarb may be cooked according to your favorite recipe or the one given below. Pour into meal-sized freezing cartons, seal, label, date, and freeze. Wash rhubarb; cut off leaves and trim root ends. Do not peel. Cut into 1-inch pieces.

Yield: 3 cups

4 cups (about 2 pounds) cut rhubarb
½ to 1 cup sugar, depending on type
   of rhubarb and on how sweet you
   like it
½ cup water

End slice of 1 lemon
½ cup white raisins (optional)
Few drops red food coloring, if
   necessary

Combine all the ingredients and bring to a boil. Lower heat and simmer, covered, for 10 minutes, or until tender, not mushy. Stir occasionally. Remove from heat and let stand covered until cool. Serve with cream or plain.

BAKED RHUBARB

Baked rhubarb is simple to make, and is preferred by many.

Yield: 2½ cups

4 cups cut up rhubarb   ½ to 1 cup sugar
2 tablespoons water

Preheat oven to 375° F. In a greased 1½-quart casserole or baking dish, combine the above ingredients. Bake, covered, at 375° F for 30 to 40 minutes or until tender, stirring once.

RHUBARB CRISP

With frozen rhubarb in your freezer, you may serve this delicious dessert all year long. The oatmeal gives it a nutlike flavor.

Yield: 6 servings

4 cups (about 2 pounds fresh) 1-inch   ½ cup brown sugar, packed
    sliced rhubarb   ½ cup quick-cooking rolled oats
½ to ⅔ cup sugar, depending on taste   ½ cup sifted flour
Grated rind 1 lemon   ⅓ cup cold butter or margarine
Dash salt

Combine rhubarb, sugar, lemon rind, and salt. Place in the bottom of a greased 8 x 8-inch baking dish. Combine brown sugar, rolled oats, and flour. Cut in the butter until crumbly. Sprinkle mixture evenly over rhubarb. Bake in a preheated 350° F oven for about 40 minutes or until rhubarb is tender and the top is browned. Serve warm with cream or ice cream.

STRAWBERRIES

Pick only fully ripened strawberries and process for freezing immediately. Wash and hull as quickly after picking as possible. Leave whole or slice, whichever you prefer. For every 5 cups of strawberries, add 1 cup of sugar and toss gently to cover all the strawberries. Pack in freezing cartons, leaving ½ inch of head space. Seal, date, label, and freeze immediately.

WHOLE STRAWBERRIES. Save the prettiest and largest strawberries to freeze whole. They make lovely garnishes for various desserts all year round. If you can get them with stems and leaves intact, all the better. Wash very gently and drain well. Line a large jelly-roll pan or tray with absorbent paper and let the berries dry further on this. Then pack very gently into freezer cartons, unsugared. Seal, date, label, and freeze.

TO SERVE WHEN FROZEN. Use as you would fresh strawberries, but don't let them thaw entirely. They should still have a few ice crystals in them when used.

STRAWBERRY SAUCE OR GLAZE

This sauce or glaze may be used as a frosting over an angel food cake, spooned over sponge or pound cake, or cheesecake, as well as over ice cream.

SINGLE RECIPE
Time: 7 minutes
Yield: 2½ cups
One 16-ounce package thawed frozen
  strawberries
¼ cup sugar
2 tablespoons cornstarch
¼ cup lemon juice
¼ cup orange juice
Grated rind of 1 lemon
Grated rind of ½ orange
1 tablespoon butter
1 to 2 tablespoons Cointreau (optional)

DOUBLE RECIPE
Time: 9 minutes
Yield: 5 cups, or sufficient to glaze
  a large angel food cake
Two 16-ounce packages thawed
  frozen strawberries
½ cup sugar
4 tablespoons cornstarch
½ cup lemon juice
½ cup orange juice
Grated rind of 2 lemons
Grated rind of 1 orange
2 tablespoons butter
2 to 4 tablespoons Cointreau
  (optional)

Drain juice from thawed strawberries and reserve. Mix sugar and cornstarch together thoroughly in saucepan. Stir in orange, lemon, and strawberry juices; cook, stirring constantly, until quite thick and clear. Remove from heat. Add lemon and orange rind, butter, Cointreau, and drained strawberries. Chill.

BETSY'S FROZEN THINGS

These marvelous "things" may be served as a light dessert or as a fruit salad. Particularly attractive and easy for a buffet. Don't be surprised at how quickly they disappear.

Yield: 24 individual muffin-sized
  servings
One 6-ounce can frozen orange juice
One 6-ounce can frozen lemonade
One 10-ounce can 7 Up
1 juice can water
½ cup sugar
6 bananas, diced
One 16-ounce can pineapple chunks
  with juice

Mix all the ingredients together and freeze in individual muffin tins. Remove about 20 minutes before serving and serve on lettuce leaves. Serve as many as needed and keep rest of "things" in freezer until needed.

FROZEN FRESH STRAWBERRY JAM

No-cooking freezer jams are simply marvelous. The following method won't result in a sugary type of jam, to which some people object.

SINGLE RECIPE
> *Time: 20 minutes*
> *Yield: About 6 medium-sized*
> *glasses*

2 cups crushed strawberries (about 1 quart whole fresh berries)
4 cups instant or superfine sugar
¾ cup water
1 box Sure-Jell

DOUBLE RECIPE
> *Time: 35 minutes*
> *Yield: About 12 medium-sized*
> *glasses*

4 cups crushed strawberries (about 2 quarts whole fresh berries)
8 cups instant or superfine sugar
1½ cups water
2 boxes Sure-Jell

Crush strawberries in a large bowl. Add sugar and mix well. Let stand for half an hour. Combine water and Sure-Jell. Bring to a boil and boil for 1 minute, stirring constantly. Add to fruit and stir for 3 minutes. Pour into glasses and seal (either with lids or with melted paraffin). Let jam stand for several hours before freezing.

FRUIT SALADS

SOUR CREAM STRAWBERRY SALAD

Frozen strawberries are a delight when fresh strawberries aren't in season. This mold is very attractive to serve all year round. Of course, the recipe may easily be doubled when you are serving a larger group.

> *Time: Less than 10 minutes total*
> *Yield: 6-cup mold*

One 16-ounce package frozen whole strawberries
One 6-ounce package strawberry gelatin

2 cups boiling water
One 8-ounce can crushed pineapple
1 pint commercial sour cream

Pour boiling water over gelatin and stir until dissolved. Add frozen strawberries and let stand, stirring occasionally. When the strawberries are completely thawed, add crushed pineapple and pour half the mixture into the bottom of an oiled 6-cup mold. Set in refrigerator until firm. Now spread sour cream on top of gelatin, followed with the remaining half of gelatin mixture. Return to refrigerator for several hours before serving. (To unmold, see Gelatin Molds, page 49.)

ORANGE SHERBET MOLD

Gelatin molds made with sherbet may be served as a light dessert, as well as a salad or accompaniment to the main course. Use your prettiest mold for this one.

Time: 10 minutes or less
Yield: One 6-cup mold

Two 3-ounce packages orange gelatin
  plus 1 teaspoon unflavored gelatin
1½ cups boiling water
One 11-ounce can drained Mandarin
  oranges

2 cups (1 pint) orange sherbet
1 tablespoon lemon juice
¼ cup Cointreau (optional)

Dissolve gelatin in boiling water. Cool. Meanwhile, drain oranges, reserving syrup. To the syrup, add lemon juice and Cointreau. Stir into gelatin mixture. Stir in orange sherbet just until sherbet melts. Add oranges and turn into an oiled mold. Chill several hours before serving. (To unmold, see Gelatin Molds, page 49.)

WINTER FRUIT SALAD

This is a family favorite for Sunday morning brunch during the winter months, when fresh fruit is at a premium.

1 package thawed frozen strawberries
Several sliced bananas
1 package thawed frozen peaches
  and/or
Fresh oranges, peeled and cut into
  sections

  and/or
Grapefruit segments
  and/or
Frozen blueberries

Whirl the thawed strawberries in the blender for a few seconds. Combine all the other fruit and pour blended strawberries over fruit.

INSTANT GELATIN FRUIT MEDLEY

Yield: 5 cups

May be served as a fruit salad or a dessert. Especially good served during the winter months.

SINGLE RECIPE
1 package lemon or lime gelatin
¾ cups boiling water

DOUBLE RECIPE
2 packages lemon or lime gelatin
1½ cups boiling water

One 8-ounce can crushed pineapple	Two 8-ounce cans crushed pineapple
½ cup frozen blueberrires	1 cup frozen blueberries
1 large sliced banana	2 large sliced bananas
½ cup whole frozen strawberries	1 cup whole frozen strawberries
½ cup commercial sour cream	1 cup commercial sour cream

Dissolve gelatin in ¾ cup boiling water (for single recipe). Stir thoroughly and cool. Crush enough ice to fill a measuring cup. Drain crushed pineapple over the crushed ice and add enough water to make 1 cup. Stir into gelatin mixture until all the ice is melted. Then add sour cream and stir with a wire wisk until all the sour cream is dissolved. Gently add the fruit, folding until completely mixed. Set in the refrigerator and in ½ hour it will be firm. The cold frozen fruit sets the gelatin almost immediately. Unmold and serve. (See Gelatin Molds, page 49.)

FRUIT SALAD DRESSING

This dressing is good served with Instant Gelatin Fruit Medley and also with any fresh fruit. It keeps well in the refrigerator.

| Juice of 1 orange | 1 cup sugar |
| Juice of 1 lemon | 1 egg |

Beat egg well, add sugar, and beat again. Now add juice of lemon and orange and cook in double boiler until thick.

CREAMY FRUIT SALAD DRESSING

Serve with any kind of fruit, either fresh or frozen. Especially good on all kinds of melons.

| ¼ cup commercial sour cream | 1 tablespoon lime juice |
| 2 tablespoons honey | |

Combine all three ingredients and taste. You may have to adjust the amount of honey or lime. It should have a distinctly sweet-sour taste.

FROZEN WALDORF SALAD

I've never been very fond of Waldorf salad, but this one is so good you can even serve it as a dessert.

Time: 20 minutes
Yield: 10 servings (6-cup mold)

One 8-ounce can drained crushed
  pineapple (reserve syrup)
2 slightly beaten eggs
½ cup sugar
¼ cup lemon juice
⅛ teaspoon salt
¼ cup mayonnaise

½ cup chopped dates
1½ cups diced, unpeeled apples
1 cup seedless or seeded grapes
¾ cup diced celery
½ cup coarsely chopped nuts
1 cup miniature marshmallows
1 cup whipping cream

Make sure that the crushed pineapple is well drained. Combine pineapple syrup with eggs, lemon juice, and salt. (You can give this a twirl in the blender, if you wish.) Add sugar and cook in saucepan over moderate heat until slightly thickened, stirring frequently. Remove from heat and cool. Fold in mayonnaise. Meanwhile, combine drained crushed pineapple, apples, celery, grapes, nuts, and marshmallows; toss gently. Whip cream and fold into cooled egg mixture. Pour over fruit and toss lightly. Fill a 6 to 8-cup mold and freeze at least 3 to 4 hours, or until very firm. Unmold on a bed of lettuce, garnishing with additional apple slices and grapes. (Be sure to dip apple slices in lemon juice to prevent discoloration.) Unmold about 30 minutes before serving so that it is partially thawed. Letting it stand longer at room temperature won't hurt it, but serving it frozen solid ruins it.

VARIATION. For Frozen Apple Salad, omit grapes, nuts, and marshmallows and increase apples to 2½ cups.

FROZEN STRAWBERRY-PINEAPPLE MOLD

This delicious mold may be used as a fruited salad, but it's also good served as a light and refreshing dessert.

Time: 15 minutes
Yield: 6-cup mold

One 16-ounce package frozen
  strawberries, thawed and drained
One 8-ounce can drained crushed
  pineapple
3 eggs
¼ cup lemon juice

¼ cup sugar
⅛ teaspoon salt
¼ cup mayonnaise
1 cup miniature marshmallows
1 cup heavy cream, whipped

Combine the juice from the pineapple and strawberries, adding lemon juice, eggs, sugar, and salt. Give it a whirl in the blender, or beat until eggs are well incorporated. Cook in a saucepan over moderate heat until thickened, stirring frequently. Remove from heat. Add marshmallows and cool. Fold in mayonnaise and whipped cream, strawberries and pineapple. Pour into a 6-cup mold and freeze. If marshmallows tend to float to the top of your mold, freeze for ½ hour and stir; then return to freezer until ready to serve.

TO SERVE WHEN FROZEN. When using as a salad, unmold on a bed of lettuce. When served as a dessert, unmold on a dessert platter, using whole frozen strawberries as a garnish. Unmold 30 minutes before serving, so that it will be partially thawed.

FROZEN DESSERTS

Frozen desserts are a natural for any freezer. They're usually put together very quickly and keep well in their frozen state, provided they're properly wrapped. Most frozen desserts are light—the perfect way to end a heavy meal. These cool desserts are especially pleasing in hot weather, not only because they're refreshing, but because their preparation doesn't require heating the oven.

Here again, you're limited only by your imagination. Colorful ice cream parfaits can be put together in lovely serving glasses. Frozen, they'll keep until you retrieve them from your freezer. Of course, you won't want to have all your good crystal filled and in the freezer; so it's best not to make frozen desserts too far in advance.

Except for very short storage, remember that frozen desserts need to be freezer-wrapped. For individual glasses and containers, use Saran Wrap secured with freezer tape.

POPSICLES

Popsicles are a favorite with the "tricycle set" and, as anyone knows who has treated a crowd of moppets when the Popsicle man came along, this can be an expensive treat. But they're easy and inexpensive to make, and many companies sell "kits" especially for this purpose.

If you don't happen to have any cherubs in your household, you can endear yourself as a favorite aunt or grandmother by keeping a supply of Popsicles in your freezer. When made of frozen fruit juices (orange, grape, and pineapple are favorites), they're more healthful than the sugary commercial ones. Also, mothers won't object that it will spoil their dinner.

FRUIT JUICE POPSICLES

Mix a can of frozen fruit juice according to directions on the can. Fill your popsicle molds and freeze. That's all there is to it, and what a welcome treat, especially in warm weather!

PUDDING POPSICLES

Here's another simple-to-make recipe. Prepare a package of pudding and pie filling (either cooked or instant). Fill the molds and freeze. These pudding and pie fillings come in a variety of delicious flavors, so make several kinds to keep on hand.

BRANDIED ICE CREAM

Perfect for the nonbaker or for those occasions when you find out at 5:00 P.M. that you're having unexpected guests for dinner.

SINGLE RECIPE
  Time: 2 minutes
  Yield: 4 servings
1 quart vanilla ice cream
½ cup brandy

DOUBLE RECIPE
  Time: 3 minutes
  Yield: 8 servings
½ gallon vanilla ice cream
1 cup brandy

Mix both ingredients in a blender. If you don't have a blender, soften ice cream just a bit and use your mixer. Pour into your prettiest sherbet glasses. Top with a dash of nutmeg if you wish.

VARIATION. You may wish to use one of the fruit brandies, coffee liqueur, et cetera.

CHERRY CREAM FREEZE

Pink and pretty, yet so easy to make that a child can do it. Has a rich creamy texture.

  Time: 7 minutes
  Yield: 6-cup mold

One 15-ounce can sweetened
  condensed milk
One 1-pound, 5-ounce can cherry pie
  filling

1 teaspoon lemon juice
½ teaspoon almond extract
1 cup heavy cream, whipped

If you added any lemon juice to your cream while whipping (see page 54), subtract from the teaspoon called for in recipe.

Combine all the above ingredients, blending them together until well mixed. Mixture should be a pale pink color; if not, add a drop of red food coloring. Pour into mold or individual serving dishes. Freeze. Let stand at room temperature at least 15 minutes before serving.

CHOCOLATE FREEZE

Although it is light and doesn't seem too rich, a little goes a long way with this light and smooth calorie-laden desert.

Time: 20 minutes
Yield: 12 servings

1 white angel food cake (6 to 8 ounces)	4 separated eggs
12 ounces semisweet chocolate	¼ cup sugar
	2 cups heavy cream, whipped

Line an 8x8-inch or a 9x9-inch pan with waxed paper, Saran Wrap, or foil. The simplest way of doing this is to use 2 sheets at right angles to each other. Cut angel food cake into 1-inch cubes. Melt chocolate in double boiler or over very low heat. Remove from heat before all the chocolate is melted and continue stirring until all the chocolate has been melted. Cool chocolate until it is just warm to the touch, since eggs will set if chocolate is too warm. Beat egg yolks until lemon colored; add cooked chocolate mixture, stirring until blended. Set aside. Beat egg whites until stiff; gradually add sugar and continue beating until very stiff. Fold into chocolate mixture. Whip cream and fold into chocolate mixture. Pour one-fourth of the chocolate mixture into pan and then a layer of one-third of angel food cubes. Alternate until all the ingredients are used, ending with the chocolate mixture. Cover with foil and freeze.

TO SERVE WHEN FROZEN. Remove frozen dessert from freezer and slice with a serrated knife. Serve immediately.

VARIATION. Add 1 cup chopped nuts and 1 teaspoon vanilla.

CHOCO-NUT TORTONI

The perfect way to end a heavy meal. Particularly good with Italian dishes.

SINGLE RECIPE
Preparation Time: 10 minutes
Yield: 8 servings

2 egg whites
4 tablespoons sugar
1 cup heavy cream, whipped
1 teaspoon vanilla extract
½ cup semisweet chocolate pieces
1 teaspoon shortening
½ teaspoon rum flavoring (optional)
¼ cup chopped toasted blanched
    almonds
4 maraschino or candied cherries

DOUBLE RECIPE
Preparation Time: 12 minutes
Yield: 16 servings

4 egg whites
½ cup sugar
2 cups heavy cream, whipped
2 teaspoons vanilla extract
1 cup semisweet chocolate pieces
2 teaspoons shortening
1 teaspoon rum flavoring (optional)
½ cup chopped toasted blanched
    almonds
8 maraschino or candied cherries

Beat egg whites until quite stiff. Gradually add half the sugar and continue beating until very stiff and shiny. In another bowl beat cream. When it is frothy, gradually add the rest of the sugar and vanilla; fold into beaten egg-white mixture. Set in freezer for 2 hours or more until frozen.

To toast almonds, preheat oven or broiler toaster to 350° F. Sprinkle almonds in a single layer and toast until golden brown—about 3 to 5 minutes.

Return bowl of egg whites and whipped cream to mixer and beat mixture until smooth, but not melted. Quickly fold in melted chocolate that has been mixed with shortening. Don't be surprised if the melted chocolate forms into minute particles when combined with the cold cream and egg-white mixture; that's the way it's supposed to be. Add almonds. Turn mixture into paper-lined cupcake tins. Garnish each tortoni with half a cherry. Freeze until firm. These tortonis may be kept in the cupcake tins for protection if you wish; simply cover the tops with polyethylene freezer wrap. Or you may wish to remove the filled cups and put them in another type of protective container.

FROZEN EGGNOG PARFAITS

This is especially good at holiday time, served with a platter of small cookies.

Time: 12 minutes
Yield: About 8 servings

2 cups dairy eggnog
1 cup heavy cream, whipped
¼ teaspoon nutmeg
1½ teaspoons rum extract

⅛ teaspoon salt
¼ cup confectioners sugar
Prepared Nesselrode sauce (optional)

If you have an ice cream freezer, you may wish to pour mixture into it, turning until set. Follow manufacturer's instructions.

Freeze eggnog in ice cube tray (covered with plastic wrap or foil) until crystals form ½ inch from the edge—about half an hour. Meanwhile, whip cream in chilled bowl; add nutmeg, rum extract, and salt. Continue beating until quite stiff. Return to refrigerator until ready to use. When the eggnog is properly chilled, turn into a chilled bowl and beat with mixer until mushy. Gradually add sugar, beating until stiff. Gently fold whipped cream into beaten eggnog until thoroughly mixed. Pour back into ice cube tray and freeze until crystals form ½ inch from edge, or about half an hour. Return to chilled bowl, beating until mushy. You may now return this mixture to the ice cube tray or pour it into individual parfait glasses and freeze. For a creamier mixture you may wish to beat it again after it is partially frozen.

Before serving, let eggnog parfaits stand at room temperature for about 10 minutes. You may garnish each parfait with candied or maraschino cherries. Frozen rosettes of whipped cream sprinkled with nutmeg also make a very attractive garnish.

FROZEN GRASSHOPPERS

This is an easy and light dessert.

SINGLE RECIPE	DOUBLE RECIPE
Time: 10 minutes	*Time: 12 minutes*
Yield: 6 servings	*Yield: 12 servings*
24 large marshmallows	48 large marshmallows
⅔ cup milk	1⅓ cups milk
⅓ cup crème de menthe	⅔ cup crème de menthe
3 tablespoons crème de cacao	¼ cup plus 2 tablespoons crème de cacao
1 cup heavy cream, whipped	2 cups heavy cream, whipped

In top of double boiler, over gently boiling water, place marshmallows and milk. Heat until melted, stirring occasionally. Cool. Stir in crème de menthe and crème de cacao. Chill over ice water until partly thickened. Meanwhile, whip cream and fold into thickened, cooled mixture. Turn into sherbet glasses or into Chocolate Cups (page 243) and freeze.

TO SERVE WHEN FROZEN. Serve as you would ice cream or let thaw partially.

GRASSHOPPER PIE. This makes a good filling for a pie. Use Chocolate Wafer Crust (page 318), 8 or 9-inch size. Freeze and serve either frozen or partially thawed.

FROZEN LEMON DESSERT

Quick and easy, this is a year-round favorite.

SINGLE RECIPE	DOUBLE RECIPE
Time: 20 minutes	*Time: 25 minutes*
Yield: 9 servings	*Yield: 18 servings*
2 separated eggs	4 separated eggs
⅓ cup lemon juice	⅔ cup lemon juice
Grated rind of 1 lemon	Grated rind of 2 lemons
½ cup sugar	1 cup sugar
Dash salt	Pinch salt
1 cup whipping cream	1 pint whipping cream
½ cup graham cracker crumbs	1 cup graham cracker crumbs

Beat egg yolks; add lemon juice and all but 2 tablespoons of sugar (for single recipe). Cook over low heat until thick, stirring constantly. Add lemon rind and salt. Cool. Line an 8 x 8-inch pan (for single recipe) with waxed paper, Saran Wrap, or foil, using 2 sheets at right angles to each other. Beat egg whites until stiff. Add remaining sugar and continue beating until very stiff and glossy. Fold into egg-and-lemon mixture. Whip cream and fold in. Sprinkle half of graham cracker crumbs on bottom of lined pan. Add all the lemon mixture and sprinkle the top with the remaining graham cracker crumbs. Cover dish with foil or Saran Wrap, and freeze.

TO SERVE WHEN FROZEN. Remove from freezer and cut into serving pieces. Place on individual plates and serve immediately.

DINO'S CUP (KAHLUA FUDGE SAUCE)

This grand finale requires no advance preparation. You can prepare it with a flair in front of your guests, using either a flambé pan or chafing dish.

SINGLE RECIPE
Yield: Serves 6 to 8

⅔ cup hot fudge ice cream topping	4 ounces brandy
4 ounces Kahlua or other coffee liqueur	vanilla, chocolate, or coffee ice cream

Combine hot fudge topping with Kahlua and heat until bubbly. Continue stirring for one additional minute. This can be done on your stove or in a microwave oven. Pour brandy into gravy ladle and let it run over the top of Kahlua mixture. Wait for a half minute so that the brandy becomes warmed, then ignite. Let flame burn out or blow it out so that some of the brandy remains. When flame is out, spoon over ice cream and serve.

LEMON ANGEL DESSERT

A lovely way to end a meal. Serves a crowd nicely.

SINGLE RECIPE
> Time: 30 minutes
> Yield: Three 9 x 9-inch pans or
> Two 9 x 13-inch pans

1 cup butter or margarine
1½ cups sugar
1½ teaspoons vanilla
Grated rind of 2 lemons
⅓ cup lemon juice
7 eggs, separated
½ cup sugar
1 cup heavy cream, whipped
one 10-inch white angel food cake
  (see page 143)

DOUBLE RECIPE
> Time: 43 minutes
> Yield: Six 9 x 9-inch pans or
> Four 9 x 13-inch pans

2 cups butter or margarine
3 cups sugar
3 teaspoons vanilla
Grated rind of 4 lemons
⅔ cup lemon juice
14 eggs, separated
1 cup sugar
1 pint heavy cream, whipped
two 10-inch white angel food cakes
  (see page 143)

You will need an 8-quart mixing bowl for the double recipe.

Cream butter until light in color. Add sugar and continue beating until very light and fluffy. Add vanilla, lemon rind, juice, and egg yolks. Beat thoroughly at high speed. In a separate bowl, beat egg whites until foamy; then add remaining amount of sugar. Gently fold egg whites into butter mixture. Whip cream and fold that in also. Line two 9 x 13-inch or three 9 x 9-inch pans (for single recipe) with waxed paper, Saran Wrap, or foil. (The easiest way of doing this is to use 2 sheets at right angles to each other.) Cut angel food cake into 1-inch cubes and distribute on bottom of pans. Add filling and continue alternating until all the ingredients are used. With a knife, cut through mixture to fill all air spaces. Cover with foil and freeze until firm.

TO SERVE WHEN FROZEN. Take frozen dessert from freezer and cut into serving-sized portions.

LEMON ICE CREAM

For that homemade ice cream flavor, try this. Serve with Sunshine Sauce.

SINGLE RECIPE	DOUBLE RECIPE
Time : 7 minutes	*Time: 8 minutes*
Yield: 8 servings	*Yield: 16 servings*
3 eggs	6 eggs
¾ cup sugar	1½ cups sugar
¾ cup light corn syrup	1½ cups light corn syrup
2¼ cups milk	4½ cups milk
1 cup heavy cream, whipped	1 pint heavy cream, whipped
⅓ cup lemon juice	⅔ cup lemon juice
Grated rind of 1 lemon	Grated rind of 2 lemons

Beat eggs until thick and light; add sugar gradually, beating constantly at high speed. Add milk, lemon juice, and grated rind, mixing well. Whip cream and fold into lemon mixture. (If you have an ice cream freezer, you may wish to pour mixture into it and churn till set. Follow manufacturer's directions.) Freeze in aluminum freezing trays until firm. Turn into a chilled bowl and beat until light. Return to freezing trays and freeze until firm. If you plan to keep this for some time before using, put trays in freezer bags.

TO SERVE. Serve as you would any ice cream.

SUNSHINE SAUCE

Time: 11 minutes
Yield: 4 cups

½ cup sugar	2 slightly beaten egg yolks
½ cup undiluted thawed orange juice	1 cup heavy cream, whipped
concentrate	Grated rind of 1 lemon
Pinch salt	Grated rind of ½ orange

Combine sugar, salt, and orange juice concentrate in a small saucepan. Cook over low heat until sugar is dissolved. Add a little of the hot mixture to egg yolks and blend well; then pour back into remaining hot mixture. Cook, stirring, until thickened. Cool to room temperature. Whip cream and fold into cooked mixture. Add lemon and orange peel. Serve as topping for lemon ice cream.

VARIATIONS. This sauce may also be made with lemon or lime concentrate, substituting the grated rind of a lime for the orange. It's also good served over angel food or chiffon cake. Try leftover sauce on fresh fruit salad. Delicious!

LIME TORTE

Picture-pretty, with a refreshing lime flavor.

Time: 15 to 20 minutes
Yield: 10 to 12 servings

1½ cups chocolate wafer crumbs	Juice of 3 limes
3 tablespoons melted butter or margarine	6 egg whites
	2 cups heavy cream, whipped
6 egg yolks	3 tablespoons rum
1 cup sugar	4 to 6 drops green food coloring
Grated rind of 2 limes	Shaved chocolate

Preheat oven to 350° F. Combine chocolate wafer crumbs with melted butter and press on the bottom and sides of a 9-inch spring form. Bake at 350° F for about 8 minutes.

While the crumb crust is baking, combine egg yolks, sugar, grated lime rind, and lime juice in the top of a double boiler. Cook the mixture over hot water, stirring constantly until it's slightly thickened. Set aside to cool.

When cool, fold in beaten egg whites plus whipped cream and rum. Make sure to mix well. Add sufficient food coloring for a nice lime green color. Pour this mixture into baked chocolate wafer crust and freeze. Decorate top with shavings of semisweet or bitter chocolate. For long storage, freezer-wrap, label, date and freeze. Serve frozen. Unmold from spring form and slice.

FROZEN MOCHA TORTE

This makes a very impressive and delicious dessert. It's quite rich, so serve small portions.

SINGLE RECIPE
Time: 20 minutes
Yield: One 8-inch torte

18 crushed cream-filled chocolate cookies	1 tablespoon butter
	⅔ cup evaporated milk
⅓ cup melted butter	1 quart coffee ice cream
2 squares (2 ounces) unsweetened chocolate	1 cup heavy cream
½ cup sugar	¼ cup crème de cacao

DOUBLE RECIPE
Time: 25 minutes
Yield: Two 8-inch tortes or one
    large 10-inch torte

36 crushed cream-filled chocolate
    cookies
⅔ cup melted butter
4 squares (4 ounces) unsweetened
    chocolate
1 cup sugar

2 tablespoons butter
1⅓ cups evaporated milk
2 quarts coffee ice cream
2 cups heavy cream
½ cup crème de cacao

Preheat oven to 350° F. Crush chocolate cookies to fine crumbs (takes only a minute with a blender or food processor). Add melted butter and mix well. Press around the bottom and sides of an 8-inch spring form (for single recipe). Bake in a 350° F oven for 8 to 10 minutes. Cool slightly and then chill in refrigerator or freeze.

Meanwhile, melt unsweetened chocolate and stir in sugar and butter. Slowly add evaporated milk. Continue cooking over very low heat or in top of double boiler, stirring occasionally until thickened. Chill.

Let coffee ice cream stand at room temperature until soft, but not melting. Remove cake form from the refrigerator. Spread softened ice cream on top of cookie crumb crust. Now spread cooled chocolate mixture over top. Whip cream and add crème de cacao. Spoon over surface of torte. You may wish to sprinkle top with shaved chocolate or chocolate shot. Return to freezer until ready to serve.

SHIRL'S MOCHA DESSERT

Another dessert to make ahead and have on hand; quick and easy, too.

SINGLE RECIPE
Time: 13 minutes
Yield: One 9 x 13-inch pan

16 cream-filled chocolate cookies
¼ cup (4 ounces) butter
1 cup milk
2 tablespoons instant coffee
16 large marshmallows
1 cup heavy cream, whipped

DOUBLE RECIPE
Time: 19 minutes
Yield: Three 9 x 9-inch pans or
    two 9 x 13-inch pans

32 creme-filled chocolate cookies
½ cup (8 ounces) butter
2 cups milk
¼ cup instant coffee
32 large marshmallows
2 cups heavy cream, whipped

Preheat oven at 350° F. Crush cookies, add melted butter, and press into bottom of pan, reserving 1 tablespoon to sprinkle on top. Bake at 350° F for 8 minutes. (For a softer crust, do not bake pie shell.) Heat milk to scalding; add coffee and marshmallows. Stir until dissolved. Cool. Whip cream and fold into marshmallow mixture. Pour into crumb-lined pan and freeze.

TO SERVE WHEN FROZEN. Remove from freezer and cut into serving portions. This frozen dessert tastes best if partially thawed.

FROZEN ZABAGLIONE

Zabaglione is a dessert of Italian origin that isn't very well known in this country and deserves more recognition. It's easy to make and a fine way to use egg yolks (see page 47). So, for something truly different, easy, light, and elegant, serve Frozen Zabaglione soon.

SINGLE RECIPE
    Time: 15 minutes
    Yield: 6 servings
6 egg yolks
½ cup sugar
1 cup Marsala wine

DOUBLE RECIPE
    Time: 17 minutes
    Yield: 12 servings
1 dozen egg yolks
1 cup sugar
2 cups Marsala wine

Any white wine that you like may be used; each will give you an entirely different flavor. Cream sherry, Rhine, and May wines are good alternates.

With an electric mixer, beat egg yolks and sugar at high speed until really thick and very light in color. Add wine, mixing well, and pour into the top of a double boiler. Set top of double boiler over boiling water and continue cooking until mixture begins to thicken, beating constantly with a wire whisk or rotary beater. (This should take about 5 minutes for a single recipe and a bit longer for a double recipe.) When the mixture begins to increase in volume, remove from heat and pour into sherbet glasses. Set in freezer until firm. If you wish to store these in the freezer more than a few days, be sure to cover the tops of the glasses with Saran Wrap and seal with freezer tape.

TO SERVE WHEN FROZEN. Serve immediately from the freezer or let stand at room temperature for 10 minutes, whichever you prefer. The glasses will be prettily frosted.

CHEESECAKES AND GOURMET DESSERTS

PINEAPPLE CHEESECAKE

This is a smooth, creamy cheesecake with a layer of pineapple on the bottom.

Time: 15 minutes, if you have your crumbs crushed; a little longer, if you don't.
Yield: About 12 servings

1¼ cups crushed graham crackers or vanilla wafers
⅓ cup butter or margarine
¼ cup sugar
16 ounces well-drained crushed pineapple
1½ 8-ounce packages cream cheese (at room temperature)

¾ cup sugar
2 eggs
1 tablespoon pineapple juice
2 teaspoons vanilla
Topping:
1 pint commercial sour cream
¼ cup sugar
1 teaspoon vanilla

Preheat oven to 375° F. Combine crumbs with sugar and add melted butter. Mix well and spread on bottom and sides of a 9-inch spring form. Spread the drained pineapple evenly on the bottom. Beat cream cheese in electric mixer at high speed, adding about 1 rounded tablespoon of sour cream (reserving the remainder for the topping). When it is nice and creamy, add sugar, beating well; then add eggs one at a time, mixing at moderately high speed until well blended and smooth. Add vanilla and pineapple juice, mixing until well blended. Pour this cheese mixture over the crushed pineapple and bake at 375° F for about 25 minutes or until the cheese filling is firm. Remove from oven and let cool for 10 minutes. Reset oven to 475° F. In the meantime, beat remaining sour cream with ¼ cup of sugar and 1 teaspoon vanilla. Pour this sour cream topping over the baked cheesecake and return to the oven for another 10 minutes. Cool and refrigerate for about 4 to 5 hours before serving.

TO FREEZE. This is a perfect dessert to make in advance and freeze for future use. Freeze in spring form. When cake is frozen solid, remove from form and freezer-wrap, label, date, and return to freezer.

TO SERVE WHEN FROZEN. Allow ample time for thawing. Let cheesecake stand at room temperature for an hour or two and then return to the refrigerator for several hours more before serving. Or set in the refrigerator the night before you wish to serve it.

1-2-3 CREAMY CHEESECAKE (NO-BAKE)

This marvelous cheesecake can be put together from start to finish in less than 10 minutes. There are many variations to this basic recipe, all of them delicious.

Yield: One 9-inch cheesecake

1 cup cornflake crumbs
⅓ cup butter or margarine, melted
3 8-ounce packages cream cheese
1 cup confectioners sugar, sifted
1 package (1 tablespoon) unflavored
　gelatin

¼ cup water
¼ cup brandy or rum, or ½ teaspoon
　rum or brandy flavoring
½ pint (1 cup) whipping cream

You may wish to bake this crust for about 5 minutes at 375° F to give you a less crumbly crust. However, this is not necessary. In the bottom of a 9-inch springform pan, place cornflake crumbs. Pour melted butter or margarine over the crumbs and pat evenly over bottom.

Dissolve gelatin in a small Pyrex or measuring cup in water. Heat over low heat or hot water until gelatin is dissolved. Cream the cream cheese until light and fluffy. Sift in sugar and continue mixing until light and fluffy. Add dissolved gelatin and liquor or flavoring.

In a separate bowl, whip cream and fold into cream cheese mixture. Pour mixture into prepared springform pan. Refrigerate about 1½ to 3 hours before serving.

TO FREEZE. Freeze in springform pan. When completely frozen, unmold and wrap or wrap in pan for extra protection. Thaw in refrigerator.

ORANGE OR LEMON CHEESECAKE. Frozen orange juice or lemonade concentrate, thawed, can be substituted for the water or brandy when dissolving the gelatin. Add an additional ¼ cup frozen concentrate to the cream cheese mixture, making a total of ½ cup.

STRAWBERRY CHEESECAKE. Thaw one 10 or 16-ounce package of frozen strawberries. Use ¼ cup of the juice to dissolve the gelatin. Put remaining strawberries and juice in blender or food processor and blend until smooth. Add to cream cheese mixture, along with gelatin.

CREAMY CHOCOLATE CHEESECAKE. Substitute ¼ cup crème de cacao for liquor. Add 1 teaspoon vanilla to cream cheese mixture, along with an additional ¼ cup crème de cacao (optional). Over very low heat, melt 1½ bars (6 ounces total) of semisweet German chocolate or semisweet morsels. Fold into cream cheese mixture before adding the whipped cream.

ST. PATRICK'S DAY SPECIAL. Add some green food color and some Irish whiskey in place of the brandy. Creme de menthe would be another good flavor to use.

OTHER VARIATIONS. As you can see, the variations are infinite. Make a vanilla cheesecake and top with Blueberry Topping (page 209), Strawberry Glaze (page 218), or a can of cherry or blueberry pie filling. The lemon cheesecake is also terrific topped with Strawberry Glaze.

CREAM PUFFS AND ÉCLAIRS

These puffs are simple to make and can be frozen either filled or unfilled. Fill them with ice cream or whipped cream. Cream-filled, they can be kept frozen for 4 weeks. Filled with ice cream, they will keep for 3 months in the freezer.

SINGLE RECIPE
Time: 10 minutes
Yield: 12 puffs or éclairs

1 cup water	1 cup flour
7 tablespoons butter or margarine	4 eggs
⅛ teaspoon salt	

DOUBLE RECIPE
Time: 12 minutes
Yield: 24 puffs or éclairs

TRIPLE RECIPE
Time: 14 minutes
Yield: 36 puffs or éclairs

2 cups water	3 cups water
14 tablespoons (2 sticks less 2 tablespoons) butter or margarine	21 tablespoons (3 sticks less 3 tablespoons) butter or margarine
¼ teaspoon salt	¼ rounded teaspoon salt
2 cups flour	3 cups flour
8 eggs	1 dozen eggs

Preheat oven to 450° F. Bring water to boil, add butter or margarine, gently boil until dissolved. Add flour all at once. Add salt. Stir vigorously with a wooden spoon until paste gathers and leaves the sides of the pan. Remove from heat and allow to cool slightly. Add eggs one at a time, beating well after each addition until paste is smooth and glossy. (Using an electric mixer or food processor will save time, especially with the large recipes.) Each egg must be completely incorporated before the next one is added. If dough is too soft, chill for 30 minutes.

PUFFS. Butter cookie sheets and drop dough into 12 equal mounds for cream puffs (for a single recipe). Smooth mounds with a wet spatula, making them as tall as possible. Leave ample spaces between each because they really spread. Bake in 450° F oven for 15 minutes; reduce heat to 325° F and bake for 25 minutes longer. For crisper cream puffs, turn oven off after baking. Cut tops off puffs, and return to oven for 15 minutes to dry.

ÉCLAIRS. Using a pastry bag or tube, it's easy to shape éclairs and give them a professional look. Moisten bag or tube before filling with dough. Put dough through a plain round tube that has a ½-inch opening. Pipe dough on a buttered baking sheet in 2½-inch lengths. For baking, follow instructions for cream puffs, making sure that they're a golden brown, dry, and crisp. Make a slit on the side of each éclair, fill, and cover. For crisper éclairs, make slit in side and return to oven (which has been turned off) for 15 minutes. Should your puffs or éclairs become soft (which is very likely in humid weather), just crisp them in the oven for a few minutes.

FILLINGS AND ICINGS FOR CREAM PUFFS AND ÉCLAIRS. The variety is limited only by your imagination. French cream fillings are popular, but they don't freeze well unless made with Clearjel. (The French Cream Fillings on page 323 can be frozen.) Freeze puff shells plain and then fill just before serving. Whipped cream fillings are ideal and can be varied by adding 3 tablespoons of various flavored liqueur to half pint of whipping cream. If you stabilize the whipped cream with gelatin, you won't have to worry about the whipped cream becoming soggy.

Top these luscious desserts with a chocolate icing (page 159), Kahlua sauce (page 239), mocha icing, or coffee icing.

TO FREEZE. Either filled or plain puff shells should be frozen before being wrapped. Set on a cookie sheet until frozen, wrap in moisture-vapor-proof material, and place in a carton. Be sure to label the type of filling, topping, and so on, that you've used.

TO SERVE WHEN FROZEN. Thaw on serving plates or platter at room temperature for about 15 minutes. Filling should be just slightly soft. Longer thawing may result in soggy puffs or éclairs.

VELVETY CREAM CHEESE FILLING

This smooth, rich filling is quick and easy to make, and it freezes well.

SINGLE RECIPE
Preparation Time: 5 minutes
Yield: Filling for 1 dozen puffs

one 8-ounce package cream cheese
1⅓ cups sweetened condensed milk
⅓ cup lemon juice

1 teaspoon lemon rind
1 teaspoon vanilla extract

DOUBLE RECIPE
Preparation Time: 7 minutes
Yield: Filling for 2 dozen puffs

two 8-ounce packages cream cheese
2⅔ cups sweetened condensed milk
⅔ cup lemon juice
2 teaspoons lemon rind
2 teaspoons vanilla extract

TRIPLE RECIPE
Preparation Time: 10 minutes
Yield: Filling for 3 dozen puffs

three 8-ounce packages cream cheese
4 cups sweetened condensed milk
1 cup lemon juice
1 tablespoon lemon rind
1 tablespoon vanilla extract

Soften cream cheese at room temperature and whip until fluffy. Gradually add sweetened condensed milk; continue beating constantly. Add lemon juice, lemon rind, and vanilla. Blend well. Pour into prepared puffs. Glaze and chill until serving time.

JIFFY CHOCOLATE GLAZE

This is a nice light and shiny glaze that is good on anything from doughnuts to pound cake.

SINGLE RECIPE
Time: 10 minutes
Yield: ¾ cup

one 4-ounce package sweet cooking
  chocolate
or
⅔ cup semisweet chocolate morsels

1½ tablespoons butter
3 tablespoons water
1 cup sifted confectioners sugar
Pinch salt
½ teaspoon vanilla

Melt chocolate and butter in water, over moderate heat. Remove from heat. Add salt and stir until combined. Sift sugar into the chocolate mixture, mixing well after each addition. When well blended, add vanilla and mix well. Glaze sets up rapidly, so work quickly.

DREAM CREAM PUFF FILLING

Absolutely heavenly to eat and divinely simple to make.

Yield: Filling for about 8 large
  cream puffs

1 pint heavy cream
½ cup Kahlua

8 large cream puff shells (see page 236)

Beat cream until quite stiff. This is very important; otherwise, your cream will break down and become watery. Or you can stabilize your whipping cream (see page 54). Add Kahlua, 1 tablespoon at a time, whipping slowly. When all the liqueur has been added, chill until ready to serve.

KAHLUA SAUCE

Yield: 1½ cups

1 cup hot fudge sauce   ½ cup Kahlua

Pour fudge sauce into a small skillet or saucepan and warm gently over low heat. Add Kahlua, stirring until mixture is well blended and warm. Remove from heat and set aside until serving time.

TO SERVE. Slice tops off cream puffs, fill with Dream Cream Puff filling, place tops on, and refrigerate until serving time. Just before serving, spoon Kahlua sauce over cream puffs.

MERINGUE SHELLS

Meringue shells freeze very well and they're not so delicate that they need a lot of extra protection when frozen. They can be made in small individual shells or in a large pie-sized shell. A single recipe will make eight 3½-inch individual shells or six 4-inch shells. Whatever you decide, make several while you're at it. It's a fine way to use up any frozen egg whites.

SINGLE RECIPE
Time: 5 minutes to mix
Yield: One 9-inch shell

4 egg whites
1 teaspoon vanilla extract
½ teaspoon cream of tartar
⅛ teaspoon salt
¾ to 1 cup superfine sugar

DOUBLE RECIPE
Time: 5 minutes to mix
Yield: Two 9-inch shells

8 egg whites
2 teaspoons vanilla extract
1 teaspoon cream of tartar
¼ teaspoon salt
1½ to 2 cups superfine sugar

Superfine sugar will cut the beating time 15 to 20 minutes. If you don't have superfine sugar and must use granulated sugar, you'll have to increase the beating time 15 to 20 minutes, or until all the sugar is dissolved. Rub a little meringue mix between your fingers to make sure that the sugar is completely dissolved; otherwise your meringue will "weep."

Preheat oven to 250° F. Have egg whites at room temperature. Put egg whites into mixing bowl; add vanilla, cream of tartar, and salt. Beat at medium speed until egg whites are frothy and about double in volume. Increase speed to highest setting, and add sugar, 1 tablespoon at a time. After all the sugar has been added, beat an additional 2 minutes, or until egg whites are very thick and shiny and peaks are stiff. Meanwhile, line a cookie sheet with brown paper. With a pencil, mark off circles, either 9 inches for a large meringue shell or 3½ to 4 inches for small individual shells. Spoon meringue onto paper-lined circles and with spoon make a well in center. (Or use a pastry bag to form fancy fluted shells.) Bake at 250° F for 1¼ hours; turn off heat and leave in oven for an additional hour. Cool and remove from paper. (They will simply lift off.)

If it's a humid day, be sure to put meringues into the freezer in an air-tight container immediately after removing them from the oven or they will soften. Also, be sure that your utensils, bowl, and beater are clean and dry. The tiniest speck of grease or fat will spoil meringues.

TO SERVE. Fill with ice cream, fruit, or pudding. An elegant-looking dessert is a fruit-topped sundae, served in the meringue shells. For a gourmet touch add Cointreau or May wine to the fruit, marinating it at least 1 hour before serving. To an 10-ounce package of strawberries, for example, add ¼ cup of wine or Cointreau.

TO FREEZE. The meringue shells may be frozen plain or filled with ice cream. If filled when frozen, be sure to thaw them at room temperature 10 minutes before serving. To freeze plain (my preference), put into freezer bags and seal. You can put these bags into a regular cardboard cake or pastry box for a little added protection. If the meringue shells seem a bit soggy or soft when defrosted, simply put them in a low oven for 10 or 15 minutes.

CHOCOLATE MERINGUE SHELLS. Add 1 tablespoon cocoa combined with the cream of tartar.

SPICY MERINGUE SHELLS. Add ½ teaspoon cinnamon and 1 pinch nutmeg. This is good with cinnamon ice cream and may be topped with Apple Topping (page 203).

OTHER VARIATIONS. To a single recipe, add 2 tablespoons flavored gelatin for color and flavor. Decrease sugar by an equal amount.

CHOCOLATE GLAZE

SINGLE RECIPE

2 squares (2 ounces) unsweetened
    chocolate
¼ cup granulated sugar

3 tablespoons water
½ teaspoon lemon extract

DOUBLE RECIPE

4 squares (4 ounces) unsweetened
    chocolate
½ cup granulated sugar
¼ cup plus 2 tablespoons water
1 teaspoon lemon extract

TRIPLE RECIPE

6 squares (6 ounces) unsweetened
    chocolate
¾ cup granulated sugar
½ cup plus 1 tablespoon water
1½ teaspoons lemon extract

Melt chocolate. Combine sugar and water, bring to a full rolling boil, and then remove from heat. Cool. When it is lukewarm, stir into chocolate, blending well. Add lemon extract. Cool—don't chill—stirring often until thick enough to spread. Then spread immediately on tops of filled Cream Puffs. Immediately freeze those that you're not going to serve, and chill the remainder until serving time.

CHOCO-SCOTCH FILLING

This is an interesting filling. Instead of slicing off the tops of the puffs, use a sharp knife and cut a small hole about 1½ inches in diameter. The filling will mound above this hole and make the puffs very attractive.

Time: 12 minutes
Yield: Enough for a single recipe
    of Choco-Scotch Puffs or filling
    for one 9-inch pie

1 cup semisweet chocolate morsels
1 cup butterscotch morsels
¼ cup milk
¼ cup sugar

⅛ teaspoon salt
4 separated eggs
1 teaspoon vanilla

Combine chocolate, butterscotch, milk, sugar, and salt in top of double boiler. Cook over hot water until mixture is blended and smooth. Cool slightly. Add egg yolks one at a time, beating well after each addition. Blend in vanilla. Beat egg whites until stiff. Fold into chocolate mixture, blending thoroughly. Fill puff shells until almost full. Chill or freeze. (For freezing instructions, see page 237). Because this filling has beaten egg whites in it, it is best when frozen less than 3 weeks.) Just before serving, top with swirls of whipped cream. Chocolate shavings may be added as a decorative touch.

TO SERVE WHEN FROZEN. Thaw at room temperature for an hour or for several hours in the refrigerator. Garnish with whipped cream, following instructions above.

CREAM PUFF LOG

This is a very simple but festive dessert. Make one large log of a single recipe of the chocolate puff dough. These logs freeze very well; so make several.

Follow the directions for the Cream Puff dough until you have all the eggs incorporated and the dough chilled. Butter a jelly-roll pan. Place dough in center of pan and form a long roll about 2½ inches wide. With a wet spatula, smooth and shape until you have a nice smooth log down the center of your pan. Bake at 450° F for 15 minutes, 425° F for 15 minutes, and 400° F for 15 minutes. After this time, puncture the log in several places with a sharp knife and let it remain in the oven with heat off and door slightly ajar for about 30 minutes. Remove from oven and allow log to become cold before filling. With serrated knife, cut top off the log lengthwise, leaving top in one long piece. Pour full recipe of filling into log. Place upper part of log on filling. Ice with Chocolate Glaze (see page 241) or Kahlua Sauce (page 239) and chill or freeze until ready to serve.

TO SERVE. Cut into serving portions with a serrated knife, using a sawing motion.

CHOCOLATE CREAM FILLING

SINGLE RECIPE	DOUBLE RECIPE
Preparation Time: 10 minutes	*Preparation Time: 12 minutes*
Yield: 1 log	*Yield: 2 logs*
⅔ cup sugar	1⅓ cups sugar
⅓ cup cocoa	⅔ cup cocoa
2 cups heavy cream	4 cups heavy cream
½ teaspoon rum extract	1 teaspoon rum extract
2 teaspoons plain gelatin	1 package plus 1 teaspoon gelatin
¼ cup very cold water	½ cup very cold water

 Combine gelatin and cold water and let stand until thick. Then remelt over simmering water, being sure that gelatin is completely dissolved. While this is cooling, beat the cream until it's of medium consistency. Add sugar, cocoa, rum extract, and gelatin all at once. Beat only until cream clings to bowl. Pour into log.

CHOCOLATE CUPS

For a truly impressive dessert (and don't we all want to impress people occasionally?) make these easy chocolate cups and fill them with some frozen dessert. My favorite is Frozen Grasshoppers, page 227. Coffee Ice Cream, Frozen Eggnog Parfaits, page 226, and Lemon Ice Cream, page 230, are also very good choices. For a large crowd you may wish to make several varieties.

SINGLE RECIPE
  Time: Less than 10 minutes
  Yield: 5 cups

1 cup chocolate chips   5 paper cupcake or muffin liners

DOUBLE RECIPE   TRIPLE RECIPE
  Time: 15 minutes   *Time: 20 minutes*
  Yield: 10 cups   *Yield: 15 cups*

2 cups chocolate chips   3 cups chocolate chips
10 paper cupcake or muffin liners   15 paper cupcake or muffin liners

Melt chocolate over low heat or in the top of a double boiler. Remove from heat when the chocolate begins to get soft and continue stirring it until all the pieces of chocolate are melted.

Divide the chocolate among the paper muffin liners (set inside muffin tins). Using a narrow rubber spatula (see page 15) or the back of a teaspoon, spread the chocolate on the sides and bottoms as evenly as possible. Make sure that all the crinkled edges are filled and covered with chocolate. Set into the freezer to harden.

After the chocolate cups have hardened, fill them and store in protected container or carton, as they are quite fragile. For long storage, put chocolate cups into freezer bags and seal.

TO SERVE WHEN FROZEN. The morning before you wish to serve them, peel the paper off the chocolate cups and return to the freezer. Serve directly from the freezer or let set at room temperature for 10 to 15 minutes, whichever you prefer.

VARIATIONS. Use half butterscotch and half chocolate chips.

CHOCOLATE GARNISHES

For an added festive touch, make garnishes as follows to top your filled Chocolate Cups: Spread melted chocolate ⅛ inch thick on a sheet of aluminum foil. When it has hardened, cut designs with an aspic cutter. Don't use the miniature aspic cutters, since they're too small and the chocolate is likely to break (see page 44).

TARTLETS

These small tart shells are made of a cookielike dough pressed into place with the fingers. Baked and frozen, they can be filled at a moment's notice with a variety of puddings, pie fillings, and various fruits. An assortment of them makes a most impressive dessert plate. Although preparing them in quantity takes time, you needn't make all of them at one sitting, and it's a sitting-down, fun-type job. It's the perfect job to be doing while you're making a few time-consuming phone calls.

If you don't have tart tins, use small-sized muffin tins. However, put these little fancy tart pans on your list of things to get. They're inexpensive, and the fancy shapes make your dessert platter look very elegant and professional.

SINGLE RECIPE
Yield: *Approximately 3 to 3½ dozen*
1 cup plus 2 tablespoons butter
1 cup sugar
1 egg
1 tablespoon cream
3¼ cups sifted flour
1 teaspoon almond extract

DOUBLE RECIPE
Yield: *Approximately 6 to 7 dozen*
2¼ cups butter
2 cups sugar
2 eggs
2 tablespoons cream
6½ cups sifted flour
2 teaspoons almond extract

Preheat oven to 350° F. Cream butter and sugar. Add egg, creaming and beating well. Add almond extract; add flour, a little at a time. Press dough (about ⅛ to ¼ inch thick) into tart pans and bake until golden brown—about 15 to 20 minutes in a 350° F oven. Cool before unmolding from tart pans. Invert; give the tins a little squeeze and they will pop out. May be frozen filled or unfilled.

LEMON TART FILLING

You'll enjoy this not-too-sweet lemon filling.

Yield: Filling for approximately
25 or more tartlets

½ cup butter or margarine
½ cup sugar (for sweeter tarts add
  another ½ cup sugar)
4 eggs

1 tablespoon Clearjel (see page 70) or
  1 tablespoon flour
⅓ cup lemon juice
Grated rind of one lemon

Cream butter and sugar. Add eggs one at a time, beating until well blended after each addition. Add flour or Clearjel, mixing well; then add lemon juice and grated lemon rind. Fill pastry-lined tart pans or muffin tins almost to the top. They will rise slightly.

Made with Clearjel, these tartlets freeze beautifully. If you don't have Clearjel, you may try making them with flour for the freezer also. I've done this quite successfully.

CREAM-FILLED TARTLETS

Use any of the French Cream Fillings (see page 323). A drop of raspberry jelly on top of plain vanilla cream filling is very attractive.

The next time you whip some cream, make an extra cup of stabilized whipping cream (see page 54) and freeze little flowerettes of the whipped cream. Use these on top of the chocolate or mocha-filled tartlets. They thaw in a matter of minutes and add a glamorous touch.

FRUIT FILLINGS

Canned fruit pie filling may also be used to fill tartlets. An assortment of mincemeat, cherry, and blueberry filling gives a nice variation of color and flavor. Fill the tarts with the pie fillings and freeze, or serve at once, if you wish. The mincemeat filling should be put into unbaked shells and then baked either before or after freezing. A whipped cream flowerette on top of these fruit-filled tartlets enhances the flavor.

Frozen fruit, such as sweet cherries, strawberries, raspberries, and peaches, may also be used. Thaw a 10-ounce package of frozen fruit according to manufacturer's instructions. Drain juice and measure (usually between ⅓ and ½ cup). For every ½ cup of juice or syrup, add 3 teaspoons cornstarch or Clearjel (see page 70) and 1 teaspoon lemon juice. Mix until all the Clearjel or cornstarch is dissolved. Cook over moderate heat until syrup thickens and becomes clear. Lower heat and simmer for a minute or two. The syrup will seem very thick, but it thins when added to the fruit. Pour syrup over drained fruit, mixing well but gently. Cool. Spoon into tart shells. Chill and serve.

BLUEBERRIES. For blueberry filling, use recipe for Blueberry Topping on page 209.

SOUR CHERRIES. When using unsweetened frozen sour cherries (they usually come in a 20-ounce package), add sugar to taste to the liquid and add 1 tablespoon cornstarch or Clearjel (see page 70). Cook until thick; cool. Optional: add 1 teaspoon almond flavoring and or a few drops of food coloring.

OTHER VARIATIONS. Pecan pie filling, almond filling (see page 116), et cetera, are also good choices. When using almond filling, add 2 additional eggs and use brown sugar for color.

QUICK AND EASY STRUDEL

Although the texture is a bit different from that of the old-fashioned genuine strudel dough (which is pulled out into paper-thin sheets as large as a table), it's so close as to be hardly discernible. This recipe is so simple, quick, and easy that I can't imagine going to all the trouble and work that the old-fashioned strudel requires. Included are two different strudel fillings, but cherry or blueberry pie filling, raspberry pastry filling, et cetera, may also be used. When I make a triple batch, I always use three different fillings for variety. The time indicated is for mixing the batter, which is very quick and easy. To roll out and fill 8 strudels (a double recipe) takes less than an hour.

SINGLE RECIPE
Preparation Time: 21 minutes
Yield: 4 strudels

½ pound butter   1 teaspoon salt
½ pint commercial sour cream   2 cups flour

DOUBLE RECIPE   TRIPLE RECIPE
Preparation Time: 40 minutes   *Preparation Time: 58 minutes*
Yield: 8 strudels   *Yield: 12 strudels*

1 pound butter   1½ pounds butter
1 pint commercial sour cream   1½ pints commercial sour cream
2 teaspoons salt   3 teaspoons salt
4 cups flour   6 cups flour

Cream butter and add sour cream. Beat well and sprinkle salt on top; then add flour. When well blended, make a ball of the dough, cover, and refrigerate overnight. Let stand an hour or less at room temperature before rolling out. Cut dough into 4 parts. On a floured board or pastry cloth, roll one part as thin as possible in an oblong shape about the size of a jelly-roll pan, 15 x 18 inches. Place filling on the edge of the longer side and then roll up in jelly-roll fashion, being careful not to break dough. Tuck in sides and gently place on a cookie sheet or other large greased baking pan. Bake at 300° F for 1 hour. Sprinkle with confectioners sugar.

After the strudels are baked, dust with powdered sugar, and cool. Wrap gently in foil and freeze. They slice better still partially frozen.

APRICOT FILLING (enough for 4 strudels):

1 pound jar apricot preserves	1 cup yellow raisins (optional)
2 cups chopped nuts	or
	¾ cup coconut

Mix all ingredients and divide into fourths, using ¼ for each strudel. If you wish, coconut and/or raisins may be omitted.

APPLE FILLING (enough for 4 strudels):

4 cups sliced apples	2 tablespoons sugar (or more,
1 tablespoon lemon juice	depending on apples)
½ cup raisins or currants	½ teaspoon cinnamon
½ cup chopped pecans	⅛ teaspoon nutmeg

Combine all ingredients, mixing well. Use ¼ for each strudel. This is enough filling for a single recipe.

See page 82 for Hot Chicken Liver Strudel.

RICE PUDDING

This seems to be particularly good on a cold winter evening.

SINGLE RECIPE	DOUBLE RECIPE
Time: 10 minutes	*Time: 15 minutes*
Yield: 4 to 5 cups	*Yield: 8 to 10 cups*
3 cups cooked rice (to measure leftover rice, pack down firmly)	6 cups cooked rice (to measure leftover rice, pack down firmly)
2 eggs	4 eggs
1 cup milk	2 cups milk
Grated rind of 1 lemon	Grated rind of 2 lemons
3 tablespoons lemon juice	⅓ cup lemon juice
½ cup sugar (more, if desired)	1 cup sugar (more, if desired)
½ teaspoon vanilla extract	1 teaspoon vanilla extract
½ teaspoon lemon extract (optional)	1 teaspoon lemon extract (optional)
¾ cup raisins (optional)	1½ cups raisins (optional)

When cooking rice for dinner, make a big batch and then use the leftover rice for Rice Pudding, making enough to freeze some of it.

Combine eggs, milk, lemon rind, lemon juice, and sugar; twirl in the blender for a few seconds. (If you don't have a blender, beat eggs, adding milk and other ingredients gradually in mixing bowl.) Combine egg and milk mixture with rice, folding in raisins (if you wish). For single recipe pour into 1½-quart casserole or baking dish (or divide into individual portions in smaller baking dishes). Bake in preheated oven at 350° F for about 45 minutes, less for smaller dishes. Pudding may still seem soft, but it will harden as it cools. Serve either warm or cold.

TO FREEZE. When rice pudding has cooled, freezer-wrap, date, label, and freeze.

TO SERVE WHEN FROZEN. Simply remove from freezer and thaw at room temperature or in the refrigerator.

POPPY SEED BREAD PUDDING

This is an old German recipe that has been handed down in our family. Traditionally, it's served during the holidays, although it's good any time of the year. If you like poppy seed, you'll love this pudding. May be made up in large quantities because it freezes well.

SINGLE RECIPE	DOUBLE RECIPE
Time: 15 minutes	*Time: 20 minutes*
Yield: About 2 quarts	*Yield: 4 quarts*
¾ pound loaf of day-old French bread	1½ pound loaf of day-old French bread
One 12-ounce can prepared poppy seed pastry filling	Two 12-ounce cans prepared poppy seed pastry filling
¾ cup sugar	1½ cups sugar
1 quart milk (4 cups)	2 quarts milk (8 cups)
2 ounces whole sweet almonds	4 ounces whole sweet almonds
Grated rind of 1 lemon	Grated rind of 2 lemons

If bread is quite dry, you will need the full amount of milk; less milk will be required if bread is moist.

Mix poppy seed with sugar and add to milk. Warm over moderate heat until the milk is almost scalded. Add lemon rind. While the poppy seed, sugar, and milk are cooling, break or slice bread into pieces that are no more than 1 inch thick. Cover bottom of serving dish with French bread and pour the milk mixture over it. Repeat layering until all the ingredients are used, topping each layer with a portion of the almonds cut into small slivers. Let the bread pudding cool at room temperature for about an hour and then refrigerate overnight.

TO FREEZE. Allow the bread pudding to cool and stand at room temperature for about 1½ hours before freezing. Freezer-wrap dish, date, label, and freeze.

TO SERVE WHEN FROZEN. Let thaw, covered, at room temperature for an hour or more and then refrigerate until serving time. Pudding should be cold when served.

Meats

✳✳✳✳✳✳✳✳✳✳✳✳✳✳✳✳✳✳✳✳✳✳✳✳✳✳✳✳

BUYING AND FREEZING MEATS

Although freezing has a slight tenderizing effect on meats, it will not change poor quality meat into prime. Whether you buy your meat in large parts of a carcass or small cuts at the local market, always select high quality meat. Choose your butcher with care. Unless you're very knowledgeable about meat (or skilled in butchering), this is very important. Select a butcher you feel confident you can trust. Then tell him what your wishes are and he'll advise you accordingly. Meat is the highest-priced single item in your food budget, so it's worth exercising great care to see that you get the most for your money.

It's very important to buy only meat that has been properly slaughtered under sanitary conditions. Any kind of contamination will greatly reduce the keeping qualities of meat. It's also of the utmost importance that your meat has been properly cooled and aged before freezing it. If you have any doubt about how the meat has been slaughtered and cured, don't hesitate to insist on seeing your butcher's facilities. If he's a first-class butcher, he'll welcome your interest.

Meanwhile, read everything you can find on meat cookery, study meat charts, and become familiar with each cut and the part of the carcass it comes from. Try the cuts that are unfamiliar; each cut has a flavor and texture all its own. Look upon this experimenting as an adventure in cooking and get your family interested in it too. You'll be amazed at some of the treats in store for you; if there are some cuts you don't care for, then cross them off your list or, better yet, try them once more, using a different recipe. Everyone likes variety and, as your knowledge expands, the food you prepare will become more and more interesting.

The clear wrapper that your meat comes wrapped in from most retail meat counters is designed for holding meat in the refrigerator for 2 to 4 days. It is suitable for freezing for a week or two, but any longer than that will result in drying out and general deterioration of your meat, especially in a frost-free freezer. This is not a vapor-proof wrapper; hence, freezer burn will occur. For longer freezer storage, select a moisture-vapor-proof wrapping and wrap it over your package. Be sure to label and date. (See Wrapping and Packaging, page 31.)

The condition called "freezer burn" is caused by dehydration of meat (meaning that there is a loss of moisture). This toughens the muscle fibers and makes them unpalatable. If meat is stored long enough without proper protection your entire cut of meat may be ruined.

Always have your meat cut and wrapped in meal-sized portions. Also, have some larger portions on hand to use when entertaining.

When wrapping several pieces of meat in one package (such as steaks, chops, cutlets), always put a double thickness of paper between the pieces of meat. This will allow frozen pieces to be easily separated without thawing.

Boned meats are easier to serve. They also take up less space in the freezer and packages are more regular in size. You won't have to worry about protecting protruding bones when wrapping your meat for the freezer. If you like, you can have the butcher bone your meat and wrap the bones separately for freezing. Later, at a convenient time, use these bones when making stock for soups, sauces, and gravies.

Resist the temptation to freeze your meat in the butcher's wrap. (I'm not referring to the special freezer-wrapping done by your local freezer locker or wholesale butcher.) Although some of these meats are wrapped attractively, they're not satisfactory for long-term storage. Remove meat from the butcher's wrap and rewrap in your favorite moisture-vapor-proof packaging material.

Local supermarkets usually have some meats on sale each week, often at 20 to 25 percent less than the regular prices. Taking advantage of these sales or "loss leaders," as they are often called, can mean a great saving. However, make sure that the meat you're buying really is "on sale." If a 1-pound T-bone steak, normally priced at $2.59 a pound, is on sale for $1.99, check to be sure that the usual amount of fat and bone is trimmed off. If the butcher trims it very sparingly, the same steak could weight 1¼ pounds and would make the total price $2.49 a pound. This applies to all cuts of meat. Be watchful. With competition as keen as it is today, there are all kinds of tricks to the trade. For instance, top round will usually sell for the same price as round steak or, at the most, 10 cents a pound more. It is more tender and can even be dry roasted. The eye of the round, on the other hand, is quite expensive and not tender at all. This is why it's very important to learn about the different cuts of meat so that you can be a knowledgeable buyer.

RETAIL BEEF CUTS

Cut	Preparation
CHUCK	
Boneless chuck eye roast* Chuck short ribs Blade roast or steak Arm potroast or steak Boneless shoulder potroast or steak Cross rib potroast Beef for stew Ground beef*	Braise, cook in liquid
RIB	
Rib roast Rib steak Rib steak, boneless Rib eye (Delmonico) roast or steak	Roast, broil, panbroil, panfry
SHORT LOIN	
Top loin steak T-bone steak Porterhouse steak Boneless top loin steak Tenderloin (filet mignon) steak or roast	Roast, broil, panbroil, panfry
SIRLOIN	
Pin bone sirloin steak Flat bone sirloin steak Wedge bone sirloin steak Boneless sirloin steak	Broil, panbroil, panfry
ROUND	
Round steak Heel of round Top round steak* Boneless rump roast (rolled) Bottom round roast or steak* Cubed steak* Eye of round* Ground beef*	Braise, cook in liquid
FORE SHANK	
Shank crosscuts Beef for stew (also from other cuts)	Braise, cook in liquid

RETAIL BEEF CUTS, *continued*

Cut	Preparation

BRISKET

Fresh brisket Corned brisket	Braise, cook in liquid

SHORT PLATE

Short ribs Skirt steak rolls* Beef for stew (also from other cuts) Ground beef*	Braise, cook in liquid

FLANK

Ground beef* Flank steak* Flank steak rolls*	Braise, cook in liquid

TIP

Tip steak Tip roast Tip kabobs	Braise, roast, broil, panbroil or panfry

NOTE: This chart approved by and used with permission of the National Live Stock and Meat Board.

* May be roasted (baked), broiled, panbroiled or panfried from high quality beef.

RETAIL VEAL CUTS

Cut	Preparation

SHOULDER

Large and small pieces for stew*	Braise, cook in liquid
Arm steak Blade steak	Braise, panfry
Boneless shoulder roast Arm roast Blade roast	Roast, braise

RIB

Boneless rib chop Rib chop	Braise, panfry
Crown roast Rib roast	Roast

RETAIL VEAL CUTS, *continued*

Cut	Preparation
LOIN	
Top loin chop Loin chop Kidney chop	Braise, panfry
Loin roast	Roast
SIRLOIN	
Cubed steak† Sirloin chop	Braise, panfry
Boneless sirloin roast Sirloin roast	Roast
ROUND (LEG)	
Cutlets Rolled cutlets Round steak	Braise, panfry
Boneless rump roast Rump roast Round roast	Roast, braise
SHANK	
Shank Shank crosscuts	Braise, cook in liquid
BREAST	
Breast Stuffed breast	Roast, braise
Riblets Boneless riblets	Braise, cook in liquid
Stuffed chops	Braise, panfry
VEAL FOR GRINDING OR CUBING*†	
Rolled cube steaks	Braise
Ground veal Patties	Roast (bake), braise, panfry
Mock chicken legs City chicken Choplets	Braise, panfry

NOTE: This chart approved by and used with permission of the
National Live Stock and Meat Board.
* Veal for stew or grinding may be made from any cut.
† Cube steaks may be made from any thick solid piece of boneless
veal.

RETAIL PORK CUTS

Cut	Preparation
BOSTON SHOULDER	
Cubed steak* Pork cubes	Braise, cook in liquid, broil
Blade	Braise, panfry
Smoked shoulder roll	Roast (bake), cook in liquid
Boneless blade Boston roast Blade Boston roast	Braise, roast
CLEAR PLATE/FAT BACK	
Fat back	Panfry, cook in liquid
Lard	Use for pastry, cookies, quick breads, cakes, frying
LOIN	
Blade chop Rib chop Loin chop Sirloin chop Cubed steak* Butterfly chop Top loin chop Sirloin cutlet	Braise, broil, panbroil, panfry
Country-style ribs Back ribs	Roast (bake), braise, cook in liquid
Smoked loin chop Canadian-style bacon	Roast (bake), broil, panbroil, panfry
Boneless top loin roast Boneless top loin roast (double)	Roast
Tenderloin	Roast (bake), braise, panfry
Blade loin Center loin Sirloin	Roast

RETAIL PORK CUTS, *continued*

Cut	*Preparation*
LEG (FRESH OR SMOKED HAM)	
Boneless leg (fresh ham)	Roast
Sliced cooked "boiled" ham	Heat or serve cold
Boneless smoked ham Canned ham	Roast (bake)
Boneless smoked ham slices Center smoked ham slice	Broil, panbroil, panfry
Smoked ham, rump (butt) portion Smoked ham, shank portion	Roast (bake), cook in liquid
JOWL	
Smoked jowl	Cook in liquid, broil, panbroil, panfry
PICNIC SHOULDER	
Fresh arm picnic	Roast
Smoked arm picnic	Roast (bake), cook in liquid
Arm roast	Roast
Ground pork*	Roast (bake), panbroil, panfry
Fresh hock Smoked hock	Braise, cook in liquid
Neck bones	Cook in liquid
Arm steak	Braise, panfry
Link and roll sausage*	Panfry, braise, bake
SPARERIBS/BACON (SIDE PORK)	
Spareribs Salt pork	Bake, broil, panbroil, panfry, cook in liquid
Slab bacon Sliced bacon	Bake, broil, panbroil, panfry

NOTE: This chart approved by and used with permission of the National Live Stock and Meat Board.

* May be made from Boston shoulder, picnic shoulder, loin, or leg.

RETAIL LAMB CUTS

Cut	Preparation
SHOULDER	
Cubes for kabobs*	Broil
Boneless blade chops (Saratoga)	
Arm chop	Broil, panbroil, panfry
Blade chop	
Cushion shoulder	
Boneless shoulder	Roast
Square shoulder	
NECK	
Neck slices	Braise
RIB	
Frenched rib chops	
Rib chops	Broil, panbroil, panfry
Crown roast	
Rib roast	Roast
LOIN	
Loin chops	
Boneless double loin chop	Broil, panbroil, panfry
Boneless double loin roast	
Loin roast	Roast
SIRLOIN	
Sirloin chop	Broil, panbroil, panfry
Boneless sirloin roast	
Sirloin roast	Roast
LEG	
Leg chop (steak)	Broil, panbroil, panfry
Combination leg	
Center leg	
Boneless leg (rolled)	
American-style leg	
Sirloin half of leg	Roast
Shank half of leg	
French-style leg	
French-style leg, sirloin off	

RETAIL LAMB CUTS, *continued*

Cut	Preparation
FORE SHANK	
Fore shank	Braise, cook in liquid
BREAST	
Breast Rolled breast	Roast, braise
Stuffed breast	Roast
Riblets Boneless riblets	Braise, cook in liquid
Spareribs Stuffed chops	Braise, roast (bake), broil, panbroil, panfry
HIND SHANK	
Hind shank	Braise, cook in liquid
GROUND OR CUBED LAMB	
Large and small pieces for stew†	Braise, cook in liquid
Lamb patties† Cubed steak*	Broil, panbroil, panfry
Ground lamb†	Roast (bake)

NOTE: This chart approved by and used with permission of the
National Live Stock and Meat Board.
* Kabobs or cube steaks may be made from any thick solid piece
of boneless lamb.
† Lamb for stew or grinding may be made from any cut.

Freezing Cooked Meats

According to the University of Illinois extension service in Agriculture and Home Economics, "Freezing cooked meat, except in combination dishes where the meat is packed in sauces, gravies, et cetera, is not recommended. Work carried on in the Foods Research Laboratory of the University of Illinois, as well as in other foods laboratories, indicates that higher quality is obtained if uncooked rather than cooked poultry and meats are frozen. Carefully controlled experiments have shown that this is true for deep-fat and oven-fried chicken, braised beef, round steaks, ham patties and loaves, and rib and loin pork roasts. In general, poultry and meat roasted or fried after freezing has a more attractive appearance and better flavor than that cooked before freezing."

Variety Meats

All meats can be frozen; however, variety meats, such as heart, liver, brains, tongue, sweetbreads, et cetera, will not keep so long as other cuts of meat. Two to three months is about the maximum recommended storage period for variety meats.

THAWING FROZEN MEATS

Most meats can be cooked while still frozen; however, it's more difficult to judge the time needed to cook frozen meat. It also uses extra energy. Try to have a roast thawed; then insert your meat thermometer into the heart of the roast, making sure that it isn't touching any bone. This is the most accurate way to time the cooking of your meat, especially if it's in some stage of thawing. (Do not force the meat thermometer into frozen or partially thawed meat; it may break if the roast is still hard-frozen in the center.) Steaks and chops that are broiled while still frozen should be cooked farther away from the source of heat than usual, so that the outside won't burn before the inside is thawed. You'll have to practice to get the knack of broiling frozen meat; however, you can avoid the problem completely by remembering to thaw all meat well in advance of cooking it.

REFRIGERATOR. The American Meat Institute recommends that frozen meat be thawed in the refrigerator. Thawing in the refrigerator requires 3 to 8 hours per pound, depending on the size, shape, and thickness of the meat: for large roasts, 4 to 7 hours per pound; for small roasts, 3 to 5 hours per pound; about 12 hours for a 1-inch steak. Never immerse unwrapped meat in water for thawing, unless it's to be cooked in the water, as for stews. All meat should be cooked as soon as it's completely thawed. Once meat has thawed completely, it should *not* be refrozen, because juices are lost during thawing and because the meat may deteriorate between the time of thawing and refreezing. If meat has partially thawed and still shows ice crystals, refreezing is possible, but not advisable. If refrozen, be sure to use within one week. Meat may be refrozen after cooking.

Freeze the prepared food in family-sized packages or smaller. If your family uses, say, one quart of spaghetti sauce per meal, freeze sauce in pint containers. This will allow you to add some easily, if the children bring a few friends home for dinner. The converse is also true; if some of the family are away, you can still cook from your freezer. Also, the smaller cartons thaw more quickly.

MICROWAVE OVEN. The microwave oven allows you to thaw meat quickly and safely, especially if you have a defrost cycle on your model. Follow manufacturer's instructions. If you don't have a defrost cycle, here is a formula you can use which will eliminate cooking meat before it is completely thawed. Multiply the number of pounds of meat by 1½ minutes and cook for that amount of time. Let meat set an equal number of minutes. Then reduce that amount of time by half and cook that number of minutes, continuing until meat is thawed. For example: a 3-pound roast x 1½ minutes = 4½ minutes. Cook 4½ minutes and let set 4½ minutes. Then $4.5 \div 2 = 2\frac{1}{4}$ minutes. Now cook meat in your microwave oven for 2¼ minutes (2 minutes, 15 seconds) and let rest the same number of minutes. Now you again, divide 2 minutes, 15 seconds in half and cook meat 1 minutes, 8 seconds, then let rest same amount of time. Continue until meat is completely thawed. Naturally, the defrost cycle is much easier and faster; this is just for those of you who do not have a defrost cycle on your microwave oven.

ROOM TEMPERATURE. Thawing at room temperature is faster than in the refrigerator. Keep meat covered and start cooking meat as soon as thawed. Remember, bacteria thrive at room temperature.

Another, quicker way is to seal meat in a plastic bag (to prevent water from seeping onto meat) and set in warm water, changing water frequently. Remove any plastic tray or soft paper from meat, as this tends to insulate it.

OVEN DEFROSTING. Use your oven to defrost meat. Set oven at 150° F. To thaw completely, figure about 1 hour per pound. This is 6 to 7 times faster than in the refrigerator. Rub meat with vegetable oil to keep juices in and meat from drying out.

Preparation

The roasting, simmering, and braising times are not included in the Preparation Time for the meat recipes in this chapter, since during this time you're free to do other things.

Rub a light film of vegetable oil on your frozen meat immediately after removing it from the freezer. This light coat of oil will seal in all the juices while the meat is thawing. You may also wish to season your meat at this time. Rubbing oil on your meat is a good practice whether or not your meat is frozen, as it seals in the juices and makes your meat more succulent.

ROASTING BEEF, LAMB, AND PORK

The chart in this section is only a guide; to roast meat accurately, use a meat thermometer whether you are cooking lamb, pork, or beef. The price of one ruined roast would more than pay for buying a good meat thermometer (see page 16). There are many variables that make timetables an estimate. For instance, the temperature of the meat: Has it completely thawed, is it 40° F, or is it still in the icy stages around 32° F? Has it warmed to room temperature on your kitchen counter? Oven temperatures also are not necessarily uniform. There often is a 25-degree variation on either side of the oven control.

To be absolutely sure that your meat is done to the degree that you wish, use a meat thermometer and insert it in the thickest part of the roast. It should be in the center of the meat and not touching any bone. Turn it so that you can read it easily through your glass oven window or at a quick glance if the oven door must be opened. There will not be too much temperature variation during the first half of the roasting period; however, thereafter the temperature will slowly creep upward. When the reading is between five and seven degrees from the desired temperature, remove the roast from the oven and let it stand for 10 or 15 minutes. The internal temperature will usually rise to the degree that you want, because the internal heat intensifies and causes the meat to continue cooking. Meat also should set for awhile before slicing; this allows the meat to firm up, facilitating carving. Allow 20 to 25 minutes for rare meat, 15 minutes for medium, and 10 minutes for well done.

Pork Cookery

After extensive research, Iowa State University, along with several other universities and in conjunction with the National Livestock and Meat Board, now recommends an internal temperature of 170° F for all fresh pork roasts. The meat should be roasted in a 325° F oven. The results show that pork roast, cooked to a final internal temperature of 170° F, is comparable in flavor and tenderness, higher in juiciness, and has a lower cooking loss than pork roasted to an internal temperature of 185° F. Another advantage is the shorter cooking time required. For fully thawed meat, the roasting time can be shortened as much as 6 to 8 minutes per pound.

Some meat thermometers are marked with these new temperatures; however, some are not. So make a mental note of these temperature changes the next time you're fixing a pork roast. Your pork loin roast may be placed in the oven completely frozen. Don't try to insert the meat thermometer until the meat is completely thawed.

TIMETABLE FOR ROASTING FULLY THAWED MEATS

Cut	Approximate Weight in Pounds	Oven Temperature Constant (F)	Interior Temperature when Removed from Oven (F)	Approximate Cooking Time (Minutes per Pound)
BEEF				
Beef rib roast, large end*	6 to 8	300° to 325°	140° (rare)	23 to 25
			160° (medium)	27 to 30
			170° (well done)	32 to 35
Beef rib roast, small end	4 to 6	300° to 325°	140° (rare)	26 to 32
			160° (medium)	34 to 38
			170° (well done)	40 to 42
Beef rib roast	5 to 7	300° to 325°	140° (rare)	32
			160° (medium)	38
			170° (well done)	48
Beef rib eye roast	4 to 6	350°	140° (rare)	18 to 20
			160° (medium)	20 to 22
			170° (well done)	22 to 24
Beef loin tenderloin roast	4 to 6	425°	140° (rare)	45 to 60 (total time)
Beef loin tenderloin roast	2 to 3	425°	140° (rare)	45 to 50 (total time)
Beef round rump roast, boneless	4 to 6	300° to 325°	150° to 170°	25 to 30
Beef round tip roast	3½ to 4	300° to 325°	150° to 170°	35 to 40
VEAL				
Veal leg round roast	5 to 8	300° to 325°	170°	25 to 35
Veal loin roast	4 to 6	300° to 325°	170°	30 to 35
Veal rib roast	3 to 5	300° to 325°	170°	35 to 40
Veal shoulder roast, boneless	4 to 6	300° to 325°	170°	40 to 45

PORK, FRESH

Loin

	Pounds	Oven Temperature	Internal Temperature	Minutes per Pound
Pork loin center rib roast	3 to 5	325° to 350°	170°	30 to 35
Pork loin sirloin half	5 to 7	325° to 350°	170°	35 to 40
Pork loin blade roast	3 to 4	325° to 350°	170°	40 to 45
Pork shoulder arm picnic	5 to 8	325° to 350°	185°	30 to 35
Pork loin top loin roast, boneless	3 to 5	325° to 350°	185°	40 to 45
Cushion style	3 to 5	325° to 350°	185°	35 to 40
Pork shoulder blade Boston roast	4 to 6	325° to 350°	185°	45 to 50

Leg (fresh ham)

Pork leg, whole	10 to 14	325° to 350°	185°	25 to 30
Pork leg, roast, boneless*	7 to 10	325° to 350°	185°	35 to 40
Pork leg, shank half	5 to 7	325° to 350°	185°	40 to 45

PORK, SMOKED

Ham (cook before eating)

Smoked ham, whole	10 to 14	300° to 325°	160°	18 to 20
Smoked ham rump, half	5 to 7	300° to 325°	160°	22 to 25
Smoked ham, shank portion	3 to 4	300° to 325°	160°	35 to 40

Ham (fully cooked)†

Smoked ham shank half	5 to 7	325°	130°	18 to 24
Smoked pork shoulder picnic, whole	5 to 8	300° to 325°	170°	35
Smoked pork shoulder roll	2 to 3	300° to 325°	170°	35 to 40
Smoked pork loin canadian-style bacon	2 to 4	300° to 325°	160°	35 to 40

LAMB

Lamb leg roast, boneless	5 to 8	300° to 325°	175° to 180°	30 to 35
Lamb shoulder arm roast	4 to 6	300° to 325°	175° to 180°	30 to 35
Lamb shoulder roast, boneless	3 to 5	300° to 325°	175° to 180°	40 to 45
Lamb shoulder cushion roast, boneless	3 to 5	300° to 325°	175° to 180°	30 to 35

* Ribs that measure 6 to 7 inches from chine bone to tip of rib.
† Allow approximately 15 minutes per pound for heating whole cooked ham to serve hot.

BEEF

Ground Beef

Ground lean beef seems to be the mainstay of the American diet, so here are a few tips on buying ground beef. Under the new uniform meat-type identity labeling laws, all ground beef will be labeled "ground beef," rather than ground round, ground chuck, ground sirloin, or hamburger. Along with the ground beef title, you will also see a sign that says, "not less than 75 percent lean, not less than 80 percent lean, not less than 85 percent lean." In order to utilize and not waste perfectly good meat trimmings and keep the cost down, butchers have been using trimmings from all parts of the carcass and putting it in their ground beef. Watch your ground beef label. Next to freshness, the label is the most important consideration in the ground beef you buy. It tells you everything you need to know in order to select ground beef that best fits the particular dish or meal you're planning. *Look for the name and the lean meat content.* Ground lean beef is plain ground beef under the Nationwide Uniform Retail Meat Identity Standards Code Meat Labels. Ground beef must be pure beef, ground only from skeletal meat (beef muscle attached to the skeleton, no variety meats, other meats, or ingredients added). Don't be surprised if sometimes you still find it labeled ground beef chuck, ground beef round, or ground beef sirloin. This tells you it is still ground beef, but that it was ground from a specific primal area.

Percent of lean on the label assures the lean-to-fat ratio in the package, and is an important factor to consider when shopping for ground meat. Not less than 75 percent or 85 percent lean means that 75 percent or 85 percent of the meat in the package is actually lean ground beef. The new standards specify that ground beef can contain varying degrees of leanness, having a minimum content of 70 percent to 90 percent or more, but never less than 70 percent minimum, and it must be labeled accordingly. Lean-to-fat ratio is important in selecting ground beef for certain recipes; it also affects the retail price (the less lean, the more fat, the lower the price per pound). Ground beef with high fat content won't freeze as well as that with a lower fat content. Since ground meats have a greater exposed surface, they're more subject to loss of quality through oxidation. A high fat content hastens rancidity.

When using ground hamburger in casseroles and prepared dishes, you'll have to cool the food and skim off the fat before freezing; otherwise, the fat will tend to become rancid. I find that using the leaner meats is a great timesaver and almost as economical as using cheaper cuts, because there's little or no waste (i.e., fat which has to be skimmed off and thrown away). Those of you who are diet conscious should also remember that the more fat ground beef has, the more calories. However, some fat is necessary or the meat will be too dry. A 10 percent to 12 percent fat content is most desirable for casserole dishes.

Hamburgers

For good hamburgers, your meat must be top quality. Everybody has a preference; however, I prefer 75 percent to 80 percent lean meat for hamburgers. This seems to give just enough fat for juices and tenderness. If your meat is too fat, shrinkage will be excessive. Beef should be freshly ground. Buy a minimum of 5 pounds (when on sale, of course), shape hamburger patties, freezer-wrap, and freeze. Ground meat should be used or frozen the same day it is ground, because it quickly loses its flavor and quality.

Several devices for making round and uniformly shaped hamburgers are on the market. These gadgets are nice to have and they certainly save time. However, they're not really necessary. To shape a large batch of hamburgers, simply roll the meat out on waxed paper to the desired thickness with a rolling pin. Then, using a clean tin can for a cutter, cut out your hamburgers. Any 8-ounce (#1 flat size) crushed or sliced pineapple can should be about the right size; a tuna fish can also works nicely. Patties can be stacked, but always insert a double piece of aluminum foil or freezer paper or double waxed paper between the patties, so that you can easily remove just the number of patties needed at any given time. Cut a number of 4 x 4-inch pieces of paper and cover each patty, top and bottom. Lay them on a cookie sheet and quick-freeze. When completely frozen, pack in bags or wrap in family-serving-sized packages. (Remember to date and label.) These patties need not be thawed before cooking. Simply add 5 to 10 minutes to the broiling time, depending on the thickness of the meat patty.

Seasoning may be added at cooking time, or you can season the hamburgers at the time of shaping. A good general rule for salting ground meats of any kind is 1 teaspoon of salt for each pound of ground meat and ¼ teaspoon of ground pepper per pound. If meat patties are to be kept for periods of more than a month, omit salt. The salt seems to hasten the development of rancidity in the fatty portion of the meat. Other spices and seasonings can be added as usual; in fact, they sometimes act as preservatives. Onions, catsup, bread crumbs, wine, milk, sour cream, herbs, et cetera, may all be added before freezing. Monosodium glutamate also may be added. Experiment until you find the formula that most appeals to your family.

For barbecuing, it's best to shape hamburgers 1 inch thick, since they're easier to handle. It also enables the chef to brown the outside, leaving the inside pink, which is the best way to prepare them. The more a hamburger is cooked, the more the natural juices are lost.

Hamburger Appetizers

The above instructions may be used in making small hamburgers for party serving or appetizers. The meat patties may be put into the broiler frozen. Just count on an additional 5 to 10 minutes of cooking time, depending on the thickness of the hamburger. The buns may be ordered at any bakery and may vary in size according to what you would like, from 1½ to 2½ inches in diameter. I prefer to use the smaller buns as appetizers and the larger ones as a late-evening snack or party dish. Have the rolls in the freezer since hamburgers make an excellent "little something" to offer unexpected guests.

BASIC MEATLOAF

Besides being real budget stretchers, meatloaves can be time-savers as well. They can be arranged attractively on a platter, which will give them a company-is-coming look. They don't need a lot of attention when they're cooking and they keep well if dinner is delayed. And what's better than cold slices of meatloaf for sandwiches later in the week?

There are probably as many varieties of meatloaf as there are cooks who prepare them. That's the fun of making meatloaves; you can vary them a little each time you make a new batch.

Buy ground meat when it's on sale in a quantity that will serve your family adequately for at least 3 meals. Make sure the meat is fresh and of good quality; be sure to mix and freeze your meatloaf the same day it is purchased. Use a bowl that's sufficiently large and combine all the ingredients; now shape your loaves into sizes that suit your particular family. This is where the small bread tins really come in handy for a small family. Insert a long piece of foil up and down the long side of the bread pan. Put meat mixture into pan and set it in the freezer until solidly frozen. Remove meatloaf from pan and wrap in suitable moisture-vapor-proof freezer wrap. Date, label, and return to the freezer. For quicker cooking, you may prefer to freeze the meatloaves in individual portions. Muffin tins and glass custard cups make excellent molds for this purpose. The smaller loaves will also cook more quickly whether or not they're frozen (see page 10).

The basic recipe for meatloaf can be varied by adding a number of other ingredients, as indicated on page 268. Naturally, you won't be able to use all these ingredients at one time, but it'll be fun to experiment, adding something different each time you make meatloaf.

SINGLE RECIPE
Yield: 8 servings

2 pounds ground beef
1 egg
1 cup bread crumbs
½ can condensed tomato soup
½ cup chopped onions

¼ cup chopped parsley
1 teaspoon salt*
Pepper to taste
½ can condensed tomato soup

DOUBLE RECIPE
Yield: 16 servings

4 pounds ground beef
2 eggs
2 cups bread crumbs
1 can condensed tomato soup
1 cup chopped onions
½ cup chopped parsley
2 teaspoons salt*
Pepper to taste
1 can condensed tomato soup

TRIPLE RECIPE
Yield: 24 servings

6 pounds ground beef
3 eggs
3 cups bread crumbs
1½ cans condensed tomato soup
1½ cups chopped onions
¾ cup chopped parsley
3 teaspoons salt*
Pepper to taste
1½ cans condensed tomato soup

Mix the first 8 ingredients thoroughly. Shape into whatever size loaves you prefer. Make one meatloaf for your dinner, pouring remaining tomato soup over the top of the loaf about halfway through the baking. Bake a loaf made from a single recipe about one hour at 350° F. Smaller loaves will require less time. If you don't have an electric knife, let loaf cool for 10 minutes for even, more attractive slices.

TO FREEZE. If you're going to shape your loaves in some fancy way, unmold on a lined cookie sheet and freeze first; then wrap. Otherwise you can mold your meat loaves on foil and wrap.

TO SERVE WHEN FROZEN. Simply unwrap meatloaf and put into a baking dish. For a large frozen meatloaf (2-pound size), add 30 to 45 minutes to the regular baking time. Meatloaf may also be partially thawed before putting it into the oven; thus you will shorten the baking time.

---

* If meatloaves are to be stored in the freezer for periods of over a month, salt lightly to avoid the development of rancidity.

MEATLOAF VARIATIONS

The following list of ingredients gives the proper quantity to add to 2 pounds of meat as variations in flavor. Naturally, you'll add only one, two, or three of these for any one meatloaf!

½ cup chopped celery
½ cup chopped green peppers*
½ cup grated raw carrots
½ cup chopped parsley
½ cup chopped dill pickles
1 package frozen mixed vegetables
1 small jar pimento, either chopped or cut into strips
1 can or 4 ounces sliced mushrooms
½ pound sharp Cheddar cheese, cut in ½-inch cubes
1 can deviled ham
1 tablespoon prepared horseradish
2 teaspoons basil
½ teaspoon sage*
1 teaspoon dry mustard
½ teaspoon celery salt
½ teaspoon paprika
½ teaspoon oregano
1 envelope salad dressing mix (any flavor)
1 clove garlic*
1 teaspoon chili powder
1 tablespoon cumin seed
2 tablespoons lemon juice

¼ cup chili sauce
1 tablespoon steak sauce or Worcestershire sauce
¼ to ½ cup catsup
2 tablespoons prepared mustard
1 can tomato sauce
½ cup toasted sesame seeds
1 can condensed tomato soup
1 envelope dry mix spaghetti sauce
1 can pizza sauce
⅔ cup (1 small can) evaporated milk
¼ cup commercial sour cream
1½ cups bread cubes, crumbs, or slices that have been soaked in milk. (Different types of bread will give flavor variations. You can use rye, whole wheat, French bread, et cetera.)
1 cup quick-cooking rolled oats (a bread substitute), bran or wheat germ
1 cup ready-mix bread stuffing
1 cup seasoned Italian bread crumbs
1 cup crushed cornflake crumbs
1 cup cooked rice
1 cup grated raw potatoes (peeled)

You can also vary your meat, from pure ground round steak to plain hamburger, ground chuck, or combinations of veal, pork, and beef. Fresh Italian sausage, pork sausage, bacon, et cetera, can also be used and will give great flavor variations.

Remember, when adding liquids, such as 1 can tomato sauce, to add also bread or crumbs or an additional egg to help hold your meat loaf together. Some people like their meatloaves rather crumbly and that's fine too. However, crumbly loaves are more difficult to slice when making sandwiches later.

* The flavors of these items get stronger with freezing; so beware, and use with a light hand, especially if you plan to freeze your meatloaf for long periods of time (up to 3 months).

SHAPING MEATLOAVES. Meatloaves can be made in various shapes and sizes. Individual loaves can be made by molding them in custard cups; turn these out on a lined cookie or baking sheet before freezing. A ring mold will give your meatloaf an attractive shape. After it's baked, it can be filled with mashed potatoes or some colorful vegetable. Casserole and bread pans are very convenient to use when making larger-sized meatloaves.

GARNISHING MEATLOAVES. Meatloaf may be served plain. However, I like to dress it up, giving it added status and eye appeal. Tomato soup, chili sauce, catsup, et cetera, can be basted over the top, which will give it a glazelike finish. Pimento strips, green pepper slices, a row of sliced green olives down the center, onion rings, whole small white onions, or mushroom caps are all ways of decorating your meatloaves. Serve your meatloaf on a large platter surrounded with colorful vegetables and potatoes, garnished with sprigs of parsley.

SPAGHETTI MEAT SAUCE

This universally favorite dish can be a Monday night supper, as well as the main course at an informal dinner party. Served with an elegant *antipasto*, wine, salad with anchovies, vinegar-and-oil dressing, garlic bread (page 93) and a light frozen dessert, such as Choco-nut Tortoni (page 225), who could ask for anything more?

SINGLE RECIPE
Preparation Time: 20 minutes
Yield: 6 servings (2½ quarts)

½ cup onion slices or chopped onions
2 tablespoons olive oil
2 pounds ground beef
2 minced or pressed garlic cloves
Two 1-pound cans stewed tomatoes (4 cups)
One 8-ounce can seasoned tomato sauce
One 6-ounce can tomato paste
One 3-ounce can mushrooms or 1 cup fresh sliced mushrooms

¼ cup finely cut parsley
1½ teaspoons oregano
1 teaspoon salt
½ teaspoon monosodium glutamate
¼ teaspoon thyme
1 bay leaf
2 teaspoons fennel
Water (optional)

DOUBLE RECIPE
Preparation Time: 25 minutes
Yield: 12 servings (5 quarts)
1 cup onion slices or chopped onions
¼ cup olive oil
4 pounds ground beef
3 minced or pressed garlic cloves
Four 1-pound cans stewed tomatoes
(8 cups)
Two 8-ounce cans seasoned tomato
sauce
Two 6-ounce cans tomato paste
Two 3-ounce cans mushrooms or 2
cups fresh sliced mushrooms
½ cup finely cut parsley
1 tablespoon oregano
2 teaspoons salt
1 taspoon monosodium glutamate
½ teaspoon thyme
2 bay leaves
1 tablespoon plus 1 teaspoon fennel
Water (optional

TRIPLE RECIPE
Preparation Time: 35 minutes
Yield: 7½ to 8 quarts
1½ cups onion slices or chopped
onions
⅓ cup olive oil
6 pounds ground beef
4 minced or pressed garlic cloves
Six 1-pound cans stewed tomatoes (12
cups)
Three 8-ounce cans seasoned tomato
sauce
Three 6-ounce cans tomato paste
Three 3-ounce cans mushrooms or 3
cups fresh sliced mushrooms
¾ cup finely cut parsley
1 tablespoon plus 1½ teaspoons
oregano
3 teaspoons salt
1½ teaspoons monosodium glutamate
¾ teaspoon thyme
3 bay leaves
2 tablespoons fennel
Water (optional)

Onion slices add a nice texture to the spaghetti sauce. However, in the interest of saving time, chopped frozen onions will do nicely.

Be sure your kettle has a capacity of at least 10 quarts for the triple recipe.

Cook onion in hot oil until golden. Add meat and garlic; brown lightly. Add remaining ingredients and simmer uncovered 2 to 2½ hours, or until sauce is thick. Stir occasionally. If sauce becomes too thick, add water. Remove bay leaves. Serve over hot cooked spaghetti. Pass bowl of grated Parmesan cheese.

After dinner, let the remainder of the sauce cool; then quickly put it into meal-sized containers, date, label, and freeze.

Because the sauce has been completely cooked, it will need only to be heated through before serving at some future date.

CHILI CON CARNE

This is a meaty, dark chili con carne. More beans may be added, if desired. For a more soupy consistency, add tomato juice. Frozen chopped onions and peppers were used in figuring the preparation time.

SINGLE RECIPE
Preparation Time: 15 minutes
Yield: 1⅓ quarts without beans

1 tablespoon olive oil
1 pound ground beef
½ cup chopped onions
½ cup chopped green peppers
1 minced clove garlic
½ cup diced celery
½ ounce unsweetened chocolate

One 8-ounce can tomato sauce
1 pound canned stewed tomatoes
1 tablespoon sugar
2 teaspoons salt
2 tablespoons chili powder (or less)
1 pound canned kidney beans

DOUBLE RECIPE
Preparation Time: 20 minutes
Yield: 2⅔ quarts without beans

2 tablespoons olive oil
2 pounds ground beef
1 cup chopped onions
1 cup chopped green peppers
2 minced cloves garlic
1 cup diced celery
1 ounce unsweetened chocolate
Two 8-ounce cans tomato sauce
2 pounds canned stewed tomatoes
2 tablespoons sugar
4 teaspoons salt
¼ cup chili powder (or less)
2 pounds canned kidney beans

TRIPLE RECIPE
Preparation Time: 25 minutes
Yield: 4 quarts without beans

3 tablespoons olive oil
3 pounds ground beef
1½ cups chopped onions
1½ cups chopped green peppers
3 minced cloves garlic
1½ cups diced celery
1½ ounces unsweetened chocolate
Three 8-ounce cans tomato sauce
3 pounds canned stewed tomatoes
3 tablespoons sugar
2 tablespoons salt
⅓ cup chili powder (or less)
3 pounds canned kidney beans

Brown beef in oil, then add onions and green peppers. Sauté until onions are transparent. Add remaining ingredients, cover pan, and bring to a quick boil. Lower heat and simmer slowly for 30 minutes.

FOR DOUBLE AND TRIPLE RECIPES. Brown meat in a very large skillet. Heat oil and then add meat. Meanwhile, combine all other ingredients, except the kidney beans, and heat in a very large kettle. When meat is brown, add onions and peppers. Sauté until onions become transparent, then add to heated tomato mixture. Bring to a boil, lower heat and simmer for 30 minutes.

Separate the amount you intend for immediate use and add a proportionate amount of beans to this. Divide remaining chili sauce into family-sized containers. Label, date, cool, and then freeze them.

Chili may be frozen with beans; however, not only does it take more room in the freezer, but the beans have a tendency to get mushy when thawed and reheated. Simmer beans in chili sauce about 30 minutes before serving.

STUFFED CABBAGE LEAVES

Here's another budget stretcher; it's a one-dish meal that's easy on the chef, as well as the pocketbook.

SINGLE RECIPE
Preparation Time: 15 minutes
Yield: 8 to 10 cabbage rolls

8 very large or 10 smaller cabbage leaves
1 cup cooked rice
1 pound ground beef
1 egg
½ cup chopped onion
¼ cup chopped parsley
1½ teaspoons salt
1 teaspoon caraway seeds
Pepper to taste
One 1-pound can stewed tomatoes
One 8-ounce can tomato sauce
2 teaspoons bouillon granules
2 tablespoons brown sugar
1 tablespoon vinegar
1 tablespoon cornstarch
1 tablespoon cold water

DOUBLE RECIPE
Preparation Time: 22 minutes
Yield: 16 to 20 cabbage rolls

16 very large or 20 smaller cabbage leaves
2 cups cooked rice
2 pounds ground beef
2 eggs
1 cup chopped onion
½ cup chopped parsley
3 teaspoons salt
2 teaspoons caraway seeds
Pepper to taste
Two 1-pound cans stewed tomatoes
Two 8-ounce cans tomato sauce
4 teaspoons bouillon granules
¼ cup brown sugar
2 tablespoons vinegar
2 tablespoons cornstarch
2 tablespoons cold water

Cover cabbage head with boiling water and steam for about 5 minutes, no more. Remove cabbage leaves from head; leaves should be pliable enough to be rolled. If the leaves in center of head are still too firm for this, return to boiling water for another minute. Meanwhile, combine meat, rice, onions, parsley, caraway seeds, egg, salt, and pepper. For a single recipe, divide meat filling into 8 or 10 even portions (depending on the size of leaves). Fold over the sides of cabbage leaves and then bring up the top and bottom, envelope style. Insert a toothpick to keep leaves closed.

In a large skillet, combine tomatoes, tomato sauce, bouillon granules, brown sugar, and vinegar. Simmer gently until bouillon granules are dissolved. Cut any remaining cabbage into wedges; add to sauce along with cabbage rolls. Cover with a tight-fitting lid and simmer for 45 minutes. Remove cabbage and cabbage rolls to serving plate. Add cornstarch mixed in water to tomato gravy and stir until thickened. Pour over cabbage rolls and serve.

TO FREEZE. As soon as the cabbage rolls have been formed (before cooking), pack them into a freezer container. You may also want to include some cabbage wedges; simply parboil these wedges with the cabbage leaves. This is the same as blanching them. Seal container, label, date, and freeze immediately. If the ground beef has been frozen or if you're cooking for a very small number of people, you should cook all the cabbage in the tomato gravy and then freeze it in its own sauce in meal-sized portions.

TO SERVE WHEN FROZEN. Remove uncooked cabbage rolls and wedges from freezer container and place in skillet. Pour tomatoes, tomato sauce, bouillon granules, brown sugar, and vinegar over cabbage and bring to a boil. Turn heat down, cover with a tight-fitting lid and simmer for 1 hour for small cabbage rolls and for 1¼ hours for the larger-sized cabbage rolls. Follow the above instructions for making gravy and serving.

BEEF-STUFFED GREEN PEPPERS

These are wonderful to prepare when green peppers are plentiful and reasonable. They're almost a meal in themselves and need only an accompaniment of soup or salad to make a substantial dinner or supper.

SINGLE RECIPE
>   *Preparation Time: 30 minutes*
>   *Yield: 1 dozen stuffed peppers*

1½ pounds ground beef
1 tablespoon oil
12 large green peppers
1 can condensed tomato soup
Two 1-pound cans stewed tomatoes
3 minced cloves garlic (or less if desired)

1 tablespoon oregano
1 teaspoon thyme
½ teaspoon salt
3 cups cooked rice
Bread crumbs
Butter

DOUBLE RECIPE	TRIPLE RECIPE
Preparation Time: 40 minutes	*Preparation Time: 50 minutes*
Yield: 2 dozen stuffed peppers	*Yield: 3 dozen stuffed peppers*
3 pounds ground beef	4½ pounds ground beef
2 tablespoons oil	3 tablespoons oil
2 dozen large green peppers	3 dozen large green peppers
2 cans condensed tomato soup	3 cans condensed tomato soup
Four 1-pound cans stewed tomatoes	Six 1-pound cans stewed tomatoes
4 minced cloves garlic (or less if desired)	5 minced cloves garlic (or less if desired)
2 tablespoons oregano	3 tablespoons oregano
2 teaspoons thyme	1 tablespoon thyme
1 teaspoon salt	1½ teaspoons salt
6 cups cooked rice	9 cups cooked rice
Bread crumbs	Bread crumbs
Butter	Butter

If you're planning to freeze this, use converted rice. Research has shown that converted rice keeps its shape and texture better during freezing than do the regular or quick-cooking rices.

Sauté beef in oil until nicely browned. Meanwhile, cut the tops off green peppers and remove seeds. Blanch peppers (also tops) for 5 minutes. When doing a large batch, have a large kettle half-filled with boiling water. Put in only enough green peppers at a time so that they're at least half-filled with the boiling water. Combine all other ingredients, except the rice, bread crumbs, and the butter. Add the cooked rice and then the browned meat. Mix well. Put peppers on a large tray or cookie sheet. Fill with rice mixture, and top with bread crumbs and a dab of butter. Then add the green pepper tops. Set tray of green peppers in freezer. When completely frozen, wrap either individually or in family-sized portions in plastic heat and seal bags, or heavy-duty foil. Seal, label, date, and return to freezer.

To bake unfrozen peppers (when you've just prepared them), place them upright in a covered casserole dish. Bake in a moderately hot oven (375° F) for 30 minutes. Uncover casserole for last 10 minutes to brown.

To bake frozen, see above and add 25 minutes to baking time. If a tomato sauce is desired, you may add a can of tomato soup or tomato sauce to the bottom of the casserole dish.

VARIATION. Parmesan cheese may be mixed with 2 parts of Italian bread crumbs for topping.

ITALIAN MEATBALLS

Here's another favorite which uses ground meat, the proverbial budget stretcher. Because of the bulky meatballs, you'll need larger freezer containers or several smaller ones to freeze in family-sized portions. Heat and seal bags are especially convenient for small or individual-size portions. Quick and easy to prepare; make in large quantities for future meals.

SINGLE RECIPE
4 slices dry bread
1¼ pounds ground beef
2 eggs
½ cup grated Parmesan cheese
2 tablespoons chopped parsley
1 small minced or pressed clove garlic

1 teaspoon crushed oregano
1 teaspoon sweet basil
1 teaspoon salt
Dash pepper
2 tablespoons olive oil

DOUBLE RECIPE
8 slices dry bread
2½ pounds ground beef
4 eggs
1 cup grated Parmesan cheese
¼ cup chopped parsley
1 large or 2 small minced or pressed
   cloves garlic
2 teaspoons crushed oregano
2 teaspoons sweet basil
2 teaspoons salt
⅛ teaspoon pepper
3 tablespoons olive oil

TRIPLE RECIPE
12 slices dry bread
3¾ pounds ground beef
6 eggs
1½ cups grated Parmesan cheese
¼ cup plus 2 tablespoons chopped
   parsley
2 minced or pressed cloves garlic
1 tablespoon crushed oregano
1 tablespoon sweet basil
1 tablespoon salt
¼ teaspoon pepper (slight)
3 tablespoons olive oil

When you are cooking in large quantities, a real time-saver is to put as many meatballs as you can on your broiling pan. Broil until just nice and brown; then turn and broil on the other side. Put a little water in the bottom of the broiling pan first; then, when you're through, add the drippings and the water to your meat sauce.

Soak bread in some water for a few minutes; then squeeze out moisture. Combine bread with remaining ingredients, except the oil, mixing well. Form into balls. (A single recipe will make about 20 small meatballs; however, when you are making a large batch, it saves time to make meatballs larger.)

Brown meatballs slowly in hot oil. Add to spaghetti sauce (see below). Serve over hot spaghetti or try serving the meatballs over mashed potatoes for variety—it's really good.

Sauce

SINGLE RECIPE
Preparation Time: 20 minutes
Yield: 6 servings

¾ cup chopped frozen onions
1 pressed or minced clove garlic
3 tablespoons olive oil
Two 1-pound cans (4 cups) tomatoes
Two 6-ounce cans (1⅓ cups) tomato paste

1 cup water (optional)
1 tablespoon sugar
1 teaspoon salt
¼ teaspoon pepper
2 teaspoons crushed oregano
1 bay leaf

DOUBLE RECIPE
Preparation Time: 30 minutes
Yield: 12 servings

1½ cups chopped frozen onions
2 small or 1 very large pressed or minced garlic clove
3 tablespoons olive oil
Four 1-pound cans (8 cups) tomatoes
Four 6-ounce cans (2⅔ cups) tomato paste
2 cups water (optional)
2 tablespoons sugar
2 teaspoons salt
½ teaspoon pepper
4 teaspoons crushed oregano
2 bay leaves

TRIPLE RECIPE
Preparation Time: 40 minutes
Yield: 18 servings

2 cups chopped frozen onions
2 pressed or minced cloves garlic
3 tablespoons olive oil
Six 1-pound cans (12 cups) tomatoes
Six 6-ounce cans (4 cups) tomato paste
3 cups water (optional)
3 tablespoons sugar
1 tablespoon salt
¾ teaspoon pepper
2 tablespoons crushed oregano
3 bay leaves

Cook onion and garlic in hot oil until tender, but not brown. Stir in remaining ingredients. Simmer uncovered for 30 minutes; remove bay leaf. Add meatballs and cook 30 minutes longer.

TO FREEZE. Fill containers with meatballs and add enough sauce to cover. If you're running short of sauce, you can then add the optional water mentioned in the recipe.

SWEDISH MEATBALLS

Swedish meatballs and buffet dinners seem to go hand in hand; they're easily made in advance and are always a nice "something hot" to serve on these occasions. Serve them in either a chafing dish or a serving dish that has its own warming candle. You may also serve them at cocktail parties with toothpicks, letting each guest spear his own.

SINGLE RECIPE
> *Time: 20 minutes*
> *Yield: 50 to 55 meatballs*

1 beaten egg
¾ cup milk
4 slices day-old bread
1 teaspoon salt
⅛ teaspoon pepper
½ teaspoon nutmeg
1 teaspoon minced onion
1 pound ground round beef
½ teaspoon monosodium glutamate
⅓ cup salad oil
2 tablespoons flour
> or

1 tablespoon Clearjel (see page 70)
> plus 1 tablespoon flour

2 cups milk
⅛ teaspoon pepper
2 teaspoons bouillon granules
2 tablespoons dry onion soup mix
½ cup commercial sour cream
> (optional for added flavor and
> richness)

DOUBLE RECIPE
> *Time: 35 minutes*
> *Yield: 100 to 110 meatballs*

2 beaten eggs
1½ cups milk
8 slices day-old bread
2 teaspoons salt
¼ teaspoon pepper
1 teaspoon nutmeg
2 teaspoons minced onion
2 pounds ground round beef
1 teaspoon monosodium glutamate
⅓ cup salad oil (more if needed)
4 tablespoons flour
> or

2 tablespoons Clearjel (see page 70)
> plus 2 tablespoons flour

4 cups milk
¼ teaspoon pepper
4 teaspoons bouillon granules
4 tablespoons dry onion soup mix
1 cup commercial sour cream
> (optional for added flavor and
> richness)

Put eggs, milk, salt, pepper, nutmeg, and onions in blender. Blend well and pour over bread slices in a large mixing bowl. Let stand for 5 to 10 minutes. Add meat and blend well. Using an electric mixer makes the meatballs light. Form into small balls. If meat mixture is chilled first, the balls will be easier to shape. Keeping your hands wet also helps when you are forming the balls.

To save time when browning the meatballs, instead of using a skillet or top of the stove, you may wish to arrange meatballs on the rack of your broiling pan and bake them in 350° F oven for 10 to 20 minutes (until nicely browned). Put about ¼ inch of water in the bottom of your broiling pan, so that drippings won't burn. Repeat until all the meatballs are browned. With this method you will not need the ⅓ cup of salad oil (for a single recipe), which will also reduce the calorie content of your finished product. Otherwise, heat oil, et cetera.

Heat oil and drop balls into skillet, making sure not to overcrowd. Shaking the skillet often helps to keep the balls round, at the same time turning and browning them on all sides. Repeat until all the meatballs are browned.

To make gravy from the pan drippings, add flour to drippings and stir with a wooden spoon until it's all dissolved. Add milk slowly, stirring all the while. Add pepper, onion soup mix, and bouillon granules. Cook until completely dissolved and the sauce is creamy. If desired, add sour cream now and stir until completely blended. Return meatballs to this sauce and simmer for 30 minutes before serving.

TO FREEZE. Pour meatballs and sauce into meal-sized or party-sized portions. Cool and freeze. I find that the half-gallon freezer containers are perfect for freezing party-sized portions.

TO SERVE WHEN FROZEN. Thaw completely before heating. Additional milk may be added to the gravy, as needed. Warm over low heat or in a double boiler, until heated through; then serve.

LASAGNE CASSEROLE

Even the single recipe makes quite a bit, but it lends itself so well to freezing that it can be divided into smaller dishes. However, because the lasagne noodles are so large this won't make up into individual dishes or servings very readily. Since there's no last-minute preparation, and only a salad and a loaf of garlic bread (see page 93) are needed as accompaniment, it's marvelous to serve when you are entertaining.

MEAT SAUCE

SINGLE RECIPE
Preparation Time: 15 minutes
Yield: 12 servings or one 9 x 13 x 2
inch baking dish

1 pound Italian sausage (in bulk, if possible)
½ pound ground beef
1 minced clove garlic
1 tablespoon whole basil
1½ teaspoons salt
One 1-pound can (2 cups) stewed tomatoes
Two 6-ounce cans (1⅓ cups) tomato paste

DOUBLE RECIPE
Preparation Time: 20 minutes
Yield: 24 servings or two
9 x 13 x 2-inch baking dishes

2 pounds Italian sausage (in bulk, if possible)
1 pound ground beef
2 minced cloves garlic
2 tablespoons whole basil
2 teaspoons salt
Two 1-pound cans (4 cups) stewed tomatoes
Four 6-ounce cans (2⅔ cups) tomato paste

Brown meat slowly; spoon off fat. Add remaining ingredients. Simmer uncovered for half an hour, stirring occasionally. Meanwhile, cook the Lasagne noodles and prepare cheese filling.

LASAGNE

For a single recipe, cook about 6 of the large wide noodles, 12 for a double recipe. (Use just enough noodles to cover your casserole dish twice; they stretch a little while cooking.) Cook noodles in a large kettle of boiling, salted water for 15 to 20 minutes. Add a tablespoon of olive oil to the water. If you're going to freeze the casserole, undercook the noodles a little.

CHEESE FILLING

SINGLE RECIPE
Preparation Time: 7 minutes

2 cups fresh ricotta or creamy cottage cheese
½ cup grated Parmesan or Romano cheese
2 tablespoons snipped parsley
2 beaten eggs
2 teaspoon salt
½ teaspoon pepper
1 pound thinly sliced mozzarella cheese

DOUBLE RECIPE
Preparation Time: 10 minutes

4 cups fresh ricotta or creamy cottage cheese
1 cup grated Parmesan or Romano cheese
¼ cup snipped parsley
4 beaten eggs
1 tablespoon plus 1 teaspoon salt
1 teaspoon pepper
2 pounds thinly sliced mozzarella cheese

Mix first 6 ingredients of the cheese filling. Place half of the cooked noodles in a 13 x 9 x 2-inch baking dish; spread with half of the cheese filling. Cover with half of the mozzarella cheese and half of the meat sauce. Repeat layers. Bake at 375° F for 30 minutes. Before cutting in squares, let stand 10 minutes so that filling will set, which makes it easier to serve. Layering a single recipe takes about 8 minutes and a double recipe about 15 minutes.

TO FREEZE. Wrap, date, label and freeze immediately, without baking.

TO SERVE WHEN FROZEN. If dish is slightly thawed or of a smaller size, reduce the baking time. Dish should be bubbling for about 15 minutes before you remove it from the oven. Large casseroles especially bake more evenly when completely thawed (see page 368).

AMERICAN PIZZA

This is a delicious thin-crusted American pizza. A single recipe yields three; it seems foolish to make only one at a time, since pizzas are easily frozen. For those who happen to have enough pizza platters, a double recipe is included.

A food processor will cut your preparation time in half! Mix dough for single recipe, as well as all slicing and shredding of cheese, in processor. A fun party idea—have all dough rolled out and in pans. Have all other ingredients in various bowls and let each guest make his own: small individual pizzas for a singles or teen party, shared 12″ pizzas for a couples group.

CRUST

SINGLE RECIPE	DOUBLE RECIPE
Time: 50 minutes	*Time: 70 minutes*
Yield: Three 12-inch pizzas	*Yield: Six 12-inch pizzas*
One ¼-ounce package dry yeast	Two ¼-ounce packages dry yeast
2 tablespoons lukewarm water (110° to 115° F)	¼ cup lukewarm water (110° to 115° F)
1⅓ cups hot water (130° to 140° F)	2⅔ cups hot water (130° to 140° F)
2 teaspoons salt	1 tablespoon plus 1 teaspoon salt
⅓ cup olive oil or shortening	⅔ cup olive oil or shortening
4 cups flour	8 cups flour

Crumble yeast into lukewarm water and let stand 5 minutes. Into mixing bowl pour hot water over shortening and salt; add yeast. Blend in flour, a cup at a time, until dough is smooth. Let dough rise until somewhat light—about half an hour. Divide dough into thirds for single recipe (6 equal parts for double recipe). Punch with fists for several minutes; then lift and throw it back into bowl several times. Roll it out with rolling pin on floured pastry cloth or board. This dough is very elastic and doesn't roll easily; so pick it up and carefully stretch it without tearing it. Lay dough on the back of your right hand and, with the left hand, turn it, gently pulling and stretching it. Have pan ready, brushed with olive oil; shape to pan. Avoid any thick edges; cut them off, if possible.

PIZZA TOPPING

SINGLE RECIPE	DOUBLE RECIPE
One 8-ounce can pizza sauce	Two 8-ounce cans pizza sauce
1 pound mozzarella cheese	2 pounds mozzarella cheese
1 Spanish onion	2 Spanish onions
2 pounds Italian sausage	4 pounds Italian sausage
2 large green peppers	4 large green peppers
1 can anchovies	2 cans anchovies
¼ pound fresh mushrooms	½ pound fresh mushrooms
Salt and pepper to taste	Salt and pepper to taste
Dried oregano	Dried oregano
Basil	Basil

Precook sausage to eliminate excess fat; simmer for 30 minutes. If sausage is in a casing, remove casing before cooking. (I find it easier to remove before cooking.) Also precook green peppers for 5 minutes. Slice sausage and julienne the green peppers. Peel onion and cut into thin slices; separate the rings. Wash and slice mushrooms and open can of anchovies. Do all of these things while your dough is rising.

Now, after you've fitted the dough to the pan, you're ready to make your pizzas in assembly-line fashion. First, generously brush the pizza sauce over the dough. Arrange the sausage evenly over all the pizzas; then the green pepper, onion rings, anchovies, and mushroom slices and spices. Cover this array with the mozzarella cheese, either thinly sliced or shredded. Smother the pizzas with this cheese. Now you're finished!

Bake one for immediate use and freeze the rest. Bake at 450° F for 10 to 15 minutes, or until done. A frozen pizza should not take much longer than 15 minutes to cook. They should be bubbly and the crust a little brown when finished.

TO FREEZE. To wrap for the freezer, always cover the cheese with a layer of waxed paper and then use heavy-duty aluminum foil. The cheese will attack the aluminum, so be sure to use waxed paper first.

TACOS

Tortillas are generally available in the frozen food section of larger supermarkets. Should you find them unavailable in your area, you may wish to substitute Arabian (pita) bread or hard rolls. This will make a very tempting sandwich.

The taco meat sauce can be made from either fresh or frozen meat, and may be frozen after it has been prepared.

Meat Filling

SINGLE RECIPE
Preparation Time: 12 minutes
Yield: Meat filling for 12 tacos

1 cup chopped onions
1 pound ground beef
1 minced clove garlic
3 tablespoons shortening
1 teaspoon salt
2 teaspoons chili powder
¼ teaspoon cumin
1 dozen tortillas
Vegetable oil for frying tortillas

DOUBLE RECIPE
Preparation Time: 15 minutes
Yield: Meat filling for 24 tacos

2 cups chopped onions
2 pounds ground beef
2 minced cloves garlic
3 tablespoons shortening
2 teaspoons salt
1 tablespoon plus 1 teaspoon chili powder
½ teaspoon cumin
2 dozen tortillas
Vegetable oil for frying tortillas

Melt shortening, add meat, and brown; then add onions and garlic. Continue cooking until onions are limp. Add seasonings and ¼ cup of taco sauce or Mexican chili sauce (see below). Continue cooking over low heat. In another pan, start frying the tortillas. Use a fairly high heat. With a small amount of shortening (about 2 tablespoons) in your skillet, put one tortilla in at a time. If you are using a very large skillet, you may fry two tortillas at a time. (Using this system, you can fry 12 in 15 to 20 minutes.) When the tortilla becomes soft and flexible, quickly turn over for a few seconds. Then, using tongs and spatula, fold tortilla over, making a double half circle. Continue frying until the tortilla is crisp.

Drain on absorbent paper. Set oven thermostat at 200° F (or less if you have a warming setting on your oven) and put in the oven a large ovenproof platter or tray that has been lined with paper towels. After the tortillas have been drained, place them on this platter in the oven until you are ready to serve them. Repeat this process until all the tortillas have been fried.

ACCOMPANYING INGREDIENTS

Yield: Sufficient filling for 12
   tacos

½ head lettuce
1 large chopped tomato

½ pound shredded Cheddar cheese
Taco sauce or Mexican chili sauce

TO SERVE. With a sharp knife, shred the half head of lettuce fairly coarsely. The cheese can be shredded with a grater in just a few minutes. Chop tomatoes. Put each ingredient—lettuce, cheese, and tomatoes—in separate serving bowls. Serve meat and fried tortillas immediately (also in separate serving dishes).

TO EAT. Holding half-moon-shaped taco in the hand, spoon meat filling in the bottom of taco; then add grated cheese, lettuce, and chopped tomatoes. A little more taco sauce on top is optional. Eat these with your fingers, just as you would a sandwich. That's what it is—a Mexican-type sandwich.

If you can't find any commercial taco sauce or Mexican chili sauce, here is a recipe for making your own.

TACO SAUCE OR MEXICAN CHILI SAUCE

SINGLE RECIPE
   Time: 5 minutes
   Yield: 1½ cups
1 cup tomato purée
¾ cup chopped onions
2 tablespoons chili powder or more
2 tablespoons olive oil
¼ teaspoon oregano

DOUBLE RECIPE
   Time: 6 minutes
   Yield: Approximately 3 cups
2 cups tomato purée
1½ cups chopped onions
¼ cup chili powder (or more)
¼ cup olive oil
½ teaspoon oregano

¼ teaspoon cumin	½ teaspoon cumin
1 teaspoon salt	2 teaspoons salt
1 clove garlic	2 cloves garlic
1 tablespoon vinegar	2 tablespoons vinegar
Several drops Tabasco sauce	Tabasco sauce to taste (it should taste hot)

Put all these ingredients in a blender and whirl until completely blended. Pour into a saucepan and heat through. Turn heat down, and simmer for 5 additional minutes. Cool. Sauce is usually served cold. Keeps well in the refrigerator or it may be frozen.

LUCIA'S ITALIAN BEEF

A neighbor gave me this delicious recipe and I always make another big batch just as soon as the previous one is finished. This recipe takes very little time to make, and it can be served in many different ways.

I prefer top round. It's cheaper and has its own layer of fat on top, which is important for a good gravy. If you choose to buy the sirloin, put a few slices of bacon over the top of the roast.

One large (10 to 15 pounds) boned sirloin tip or top round	1 large sliced Bermuda onion
2 tablespoons crushed oregano	Salt
1 tablespoon basil	¼ to ⅓ cup flour
1 teaspoon thyme	2 to 3 large 1-pound cans stewed tomatoes
2 teaspoons garlic salt	2 teaspoons bouillon granules

Mix all the seasonings together and sprinkle or rub over entire piece of meat; cover with several onion slices and put the rest in bottom of pan, where they'll cook in the drippings. Put meat in a large roasting pan and bake at 325° F until your meat thermometer registers the desired internal temperature. If you like your meat rare, remove from oven a short time before the thermometer registers "rare," since the meat will continue to cook awhile, even though you've removed it from the oven. Such a large piece of meat takes time to cook, but it doesn't need close watching. Put fatty side up, and figure about 28 to 30 minutes per pound, for rare beef.

When the meat is done, remove from pan, along with onion slices. Take drippings from pan, add just enough flour to absorb the grease in the drippings. Salt to taste, and add 1 cup of boiling water in which 2 teaspoons bouillon granules have been dissolved. Add 2 or 3 large cans of stewed tomatoes (depending on the size of your piece of meat) and cook until thick. Now add onion slices and put the mixture into your blender or food mill. You'll have a most scrumptious gravy.

TO SERVE. For the first meal, carve the meat as you would any roast; serve with potatoes, salad, vegetables, and some of the good gravy. Refrigerate the meat overnight. (This is important if you like thin slices of beef.) The next day take this meat back to your butcher and have him slice it very thin. Wrap slices in meal-sized portions for sandwiches. Freeze the gravy separately or freeze individual portions in freeze-and-seal bags with gravy.

Because this meat is so versatile, you'll discover many ways to serve it. For large crowds—a buffet meal, say—it makes an impressive platter. Carve as you serve. Have the gravy in a separate bowl or pitcher. When serving the meat that has been frozen, thaw meat slightly and heat the gravy. When the gravy is bubbly, add meat just long enough to warm it through (otherwise your meat won't stay rare, medium rare, et cetera). Put meat and gravy in shallow bowl or platter and serve immediately; have plenty of warm Italian bread or rolls to go with this.

The sliced meat can also be thawed and served plain as cold beef slices.

QUICK AND EASY POTROAST

This is a delicious all-in-one meal that needs only a salad for an accompaniment. Wonderful for those days when you don't have time to cook.

Preparation Time: 7 minutes
Yield: 6 servings

3 pounds pot or Swiss roast	6 medium-sized potatoes
1 package dried onion soup mix	½ cup water
½ pound carrots, cut into long, thin strips	1 cup frozen peas (optional)

Take your meat right out of the freezer and put it into a large ovenproof pan (preferably one with a lid). Sprinkle with onion soup mix and arrange carrots and potatoes around the meat in the bottom of the pan. Cover; if your pan doesn't have a lid, secure heavy-duty aluminum foil over the top. Cook in a 275° F oven for 6 to 8 hours, depending on whether or not the meat is frozen. Check every few hours to see if there's enough liquid in the pan. If your meat is of high quality, there should be enough meat juice so that you won't have to add any more liquid. Turn potatoes once or twice, so that they'll become a nice deep brown while cooking in the gravy. To make a good gravy, just before serving, remove meat and vegetables; add a little flour, dissolved in cold water, to the liquid in the baking pan. This recipe would lend itself well to a slow cooker. Assemble in morning and forget until dinner time.

ROAST BEEF HASH

Roast beef hash can be prepared very quickly with leftover roast beef (either chopped fine or ground) and hashed brown potatoes. Add some frozen chopped onions, frozen green pepper, and chopped celery, if you wish. Add seasoned stewed tomatoes, mixing well. Dot with butter and bake in a 350° F oven until mixture is heated through and bubbly. This is especially good made with leftover corned beef.

BEEF STEW IN WINE

This stew is good enough for company fare, although it's a budget meal. It doesn't need any attention while cooking, which makes it the dream of the working woman or the homemaker who is going to be away or busy all day.

SINGLE RECIPE
    Time: 10 minutes
    Yield: Serves 6
2 pounds beef stew meat, cut into
    2-inch cubes
One 1-pound can stewed tomatoes
1 bay leaf
Pinch thyme
Pinch marjoram
1 teaspoon salt
¼ teaspoon pepper
1 large sliced Spanish onion
4 carrots
½ pound fresh mushrooms (optional)
1 cup dry red wine
2 tablespoons flour or Clearjel (see
    page 70)

DOUBLE RECIPE
    Time: 15 minutes
    Yield: Serves 12
4 pounds beef stew meat, cut into
    2-inch cubes
Two 1-pound cans stewed tomatoes
2 bay leaves
⅛ teaspoon thyme
⅛ teaspoon marjoram
2 teaspoons salt
½ teaspoon pepper
2 large sliced Spanish onions
8 carrots
1 pound fresh mushrooms (optional)
2 cups dry red wine
¼ cup flour or Clearjel (see page 70)

Your stew meat need not be thawed. Simply put it into a heavy kettle that has a tight-fitting lid. Add all the other ingredients, except flour or Clearjel, cover, and place in oven or slow cooker. Have your timer set to turn the oven on about 5 hours before you want to serve. Set temperature control at 275° F.

This stew is good served with noodles, dumplings, or potatoes. If you wish, you may add half a dozen peeled potatoes to the stew about 1 hour before it's done. Just before serving, remove meat and vegetables with slotted spoon. Dissolve flour or Clearjel in water and add to gravy, cooking until thickened.

TO FREEZE. Spoon into freezer containers, seal, date, and label. Do not freeze with potatoes, because they tend to become mealy.

TO SERVE WHEN FROZEN. Partially thaw and heat through, adding potatoes if you wish.

BARBECUED BRISKET OF BEEF

It's a good idea to buy brisket of beef when it's on sale, so that you'll have it on hand in your freezer for this easy yet tasty meal. When you are serving a large group at informal gatherings, it makes a pleasant change. Cold leftovers are delicious for sandwiches.

Yield: 10 ample servings
Time: 10 to 15 minutes total

5 to 6-pound brisket of beef	2 tablespoons Worcestershire sauce
Celery salt	½ cup barbecue sauce
Onion salt	Water (if needed)
Garlic salt	2 tablespoons flour
Salt and pepper	½ cup water
3 ounces liquid smoke	

Thaw brisket the day before. Put meat in shallow baking dish and sprinkle generously with celery, onion, and garlic salts. Pour liquid smoke over meat, cover, and refrigerate overnight.

Six hours before serving, preheat oven to 275° F. Remove meat from refrigerator and sprinkle with salt and pepper to taste; add Worcestershire sauce. Cover dish with foil, sealing edges, and bake for 5 hours at 275° F. Uncover meat and pour barbecue sauce over it. Continue baking 1 more hour uncovered, adding water, if it's needed. Remove meat to warm platter. Skim or pour some of the grease off drippings. Add flour and water mixture to meat drippings, and more barbecue sauce to taste. Pour some of this gravy over the meat, and serve the remainder of the gravy in a separate bowl. Especially good with noodles.

BAKED STUFFED FLANK STEAK

This is another easy meal; once it's in the oven, you can virtually forget it until serving time.

Time: 15 minutes
Yield: Serves 6

1½ to 2-pound thawed flank steak
¼ pound bacon, cut into cubes
or
About ⅓ cup frozen bacon pieces (see page 41)
½ cup chopped frozen onions
½ cup chopped celery
1 cup seasoned poultry stuffing
¼ pound sliced mushrooms

½ teaspoon salt
¼ teaspoon pepper
½ teaspoon poultry seasoning
One 4-ounce jar pimiento, cut into strips
1 egg
1 can beef broth
½ Bermuda onion, cut into thin slices

Fry bacon in skillet until almost crisp. Meanwhile, in a bowl combine onions, mushrooms, celery, seasonings, pimiento, egg, and poultry stuffing. Drain bacon and add, mixing well.

Flank steak should bere moved from the freezer early enough to be well thawed before stuffing. If flank steak is thick, have the butcher cut a pocket in it. Fill pocket with stuffing, closing the opening with toothpicks. Otherwise, simply spread the stuffing down the center of the flank steak; roll and tie securely with twine. Brown meat on all sides in a heavy kettle, using oil or bacon fat. Top meat with sliced onions and add beef broth. Preheat oven to 350° F. Cover and bake for 2 hours. To shorten cooking time, you may wish to sprinkle meat with tenderizer when wrapping it for the freezer. Meat should be nice and tender when cooked 1 to 1½ hours.

During the last 15 minutes you may want to add noodles to the broth. Add enough water to cover the noodles just barely. Dumplings or potatoes are also good additions that can be cooked in the same kettle. Thicken gravy if you wish.

When meat is done, remove to serving platter; cut and remove string. Slice meat into 1-inch slices.

AUNT ADDIE'S STEAK MARINADE

This marinade will give your steaks an Oriental flavor. Also good for lamb chops, shish kebabs, et cetera.

Time: 7 minutes
Yield: About 1¾ cups

⅔ cup dry vermouth
One 3-ounce bottle soy sauce
1 teaspoon Worcestershire sauce
½ teaspoon dry ginger (or more to taste)

¼ cup brown sugar
¼ teaspoon chili powder
1 pressed clove garlic

In a small saucepan, combine soy sauce and all the ingredients, except the dry vermouth. Heat until sugar is completely dissolved. Cool slightly and add vermouth. Steaks should be well thawed before marinating. Cut steak into serving pieces and marinate before broiling. Half an hour is sufficient time to marinate steaks, such as T-bone, sirloin, sirloin tip, strip steaks, et cetera. However, if you wish to use some of the economy cuts, let them marinate for at least an hour. A teaspoon of meat tenderizer may be added to the sauce for these cuts. For a stronger flavor, increase marinating time.

BEEF STROGANOFF

Here's another dish that lends itself well to entertaining, since it needs no last-minute preparation. Made in quantities and frozen, it's an elegant meal from the freezer.

Many meat markets will have the beef round tip steak thinly sliced and call it sandwich steak.

SINGLE RECIPE
Time: 15 minutes to prepare meat and vegetables;
15 minutes to sauté everything
Yield: 6 to 8 servings

1½ pounds thinly sliced beef round tip steak
2 tablespoons vegetable oil
1 pound sliced mushrooms
2 large julienne-sliced green peppers
½ cup chopped onions
1 minced clove garlic
2 tablespoons flour
1½ cup water

DOUBLE RECIPE
Time: 25 minutes to prepare meat and vegetables;
20 minutes to sauté everything
Yield: 14 to 16 servings

3 pounds thinly sliced beef round tip steak
3 tablespoons vegetable oil
2 pounds sliced mushrooms
4 large julienne-sliced green peppers
1 cup chopped onions
2 minced cloves garlic
4 tablespoons flour
3 cups water

Salt and pepper to taste
2 teaspoons beef bouillon granules
1 cup commercial sour cream

Salt and pepper to taste
4 teaspoons beef bouillon granules
1 pint commercial sour cream

Partially thaw beef round tip; then, using a sharp knife, slice into long thin slices. This is done very easily and quickly when the meat is partially frozen. Remove any fat from meat. Prepare mushrooms and peppers. In a very large skillet, heat oil and quickly brown meat at high temperature. Remove meat from skillet and put aside; now put prepared vegetables and garlic in skillet and sauté for 5 minutes. Remove vegetables from skillet and make a paste of flour and drippings in the pan. Slowly add water and bouillon granules, stirring constantly. When mixture becomes thick and bubbly, lower heat and add sour cream, blending well. Add all the vegetables and the meat, cover, and simmer over very low heat for 30 minutes.

TO FREEZE. Put the Beef Stroganoff into containers before the last 30-minute simmer. Label, date, and freeze.

TO SERVE WHEN FROZEN. Partially thaw Beef Stroganoff; pour into a skillet or pan and cover. Gently warm entire mixture, stirring from time to time. Then simmer another 30 minutes. Delicious served over wild rice. May also be served with parsleyed rice, noodles, or pilaf.

ORIENTAL PEPPERED BEEF

For those of you who like Oriental cookery, here's a good all-in-one dish. Serve with fluffy rice and/or Chinese noodles. Nothing else is necessary.

SINGLE RECIPE
  Time: 15 minutes
  Yield: 6 servings

2 tablespoons vegetable oil
1 small minced or pressed clove garlic
1 teaspoon powdered ginger
2 pounds beef round tip, sliced thin,
  or beef flank steak cut into very thin
  diagonal slices or sandwich steaks
2 large julienne-sliced green peppers
¾ cup chopped onions
½ cup water
3 tablespoons soy sauce
1 tablespoon Chinese bead molasses
Dash pepper
1 can (1 pound, 3 ounces) Chinese
  mixed vegetables
½ cup water
3 tablespoons cornstarch
1 large or 2 medium-sized tomatoes,
  cut in pieces
¼ cup cashew nuts

DOUBLE RECIPE
  Time: 20 minutes
  Yield: 12 servings

3 tablespoons vegetable oil
2 small or 1 large minced or pressed
  clove garlic
2 teaspoons powdered ginger
4 pounds beef round tip, sliced thin,
  or beef flank steak cut into very thin
  diagonal slices or sandwich steaks
4 large julienne-sliced green peppers
1½ cups chopped onions
1 cup water
⅓ cup soy sauce
2 tablespoons Chinese bead molasses
⅛ teaspoon pepper
2 cans (1 pound, 3 ounces each)
  Chinese mixed vegetables
1 cup water
⅓ cup cornstarch
2 large to 4 medium-sized tomatoes,
  cut in pieces
½ cup cashew nuts

Heat oil, garlic, and ginger together in a large skillet. Add meat; cook over high heat 5 minutes, stirring constantly. Remove meat. Add peppers and onions to remaining oil in skillet; cook 2 minutes. Add soy sauce, water, molasses, and pepper; cook 3 minutes. Add meat, Chinese vegetables, and cook 2 minutes longer, or until mixture is heated through. Add cornstarch that has been mixed with water until the sauce is thick and clear. Now add tomatoes and nuts; cook 1 minute and serve over fluffy rice and/or Chinese noodles.

TO FREEZE. If you're going to freeze part of your recipe, eliminate the nuts and tomatoes. Remove from heat as soon as the sauce has thickened and put into freezer containers. When you label, write a notation about the quantity of tomatoes and nuts that are to be added when reheating. Try to thaw this dish completely before warming so that the meat and vegetables won't be overcooked.

SUKIYAKI

If you've never tried sukiyaki (skee-yah-kee), you have a treat in store. Try it soon. It's very quick and easy to prepare and can be served as an unusual yet elegant company meal. However, I wouldn't try to serve sukiyaki to more than 8 people at a time. If you have an electric wok or skillet, cook the meal at the table; it will add showmanship to the whole performance!

SINGLE RECIPE
Time: 15 minutes
Yield: 4 servings

1½ pounds very thinly sliced beef round tip steak or sandwich steaks
4 ribs of celery, cut diagonally into ½-inch pieces
1 bunch green onions, cut diagonally in 2-inch lengths, including the green tops
1 cup sliced fresh mushrooms
1 bunch watercress sprigs
One 6-ounce can drained water chestnuts
½ pound fresh or 1 package frozen leaf spinach, thawed
1 julienne-sliced green pepper

DOUBLE RECIPE
Time: 20 minutes
Yield: 8 servings

3 pounds very thinly sliced beef round tip steak or sandwich steaks
8 ribs of celery, cut diagonally into ½-inch pieces
2 bunches green onions, cut diagonally in 2-inch lengths, including the green tops
2 cups sliced fresh mushrooms
2 bunches watercress sprigs
Two 6-ounce cans drained water chestnuts
1 pound fresh or 2 packages frozen leaf spinach, thawed
2 julienne-sliced green peppers

Take your beef round tip steak out of the freezer and, while it's still icy but partially thawed, cut it into very thin slices. The partially frozen meat will slice easily, especially if you're using a sharp knife. Arrange cut, uncooked beef on a platter. Prepare all the vegetables, arranging them attractively on a large tray. All this can be done early in the day, if you wish. Cover with Saran Wrap and refrigerate to keep fresh. Prepare sauce.

SUKIYAKI SAUCE

SINGLE RECIPE
¼ cup soy sauce
¼ cup white wine
½ cup water
1 tablespoon Chinese bead molasses

DOUBLE RECIPE
½ cup soy sauce
½ cup white wine
1 cup water
2 tablespoons Chinese bead molasses

Combine all ingredients of the sauce and cook for 2 minutes. Have a large bowl of fluffy rice at the table and set your electric skillet at 420° F or highest setting on your skillet. After everyone is seated, put about 2 tablespoons of olive oil in the skillet and wait until it's very hot. Now add two thirds of your vegetables (except for the watercress) and pour half of your sauce over the vegetables. Turn ingredients gently while cooking 5 to 6 minutes. Now add the remaining vegetables and meat and cook for 1 to 2 minutes more. (If you don't like your meat fairly rare, add the meat shortly after you have started cooking the vegetables. However, the meat is sliced very thin and cooks rapidly at this high temperature. Be sure not to overcook the vegetables, since they should be a bit crunchy.) Add watercress and cook for 1 more minute. Remove to large platter. Put remaining sauce in a pitcher and pass with the sukiyaki. You may prefer to double the amount of sauce if you like your rice fairly moist.

When serving a double recipe, cook only half the ingredients at a time; if your electric skillet is small, you may want to do this even with a single recipe.

This is really a fun meal for children and adults alike. If you don't have an electric skillet, don't let that deter you. Just cook it on the stove, following the above directions and using a very hot skillet.

ROULADEN OR BEEF BIRDS

This is a tasty dish that's good when prepared in quantity. Freeze part of it for future heat-'n-serve meals.

SINGLE RECIPE	DOUBLE RECIPE
Time: 30 minutes	*Time: 45 minutes*
Yield: 12 large beef birds	*Yield: 24 large beef birds*
3 pounds of beef round steak, cut ¼ inch thick	6 pounds beef round steak, cut ¼ inch thick
2 teaspoons salt	4 teaspoons salt
½ teaspoon pepper	1 teaspoon pepper
1 large sweet onion, cut into 12 strips	2 large sweet onions, cut into 24 strips
3 large dill pickles, cut into 12 strips	6 large dill pickles, cut into 24 strips
2 carrots, cut in half and then into 12 equal strips	4 carrots, cut in half and then into 24 equal strips
2 teaspoons bouillon granules	4 teaspoons bouillon granules
1½ cups boiling water	3 cups boiling water

When you bring the meat home from the butcher, trim off any fat and pound it lightly with a meat hammer or mallet. Lay double thickness of waxed paper between meat slices, freezer-wrap, and freeze. When ready to cook, separate the meat and let it thaw. Meanwhile, prepare the vegetables. For a single recipe cut the meat into 12 rectangles. (Each pound of meat is usually 1 slice; so just divide each slice into about 4 equal parts.) In the center of each piece of meat put a strip of onion, carrot, and dill pickle. Roll up and secure with wooden picks or string. Brown beef birds on all sides in melted fat or oil. Put the beef birds in a large pan (for a double recipe a turkey roasting pan is ideal), and cover with boiling water in which bouillon granules have been dissolved. Simmer for 1 hour, or until meat is tender. Thicken pan liquids with flour for gravy, if you wish.

TO FREEZE. Divide beef birds into family-sized portions and pack into freezer containers. Pour a proportionate amount of gravy over them. Seal, label, date, and freeze.

TO SERVE WHEN FROZEN. Partially thaw and warm at low temperature until heated through.

VEAL

VEAL LOIN CHOPS IN SOUR CREAM

Another oven meal that requires little attention or preparation.

Time: 10 minutes
Yield: 4 servings

4 thawed lean veal loin chops
2 tablespoons butter
Salt and pepper to taste
4 large slices sweet onion

¼ cup water or white wine
1 cup commercial sour cream
Grated Parmesan cheese

Brown chops in butter. Arrange in baking dish. Season with salt and pepper to taste and place 1 slice of onion on top of each chop. Mix water or wine with drippings in frying pan and pour over chops. Bake covered in a 350° F oven for 45 minutes. Remove cover, spread sour cream over chops, and sprinkle generously with grated Parmesan cheese. Return to oven, uncovered, for another 20 minutes or until brown.

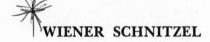

WIENER SCHNITZEL

The most popular ways of serving veal cutlets are Veal Parmesan, Veal Florentine, and Wiener Schnitzel, each named for the place of its origin. They're all very simple to prepare and are basically the same dish with variations. All make marvelous entrées for entertaining.

Time: About 15 to 20 minutes
Yield: 4 to 6 servings

1 pound veal cutlets or steaks cut ½ inch thick	1 tablespoon milk or cream
1 well beaten egg	1 cup bread crumbs
Salt and pepper to taste	Vegetable oil

Thaw meat and pound with meat hammer or mallet. Cut into serving-sized pieces. Combine beaten egg with cream or milk and add salt and pepper. Dip meat into egg mixture and then into bread crumbs. Let stand on waxed paper for 15 to 20 minutes to set crumbs. In large skillet, brown meat in shortening, first one side and then the other. Lower heat, cover, and continue cooking for another 5 minutes or until done. Garnish each piece of meat with a lemon slice and anchovy fillet. Serve immediately.

VEAL PARMESAN

Follow the instructions for Wiener Schnitzel, using olive oil for shortening. After meat has finished cooking, remove it from pan. Add a little more olive oil, if necessary, and 1 minced or pressed clove of garlic plus a tablespoon of instant minced onions. Sauté until lightly brown. Add an 8-ounce can of seasoned tomato or pizza sauce. Return meat to sauce and place a generous slice of mozzarella cheese on top of each piece of meat and sprinkle with Parmesan cheese. Cover and continue cooking at moderate heat until cheese is entirely melted. Serve immediately.

VEAL FLORENTINE

Prepare veal as in Wiener Schnitzel. While meat is cooking, prepare one 10-ounce package of frozen spinach in cream sauce. When meat has finished cooking, spoon an equal amount of spinach on each piece of breaded veal and top with a generous slice of Swiss cheese. Cover and continue cooking until cheese melts. Serve immediately.

VEAL SCALOPPINE

This is a quick but elegant meal that can be served to family and company alike. Keep the prepared veal round in your freezer and it can be cooked on very short notice.

Time: 10 minutes
Yield: 4 servings

1 pound veal round, cut in ¼-inch slices	1 cup thinly sliced fresh or frozen mushrooms
Flour	½ cup olive oil
Salt and pepper	½ cup cooking sauterne

Have your butcher slice the veal very thin into about 10 to 12 uniform pieces per pound. Using a meat hammer, pound these pieces on a bread or cutting board, until they're about ⅛ inch thick. Place meat between double thicknesses of waxed paper, freezer-wrap, date, label and freeze.

When ready to prepare Veal Scaloppine, remove from the freezer only the amount of meat needed. Because the meat is so thin, it will thaw very quickly. Sprinkle with salt and pepper and then flour lightly. In a large skillet, cook mushrooms in 2 tablespoons of olive oil until tender, about 4 to 5 minutes. (I use the olive oil from my cruet in which I have a clove of garlic soaking. See page 49. This gives just a hint of garlic flavor.) Remove mushrooms and keep warm. Add remaining olive oil to skillet and, when hot, put in several pieces of the veal and brown over high heat about 1 minute per side. Keep the cooked meat warm while browning remainder. When all the meat is browned, return mushrooms and meat to pan; add cooking sauterne and cook at high heat an additional minute. Remove from heat and arrange meat and mushrooms on a warmed platter. Scrape bottom of pan, stirring to mix the drippings with the sauterne; pour over meat.

PORK

CROWN PORK ROAST WITH DRESSING

This is a truly festive, delicious, and elegant entree. Because a crown roast weighs about 7 pounds or more, it's best to serve it when you're entertaining. It's just as easy to make two of these at the same time, and plan another dinner party soon. The dressing can be made the day of the dinner or a week ahead; fill the crown roast and freeze until used.

SINGLE RECIPE	DOUBLE RECIPE
Time: 20 minutes	*Time: 25 minutes*
Yield: 1 crown roast and dressing	*Yield: 2 crown roasts and dressing*
1 pound ground beef	2 pounds ground beef
½ pound pork sausage	1 pound pork sausage
½ cup chopped Spanish onion	1 cup chopped Spanish onion
2 tablespoons butter or drippings	3 tablespoons butter or drippings
¼ cup each of uncooked white, brown, and wild rice	½ cup each of uncooked white, brown, and wild rice
2 cups finely chopped celery	4 cups finely chopped celery
½ cup minced parsley	1 cup minced parsley
½ cup whole white raisins	1 cup whole white raisins
1½ teaspoons salt	1 tablespoon salt
¼ teaspoon pepper	½ teaspoon pepper
1 can (1 pound, 12 ounces) tomatoes	2 cans (1 pound, 12 ounces each) tomatoes
½ cup chopped pecans	1 cup chopped pecans
1 crown pork roast (about 7½ pounds)	2 crown pork roasts (about 7½ pounds each) or 3 (about 5 pounds each)

Have your butcher make up your crown pork roasts. They can be made up as small as 5 pounds and as large as 9 to 10 pounds. It's advisable to order these roasts in advance.

Cook ground beef, sausage, and onions in butter for 10 minutes, stirring frequently. Add rice, celery, parsley, raisins, seasonings, and tomatoes; cook to boiling. Cover and cook at low heat for 45 minutes, adding water if needed. Stir in nuts.

Season roast with salt and pepper; place in shallow roasting pan. Fill hollow with dressing; cover bone tips and dressing with foil. Bake at 325° F until meat thermometer registers 170° F (about 35 to 40 minutes per pound). Carefully remove roast to serving platter, using a spatula or two to keep dressing intact.

For a more festive look, arrange red spiced apples and parsley around the roast.

ORIENTAL SWEET-SOUR PORK

Even if you don't as a rule like pork loin, try this, especially if you like the sweet-sour pork in Chinese and Cantonese restaurants. When served with Cantonese Fried Rice (page 407), this is truly an elegant meal and yet very simple to prepare.

SINGLE RECIPE
Time: 5 minutes
Yield: 5 servings

2 pounds frozen pork loin tenderloin
1 cup apricot preserves
2 tablespoons soy sauce
1 tablespoon vinegar
1 teaspoon Chinese bead molasses

DOUBLE RECIPE
Time: 6 minutes
Yield: 10 servings

4 pounds frozen pork loin tenderloin
2 cups apricot preserves
4 tablespoons soy sauce
2 tablespoons vinegar
2 teaspoons Chinese bead molasses

Pork loin tenderloins are often frozen before they reach the meat markets—in which case, make sure that you request frozen pork loin tenderloins if you want to freeze them. Bring them home in their frozen state, freezer-wrap, and return to the freezer. You may bake these without thawing, if you allow additional baking time.

Arrange pork loin tenderloin in an 8 x 8 or 9 x 9-inch baking dish. (Use 9 x 13-inch pan for double recipe.) Insert meat thermometer and bake at 325° F for about 45 minutes. Combine all the remaining ingredients and mix well. Pour over the pork loin tenderloin. Return to oven and continue baking until meat thermometer registers 170° F, basting occasionally.

Remove meat from sauce and let cool for about 5 minutes. Then slice into very thin slices. You may wish to serve the meat arranged on a platter with the sauce as an accompaniment or slice the meat and return it to the sauce and serve.

ROLLED PORK ROAST

Preheat oven to 325° F. Put frozen meat in a shallow baking dish and brush liberally with Kitchen Bouquet. Now pour about half a cup of soy sauce over the roast and continue basting occasionlly while baking. Roast until meat is completely thawed and then insert meat thermometer. Continue roasting until meat thermometer registers 170° F.

The drippings in the pan will make a most delicious gravy. Thicken with flour mixed with water, and season to taste.

BROILED PORK LOIN CHOPS

If pork loin chops have been wrapped properly, they will separate easily and you may broil them while they are still frozen. Season chops liberally with herbs and pepper on both sides. Spread pork chops on broiler pan (pork loin chops should be about 1½ inches thick) and broil at 500° F until they're nicely browned. Turn and repeat on other side. Turn oven down to 350° F and bake for about 1¼ hours. (In gas stoves, chops should be put on center rack of oven to bake. In electric stoves this move to the center rack isn't necessary.) Thinner chops will require less time. Chops should be juicy on the inside.

VARIATIONS. Lamb loin chops can be broiled in the same manner, if you reduce baking time to about ½ hour, depending on thickness of chops.

STUFFED PORK LOIN CHOPS

It's just as easy to make these stuffed pork loin chops by the dozen as to prepare a few. You can then freeze them and cook them whenever the mood strikes. So the next time there's a sale on pork loin chops, buy in quantity! This recipe makes pork loin chops into a rather festive dinner.

SINGLE RECIPE
  Time: 15 minutes
  Yield: 4 stuffed pork loin chops

4 double pork loin chops
½ cup chopped onions
3 tablespoons butter
⅓ cup chopped mushrooms
¼ cup finely chopped celery
Pinch thyme
2 tablespoons chopped parsley
½ cup toasted bread crumbs
½ teaspoon salt
Pepper to taste
1 egg
Soy sauce

DOUBLE RECIPE
  Time: 20 minutes
  Yield: 8 stuffed pork loin chops

8 double pork loin chops
1 cup chopped onions
6 tablespoons butter
⅔ cup chopped mushrooms
½ cup chopped celery
Pinch thyme
¼ cup chopped parsley
1 cup toasted bread crumbs
1 teaspoon salt
Pepper to taste
2 eggs
Soy sauce

TRIPLE RECIPE
  Time: 25 minutes
  Yield: 12 stuffed pork loin chops

12 double pork loin chops
1½ cups chopped onions
¼ pound plus 1 tablespoon butter
1 cup chopped mushrooms
¾ cup finely chopped celery
Pinch thyme
⅓ cup chopped parsley
1½ cups toasted bread crumbs
1½ teaspoons salt
Pepper to taste
3 eggs
Soy sauce

Ask your butcher to cut a pocket in each double chop. Sauté chopped onions in melted shortening until onions are limp. Add chopped mushrooms, celery, thyme, and parsley, and continue cooking for 5 additional minutes. Stir in bread crumbs, salt, and pepper. Remove from heat and add slightly beaten eggs. Fill chop pockets with this mixture. You may want to use toothpicks as skewers to hold stuffing in the chops. Another easy way is simply to take a stitch or two with some heavy thread. Brush pork loin chops liberally with soy sauce and broil on both sides until just nicely browned. Transfer to baking dish, cover with a lid or foil, and bake for 1 hour at 325° F. Remove cover and continue baking 20 minutes longer. Allow 1 pork loin chop per serving.

TO FREEZE. Pork loin chops can be wrapped individually or in meal-size portions. Insert a double thickness of freezer wrap between the chops so that they'll separate easily while still frozen.

TO COOK AFTER FREEZING. Unwrap frozen package of stuffed pork loin chops and thaw in refrigerator. To cook while still frozen, brush liberally with soy sauce and put under the broiler until just nicely browned on both sides. Bake, uncovered, for about 30 minutes, and then covered for about 1 hour. Uncover for the last 15 to 20 minutes.

PORK CHOP SUEY

This is another tasty recipe, easy to make in batches and freeze. Because of all the different vegetables in this dish, it's really a meal in itself. A salad isn't necessary. Besides the rice and the Chinese noodles, plain sliced tomatoes make a nice accompaniment. In other words, it's a quick and easy meal to pop out of the freezer any day you're too busy to take much time for cooking.

Note that it takes less time to make a triple recipe than it does to make a double one; the reason is that, when you are making the larger quantities, you can use two pots at the same time, one for browning the meat and another for cooking the vegetables. Put all the vegetables in a large kettle and start heating them; meanwhile, in a large skillet, brown meat at high temperature, about 2 pounds of meat at a time. As meat is browned, add to vegetable mixture.

SINGLE RECIPE
Time: 25 minutes
Yield: 2 quarts

2 pounds cut-up lean pork
1 tablespoon fat or cooking oil
1 can (1 pound, 3 ounces) Chinese
mixed vegetables
1 cup diagonally sliced celery
1 large julienne-sliced green pepper
½ cup hot water
2 teaspoons beef bouillon granules
4 green diagonally sliced onions,
including tops

¼ pound fresh or frozen sliced
mushrooms (optional)
1 teaspoon sugar
½ teaspoon salt
1 tablespoon Chinese Bead Molasses
2 ounces soy sauce
¼ cup cornstarch
¼ cup cold water

DOUBLE RECIPE
Time: 40 minutes
Yield: 4 quarts

4 pounds cut-up lean pork
2 tablespoons fat or cooking oil
2 cans (1 pound, 3 ounces each)
Chinese mixed vegetables
2 cups diagonally sliced celery
2 large julienne-sliced green peppers
1 cup hot water
4 teaspoons beef bouillon granules
8 green diagonally sliced onions,
including tops
½ pound fresh or frozen sliced
mushrooms (optional)
2 teaspoons sugar
1 teaspoon salt
2 tablespoons Chinese Bead Molasses
4 ounces soy sauce
½ cup cornstarch
½ cup cold water

TRIPLE RECIPE
Time: 30 minutes
Yield: 6 quarts

6 pounds cut-up lean pork
2 to 3 tablespoons fat or cooking oil
3 cans (1 pound, 3 ounces each)
Chinese mixed vegetables
3 cups diagonally sliced celery
3 large julienne-sliced green peppers
1½ cups hot water
6 teaspoons beef bouillon granules
12 diagonally sliced green onions,
including tops
¾ pound fresh or frozen sliced
mushrooms (optional)
1 tablespoon sugar
1½ teaspoons salt
3 tablespoons Chinese Bead Molasses
6 ounces soy sauce
¾ cup cornstarch
¾ cup cold water

Brown meat in hot fat. Add seasonings, vegetables, sugar, soy sauce, water in which bouillon granules have been dissolved, and molasses. Bring this mixture to a gentle boil. Dissolve cornstarch in cold water and add slowly to boiling chop suey mixture, stirring constantly, until mixture is thick and clear, adding more water as necessary. Reduce heat, cover, and simmer for 40 minutes, adding more water as necessary. Serve piping hot over fluffy rice and or Chinese noodles.

TO SERVE WHEN FROZEN. This can be frozen in freezer-to-oven containers or in plastic ones. I use the latter and take the chop suey out of the freezer in the morning and let it thaw in the refrigerator. Add a little water and put on low flame to heat through before serving. To quick-thaw chop suey, put plastic container in hot water until thawed, before warming chop suey on top of stove, or thaw and heat in microwave unit.

BARBECUED PORK SPARERIBS OR PORK LOIN BACK RIBS

This is a simple, quick way to prepare frozen pork spareribs on short notice. It's especially nice when you've forgotten to thaw something for dinner. Because cooked meats don't freeze well, cook only the amount you plan to eat. Because these ribs are parboiled, they are never greasy.

Before putting the pork spareribs or pork loin back ribs into the freezer, cut them into 2 or 3-rib servings. When you take them from your freezer to use, put these frozen ribs into a large kettle of boiling water. Leave heat on high until the water begins to boil again. Now lower heat and simmer for 30 to 45 minutes. Drain and arrange the ribs on your broiling pan. Broil until brown and then turn. Brush liberally with a barbecue sauce (either your own or a commercially prepared product) and return to broiler until bubbly. May be served with the traditional baked beans, sauerkraut, or potato salad.

This shouldn't take more than 1 hour and 15 minutes from beginning to end, and you can use the time the meat is simmering to make your potato salad or beans and to set the table.

HAM

When baking a whole or half ham, there will always be a lot of juice and drippings. Strain these into a container and refrigerate, then remove the fat. Pour into ice-cube trays and freeze. When frozen, put cubes in plastic freezer bags (don't forget to label and date). Then when you want some ham seasoning for soup or vegetables, such as beans, just take out a couple of cubes. The broth is usually a bit salty, so remember this when adding it to another dish. For leftover ham recipes, see Hot Ham 'n Cheese Burgers (page 93); Leek and Ham Soup (page 400).

SCALLOPED POTATOES AND HAM AU GRATIN

This is a good recipe to use when you have a lot of ham left over from a baked ham dinner. I like to freeze it in serving casseroles that are just large enough for a meal. Making these in quantity is a real timesaver.

SINGLE RECIPE
> *Time: 20 minutes*
> *Yield: Two 2-quart casseroles*

3 tablespoons butter
3 tablespoons flour
2 to 2½ cups milk
½ teaspoon salt
2 teaspoons bouillon granules
1 tablespoon Worcestershire sauce
4 average or 3 large peeled Idaho potatoes
8 ounces sliced sharp Cheddar cheese (optional)
2 julienne-sliced green peppers
Cooked or leftover ham, sliced thin (about 1 pound, more or less)
Bread crumbs
Butter

DOUBLE RECIPE
> *Time: 30 minutes*
> *Yield: Four 2-quart casseroles or equivalent*

⅓ cup butter
⅓ cup flour
4 to 5 cups milk
1 teaspoon salt
4 teaspoons bouillon granules
2 tablespoons Worcestershire sauce
8 average or 6 large peeled Idaho potatoes
1 pound sliced sharp Cheddar cheese (optional)
4 julienne-sliced green peppers
Cooked or leftover ham, sliced thin (about 2 pounds, more or less)
Bread crumbs
Butter

Melt butter and add flour, stirring until dissolved. Gradually add milk and seasonings, stirring occasionally until thickened. While this is simmering, grease two casseroles (about 1½ to 2-quart size for a single recipe) or any number of casseroles in the sizes you use that would equal approximately 4 quarts.

Precook potatoes 10 to 15 minutes, depending on size, for any casseroles that are to be frozen before baking. Otherwise, cut raw potatoes into thin slices and arrange in bottom of casseroles. Add a layer of ham, then cheese and green peppers, topped with some of the sauce. Continue alternating layers until all the ingredients are used. The top layer should be potatoes, with remaining sauce poured on top. Sprinkle with dry bread crumbs and dot with butter. Bake in a 400° F oven until just bubbly. Remove the casseroles that you're going to freeze, and cool them. Wrap and freeze. Continue cooking the casserole that you're going to use immediately, until the potatoes are tender. (Depending on the size of your casserole dish, it should be done in 15 to 30 extra minutes.) With the addition of a salad, your meal will be complete.

TO SERVE WHEN FROZEN. It's best to thaw casserole as much as possible, especially the larger-sized dishes, because the outside will start to cook before the center is thawed. However, in case of emergency, you can put the casserole into the oven straight out of the freezer. Be sure to remove any aluminum covering or casserole tops, since this will keep it from heating through uniformly. Test potatoes to make sure they're done.

HAM AND MACARONI CASSEROLE

Here is another way to use leftover ham. It's practically a meal in itself. With all the meat, cheese, vegetables, and macaroni, you'll need only a tossed salad for an accompaniment.

SINGLE RECIPE
Time: 25 minutes
Yield: Two 1½-quart casseroles

3 cups ground or cubed ham
One 8-ounce package macaroni
¼ cup margarine or butter
¼ cup flour
Two 1-pound cans stewed tomatoes
Milk
½ pound sharp Cheddar cheese (optional)
1 teaspoon salt (less if ham is salty)
1 teaspoon dry mustard
2 tablespoons Worcestershire sauce
1 minced clove garlic
Bread crumbs
Butter

DOUBLE RECIPE
Time: 35 minutes
Yield: Four 1½-quart casseroles

6 cups ground or cubed ham
Two 8-ounce packages macaroni
½ cup margarine or butter
½ cup flour
Four 1-pound cans stewed tomatoes
Milk
1 pound sharp Cheddar cheese (optional)
2 teaspoons salt (less if ham is salty)
2 teaspoons dry mustard
¼ cup Worcestershire sauce
2 minced cloves garlic
Bread crumbs
Butter

Cut meat from ham bone and grind or cut in cubes. Cook macaroni for 3 minutes. (Cook 3 minutes if you're using the quick-cook "7 minute" type macaroni. Some macaroni is the longer-cooking type and should be cooked just enough so that it's soft and about double in volume.)

In large skillet, melt shortening and add flour. Stir until completely dissolved and bubbly. Drain tomatoes and add enough milk to juice to make 1½ cups (for single recipe). Add liquid to flour mixture, stirring constantly so that there are no lumps. When bubbly and thick, lower heat and add cheese that has been cut into thin slices. Cook until melted. Add salt, mustard, Worcestershire sauce, and garlic. Then add ham and tomatoes. (If tomatoes are whole, break up into smaller pieces.) Mix all ingredients together in a very large container and divide into family-sized portions. Put into greased casseroles, cover with bread crumbs, and dot with butter. Bake in 350° F oven for 45 minutes or until nice and bubbly.

TO FREEZE. If you don't have enough bake-and-serve dishes, line dishes with foil, fill, and then freeze. After the casserole is frozen, remove it from container, wrap in freezer wrap, date, label, and return to freezer.

TO SERVE WHEN FROZEN. Depending on the size of the casserole, an additional 30 to 45 minutes baking time is usually adequate for the frozen casseroles. *Always bake uncovered!*

SPAGHETTI CASSEROLE

Because it's made with bacon and ham, this spaghetti casserole has an unusual flavor. This is one more way to use your ham leftovers.

SINGLE RECIPE	DOUBLE RECIPE
Time: 15 minutes	*Time: 20 minutes*
Yield: 2 quarts	*Yield: 4 quarts*
4 slices of bacon or ¼ cup crumbled bacon (see page 41)	8 slices of bacon or ½ cup crumbled bacon (see page 41)
1 cup chopped or ground ham	2 cups chopped or ground ham
½ cup chopped onion	1 cup chopped onion
1 coarsely chopped green pepper	2 coarsely chopped green peppers
1 minced clove garlic	2 minced cloves garlic
½ pound ground beef	1 pound ground beef
One 8-ounce can tomato sauce	Two 8-ounce cans tomato sauce
One 1-pound can stewed tomatoes	Two 1-pound cans stewed tomatoes
8 ounces spaghetti	1 pound spaghetti
1 cup grated or shredded sharp cheese	2 cups grated or shredded sharp cheese

Cook bacon until almost crisp; then remove from pan and set aside. Drain off most of the drippings. Add onions, peppers, and garlic, and sauté for about 3 minutes. Add beef; continue stirring until beef is done. Meanwhile, cook spaghetti in boiling water. Remember to undercook, especially if you plan to freeze part of the recipe. Add bacon, ham, tomato sauce, and stewed tomatoes, as well as spaghetti and cheese. Pour into casseroles. Bake for 30 minutes at 350° F.

TO FREEZE. Simply cool casserole, wrap, label, and date.

TO SERVE WHEN FROZEN. Bake in 350° F oven for 1¼ hours, if casserole is taken directly from the freezer. Baking time may be shortened somewhat if the casserole is first allowed to thaw partially.

LAMB

Lamb is often called the forgotten meat. While it is delectable, too often it is ordered only when dining out and completely "forgotten" when cooking at home. Roasting lamb is no more difficult or mysterious than any other meat; it is a young meat and requires only a minimum of cooking time. Often lamb is overcooked at home. When broiling or roasting lamb, try cooking it to an internal temperature of 165° F to 170° F for rare; medium-well is 170° F to 175° F; 175° F to 180° F is considered very well done. I strongly recommend that you try cooking lamb on the rare side, so that it is a little pink on the inside. This gives lamb an entirely different and desirable texture and flavor. Lamb can be roasted, broiled, braised, and/or simmered, depending on the cut and recipe you select.

Buying and Storing Lamb

Most often you will find "spring lamb" which has been slaughtered at approximately 6 months. Year-round lamb also is available and that generally is 5 to 11 months old. New Zealand and Australian lamb is imported and is also considered a very good quality of lamb, usually purchased frozen. Lamb should be light pink to a darker rose color, according to age; texture should be very fine with a velvety look to it, and fat should be smooth, firm, and white. Unless you plan to use the lamb within 2 or 3 days, it is best to freeze it. Label and wrap lamb in proper vapor-moisture-proof material before freezing. This especially is a good idea at that time of the year (mostly in the spring) when lamb is on sale. Remember when you are buying meat for the freezer that boned roasts and meat take up less room.

LEG OF LAMB

Lamb is a favorite in the Near East countries and we can learn a great deal from how they prepare it. This recipe originates in the Mediterranean area and is exceptionally good.

Yield: Serves 6 to 8

1 leg of spring lamb (4 to 5½ pounds)	½ cup chopped frozen onions
⅛ teaspoon black pepper	4 sprigs of parsley
1 teaspoon oregano	1 clove of garlic, halved
¼ cup butter or margarine	1 cup hot water
Juice of 1 lemon	

Rub leg of lamb with pepper and oregano, melt butter and mix with lemon juice. Brush over meat. Put lamb in a roasting pan and add the onions, parsley, garlic, and hot water. Insert meat thermometer and roast in a preheated 400° F oven for 20 minutes. Lower temperature to 350° F and bake to 165° F to 170° F for rare, 170° F to 175° F for medium, or 175° F to 180° F for well done, as you prefer. (Do not confuse rare lamb with rare beef, which is cooked to only 140° F and is still a bit bloody.) Baste several times during the baking. Serve with pilaf if you wish.

TURKISH LAMB SHISH KABOB

A Mideast recipe that is also becoming a favorite here. Very easy to prepare and marvelous for a summer barbecue. Very little else is needed in the way of side dishes. Serve with a large bowl of buttered and seasoned rice.

Yield: 6 servings

½ cup vegetable or olive oil
⅓ cup lime juice
1 teaspoon dry mustard
¼ teaspoon thyme
1 bay leaf, crushed
⅛ teaspoon rosemary
½ teaspoon salt
⅛ teaspoon pepper

1 tablespoon dehydrated chopped onion
2 pounds lean, boned lamb (from shoulder or rump) cut in 1½-inch cubes
½ pound fresh large mushrooms
1 dozen (approximately) small white onions (1 to 1½ inches in diameter)
2 green peppers, cut in eighths

Combine oil, lime juice, seasonings, and dehydrated onions in a bowl. Add cubed lamb. (To save time, have your butcher prepare lamb for you.) Marinate 5 hours or overnight. Drain, reserving marinade.

On long skewers, alternate cubes of lamb with whole onions, mushroom caps, and pieces of green pepper until all the ingredients are used. Place kabobs on rack 3 inches from heat when coals are grey. Broil approximately 20 minutes, turning once, basting with remaining marinade. Onions will become somewhat blackened, but don't worry about it. Simply remove outer peelings after they are removed from skewers. You can also make these under your broiler in the oven. Place at least 3 inches from source of heat and watch closely.

TO FREEZE. Although shish kabobs don't freeze well, you can keep the lamb cubes in the freezer for unexpected company. (Buy when on sale.) Let lamb thaw in marinade in refrigerator.

LAMB PILAF

A marvelous all-in-one dish with a distinctive Mediterranean flavor.

Yield: 6 to 8 servings

4 tablespoons butter or margarine
3 pounds boned lean lamb, cut into
   1-inch cubes
1 large Spanish onion, sliced thinly
   and separated into rings
½ teaspoon cinnamon
½ teaspoon pepper
1 cup raw rice
1 cup white raisins

1 teaspoon salt
One 10½-ounce can consomme
1 cup water
¼ cup lemon juice
1 cup (two 3-ounce packages) sliced
   almonds, toasted
½ cup chopped or snipped parsley

Preheat oven to 400° F. Melt half the butter or margarine in a large heavy skillet. Sauté half the lamb over very high heat until browned. Remove lamb from skillet and drain on paper toweling. Remove excess fat from the skillet. Add remaining butter or margarine and repeat with remaining lamb. Lower heat. Sauté onions. Add cinnamon and pepper, and continue cooking over medium low heat for 3 to 5 minutes, until the onions become soft.

For a single recipe, butter a 2½-quart casserole lightly. Sprinkle the bottom lightly with ¼ cup raw rice and ¼ of the raisins, meat, and onions. Repeat layers. Sprinkle top with salt. Add combined consomme and water. Pour over the mixture, along with lemon juice. Cover. Bake at 400° F for 50 minutes. Remove cover. Sprinkle top with almonds and parsley. Bake 10 minutes longer. Serve immediately.

TO FREEZE. Arrange pilaf in casserole dish, omitting almonds and parsley. Freezer-wrap, label, date and freeze.

TO SERVE WHEN FROZEN. Bake frozen casserole in a preheated 400° F oven for 1 hour and 35 minutes. Remove cover, add almonds and parsley, and continue baking for another 10 minutes. Smaller casserole dishes require less baking time.

Pies

✳✳✳✳✳✳✳✳✳✳✳✳✳✳✳✳✳✳✳✳✳✳✳✳✳✳✳

There are many kinds of pies and the single-crusted types are known by many different names: they're often called flans, tortas, quiches, and the smaller varieties are called tarts and tartlets. They can be filled with meats and vegetables, as well as sweets. They may be served hot or cold, and in some cases they're served frozen. They can be served as the first, main, or dessert course, and can be served with any meal, including brunch. We will, however, concern ourselves here mainly with the dessert pie in its various forms.

After much deliberation, I've decided to confess that my pastry-crusted pies leave something to be desired. Oh, it isn't that they don't taste good—my crust is light and flaky and the fillings are delicious too—but, from a purely aesthetic point of view, they're not all they could be. I don't know what it is that I'm lacking, but my pies never seem to look like the pictures you see in magazines.

You'll notice that most of the pies here are of the open-face type. They're preferable if you're watching calories, and also are easier and faster to make.

The following are some piecrust recipes that I frequently use. I also want to make it clear that I'm not above using piecrust mix, especially when I'm in a hurry. All pircrust mixes are not the same, so try several until you find the one that best suits your taste. The Py-O-My ready mix is my favorite brand, but it's difficult to find at times.

FREEZING PIES AND PIECRUSTS

Because piecrusts freeze well, either baked or unbaked, it's a good idea to make several at a time and put them into the freezer. When you consider all the time and effort (getting out the pastry cloth, rolling pin, et cetera), it takes to make a single crust, it would be prudent always to make the larger recipes. Each additional crust takes only about 4 minutes to make. If your family is small, you may prefer to cut the extra dough into 4-inch circles for tarts and freeze them flat (which will be explained below), especially if freezer space is at a premium.

Unbaked Piecrusts

Unbaked pie crusts can be frozen in two different ways; the first takes up the least room in your freezer. You simply roll out the dough to a size that will fit your pie tin, allowing for the fluted edge, trim it with a pastry wheel, and lay it on a piece of cardboard. Save the heavy cardboard backings from large commercially prepared pizza pies. These are just the right size and thickness to give you piecrusts perfect protection for their stay in your freezer. Several pieces of pastry may be frozen in this manner, one on top of the other. Be sure to insert a double thickness of freezer paper between the layers; then wrap with foil or freezer wrap, and store. The pie dough will keep in the freezer for about 3 months. Simply remove the dough as you need it, making sure always to seal the package securely each time you open it to remove a sheet of pastry. It takes about 15 minutes to thaw the dough enough to fit into a pan.

The second way will work only for single-crust pies. You put the crust in the pie tin, flute it, and then freeze it. Aluminum pie tins are inexpensive, so keep several on hand for this purpose. Remember, the frozen crust will break easily; after they're wrapped, be sure to store them where they're not apt to get jostled or knocked around. A strip of cardboard taped around the edges will also protect the frozen piecrust.

When freezing a double-crusted pie, don't put slits in the upper crust. Set all unbaked pies (single and double-crusted) in the freezer until firm, then wrap in moisture-vapor-proof material, label, date, and freeze.

Baked Pie Shells

Prepare and bake pie shells according to recipe directions. Cool completely and then wrap for the freezer, seal, date, and label.

Baked Pies

Prepare baked pies according to the directions in your recipe. Completely cool pie, freezer-wrap, date, label, and freeze.

Chiffon Pies

Chiffon pies are frozen after they have been made according to directions. If the recipe calls for a whipped cream topping, omit it or stabilize the whipped cream according to directions on page 54 before freezing. Again, set pie or pies in the freezer until very firm, then freezer-wrap, date, label, and freeze.

Crumb Crusts

If your crumb crusts are going to be used with fillings that don't require baking, then bake the crusts before putting them into the freezer. All crumb crusts should be left in their original pie plates. This gives the crust sufficient protection while it's in the freezer. Insert your piecrust (with its plate) in a plastic freezer bag. Seal, date, and label. Crumb crusts can be stored in this manner one on top of another, thereby taking up very little space in your freezer.

Custard and Fruit Pies

Cream and custard pies do not freeze well unless made with Clearjel (see page 70). Fruit pies freeze well either baked or unbaked. However, I prefer to bake mine just before serving them; then they have that just-out-of-the-oven flavor. Chiffon pies may also be frozen; you may notice that the texture is a bit heavier after they've been frozen.

USING FROZEN PIE SHELLS AND PIES

Unbaked Pie Shells

If you're going to bake the shell without a filling, prick holes with a fork all around the shell. Immediately bake frozen pie shell for about 20 minutes, or until golden brown, in a preheated oven at 450° F. Let it cool completely and fill as you wish.

When pie shell is going to be baked with a filling, simply let lined pie plate thaw at room temperature or in the refrigerator. Fill and bake according to recipe directions.

If you're working with flat-frozen pie dough, see instructions in paragraph 2 on page 309.

Baked Pie Shells

Remove freezer wrappings and let the shells thaw at room temperature, or fill them while still frozen and refrigerate, or let stand at room temperature until you're certain that the crust has thawed completely before serving. This is usually just a matter of 10 minutes or so.

Crumb Crusts

Let crust stand at room temperature to thaw. If baking is necessary, fill and bake, or bake empty according to recipe directions.

Filled Unbaked Pies

To serve a double-crusted pie from the freezer, make slits in top crust and put directly into a preheated oven at 425° F. Bake about 1 hour (the time will vary, depending on the size of the pie), or until crust is golden brown and the fruit is bubbly. Single-crusted fruit pies are baked in the same manner and removed when the fruit seems tender.

Filled Baked Pies

Baked pies are best when completely thawed and then, perhaps, warmed for 10 to 15 minutes in a preheated oven at 375° F. A solidly frozen baked pie can be thawed in the oven in about 30 to 40 minutes at 375° F. However, the crusts seem to get a bit overdone and the pie tends to dry out when this method is used.

Chiffon, custard, and cream pies are best thawed in the refrigerator. To hurry the thawing time, you may let them stand at room temperature for about 2 hours and then put them in the refrigerator to finish thawing. Chiffon pies take about 1½ hours to thaw in the refrigerator after thawing at room temperature for 1½ hours. Cream and custard pies take longer to thaw, depending on how light or heavy the filling is. Some custard pies take 3 hours or more, even if you have let them stand for 2 hours at room temperature. It is not recommended that you thaw chiffon, custard, or cream pies in microwave oven unless your unit has a defrost cycle, and then thaw only partially.

A Gourmet Touch

The next time you make whipped cream to top your pies, add any *one* of the following ingredients for a real taste treat.

To 1 cup (½ pint) of heavy cream, whipped, add:

1 teaspoon of grated lemon rind	Good on apple pies and desserts, as well as some chocolate ones
2 teaspoons of crème de menthe	Especially good with peach pies
2 teaspoons of orange curaçao or Cointreau	Very good with strawberry or blueberry pies
2 teaspoons of sherry	Good with apple pies and cherry pies and desserts
2 teaspoons of brandy	Serve with mincemeat pies and desserts, also eggnog dishes
2 teaspoons of rum	Delicious with chocolate pies and desserts
2 drops of almond flavoring	Blends well with either cherry or apricot pies and desserts

If you don't like the chemical flavor of frozen whipped topping, but are worried about the calories of real whipped cream, here's what you can do. Whip one egg white until quite stiff. Then whip your cream in a separate bowl, add your flavoring, and fold in beaten egg white. You absolutely cannot taste the egg white, yet you will have almost twice the amount of whipping cream with virtually half the calories.

MAKING BASIC PIE AND TART PASTRY

GOOD BASIC PASTRY

For a buttery flavor, you may substitute butter for half of the lard in this recipe. However, the all-lard pastry will be lighter and flakier. If you decide to use butter, be sure to chill the dough for half an hour before rolling it out. The time given is for mixing the dough; allow 5 minutes to roll out and shape each piecrust.

Time: 6 minutes for 2 crusts
8 minutes for 4 crusts
12 minutes for 6 crusts

TWO PIECRUSTS

2 cups sifted flour	¼ teaspoon baking powder
⅔ cup lard	6 tablespoons cold milk
½ teaspoon salt	(approximately)

FOUR PIECRUSTS
4 cups sifted flour
1⅓ cups lard
1 teaspoon salt
½ teaspoon baking powder
¾ cup cold milk (approximately)

SIX PIECRUSTS
6 cups sifted flour
2 cups lard
1½ teaspoons salt
¾ teaspoon baking powder
1 cup plus 2 tablespoons cold milk
   (approximately)

Mixing Methods

ELECTRIC MIXER. If you have a mixer that will operate with only one beater, you can assemble these piecrusts in a very short time. Remove the beater toward the center of the bowl; measure in your flour and add the lard, cutting it into chunks. Sprinkle salt and baking powder over the top. Beat at moderate speed until the mixture is the size of baby peas. Remove remaining beater; add liquid, stirring with a fork, following instructions under Hand Method. Do not fold in liquid with beater.

HAND METHOD. Cut cold lard into flour with a pastry blender or knife until pieces are the size of small peas. Don't make the mixture too fine. Add salt and baking powder to the cold milk and stir. Sprinkle milk, 1 tablespoon at a time, in the center of the flour-shortening mixture, pushing the moistened part to one side. Continue until all the mixture is moistened, adding an extra tablespoon of milk if needed. If moistened dough seems too wet, roll it in the dry mixture. Don't be too generous with liquid or your dough will be difficult to handle. Gather mixture into a ball, being careful not to overwork the dough. Chill at least 20 minutes before rolling out. This step makes the dough more manageable and less sticky. It will also help keep the heat of your hands from melting the shortening, so the finished crust will be flakier. If you don't want to roll out dough at this time, it may be stored in the refrigerator overnight or longer. Roll it into a perfectly round ball and cover with plastic wrap to keep it from drying out.

FOOD PROCESSOR. Use steel blade to cut shortening into flour, turning processor off and on very rapidly. Be very careful not to overprocess at this point. Measure your liquid, turn processor on, pour liquid through the tube, and turn off processor the instant the dough forms a ball. There really is no need to measure the liquid after you get the hang of it, as you stop pouring when the pastry forms a ball. This whole process takes less than a minute.

Rolling and Baking Pastry

If dough has been refrigerated for several hours, let it stand at room temperature for 10 to 15 minutes before working with it. Over-chilled dough is difficult to roll out and breaks very easily. Put ball of pastry on a well-floured pastry cloth and flatten slightly. Now press dough with the edge of your hand, making three indentations across the ball of dough; then give the dough a quarter-turn and repeat.

Rolling the dough out to the proper size is simplified when the pastry cloth has circles drawn on it. Roll the dough in spoke fashion from the center out to the edge, using light strokes. The dough should be rolled to about 1/16-inch thickness. To transfer the pastry to the pie tin, simply roll it up on the rolling pin and gently unroll it on the pie plate. Chill for half an hour before baking.

SINGLE-CRUST PIE. Trim pastry ½ inch beyond the rim of the pie plate. Fold pastry dough under the edge and make a raised flute with your finger. To bake a single crust, be sure that the dough has not been stretched. Prick many holes with a fork in the bottom of the crust to avoid bubbling. (Another sure way to avoid this problem is to cover the finished and fluted pie shell with a large circle of waxed paper. Fill with enough dried beans or rice to cover bottom of pie shell. After pie shell is completely baked and cooled, remove waxed paper with beans or rice. Store dried beans or rice to be reused at another time.) Use as little flour as possible to prevent sticking; too much flour will result in a tough crust. A stockinette cover over your rolling pin will distribute the extra flour evenly as the dough is rolled out. If the dough should bubble while baking, simply prick with a fork.

Bake in a very hot oven, 450° F, for 10 to 12 minutes or until golden brown. These single-crust pie shells are marvelous to have on hand for chiffon, cream, and boiled custard pies, as well as no-bake cheese and fruit pies. You can keep them in airtight metal or plastic containers, as well as freeze in rigid, moisture-proof containers.

To bake frozen unbaked pastry, place in the oven while still frozen and allow a few additional minutes for baking.

TWO-CRUST PIES. Fill the shell with your choice of pie filling and then, following the above steps, make a second crust. Again lift the pastry by rolling it on the rolling pin and unroll on the filled pie. Trim pastry ½ inch larger that the pie plate. Tuck the edge of the top crust under the rim of the bottom crust and crimp. Be sure that the top crust is well vented before putting it into the oven. Pies that are to be frozen in this manner should not be vented until they are to be baked. Baking directions are given with the pie filling recipes.

PREVENTING SOGGY CRUSTS. When you are baking pies that are

liquid, such as pumpkin and custard, or some fruit and berry pies that have a lot of juice in the bottom, simply brush the crust with an egg white that has been slightly beaten with 1 teaspoon of water. Or substitute Instant Clearjel for thickening (see Clearjel, page 70). Be sure to mix Clearjel thoroughly with sugar to avoid lumps. Always chill the dough well before filling the crust. Putting the pie on the bottom of the oven, where the heat is more intense, also helps. As an extra precaution, you can also bake the piecrust for 5 minutes at 450° F before filling it, simply to set the crust. Cool crust; fill and bake according to recipe.

LEFTOVER PASTRY. A good way to use the pastry that's trimmed from a pie is to cut out decorative shapes, using aspic cutters or small cookie cutters. Place a double layer of waxed paper between layers of pastry pieces so the pieces can be separated easily after they are frozen. These decorations are nice to put on the top of casseroles and single-crust pies; baked, they can be floated in a bowl of soup. You'll find many other uses for these little garnishments.

VARIATIONS ON BASIC PASTRY. Substitute ½ cup quick-cooking rolled oats for ½ cup of flour.

Add ¼ cup of lightly toasted sesame seeds.

Substitute ½ cup of finely ground nuts for ½ cup flour.

Add ⅓ cup of grated sharp Cheddar cheese after the shortening has been cut into the flour. More water may be needed. This is really good when you are making apple pies.

Substitute ½ cup of cornmeal for ½ cup of flour. This type of crust is more suitable for meat and vegetable pies.

Common Causes of Pie Failure

If your crust is not tender and flaky: You may have overmixed or overhandled the dough. This melts the fat particles, and the pastry will not be flaky. Be sure that your liquid is ice-cold, since warm liquid also melts the fat particles.

If your crust shrinks or buckles while baking: You have probably stretched the dough when rolling or fitting into the pan. Always roll from the center to the outside edge of the dough; lay the dough into pie tin, being careful not to stretch it. Buckling of an unbaked pie shell may be caused by not pricking the crust enough.

If you have an underdone or soggy crust: A tear in the bottom crust can cause this, allowing juice or pie filling to run under the piecrust. May be caused by shiny pans, which reflect the heat away from the pie. Placing the pie on a baking sheet also deflects the heat away from the pie. Be sure to cool pie on a rack so that the air can circulate underneath pie plate and cool it quickly.

If dough doesn't hold together: You probably need to add more liquid. Also, don't cut shortening too fine. Fine particles will not absorb liquid properly and will make dough crumbly.

If dough sticks to board or rolling pin when you roll: You may have added too much liquid. Try rolling dough between layers of waxed paper. Chilling dough should also help.

TARTS

For tart shells, the pastry should be rolled a bit thicker than for pie crusts. Tart shells can be made by cutting the pastry into 4-inch circles with a pastry wheel. These circles can be fitted on the backs of inverted muffin tins or individual custard cups. A two-crust pie recipe will usually yield about 12 tarts of this size. Bake the same as single-crust pie shells.

CRUMB CRUSTS

GRAHAM CRACKER CRUST

Now that you can buy prepared graham cracker crumbs, this is the quickest of all the crumb crusts. It is also perhaps the best known and the most versatile.

SINGLE RECIPE	DOUBLE RECIPE
Time: 5 minutes	Time: 8 minutes
Yield: One 9-inch piecrust	Yield: Two 9-inch piecrusts
1½ cups graham cracker crumbs (or 18 crackers crushed)	3 cups graham cracker crumbs (or 36 crackers crushed)
2 tablespoons sugar	¼ cup sugar
½ cup melted butter or margarine	1 cup melted butter or margarine

Melt shortening. Meanwhile, measure and pour crumbs into pie plate. Add sugar and mix well. Now pour melted shortening over this mixture. Stir with a fork until all the shortening is equally incorporated in the crumb mixture. Spread mixture around evenly and press an 8-inch pie plate on top of the crumb mixture. The crumbs will shape themselves evenly. Bake at 375° F for about 8 minutes or until edges are slightly browned. A single recipe can be mixed right in the pie tin.

VANILLA WAFER CRUST

This crust is quite a bit more crunchy than the graham cracker crust and has an entirely different flavor. Cream fillings, particularly banana cream pies, are delicious in this crust.

SINGLE RECIPE
Time: 8 minutes
Yield: One 9-inch crust

1¼ cups fine vanilla wafer crumbs (about 36 cookies)
2 tablespoons sugar
⅓ cup melted butter or margarine

DOUBLE RECIPE
Time: 10 minutes
Yield: Two 9-inch crusts

2½ cups fine vanilla wafer crumbs (about 72 cookies)
¼ cup sugar
⅔ cup melted butter or margarine

Crush wafers quickly and easily in your blender or food processor. Melt shortening. Combine all the ingredients in the pie plate and mix thoroughly. Again, press an 8-inch pie plate on top of the crumbs to shape crust. (See instructions for Graham Cracker Crust.) Bake at 375° F for 8 minutes.

GINGERSNAP CRUST

This crust is particularly good with pumpkin chiffon pies and spicy raisin-type fillings.

SINGLE RECIPE
Time: 8 minutes
Yield: One 9-inch crust

1½ cups fine gingersnap crumbs (about 24 gingersnaps)
2 tablespoons sugar
¼ cup melted butter or margarine

DOUBLE RECIPE
Time: 10 minutes
Yield: Two 9-inch crusts

3 cups fine gingersnap crumbs (about 48 gingersnaps)
¼ cup sugar
½ cup melted butter or margarine

Drop gingersnaps into blender or food processor, making fine crumbs. Melt shortening and pour all the ingredients into pie plate. Mix well. (See instructions for Graham Cracker Crust and bake accordingly.)

OATMEAL CRUST

Here's another variation that has a nutty flavor and is particularly good with cream pies that have a fruit topping.

SINGLE RECIPE
Time: 5 minutes
Yield: One 9-inch crust

1½ cups quick-cooking rolled oats (uncooked)
⅓ cup firmly packed brown sugar
⅓ cup melted butter or margarine
⅓ cup chopped nuts
1 tablespoon maple syrup

DOUBLE RECIPE
Time: 8 minutes
Yield: Two 9-inch crusts

3 cups quick-cooking rolled oats (uncooked)
⅔ cup firmly packed brown sugar
⅔ cup melted butter or margarine
⅔ cup chopped nuts
2 tablespoons maple syrup

Heat oven to 350° F. Combine oats, brown sugar, melted shortening; mix well. Then add nuts and syrup. Shape. Set an 8-inch pie plate on crust before baking. Bake at 350° F for about 8 minutes. Cool and then remove 8-inch pie plate.

CHOCOLATE WAFER CRUST

This chocolate crust is good with any filling that goes well with chocolate. I happen to like lemon meringue filling in it, or the Quick-and-Easy Black Bottom Pie filling on page 319, as well as many others.

SINGLE RECIPE
Time: 8 minutes
Yield: One 9-inch crust

15 chocolate cream wafer cookies (two wafers held together with either vanilla or chocolate cream filling) or 1½ cups, crushed
3 tablespoons melted butter or margarine

DOUBLE RECIPE
Time: 10 minutes
Yield: Two 9-inch crusts

30 chocolate cream wafer cookies (two wafers held together with either vanilla or chocolate cream filling) or 3 cups, crushed
6 tablespoons melted butter or margarine

Drop cookies into the blender or food processor while it's going at high speed. Your crumbs will be ready in minutes. Combine with melted shortening and press into pie plate. Bake at 350° F oven for about 8 minutes.

QUICK-AND-EASY CHOCOLATE PIECRUST

This is a confection type of crust that's particularly good filled with French ice cream; coffee, chocolate, or peppermint ice creams are especially tasty with this crust. Garnish with whipped cream (see pages 311–12) or chocolate shot or shavings. Once frozen, the pie shells can easily be removed from the plate and stored in a protective container. They're easy to make and wonderful to have on hand at all times.

SINGLE RECIPE
   Time: 5 minutes
   Yield: One 9-inch crust

One 6-ounce package semisweet
   chocolate pieces
3 tablespoons butter
2½ cups crisp rice cereal
3 tablespoons light corn syrup

DOUBLE RECIPE
   Time: 7 minutes
   Yield: Two 9-inch crusts

One 12-ounce package semisweet
   chocolate pieces
6 tablespoons butter
5 cups crisp rice cereal
6 tablespoons light corn syrup

Melt chocolate in the top of a double boiler over hot water (not boiling); add butter and corn syrup and mix thoroughly. Add cereal and stir until all the cereal is coated. Pour into a buttered 9-inch pie plate. Press into place and freeze.

TO SERVE WHEN FROZEN. Remove from freezer at least half an hour before serving and return to pie plate. Fill with ice cream just before serving. Otherwise the crust is too hard to cut. Ice cream should be soft enough to pack into crust properly. You may want to return the pie to the freezer for 10 minutes to harden the ice cream.

FILLINGS

QUICK-AND-EASY BLACK BOTTOM PIE

This is a simplified version of the old Black Bottom Pie. It is a delightful combination of chocolate, rum, and cream filling.

Time: 17 minutes
Yield: One 9-inch pie

One 9-inch Chocolate Wafer Crust
   (see page 318)
3 tablespoons cold water
1 package unflavored gelatin
⅓ cup cold milk
3 egg yolks
⅓ cup sugar
1 tablespoon cornstarch or Clearjel

Pinch salt
⅓ cup instant nonfat dry milk
¾ cup boiling water
1 teaspoon vanilla extract
3 egg whites
Pinch cream of tartar
¼ cup sugar
1 teaspoon rum extract

If you use Clearjel (see page 70) this pie can be frozen.

Dissolve gelatin in cold water and let soften for 5 minutes. In mixing bowl or blender, combine cold milk, egg yolks, sugar, cornstarch, instant nonfat dry milk, and salt. Blend well. Add boiling water and cook in top of double boiler, stirring constantly until custard coats spoon. Remove from heat and stir in gelatin until it has dissolved. Add vanilla and chill. Meanwhile, beat egg whites until creamy; add cream of tartar and beat until moist peaks form when beater is raised. Gradually add sugar, beating until stiff and shiny. Add rum extract. Add to cooled custard mixture. Pour unto prepared chocolate piecrust and chill for 2 hours or more. Chocolate shavings on top of pie give a decorative touch.

SOUR CREAM APPLE PIE

This apple pie is a bit different, and I'm sure you'll enjoy it.

Time: 10 minutes
Yield: One 9-inch pie

One 9-inch unbaked pie shell
6 cups of thawed prepared frozen
  apples
  or
6 pared and cored tart apples
1 tablespoon lemon juice (optional)
¾ cup sugar

⅓ cup Instant Clearjel (see page 70)
  or cornstarch
1 teaspoon cinnamon
¼ teaspoon allspice
¼ teaspoon nutmeg
¼ cup cold butter
½ cup commercial sour cream

Place apples in a large bowl to thaw; apples should be sufficiently thawed so that the slices separate easily. Sprinkle with lemon juice. In another small bowl, combine Clearjel or cornstarch, sugar, cinnamon, allspice, and nutmeg, mixing well. With a pastry blender or knife, cut in the butter. Sprinkle this mixture over the apples and toss. Place in pie shell. Spoon sour cream on top. Bake in a preheated oven at 400° F for 30 minutes; then lower heat to 350° F and bake about 20 minutes longer, or until the apples are tender.

TAFFY-APPLE PIE. Combine 1 cup of caramel or butterscotch ice cream topping with sour cream. This gives the pie a taffy-apple flavor.

QUICK CHERRY OR BLUEBERRY CREAM PIE

These pies are nice to have on hand. Use a baked pie shell (either pastry or crumb), fill with French Cream Filling (page 323), top with prepared fruit pie filling of your choice, and serve. Make several while you're at it.

SINGLE RECIPE	DOUBLE RECIPE
Time: 6 minutes	*Time: 7 minutes*
Yield: One 9-inch pie	*Yield: Two 9-inch pies*
2 cups boiling water	4 cups boiling water
½ cup sugar	1 cup sugar
2 tablespoons Clearjel (see page 70)	¼ cup Clearjel (see page 70)
2 tablespoons flour	¼ cup flour
½ teaspoon salt	1 teaspoon salt
1 egg yolk	2 egg yolks
½ cup cold milk	1 cup cold milk
⅔ cup instant nonfat dry milk	1⅓ cups instant nonfat dry milk
1 tablespoon butter	2 tablespoons butter
2 teaspoons vanilla	1 tablespoon plus 1 teaspoon vanilla
1 can cherry or blueberry pie filling	2 cans cherry or blueberry pie filling

Mix sugar, flour, Clearjel, and salt. Combine egg yolk and cold milk, beating slightly with a fork. Now add to flour and Clearjel mixture. Add nonfat dry milk and stir well, making sure there are no lumps. (A wire whisk is indispensable for this purpose.) Add boiling water slowly. Continue cooking over moderately high heat, stirring all the while. Cook for several minutes (longer for a double recipe) until smooth and thick. Add butter; continue stirring until butter is completely dissolved. Now add vanilla. Cool. Pour cooled filling into baked pie shell and freeze if you wish.

TO SERVE. Pour the contents of one can of either cherry or blueberry pie filling on top of the cream filling and chill. Garnish with whipped cream, if desired, and serve.

TO SERVE WHEN FROZEN. Remove from freezer in the morning and let thaw in the refrigerator all day. Pie filling may be added at any time.

HEAVENLY FROZEN CHOCOLATE TORTE

A dessert that will not soon be forgotten.

SINGLE RECIPE
Yield: 10 to 12 servings

1 cup chopped pecans or toasted almonds	or
½ cup sugar	Two 3-ounce packages Toblerone Bittersweet Chocolate with almonds and honey nougat
½ cup water	
2 eggs	2 tablespoons cognac or brandy
6 ounces semisweet chocolate chips (1 cup)	¼ cup Kahlua
	1 cup heavy cream, whipped

Chop nuts and set aside. Combine sugar and water in saucepan and heat slowly until sugar is completely dissolved. (This can also be done in your microwave oven.) Place chocolate chips in your blender or food processor, along with eggs. Add hot syrup and blend. Add liquors and mix. Cool.

Whip cream until stiff and fold into cooled mixture. Add chopped pecans and pour into a 9-inch spring-form pan that has been greased and dusted with graham cracker crumbs or chocolate wafer cookie crumbs. Freeze several hours until frozen.

TO SERVE. Remove from freezer about 10 minutes before serving. Loosen spring-form sides immediately upon removing from freezer and let torte set for 10 minutes before serving.

VARIATIONS. Instead of Kahlua, use Swiss chocolate liqueur and add blanched, toasted, chopped almonds instead of the pecans.

CRANBERRY-APPLE PIE

Something different, nice and tart, and made in a wink.

SINGLE RECIPE
   Time: 2 minutes
   Yield: One 9-inch pie

One 9-inch unbaked pie shell
One 1-pound can prepared apple pie
   filling

2 cups thawed cranberry-orange
   relish

Either use your homemade cranberry-orange relish, fresh or frozen (see recipe on page 212), or use the commerically prepared cranberry-orange relish. Combine relish with apple pie filling and turn into pie shell. Bake in a preheated oven at 425° F for 30 minutes or until done.

CREAM CHEESE PIE WITH FRUIT TOPPING

Ready in a minute and so festive looking, this easy dessert is a pleasure to have on hand.

SINGLE RECIPE
   Time: 7 minutes
   Yield: One 9-inch pie

1 baked pastry pie shell
   or
1 crumb crust for 9-inch pie pan

DOUBLE RECIPE
   Time: 8 minutes
   Yield: Two 9-inch pies

2 baked pastry pie shells
   or
2 crumb crusts for 9-inch pie pans

One 8-ounce package cream cheese	Two 8-ounce packages cream cheese
1½ cups (15-ounce can) sweetened condensed milk	2⅔ cups (two 15-ounce cans) sweetened condensed milk
⅓ cup lemon juice	⅔ cup lemon juice
1 teaspoon vanilla extract	2 teaspoons vanilla extract
1 can cherry or blueberry pie filling	2 cans cherry or blueberry pie filling

Soften cream cheese to room temperature; then beat until light and fluffy. Gradually add sweetened condensed milk, beating continuously. When well blended, add lemon juice and vanilla extract. Pour into baked pie crust and chill or freeze. To serve without freezing, add blueberry or cherry pie filling to top of pie and refrigerate until serving time.

TO FREEZE. Set filled pie (minus fruit topping) in the freezer. After it's frozen solid, cover with freezer material, date, and label.

TO SERVE WHEN FROZEN. Remove pie from freezer about 2 hours before serving. Spread blueberry or cherry pie filling over the top of frozen pie. Let stand at room temperature for about 1 hour and then refrigerate until serving time.

FRENCH CREAM FILLING

If made with Clearjel (see page 70), this delectable French Cream Filling can be frozen without the slightest hesitation. It's good served plain as a pudding or custard, as well as in combination with other desserts, including cream puffs. It makes especially delicious fillings for pies. Using instant milk and boiling water cuts down the cooking time by about 10 to 15 minutes.

SINGLE RECIPE
Time: 6 minutes
Yield: 2⅔ cups

2 cups boiling water
½ cup sugar
2 tablespoons Clearjel
2 tablespoons flour
½ teaspoon salt
2 egg yolks
½ cup cold milk
⅔ cup instant nonfat dry milk
1 tablespoon butter
2 teaspoons vanilla

DOUBLE RECIPE
Time: 7 minutes
Yield: 5⅓ cups

4 cups boiling water
1 cup sugar
¼ cup Clearjel
¼ cup flour
1 teaspoon salt
4 egg yolks
1 cup cold milk
1⅓ cups instant nonfat dry milk
2 tablespoons butter
1 tablespoon plus 1 teaspoon vanilla

Mix sugar, flour, Clearjel, and salt. Combine egg yolks and cold milk, beating slightly with a fork. Add to flour and Clearjel mixture. Add nonfat dry milk and stir well, making sure that there are no lumps. Add boiling water slowly; continue cooking over moderately high heat, stirring constantly. Cook for several minutes (longer for a double recipe) until smooth and thick. Add butter and continue stirring until butter is completely dissolved. Now add vanilla. Cool.

CHOCOLATE FRENCH CREAM FILLING. For single recipe, add 1 ounce of bitter chocolate to hot cream filling immediately after the hot water has been added. The chocolate will be melted by the time the filling is cooked. Also, increase sugar ¼ cup.

MOCHA CREAM FILLING. Add 1 or 2 tablespoons of instant or freeze-dried coffee to French Cream Filling (for a single recipe). This is especially good for Éclairs (page 237), topped with Mocha Frosting (page 161).

BRANDIED FRENCH CREAM FILLING. Make a single recipe of French Cream Filling. Cool for 2 hours in refrigerator. When it is completely cold, beat ½ cup whipping cream and fold into cream filling. Add 1 ounce of brandy, and fold in until well blended. Keep in refrigerator until ready to serve, or freeze, as desired.

EGGNOG FILLING. This is particularly good served during the holidays. Follow recipe for French Cream Filling, omitting the vanilla flavoring and substituting ¼ cup of brandy for a single recipe. Also, add ½ cup dry instant eggnog mix to the sugar, Clearjel, and flour mixture. Top of pie may be garnished with shaved bitter chocolate or glazed fruit.

LEMON CREAM PIE

Made with timesaving frozen lemonade concentrate, this tangy and creamy Lemon Cream Pie is sure to become a family favorite.

Time: 12 minutes
Yield: One 10-inch pie

One 6-ounce can frozen lemonade
   concentrate
one envelope (1 tablespoon)
   unflavored gelatin
4 separated eggs

Dash salt
½ cup sugar
1 cup commerical sour cream
1 baked 10-inch pie shell

Let frozen lemonade concentrate defrost in saucepan. Add gelatin and let stand until gelatin is softened. Separate eggs, adding yolks to the lemon concentrate-gelatin mixture. Add salt and beat yolks with wire whisk. Heat this mixture sufficiently to dissolve gelatin. Remove from stove and add sour cream, mixing well. Set pan in refrigerator to cool. Meanwhile, beat egg whites until stiff. Gradually add sugar, 1 tablespoon at a time. Beat until mixture forms soft peaks and is glossy. Fold into cooled lemon mixture and turn into pie shell. Chill for about 2 hours.

PINEAPPLE RHUBARB PIE

When rhubarb is in season, you can make a number of these fillings and freeze them for use later in the year. Or you can use rhubarb from your freezer.

Time: 5 minutes
Yield: One 9-inch pie

One 9-inch unbaked pie shell	2 cups cut up and thawed rhubarb
3 tablespoons cornstarch or Instant Clearjel (see page 70)	One 20-ounce can crushed pineapple
½ cup brown sugar	¼ cup softened butter
¼ teaspoon salt	3 tablespoons flour
	3 tablespoons brown sugar

Combine cornstarch or Instant Clearjel with brown sugar and salt. Toss with mixture of rhubarb and pineapple. Pour into lined pie pan. Blend softened butter with flour and brown sugar for topping, and sprinkle over filling. A lattice covering makes this pie very attractive; however, it's not absolutely necessary. Bake in a preheated oven at 425° F for 40 to 45 minutes, or until nicely browned.

TO FREEZE. If you want to make a number of these pie fillings for the freezer, simply line pie plate with plastic wrap, pour in filling, and quick-freeze. When firm, remove from pie tin, wrap for the freezer, seal, label, and date. You may also freeze the filling in the pie shell, if you wish; however, it's then best to leave the pie in its tin for freezer storage.

TO BAKE WHEN FROZEN. Put frozen pie in a preheated oven at 425° F and bake approximately 1 hour and 5 or 10 minutes. Filling should be bubbly when done.

ITALIAN PLUM PIE

This can be made from fresh or frozen plums. The port wine really gives it a heady flavor.

Time: 5 minutes
Yield: One 10-inch pie

One 10-inch unbaked pie shell
4 cups thawed, pitted Italian plums
½ cup raisins (optional)
½ cup Instant Clearjel (see page 70)

1 cup sugar
¼ teaspoon nutmeg
½ teaspoon cinnamon
½ cup port

Let plums thaw in a large bowl. Combine sugar, spices, and Clearjel, mixing well. Add wine to plums and then add sugar and Clearjel mixture. Blend well. Pour into prepared pie shell. Bake in a preheated oven at 425° F for 20 minutes; reduce heat to 325° F and bake an additional 30 minutes. Cool. See page 200.

PUMPKIN PIE OR CUSTARD

Although this filling makes a delicious pie, it's good served plain as a custard. Not only does this save time, but it has a lot fewer calories without the piecrust. Delicious with vanilla ice cream. By using Clearjel, you can make this recipe in quantity and have it freezer-stored for oven or table.

SINGLE RECIPE
Time: 12 minutes
Yield: One 10-inch pie

Pastry for one 10-inch pie shell
1 cup milk
⅔ cup seedless white raisins
1 cup packed brown sugar
2 tablespoons Clearjel (see page 70)
4 eggs
½ teaspoon cinnamon
¼ teaspoon nutmeg
¼ teaspoon ginger
¼ teaspoon allspice
½ teaspoon salt
One 1-pound can prepared pumpkin
1 cup evaporated milk, cream, or half 'n half
1½ cups chopped pecans

DOUBLE RECIPE
Time: 15 minutes
Yield: Two 10-inch pies

Pastry for two 10-inch pie shells
2 cups milk
1⅓ cups seedless white raisins
2 cups (1 pound less ¼ cup) packed brown sugar
¼ cup Clearjel (see page 70)
8 eggs
1 teaspoon cinnamon
½ teaspoon nutmeg
½ teaspoon ginger
½ teaspoon allspice
1 teaspoon salt
Two 1-pound cans prepared pumpkin
2 cups evaporated milk, cream, or half 'n half
3 cups chopped pecans

Line a 10-inch pie plate with pastry. If you don't own a 10-inch pie plate, use the 8 or 9-inch size and bake any remaining pie filling as a custard in a plain baking dish.

Scald milk; add raisins. Mix sugar and Clearjel thoroughly, and add to scalded milk. In a large mixing bowl, beat eggs; add spices and then pumpkin. Mix well and add evaporated milk, cream, or half 'n half. When this mixture is thoroughly blended, add milk-raisin-and-sugar mixture. Fill pie shell or baking dishes and bake at 350° F for 1 hour, or until a silver knife inserted in center of pie comes out clean. Cool and serve.

PUMPKIN CHEESE PIE

The cream cheese in this pumpkin pie gives it a smooth, creamy texture. The sour cream topping adds just the right touch.

SINGLE RECIPE
  Time: 10 minutes
  Yield: One 9-inch pie
Prepared crust for one 9-inch pie
One 8-ounce package softened cream
  cheese
¾ cup sugar
2 tablespoons Clearjel (see page 70)
1 teaspoon cinnamon
¼ teaspoon allspice
¼ teaspoon nutmeg
¼ teaspoon ginger
½ teaspoon vanilla
2 whole eggs
2 egg yolks
One 1-pound can prepared pumpkin
Topping:
1 cup commercial sour cream
2 tablespoons sugar
1 teaspoon vanilla
½ teaspoon cinnamon

DOUBLE RECIPE
  Time: 15 minutes
  Yield: Two 9-inch pies
Prepared crust for two 9-inch pies
Two 8-ounce packages softened
  cream cheese
1½ cups sugar
¼ cup Clearjel (see page 70)
2 teaspoons cinnamon
½ teaspoon allspice
½ teaspoon nutmeg
½ teaspoon ginger
1 teaspoon vanilla
4 whole eggs
4 egg yolks
Two 1-pound cans prepared pumpkin
Topping:
1 pint commercial sour cream
¼ cup sugar
2 teaspoons vanilla
1 teaspoon cinnamon

Preheat oven to 350° F. Line pie plates. In a large mixing bowl, beat cream cheese that has been softened at room temperature. Combine Clearjel and sugar thoroughly and add to cheese. Add remaining ingredients and beat until smooth. Pour into pastry-lined pan. Bake in preheated oven at 350° F for 50 to 55 minutes, or until silver knife inserted in center of pie comes out clean. Immediately spread with topping (see below) as gently as possible. Raise oven temperature to 475° F and return pie to oven for about 5 minutes. Cool; then refrigerate for several hours before serving.

TOPPING. In a small mixing bowl, combine sour cream, sugar, vanilla, and cinnamon. Have this mixture ready when pie comes out of the oven.

TO FREEZE. Freeze Pumpkin Cheese Pie unbaked and without topping.

TO SERVE WHEN FROZEN. Remove frozen pie from freezer and put into preheated 350° F oven. Bake for about 70 minutes, or until silver knife inserted in center of pie comes out clean. Add topping and put pie back into the oven at 475° F for another 5 minutes.

SOUR CREAM RAISIN PIE OR PUDDING

This tastes great either in or out of a pie shell.

SINGLE RECIPE	DOUBLE RECIPE
Time: 15 minutes	*Time: 20 minutes*
Yield: One 9-inch pie	*Yield: Two 9-inch pies*
Prepared crust for one 9-inch pie	Prepared crust for two 9-inch pies
1 cup seedless raisins	2 cups seedless raisins
1 cup water	2 cups water
1 tablespoon cornstarch or Clearjel (see page 70)	2 tablespoons cornstarch or Clearjel (see page 70)
3 tablespoons sugar	¼ cup plus 2 tablespoons sugar
1 package lemon pie filling	2 packages lemon pie filling
¼ cup sugar	½ cup sugar
¼ cup water	½ cup water
2 egg yolks	4 egg yolks
1¾ cup boiling water	3½ cups boiling water
1 cup commercial sour cream	1 pint commercial sour cream

Pour water over raisins in a small pan. Mix sugar and Clearjel thoroughly and add to raisins. Mix well and simmer for 15 minutes or until thick. Meanwhile, in another pan combine lemon pie filling mix with ¼ cup water and 2 egg yolks (for single recipe), stirring well with wire whisk. Slowly add remaining boiling water and cook over moderate heat until filling comes to a full boil and thickens. Combine with thickened raisin mixture. Cool and fold in sour cream. Turn into a baked pastry shell and chill until firm.

TO FREEZE. My preference is to freeze and serve this as a pudding rather than a pie, since the filled and baked crust tends to get soggy with long storage in the freezer. Spoon pudding into either individual serving dishes or 1½-quart serving dish; freezer-wrap, label, date, and freeze.

TO SERVE WHEN FROZEN. Simply let it thaw in the refrigerator for half a day. To hasten thawing, you may let it stand at room temperature for an hour or so and then finish thawing it in the refrigerator.

RASPBERRY PIE

When it comes to fruit pies, nothing really beats raspberry pies, and they're so easy to make—that is, once you have the raspberries! If you're fortunate enough to find fresh raspberries, prepare a number of these pie fillings and freeze (see instructions on page 200).

SINGLE RECIPE
Yield: One 9-inch pie

Pastry for a single 9-inch piecrust
3 cups thawed raspberries and juice
Sugar to taste
1 tablespoon Instant Clearjel (see page 70)
1 tablespoon tapioca

DOUBLE RECIPE
Yield: Two 9-inch pies

Pastry for two single 9-inch piecrusts
6 cups thawed raspberries and juice
Sugar to taste
2 tablespoons Instant Clearjel (see page 70)
2 tablespoons tapioca

Combine all ingredients and fill pastry-lined pie tin. Bake at 400° F for about 25 to 30 minutes. When you are using thawed frozen raspberries, Instant Clearjel will absorb the juice immediately and will keep the crust flaky.

Poultry

✳✳✳✳✳✳✳✳✳✳✳✳✳✳✳✳✳✳✳✳✳✳✳✳✳✳

Chicken and turkey have long remained one of the best meat buys, while still lending themselves to elegant and festive meals. It's a good idea to buy in quantity when they're on sale and enjoy them all year round. Always select fresh, top-quality fowl for your freezer. Although freezing preserves poultry in its full flavor and tenderness, it won't improve the quality. Healthy young birds that have been well fed have a nice layer of fat under the skin.

Care, handling, and freezing of game birds are the same as for domestic poultry. Poultry or game birds should be cleaned and dressed immediately after killing. Leaving them in the refrigerator below 40° F for 12 hours before freezing insures maximum tenderness. When freezing whole birds, remove the giblets and livers and freeze them separately. The giblets should be used in 3 months and the livers within a month.

FREEZING POULTRY

The "drugstore wrap" is recommended when wrapping poultry for the freezer. Use freezer wrapping material that can be pressed close to the surface to eliminate air pockets. Cut poultry takes up less room than whole birds. When freezing the whole bird, try to press or tie down any protruding bones and cover these bones with crushed freezer paper.

Plastic freezer bags are also convenient for packaging poultry, especially whole birds. Put bird in freezer-weight polyethylene bag and lower three-quarters of the way into water. The water will force out all the air, leaving the plastic hugging the bird. Be sure not to get any water inside the bag.

Cooked poultry in small pieces is best frozen in rigid containers. Pack solidly to eliminate air. The addition of broth or gravy will lengthen storage life. Cooked poultry packaged without broth should not be stored for more than a month. In broth or gravy, it will keep for 6 months. For freezer storage times, see chart on pages 21–25.

NEVER FREEZE STUFFED POULTRY. Commercially stuffed birds may be purchased; these stuffed birds are frozen under carefully controlled temperature conditions not possible to attain in the home. A stuffed bird takes so long to freeze that bacterial growth may start, which would be a health hazard. A frozen stuffed bird also takes longer to thaw and cook, hence further increase in the possibility of bacterial growth.

You may observe that young birds from your freezer occasionally have darkened bones. This is caused by seepage from the bone marrow during freezing and thawing. The defect is strictly visual and has no effect on flavor or quality.

Although poultry may be cooked while frozen, it's generally agreed that thawing before cooking results in better flavor and texture. Whole birds should be completely thawed to insure uniform cooking.

TURKEY

Benjamin Franklin was of the opinion that the turkey, rather than the marauding bald eagle, should have been chosen as the symbol of the United States. Brillat-Savarin said that it "surely is one of the noblest gifts which the Old World has received from the New."

Before the days of quick-freezing, turkey was usually served only for the traditional holiday dinner. Now it's available the year round and may be served in innumerable guises—stuffed, barbecued, roasted, or braised. The meat is excellent in salads, casseroles, sandwiches, et cetera; all this at bargain prices too!

In this chapter you will find a number of recipes for this marvelous bird. Try serving it often. Most turkeys are already frozen, so all you'll have to do is date them and put them into your freezer as quickly as possible. Remember, the larger the turkey, the more meat per pound. If you prefer, your butcher will cut a large turkey in half with a power saw, or it can be quartered into "turkey roasts." This is very practical for the smaller family. If you like dark meat, be sure to take advantage of the large turkey legs and thighs that can often be found in the market at really bargain prices.

Today turkeys are plumper and larger breasted than they used to be. Some give 50 percent more meat than those offered twenty years ago. They are also juicier and more tender, which substantially reduces the cooking time. So don't use old cooking charts when cooking turkeys today or your bird will be overdone and dried out.

Quantity

When you are buying turkey, be sure to buy it in sufficient quantity to allow for planned leftovers. For smaller families, quarter and half turkeys offer the economical advantages of a large bird. The following table is based on normal servings, each amounting to approximately 3 ounces of cooked meat without bone, skin, or juices. When buying whole, ready-to-cook turkeys weighing less than 12 pounds, allow ¾ to 1 pound per serving. For larger birds, allow ½ to ¾ pound. With uncooked boneless turkey roasts, allow ⅓ pound per serving.

Ready-to-Cook Weight Whole Turkey (Pounds)	Approximate Number of Servings
5 to 8	6 to 10
8 to 12	10 to 20
12 to 16	20 to 32
16 to 20	32 to 40
20 to 24	40 to 50

Roasting Preparations

Thawing time for frozen turkey varies widely, depending on the size of the bird, or pieces, and the method used.

Thawing at room temperature, unwrapped, is *not* recommended because of the possibility of contamination.

The first recommended procedure is thawing the turkey on a tray in the refrigerator, still in the original wrap. This requires 1 to 3 days.

The second recommended procedure is to thaw the bird, still in its original watertight wrap, under cold running water, or immersed in cold water, changing the water frequently. This requires 3 to 4 hours for fryer-roaster turkeys and 6 to 7 hours for larger birds.

The quickest and easiest way, of course, is to use a microwave oven if you have one. Follow manufacturer's instructions and use defrost cycle.

Fresh uncooked turkey rolls or roasts may be thawed in a similar manner.

Trussing is the simple procedure of binding the legs and wings to the body to make the turkey compact, easier to handle, easier to cook, more attractive and to eliminate the possibility of burning wingtips and ends of drumsticks. Twist wings "hammer-lock" style, bringing wing tips onto the back. Tie a string securely around the tail to serve as an anchor. Then tie the ends of the legs to the same string. This is much easier than the "natural" truss, using the band of skin. Complete the truss after dressing has been inserted.

The "natural" truss consists of inserting the tips of the legs through the band of skin formed above the tail and below the large opening into the body cavity. When the "natural" truss is used, the band of skin should be cut during the final hour in the oven to allow complete cooking of the thick-meated joints.

Roasting*

Turkeys of any size may be roasted. Correct roasting is dry-heat cooking at low temperature. It requires no water, no searing, and no cover. A shallow pan with a rack at least ½ inch high raises the bird off the bottom of the pan, keeping it out of the juices and allowing the heat to circulate around the bird, roasting it evenly.

Always roast turkey in one continuous cooking period, until it's done. Low temperatures assure better flavor and appearance, less shrinking, and less loss of juices.

Here are the simple steps:

1. Preheat oven to 325° F (slow oven).

2. Rinse, drain, and dry the bird. Rub cavity lightly with salt, if desired. Do not salt if bird is to be stuffed.

3. If it's to be stuffed, fill wishbone area (neck) loosely and fasten neck skin to back with skewer. Sometimes the snapped-back wingtips hold the neck skin down. Fill body cavity lightly, because dressing tends to expand. Tie drumsticks to the tail. Do not stuff until ready to cook, or unwanted bacteria may develop.

(I have found the quickest and easiest way of closing a bird after it is stuffed is to simply pin it shut with large diaper pins! They are easily cleaned and stored for repeated usage.)

4. Place turkey, breast side up, on rack in shallow roasting pan. Brush skin with butter or fat. If a roast-meat thermometer is to be used, insert it so that the bulb is in the center of the inside thigh muscle or the

* Turkey roasting instructions are reprinted with permission of National Turkey Federation.

thickest part of the breast meat. Be sure that the bulb doesn't touch bone.

5. Place in preheated oven. Periodic basting or brushing with butter, margarine, or pan drippings will result in a more moist and juicy bird. (I use a stainless steel baster into which you can screw a needle. This enables you to inject the entire bird with juice, giving it marvelous flavor. The baster is available at specialty stores.) When turkey is two-thirds done, cut cord or band of skin at tail to release the legs and permit the heat to reach the heavy-meated part. Cover with a loose tent of aluminum foil or lay a fat-moistened cloth over the legs and breast to prevent excessive browning.

6. Roast until done.

7. Always allow turkey to set at least 30 minutes before carving! This allows juices to be reabsorbed and makes uniform slicing easier.

Timetable Guide

The following timetable for roasting poultry is intended only as a guide. Because of the differences in quality, shape, and tenderness of each bird, you may have to increase or decrease the cooking time. There is also a difference in the temperature of the birds when they're placed in the oven. Even the type of roasting pan you use can make a difference. If a shiny, light-colored pan is used, increase roasting time up to 1 hour. Even personal preferences vary, with some people liking a moist bird and others preferring theirs well done.

The only positive way to tell if a turkey is done is to use a properly placed meat thermometer. Much of the variation in cooking time and tenderness is due to inaccurate oven thermometers and the frequent opening of the oven door.

It's best to start the turkey roasting 30 to 45 minutes ahead of schedule. If dinner is planned for a definite hour, this avoids delay when the turkey takes longer to cook than was estimated from the guide. And the extra time allows the meat to stand and absorb juices, so the bird is easier to carve.

The roasting periods listed in the timetable are for fresh, chilled or completely thawed, stuffed turkeys (at a temperature of about 40° F) placed in 325° F preheated ovens. (For roasting in your microwave oven, see manufacturer's instructions.) Time will be slightly less (1 to 3 minutes per pound) for unstuffed birds.

There's no substitute for a meat thermometer, placed in the center of inside thigh muscle (or the thickest part of the breast). When it registers 180–185° F, the turkey is done. If the bird is stuffed, the point of the thermometer should be in the center of the stuffing and register 165° F.

The traditional "doneness" test used by many experienced cooks is a "feel" test. Turkey is done if the thickest part of the drumstick feels very soft, when pressed between protected fingers, and the drumstick moves easily up and down as the leg joint gives readily, or breaks.

APPROXIMATE TIMETABLE
(Whole Turkey)

Ready-to-Cook Weight POUNDS	Approximate Time at 325° F HOURS	Internal Temperature When Done DEGREES F
6 to 8	3 to 3½	180° to 185°
8 to 12	3½ to 4½	180° to 185°
12 to 16	4½ to 5½	180° to 185°
16 to 20	5½ to 6½	180° to 185°
20 to 24	6½ to 7	180° to 185°

Reheating Whole, Roasted Turkey

For years we have been warned not to cook a turkey ahead: "It's not safe, the turkey would be overcooked and dry, with an inferior flavor." The home economists at Swift & Company have done a good job researching these myths and have developed a technique for doing just that. So now you may cook your turkey ahead of time. This new method of cooking a turkey ahead should help more than anything in taking the turkey out of the holiday-only category. Follow instructions on how to cook your turkey on preceding pages. After the turkey has cooled slightly, the stuffing should be removed and both the turkey and stuffing wrapped and *refrigerated immediately*. Here are two ways to reheat the whole turkey, as recommended by Swift & Company. For both methods, remove the whole roasted turkey from the refrigerator and slip it into a special plastic bag made for oven roasting. Puncture the bag in three places. Tuck the open end of the bag under the bird.

CONVENTIONAL OVEN METHOD. Place cooked turkey, wrapped in a plastic oven roasting bag, on a rack in a low-sided open pan. Roast meat thermometer may be inserted through the plastic into the center of thigh next to the body. Set in a preheated 350° F. oven. Allow an hour and twenty minutes for a 12-pound bird. When meat thermometer reads 140° F, remove from oven and overwrap in foil for 10 to 20 minutes. During this standing time, the temperature will increase. Remove foil and plastic bag for carving.

MICROWAVE OVEN METHOD. Arrange turkey in a plastic oven roasting bag, breast side down on a platter suitable for microwave cooking and reheat for 15 minutes. Remove from oven and turn the turkey breast side up. Return to microwave oven and continue to reheat for about 17 minutes. Remove turkey from oven and overwrap with foil for 10 minutes. Do allow for temperature increase. Remove foil and plastic bag before carving.

Reheating Sliced Turkey

Remove turkey from the refrigerator. Slice the white meat from the breast, remove the drumsticks from thigh and carcass, slice the meat from the bones. On a large, ovenproof platter, arrange the slices of white meat in the center, dark meat on one end, and stuffing on the other end. Spoon gravy over both meat and stuffing. Cover ovenproof platter loosely with foil and heat in a preheated 350° F oven for 35 minutes.

For microwave oven method, cover platter with transparent wrap and place in microwave oven for 8 to 10 minutes, cooking on reheat set.* Keeping the turkey covered while reheating seems to be the secret to keeping the meat moist and flavorful.

Always refrigerate turkey shortly after initial roasting. The stuffing can be reheated separately by microwave or in a regular oven, as the turkey waits on the counter for carving. Or if you wish, the dressing could be prepared and baked in a casserole the day of serving. For extra flavor, baste with pan drippings.

Roasting Half and Quarter Turkeys

1. Preheat oven to 325° F.
2. Rinse turkey with cold water; drain and pat dry. Skewer skin to meat along cut edges to prevent its shrinking away from the meat during roasting. Rub cavity of turkey lightly with salt.
3. Tie leg to tail. Lay wing flat over white meat and tie string around breast end to hold wing down.
4. Place turkey on rack in shallow pan, skin side up. Brush skin with butter or fat. Place in preheated oven. If desired, baste occasionally with pan drippings or butter, especially any dry areas.
5. Continue roasting until done. (See timetable.)

* Tests were conducted in a multi-power oven on "reheat set" study which operates at 88% power or 540 to 460 watts. Foods cooked in ovens with less wattage may need extra cooking time. Check microwave oven manual or cookbook for guidance.

APPROXIMATE TIMETABLE
(Half and Quarter Turkeys)

Ready-to-Cook Weight POUNDS	Approximate Time at 325° F HOURS	Internal Temperature When Done DEGREES F
5 to 8	2½ to 3	180° to 185°
8 to 10	3 to 3½	180° to 185°
10 to 12	3½ to 4	180° to 185°

Cooking Boneless Turkey Roasts and Rolls

To thaw uncooked boneless turkey roasts or rolls, follow the general thawing directions. Leave roasts or rolls in original wrapper and thaw in refrigerator for 1 to 2 days, or under running, cold water or use your microwave oven. For roasting, remove wrap and leave string in place.

OVEN ROASTING

1. Preheat oven to 325° F (slow oven).

2. If roast is not preseasoned, rub lightly with seasoned pepper.

3. Place on rack in shallow roasting pan. Brush entire roast with melted butter or fat. Place in preheated oven. Baste or brush occasionally with butter or pan drippings, especially any dry areas. If meat becomes too brown during roasting, cover with a loose tent of foil.

4. Continue roasting until done. To test doneness, a roast meat thermometer inserted in center of roast should register 170° to 175° F (3 to 4 hours). Before carving, let turkey roast stand 10 to 15 minutes after removing from oven. Pan drippings may be used for making gravy.

ROTISSERIE ROASTING

1. If roast is not preseasoned, rub lightly with seasoned pepper.

2. Insert spit rod lengthwise through center of turkey roast. Insert end skewers firmly in roast and screw tightly. Test the balance. Roast must balance on spit so it will rotate smoothly throughout the cooking period. Place spit rod in rotisserie. Brush roast with melted butter or other shortening.

3. Follow manufacturer's directions for rotisserie temperature setting. Roast until done. To test doneness, insert a meat thermometer in center of roast, being careful not to touch the spit rod. Thermometer should register 170° to 175° F. No further basting is necessary.

For best results in slicing, allow roast to stand 20 to 30 minutes to reabsorb juices. Remove string and slice with a sharp knife or meat slicer.

APPROXIMATE TIMETABLE
(Boneless Turkey Roasts or Rolls)

Ready-to-Cook Weight POUNDS	Approximate Time (Hours)	
	OVEN	ROTISSERIE
3 to 5	2½ to 3	2 to 2½
5 to 7	3 to 3½	2½ to 3
7 to 9	3½ to 4	3 to 3½

Helpful Hints

FRESH TURKEY. Chilled fresh turkey can be held 1 to 2 days in the coldest part of the refrigerator. Make sure any wrappings are loose enough to allow some air circulation. Remove giblets (heart, gizzard, and liver), wrap loosely, and store separately. Prompt cooking of these more perishable parts is recommended.

COOKED TURKEY. As soon as possible after serving your turkey, remove every bit of stuffing from the wishbone and body cavities. Remove meat from bones; larger sliced pieces may be frozen, wrapped in foil or other freezer wrap, to be used later in sandwiches. Smaller pieces should be packed in rigid containers with gravy or broth.

TURKEY BROTH. Place bony pieces of turkey in a large kettle and fill with enough water to cover all the bones. Add celery greens, a carrot or two (cup up), a bay leaf, and a few sprigs of parsley. Simmer until meat is loosened from the bones. Strain broth, remove pieces of meat from the bones, and place in freezer cartons. Cover with broth and freeze.

TURKEY SOUP

Restaurant chefs have long known that the secret to a good soup stock is simmering over a long period of time. Restaurants that make their own soups have enormous stainless steel caldrons to which they add bones, vegetables, and other odds and ends, and just let it cook for several days sometimes. You can do the same with your turkey carcass, which will give you a rich and dark brown stock to use as a base for the soup. It is an easy way of getting rid of your bones and tidbits of leftover vegetables, gravy, et cetera, after you have carved your turkey. The actual time required to prepare the soup is minimal.

Yield: Approximately 2 quarts

Carcass of 1 turkey
2 bay leaves
½ teaspoon marjoram
½ teaspoon thyme
basil
1 medium onion, peeled and sliced
1 large sprig parsley
celery leaves

1 carrot, coarsely sliced
6 beef bouillon cubes
¼ cup barley
½ cup finely chopped celery
¼ cup butter
½ pound mushrooms, sliced
salt and pepper to taste

After you have sliced and removed all the meat from the turkey carcass, break, saw, or cut the large bones to fit in the bottom of a large kettle or soup caldron. Add herbs, onion, parsley, celery leaves, and carrots. Cover with water and simmer at least 5 hours, preferably overnight. Cooking overnight makes a big improvement in the broth. (This is perfect for a large slow cooker. It can simmer for several days.) You may wish to add leftover gravy and dressing to the stock. After it has cooked, strain broth. Add bouillon cubes, barley, and celery, and continue cooking at low temperature until the barley is tender. In a skillet, melt butter and sauté mushrooms. Add to soup, heating through. Adjust seasoning with salt and pepper and serve.

TO FREEZE. Whichever is most convenient for you, either freeze broth and make soup later or complete soup and freeze.

VARIATION. You may wish to add 1 cup of turkey bits to the soup. You may wish to cool the broth and, if it seems particularly fatty, remove the fat from the top of the soup.

SAUSAGE STUFFING FOR TURKEY

Someone once said, "A roasted turkey without dressing is like a kiss without a hug."

SINGLE RECIPE
   Time: 15 minutes
   Yield: Enough stuffing for 10 to
      16-pound bird

1 pound pork sausage
Liver and gizzard from turkey
2 cups chopped onions
1½ cups finely cut parsley
¾ loaf of dry French bread, cut into
   small pieces

¼ pound butter
6 ribs of finely chopped celery
½ teaspoon poultry seasoning
1½ teaspoons sage
1¼ teaspoons salt
1 tablespoon monosodium glutamate

RECIPE AND A HALF
> *Time: 20 minutes*
> *Yield: Enough stuffing for a*
> *24-pound bird*

1½ pounds pork sausage
Liver and gizzard from turkey
3 cups chopped onions
2¼ cups finely cut parsley
1 large loaf of dry French bread, cut
  into small pieces
12 tablespoons (⅜ pound) butter

9 ribs of finely chopped celery
¾ teaspoon poultry seasoning
2¼ teaspoons sage
1¾ teaspoons salt
1½ tablespoons monosodium
  glutamate

Put gizzard, liver, and neck of turkey in just enough water to cover; bring to a boil, lower heat, and continue cooking until gizzard is tender. Remove from broth, set neck aside, and grind or chop gizzard and liver with food grinder or food processor. Meanwhile, add pork sausage to broth and cook until done, breaking sausage up with a wooden spoon or spatula as it is cooking. Now mix all the other ingredients together in a large bowl, adding enough broth to moisten. Dressing should be just moist enough to hold together. Stuff bird lightly and roast. (Dressing expands during roasting.) Any excess dressing may be baked in a casserole dish during the last half hour of roasting.

TO FREEZE. (I usually make enough dressing at Thanksgiving to last me through the Christmas holidays.) Freeze uncooked in appropriate size containers. To use when frozen, thaw in refrigerator.

ROULA'S TURKEY DRESSING

Are you game to try something different from the dressing your mother always made? This is truly a scrumptious dressing.

SINGLE RECIPE
> *Time: 20 minutes*
> *Yield: Enough for a 10 to*
> *12-pound bird*

¾ cup uncooked rice
1½ cups chopped onions
½ medium-sized stalk of celery,
  coarsely ground or finely chopped
1 pound hamburger
½ pound pork sausage
½ cup chopped parsley
1½ teaspoons salt
¼ teaspoon pepper

DOUBLE RECIPE
> *Time: 25 minutes*
> *Yield: Enough for a 20 to*
> *24-pound bird*

1½ cups uncooked rice
3 cups chopped onions
1 whole medium-sized stalk of celery,
  coarsely ground or finely chopped
2 pounds hamburger
1 pound pork sausage
1 cup chopped parsley
1 tablespoon salt
½ teaspoon pepper

½ cup white raisins	1 cup white raisins
½ cup chopped nuts (preferably pecans)	1 cup chopped nuts (preferably pecans)
1 large can stewed tomatoes	2 large cans stewed tomatoes

Brown meat and onions. Meanwhile, combine all the other ingredients in another large kettle. Add meat and onions and bring to a boil. Lower heat and simmer until rice is cooked, adding water if necessary. Proceed to stuff bird lightly and roast. (Dressing expands during roasting.) Put any extra dressing in a casserole dish and bake for the last half hour of roasting.

CHICKEN

Most of the chickens available today are of the broiler-fryer variety. Fresh-killed poultry is best for home freezing. Look for plump birds with fat well distributed and few skin blemishes. Remember that the larger the bird, the more meat per pound; hence the more economical it is. Always select the largest birds available. When buying for the home freezer, be sure that the birds you select haven't been previously frozen. If the birds are displayed in film or tray packs, do not freeze them in these wrappings. Such wrappings are not designed for freezer storage.

When chickens are on sale, buy at least enough to last until the next sale. As soon as you get home from the market, inspect your dressed birds and remove any pinfeathers that may be left. Wash and package for your freezer in the quantity and style you intend to use. If you're going to serve fried chicken, buy cut-up pieces and package the amount you normally cook at one time. Buy whole or quartered chicken for roasting and broiling, whichever you prefer. Wrapping and packaging instructions are on page 330.

If your family likes only certain parts of the chicken, it may be more economical to buy only those pieces, such as legs and thighs, breasts or wings. However, you usually pay premium prices for selected parts. I buy whole fryers, cut up, reserve the choice pieces the family enjoys most, and put the rest of the bird into a large kettle. Cover with water and add celery greens, parsley, a bay leaf, peppercorns, a cut-up carrot or two, and some onion slices (no salt). I usually add an extra breast and/or thigh to the pot to ensure an adequate quantity of boned chicken. Simmer gently for 2 hours or until meat falls off the bones. Strain broth. Cool and remove meat from the bones; put into freezer cartons. If you intend to store this longer than a month, pour broth over the meat, date, label, seal, and freeze. Now you'll have a quantity of boned, cooked chicken in your freezer to use in the many recipes that call for it. Remember that you can substitute chicken for turkey in almost any recipe. Freeze broth in cartons also, making sure to leave ample head room.

Recipes that use boned chicken or turkey, other than those in this section, are: Chicken Sandwich Spread (page 88); Chicken Crispies (page 79); Hot Chicken Curry Sandwiches (page 89); Chicken Poinsettias (page 185).

Recipes other than those in this section that call for chicken broth are Lobster and Shrimp Cantonese (page 185); Mushroom Soup (page 385); Cantonese Fried Rice (page 407).

OVEN-FRIED CHICKEN

I can't imagine anyone cooking fried chicken any way other than in the oven. There's no watching, no spattering, no muss or fuss and fewer calories. Prepare enough for one meal and have a few pieces left over for lunch-box treats or snacks.

Thaw chicken until it's partially pliable. Preheat oven to 425° F. Dip chicken pieces in milk or evaporated milk and then into either a seasoned flour mixture or cornflake crumbs. Pour one tablespoon of vegetable oil or melted butter in a large flat baking pan, spread evenly, and arrange one layer of coated chicken pieces, skin side down, in pan. Put chicken in oven and after 25 minutes, turn each piece. In another 25 minutes your chicken will be crunchy, crisp, and table-ready. Simple enough? Once you try it, you'll never go back to the old method of frying chicken. It has fewer calories too and never a greasy flavor. For a large crowd, you can have several pans cooking at one time, which will enable you to cook 3 or 4 chickens at once.

If made in advance, reheat chicken in a 400° F oven for 15 minutes. To reheat a few leftover pieces, place chicken in broiler-toaster unit for 10 to 15 minutes. Marvelous for a quickie lunch or supper.

VARIATIONS. To the flour or cornflake crumbs, add any one of the following.

One package of dry barbecue sauce mix
One package of dry Italian spaghetti sauce mix
One package of dry garlic and cheese salad-dressing mix
3 tablespoons sesame seeds
1 tablespoon paprika
1 teaspoon curry powder
¼ cup Parmesan cheese
Substitute butter or margarine for milk and dip chicken into this first.

To ½ cup milk, add 3 tablespoons lemon juice and the grated rind of 1 lemon.

IMPERIAL CHICKEN

Another variation of oven-roasted chicken.

2 cups coarse or Italian-flavored bread
   crumbs
¼ cup chopped parsley
1 minced garlic clove
¾ cup grated Parmesan or Romano
   cheese

2 teaspoons salt
⅛ teaspoon pepper
About ¼ pound melted butter or
   shortening
2 cut-up fryers

Combine the first 6 ingredients, mixing thoroughly. Dip each piece of chicken into melted shortening, then into the crumb mixture, making sure that each piece is well coated. Arrange the pieces in a single layer in an open, shallow roasting pan. Pour any remaining shortening into pan and bake as for oven-fried chicken.

ROASTED CHICKEN

Young broiler-fryers weighing 2½ pounds or more are ideal for roasting. You may roast them stuffed or unstuffed. Any turkey stuffing is good in a roasted chicken; simply reduce the amount. For a larger meal, two chickens may be roasted together; this makes a very attractive platter to serve. If stuffing is used, fill cavities lightly; then tie drumsticks to tail. You'll need about 1½ cups of stuffing for a 3-pound broiler-fryer.

The following is a timetable for roasting, reprinted here with the permission of the Poultry and Egg National Board. Figure an extra 15 minutes for a stuffed bird.

TIMETABLE FOR ROASTED CHICKEN

Ready-to-Cook Weight	Oven Temperature (F)	Cooking Time
1½ to 2 pounds	400°	¾ to 1 hour
2 to 2½ pounds	400°	1 to 1¼ hours
2½ to 3 pounds	375°	1¼ to 1¾ hours
3 to 4 pounds	375°	1¾ to 2¼ hours

BROILED CHICKEN

Chickens must be very young and tender to be good for broiling and usually should weigh under 2½ pounds. They may be split in half, quartered, or cut up; if they are broiled on a spit, they may be done whole. The smaller pieces are particularly good if they have been soaked in a marinade for several hours before broiling. Brush generously with seasoned margarine or butter or marinade sauce before and during broiling. If you want to baste your chicken with a barbecue sauce, do so only during the last 10 or 15 minutes; otherwise, since the barbecue sauce burns easily, it will have a scorched flavor long before the chicken is done. For split, quartered, or cup-up chicken, broiling for 20 to 30 minutes is usually sufficient. Chicken should be fork-tender, brown, and crisp. The timing will vary, depending on how far the chicken is from the source of heat, and whether you're using gas, electric, or charcoal heat. Remember that chicken should be completely thawed before you start to broil it.

TIMETABLE FOR THAWED, ROTISSERIE-BROILED WHOLE CHICKEN

Ready-to-Cook Weight	Cooking Time
1½ to 2 pounds	¾ to 1¼ hours
2 to 2½ pounds	1¼ to 1½ hours
2½ to 3 pounds	1½ to 1¾ hours

DONNA'S CHICKEN BREASTS SUPREME

This simple yet elegant dish is perfect for serving to guests, whether you're having a small dinner party for 6 or serving a group of 24 buffet style. Once in the oven, it needs no attention until you put it on the table.

SINGLE RECIPE
Time: 15 minutes
Yield: 6 servings
6 boned, skinned, and halved chicken breasts
¼ cup butter
1 cup commercial sour cream
¼ pound sliced fresh mushrooms or 1 can mushroom pieces
1 can undiluted mushroom soup

DOUBLE RECIPE
Time: 20 minutes
Yield: 12 servings
12 boned, skinned, and halved chicken breasts
⅓ cup butter (or more, if needed)
1 pint commercial sour cream
½ pound sliced fresh mushrooms or 2 cans mushroom pieces
2 cans undiluted mushroom soup

TRIPLE RECIPE
Time: 25 minutes
Yield: 18 servings

18 boned, skinned, and halved
chicken breasts
½ cup butter (or more, if needed)
1½ pints commercial sour cream
¾ pound sliced fresh mushrooms or 3
cans mushroom pieces
3 cans undiluted mushroom soup

QUADRUPLE RECIPE
Time: 30 minutes
Yield: 24 servings

24 boned, skinned, and halved
chicken breasts
½ cup butter (or more, if needed)
2 pints commercial sour cream
1 pound sliced fresh mushrooms or 4
cans mushroom pieces
4 cans undiluted mushroom soup

Have the butcher bone and skin the chicken breasts. (Always ask for the bones and skin; it's surprising how much meat is still left on the bones. Wrap all bones and skin in one package, and freeze. The next time you make chicken broth, simply put the entire contents into your kettle.) Cut breasts in half and brown in butter on both sides in a large skillet; breasts should be just delicately brown. Then place them in a large baking dish, one layer thick. If you have any large oven-to-table ware, this is the ideal time to use it. After all the chicken breasts have been browned and removed to baking dishes, sauté mushroom pieces for 5 minutes, adding more butter if needed. When the mushrooms are cooked, add sour cream and mushroom soup; blend well. Try to dissolve and add all the drippings in the bottom of the skillet. Pour this mixture over chicken breasts and place in a 350° F oven for 1 hour. Sprinkle with paprika and serve. Delicious served with wild rice or what I call my "economy wild rice"—⅓ wild rice, ⅓ long-grained white rice, and ⅓ brown rice.

TO FREEZE. If you can spare the baking dishes, simply freeze, then wrap and label. Heavy-duty foil usually works quite well for large dishes. To give added protection, insert a piece of plastic wrap over the top of the dish first, secure it tightly, and then cover with the foil. You may also line your serving dish with foil, fill and freeze it; then remove and wrap the entire contents again. Always wrap in the quantity you think you'll use when serving.

TO SERVE WHEN FROZEN. I like to thaw the chicken breasts partially first and then put them in the oven. However, you may put them in frozen and increase the baking time from ¾ to 1 hour, depending on the size of baking dish you're using.

CHICKEN CHOW MEIN

Anyone who likes Oriental cuisine will enjoy this easily prepared dish. It will serve 12 amply.

SINGLE RECIPE
> *Time: 20 minutes*
> *Yield: 12 servings*

1 pound sliced mushrooms
¼ cup butter or margarine
1 green pepper, cut into half-inch squares
6 green onions with their tops
4 large ribs of celery
4 cups cooked cubed chicken
one 8-ounce can drained water chestnuts
one 1-pound can bean sprouts or mixed Chinese vegetables
1 package frozen pea pods (optional)
4 cups chicken broth
¼ cup soy sauce
2 teaspoons salt
Pepper to taste
¼ cup cornstarch or Clearjel (see page 70)
one 2-ounce jar pimento
1 cup toasted slivered almonds

DOUBLE RECIPE
> *Time: 30 minutes*
> *Yield: 24 servings*

2 pounds sliced mushrooms
⅓ cup butter or margarine
2 green peppers, cut into half-inch squares
12 green onions with their tops
8 large ribs of celery
8 cups cooked cubed chicken
two 8-ounce cans drained water chestnuts
two 1-pound cans bean sprouts or mixed Chinese vegetables
2 packages frozen pea pods (optional)
8 cups chicken broth
½ cup soy sauce
4 teaspoons salt
Pepper to taste
½ cup cornstarch or Clearjel (see page 70)
two 2-ounce jars pimento
2 cups toasted slivered almonds

Sauté mushrooms for 5 minutes. Add green pepper, green onions, and celery that has been sliced diagonally, and sauté another 5 minutes. In a large pan combine cooked chicken (4 cups equal about 4 large chicken breasts, in case you don't have enough cooked chicken on hand), water chestnuts, bean sprouts or Chinese mixed vegetables, and frozen pea pods. Add 3 cups of chicken broth (for a single recipe), salt, pepper, and soy sauce. Heat to boiling, lower heat, and simmer for 5 minutes. Add sautéed vegetables and heat thoroughly. Blend cornstarch or Clearjel with remaining cup of chicken broth, add to chicken mixture, and cook, stirring gently, until thickened and clear. Add pimento, which has been cut into strips. Cooked nuts lose their crunchiness after they have been frozen; so toast only enough nuts to serve immediately. Sprinkle on top of Chicken Chow Mein and serve with a large bowl of hot fluffy rice.

TO FREEZE. Simply spoon any remaining Chicken Chow Mein into freezer cartons in meal-sized portions, date, label, and freeze.

TO SERVE WHEN FROZEN. Partially thaw in freezer carton. Put into a pan and warm over low heat, bringing to a boil. Add toasted almonds and serve immediately with hot fluffy rice. Make sure you don't over-cook, or the vegetables will become mushy.

SIMPLE CHICKEN CASSEROLE

This is a quick, easy meal for those days when you simply don't have an extra minute to spare.

Time: 5 minutes
Yield: 5 servings

1 can undiluted chicken with rice soup
1 can undiluted mushroom soup
½ cup or 1 small can evaporated milk
one 3-ounce can chow mein noodles
1 cup thawed, cooked, boned chicken
½ cup diced celery
one 4-ounce jar pimento, cut into strips
½ cup coarsely chopped nuts

Combine all the ingredients in a 2-quart casserole dish. Bake in a 350° F oven for 45 minutes to 1 hour. If chicken pieces are large, cut into bite size or smaller.

CHICKEN DIVAN

Although this is a favorite way of using leftover chicken and turkey, I prefer using boned chicken breasts when I have guests. Quick and easy to prepare, this needs no last-minute attention; it's a "breeze" when you are entertaining.

SINGLE RECIPE
Time: 15 minutes
Yield: 6 to 8 servings

two 10-ounce packages frozen broccoli spears
or
1 large bunch (1 pound) fresh broccoli
4 large boned, cooked chicken breasts
¼ cup melted butter
1 can undiluted cream of chicken soup
1 pint commercial sour cream
one 4-ounce jar drained whole pimentos
½ pound thinly sliced Swiss cheese

DOUBLE RECIPE
Time: 20 minutes
Yield: About 14 servings

four 10-ounce packages frozen broccoli spears
or
2 large bunches (2 pounds) fresh broccoli
8 large boned, cooked chicken breasts
½ cup melted butter
2 cans undiluted cream of chicken soup
2 pints commercial sour cream
two 4-ounce jars drained whole pimentos
1 pound thinly sliced Swiss cheese

Cook broccoli according to directions on package or follow chart on page 369. Butter a 9 x 13-inch baking-serving dish (for single recipe); arrange cooked and drained broccoli in a single layer on the bottom of dish. Combine chicken soup and sour cream and spread half of the mixture over broccoli. Now lay half of the cheese over the sauce, and add sliced cooked chicken on top of the cheese. Spread remaining sauce over chicken and top with the remaining Swiss cheese. Cut pimentos into strips and arrange over the cheese. Bake at 400° F for 25 minutes; the cheese should be completely melted and the sauce hot enough to bubble.

TO FREEZE. If you're going to make this for freezing, use fresh cooked chicken, not frozen cooked chicken. Thaw frozen broccoli just enough to separate. Cool. Freezer-wrap, date, label, and freeze.

TO SERVE WHEN FROZEN. Bake frozen casserole at 400° F for 55 to 60 minutes. Sauce should be bubbly and cheese melted.

CHICKEN À LA BRIAR

This dish is festive enough to serve to guests. It makes a nice addition to any buffet or it may be made with leftover chicken or turkey as a quick dinner.

Time: 20 minutes
Yield: 6 servings

2 large (about 1 to 1½ pounds) boned chicken breasts or 2 cups boned leftover chicken or turkey
2 tablespoons butter
½ pound boiled ham, sliced ¼ inch thick or one 3-ounce package of dried beef or ham

one 2¼-ounce can sliced ripe olives
one 4½-ounce jar sliced mushrooms
½ pound sliced Swiss cheese
1 can undiluted cream of chicken or cream of mushroom soup
½ cup commercial sour cream
½ cup water or white wine

Remove the skin from boned and thawed chicken breasts. Brown lightly in butter. (When you are using cooked chicken or turkey, this step may be eliminated.) While the chicken breasts are browning, cut the ham and cheese into 1-inch strips. Drain mushrooms and olives and combine with cheese and ham strips. Combine sour cream with undiluted soup and add. Remove browned chicken breasts and cut into 1-inch strips crosswise. Add. Pour water or wine into the pan where chicken breasts were browned, dissolving all the drippings. Add to chicken mixture. Mix all the ingredients thoroughly but gently. Pour into a 2-quart buttered baking dish or casserole and bake in a preheated 350° F oven for about 30 minutes. Particularly good served with rice or noodles cooked in chicken broth or bouillon. Also good over Noodle Nests, page 406.

SCALLOPED CHICKEN AND NOODLES

This easy-to-prepare chicken dish can be made with fryers or chicken breasts, whichever you prefer. If you like dark meat as well as white, use fryers when making this dish for the family and boned breasts when cooking for guests.

Time: 10 to 15 minutes
Yield: 8 servings

2 cut-up chicken fryers, or 5 or 6 boned and halved chicken breasts
4 cups chicken stock
one 8-ounce package noodles

1 cup commercial sour cream
4 teaspoons beef bouillon granules
¼ pound butter or margarine
½ pound shredded Swiss cheese

Thaw fryers or chicken breasts. Meanwhile, cook noodles in chicken stock, adding bouillon granules. When noodles are done, remove from heat and cool slightly (don't drain the noodles). Add sour cream and pour into a large flat baking pan. Melt shortening and dip or brush chicken with it, adding more shortening if it is needed. Top noodle-sour cream mixture with chicken pieces and bake at 300° F for 2 hours. (When using chicken breasts, reduce baking time to 1½ hours or chicken breasts will be dry. If the chicken breasts are not brown enough, put them under the broiler for a few minutes.) The chicken will brown nicely and turning isn't necessary unless it's desired.

TO SERVE. Set chicken aside in a covered container; add shredded cheese to noodle mixture and stir. You may want to place this mixture under the broiler for a few minutes to help melt and brown the cheese on the noodles. Return chicken to baking dish and serve. If your large baking pan isn't of the oven-to-table variety, you may want to transfer the noodles to a large heated platter and place the chicken on top. Garnish with parsley sprigs.

CHICKEN CROQUETTES

This is a quickie and it's economical too. It's another way to use the boned cooked chicken in your freezer. These croquettes can also be rolled into bite-sized balls and used as appetizers (see page 79).

SINGLE RECIPE	DOUBLE RECIPE
Time: 10 minutes for grinding chicken, making sauce, and mixing *Yield: 12 croquettes*	*Time: 15 minutes for grinding chicken, making sauce, and mixing* *Yield: 24 croquettes*
⅓ cup butter or margarine	⅔ cup butter or margarine
⅓ cup flour	⅔ cup flour
1 teaspoon salt	2 teaspoons salt
⅛ teaspoon pepper	¼ teaspoon pepper
1¼ cups milk	2½ cups milk
2½ cups ground cooked chicken	5 cups ground cooked chicken
1 teaspoon ground onion	2 teaspoons ground onion
½ teaspoon ground coriander	1 teaspoon ground coriander
2 tablespoons minced parsley	4 tablespoons minced parsley
1 slightly beaten egg	2 slightly beaten eggs
1 cup medium-fine bread crumbs	2 cups medium-fine bread crumbs

Melt butter and add flour, mixing into a paste. Add salt and pepper. Then slowly add milk, stirring constantly. Continue cooking until sauce is thick and smooth. Remove from heat. Add chicken, onion, parsley, and coriander. Stir until well mixed. Chill mixture for about 1 hour. Shape mixture from a single recipe into about 12 cone-shaped croquettes. Roll cones in beaten egg and then in bread crumbs. Bake on a greased baking sheet at 475° F for 15 minutes. Serve with Mushroom Sauce, page 385, if you wish. Also good with Cranberry Relish, page 212.

TO FREEZE. Simply set croquettes on baking sheet or platter and freeze until firm. Put croquettes into moisture-vapor-proof bags, seal, date, label, and put back in freezer.

TO COOK WHEN FROZEN. Put frozen croquettes into a baking dish. Bake at 475° F for 25 minutes or until golden brown.

CHICKEN SOUP WITH AVOCADOS

This makes a very colorful first course for any dinner. I have always liked avocados in spreads, dips, and salads, but the idea of using them in soups, ice creams, et cetera, has never appealed to me. The first time I served this soup everyone in the family made snide remarks. But, once they'd tried it, they asked for more. It's not only delicious but very pretty with the green avocado slices floating on top of the soup.

4 cups thawed chicken broth	1 cup boned chicken
1 whole chicken breast or	2 green onions, cut fine, including greens

½ teaspoon ground coriander   ¼ teaspoon pepper
½ teaspoon oregano   2 teaspoons beef bouillon granules
½ teaspoon salt   1 ripe avocado

Heat chicken broth and add chicken breast or boned chicken. Simmer the broth for about 20 minutes if you're using an uncooked chicken breast. When it is cooked, remove it and cool slightly. Skin the chicken and cut into julienne strips with a sharp knife. Return chicken to the broth. Add onions and seasonings. Simmer for 5 minutes. Peel avocado and cut into thin slices. Add to soup just before serving. The avocado slices will float on the top.

CHICKEN TETRAZZINI BAKE

This dish can be made from fresh or frozen cooked and boned chicken or turkey. However, if you wish to make it in large quantities for the freezer, it's advisable to use fresh chicken or turkey.

SINGLE RECIPE	DOUBLE RECIPE
Time: 10 minutes	*Time: 15 minutes*
Yield: 1½ quarts	*Yield: 3 quarts*
2 cups cooked spaghetti	4 cups cooked spaghetti
¼ cup frozen chopped onions	½ cup frozen chopped onions
½ large chopped green onion	1 large chopped green onion
1 can golden mushroom soup	2 cans golden mushroom soup
2 cups diced cooked chicken	4 cups diced cooked chicken
one 4-ounce jar chopped pimento	two 4-ounce jars chopped pimento
¼ cup sauterne	½ cup sauterne
1 jar drained sliced mushrooms (optional)	2 jars drained sliced mushrooms (optional)
2 tablespoons grated Parmesan cheese	¼ cup grated Parmesan cheese

Cook spaghetti and drain. Meanwhile, combine all the other ingredients, except the Parmesan cheese, in a bowl. (If you're making a single casserole, you may mix it right in the baking dish.) Add cooked, well-drained spaghetti and mix well. Pour into buttered baking dishes and top with Parmesan cheese. Bake at 350° F for 35 minutes.

TO FREEZE. Freezer-wrap baking dishes or see instructions on page 367. Date, label, and freeze.

TO SERVE WHEN FROZEN. Bake frozen casserole in a preheated 350° F oven for about 1 hour, depending on size of casserole, or until mixture bubbles.

CHICKEN À LA KING

Here's an old standby that takes only minutes to prepare and, if boned chicken has been diced before freezing, it need not be thawed first. Especially good served over Noodle Nests, page 406.

SINGLE RECIPE
Time: 10 minutes
Yield: 5 servings

2 tablespoons butter or margarine
2 tablespoons flour
2 cups diced chicken
½ cup chicken broth
1 cup milk
¼ cup sauterne (optional)
½ teaspoon ground coriander
½ teaspoon salt
Pepper to taste
one 4-ounce jar chopped pimiento
1 cup frozen peas

DOUBLE RECIPE
Time: 12 minutes
Yield: 10 servings

4 tablespoons butter or margarine
4 tablespoons flour
4 cups diced chicken
1 cup chicken broth
2 cups milk
½ cup sauterne (optional)
1 teaspoon ground coriander
1 teaspoon salt
Pepper to taste
two 4-ounce jars chopped pimiento
2 cups frozen peas

Melt butter in a large skillet and add flour, making a paste. Add broth and milk, stirring constantly until mixture becomes thick and smooth. Add diced frozen chicken and continue cooking over low heat until chicken is completely thawed. Add wine and seasoning and simmer for 5 minutes. Add frozen peas and chopped pimiento and cook another 5 minutes. Serve immediately. This is good over rice, toast, or noodles, as well as with Noodle Nests.

CHICKEN SALAD

A luncheon favorite, this is also good for light suppers and buffet meals. It's an easy way to use frozen boned chicken (see page 342) and leftover turkey. Because this salad is stabilized with gelatin, you can make it early in the day without a worry that it will become soggy and watery. However, you may omit the gelatin and water if you are going to toss the salad just before serving it.

Time: 10 minutes
Yield: 4 to 6 servings

2 cups boned, cut-up chicken
2 cups coarsely chopped celery
2 tablespoons tarragon or Italian
   dressing
1 teaspoon gelatin

2 tablespoons cold water
1 tablespoon lemon juice
1 tablespoon commercial sour cream
1 teaspoon sugar, instant preferred
2 tablespoons mayonnaise

Salt and pepper to taste
¼ cup toasted blanched almonds or
   toasted pecans

2 teaspoons capers (if they're large,
   chop them)

Thaw boned chicken, cut it up, and add celery. Toss with tarragon
or Italian dressing. Combine cold water with gelatin and let stand for 5
minutes. Then, in top of double boiler or a heatproof custard cup set in
a saucepan of boiling water, dissolve the gelatin. Remove from heat
and combine with lemon juice, sour cream, sugar, and mayonnaise.
Add to chicken-celery mixture and toss until well covered. Add salt and
pepper to taste. Then add nuts and capers, tossing once more. Arrange
on a bed of lettuce and garnish with quartered hard-boiled or deviled
eggs, olives, and parsley.

HOT CHICKEN SALAD

This is a perfect meal to serve at a luncheon or for a light supper. It
takes only minutes to prepare, and you put it in the oven just 15 minutes before you serve it. It's a wonderful dish for the working person or
for anyone who wants to get a hot meal on the table quickly.

SINGLE RECIPE
   Time: 10 minutes
   Yield: 5 ample servings
1 cup diced cooked chicken
1 can undiluted cream of mushroom
   soup
¾ cup chopped celery
1 snipped green onion
⅓ cup mayonnaise
¾ to 1 cup cooked rice
one 4½-ounce jar sliced
   mushrooms
one 2-ounce jar sliced ripe olives

DOUBLE RECIPE
   Time: 15 minutes
   Yield: 10 ample servings
2 cups diced cooked chicken
2 cans undiluted cream of mushroom
   soup
1½ cups chopped celery
2 snipped green onions
⅔ cup mayonnaise
1½ to 2 cups cooked rice
two 4½-ounce jars sliced mushrooms
two 2-ounce jars sliced ripe olives

Mix all ingredients together and pour into a well-buttered 1½-
quart baking dish. Bake in a preheated 400° F oven for 15 minutes or
just until the casserole is heated through, leaving the onions and celery
crisp.

CHICKEN CACCIATORE

You can find many recipes for Chicken Cacciatore. However, I think you'll like this one; simple, yet very tasty.

Time: 15 minutes
Yield: 6 servings

4 thawed, boned, and skinned
  chicken breasts
2 tablespoons butter or margarine
1 pressed garlic clove
1 whole pimiento, cut into strips
½ teaspoon oregano
¼ teaspoon black pepper

About 1½ teaspoons salt
1 tablespoon flour
2 tablespoons sherry or Marsala wine
one 8-ounce can tomato sauce
¼ pound fresh or frozen mushrooms,
  sliced thick
2 tablespoons butter or margarine

Split chicken breasts in half and brown in butter over moderately high heat, adding a few drops of olive oil to the butter to keep it from burning. Remove browned breasts from skillet and stir flour into remaining butter. When it is completely blended, add remaining ingredients except for mushrooms and butter. Cover skillet and simmer for about 30 minutes, or until fork tender. Meanwhile, sauté mushrooms in butter and add them. Continue cooking uncovered if there is too much liquid. Serve with Sauce Cacciatore.

SAUCE CACCIATORE

Time: 8 minutes

2 tablespoons butter
½ cup frozen chopped onions
1 small fresh green pepper, cut into
  strips
1 teaspoon salt

¼ teaspoon black pepper
2 tablespoons Parmesan cheese
1 cup solid-packed Italian-style
  canned or frozen tomatoes
2 tablespoons finely snipped parsley

Heat butter until it is quite hot, being careful not to burn it. (You may wish to add a teaspoon of olive oil to the butter to keep it from burning.) Add onions and green pepper and sauté for about 5 minutes. Add seasoning and tomatoes; simmer, uncovered, for about 15 minutes or until mixture is quite thick. Stir occasionally, breaking up tomatoes.

TO SERVE. Arrange chicken breasts, mushrooms, and other ingredients on heated platter or in serving dish. Cover with Sauce Cacciatore, and serve with buttered spaghetti.

CHOPPED CHICKEN LIVERS

Served on a bed of lettuce, with tomato quarters and artichoke hearts, this will make a meal in itself on hot summer days. Olives and parsley make a nice garnishment. Also a good spread to be used for buffet serving or with your appetizers (see page 82).

SINGLE RECIPE	DOUBLE RECIPE
Time: 15 to 20 minutes	*Time: 20 to 25 minutes*
Yield: About 2 cups	*Yield: About 4 cups*
1 pound chicken livers	2 pounds chicken livers
3 tablespoons butter, chicken fat, or margarine	3 to 4 tablespoons butter, chicken fat, or margarine
2 hard-boiled eggs	4 hard-boiled eggs
1 tablespoon commercial sour cream	2 tablespoons commercial sour cream
1 tablespoon mayonnaise	2 tablespoons mayonnaise
½ medium-sized sweet onion	1 medium-sized sweet onion
Salt and pepper to taste	Salt and pepper to taste

Sauté livers in butter until well browned on both sides and no longer pink on the inside. Don't overcook, or they'll be dry. Put chicken livers, hard-boiled eggs, and onion through food grinder or process in your food processor. Combine mayonnaise and sour cream, mixing well. Add just enough of combined mayonnaise and sour cream to the ground chicken livers to hold the mixture together properly, being careful not to add too much. Salt and pepper to taste.

TO FREEZE. Chopped chicken livers freeze well. Freeze in the amount you're likely to use at one time.

TO SERVE WHEN FROZEN. Simply thaw.

CHICKEN OR TURKEY HASH

A truly elegant way of serving leftover chicken or turkey. Serve in crepes (see page 127), as well as in patty shells or on toast.

Yield: Serves 8

4 large chicken breasts, cooked or	½ cup flour
	1¾ cups chicken stock
4 cups boned leftover chicken or turkey	½ cup white wine
	½ cup heavy cream
¾ pound fresh mushrooms, thinly sliced	Salt and pepper to taste
	½ cup coarsely chopped pecans, sautéed in butter (optional)
¼ pound butter or margarine	

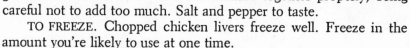

Poach chicken breasts in 2 cups of water and a little wine (optional) for 20 minutes, adding a bouquet garni (see page 41). When done, cool and strain stock; chill to remove fat. Remove skin and bones from chicken and discard. Cut chicken into medium-sized pieces. Sauté mushrooms in half the butter, season with salt and pepper. In separate pan, melt rest of shortening, add flour, and cook a few minutes. Add chicken stock and wine and stir until mixture is thickened. Gradually add cream; cook, stirring until you have a smooth, creamy sauce. Season well with salt and pepper, add mushrooms, chicken pieces, and nuts if desired. Heat well or refrigerate and bake later.

TO FREEZE. Crepes may be filled with hash and arranged in a baking dish. Cover with foil and refrigerate or freeze. It is best to thaw them in the refrigerator and bake in the oven at 350° F, covered, for about 30 minutes or until crepes are bubbly. Uncover and continue baking for about 5 additional minutes.

Leftover hash can be frozen in a freezing container or bag and used at another time. To use, thaw in refrigerator or your microwave oven and heat thoroughly before spreading on warmed crepes.

OTHER FOWL

ROCK CORNISH GAME HENS

Here's a delectable item, prepared either on the grill or in the oven, that can be served as a company or family meal. Serve with or without dressing as you wish. Plan one bird per person.

Thaw hens. Remove neck, gizzard, and liver from cavity. Clean and salt and pepper the inside. Fill with dressing if you wish (wild rice stuffing, page 357, is great with cornish hens). Truss and place on a rack in a shallow baking pan. Roast in a 400° F oven for about 1 hour or until tender. Baste several times with melted butter or sauce. For first 15 minutes, have hens lying on their sides; for next 15 minutes, lying on other side; and breast up for remaining baking time.

BASTING SAUCE

Yield: 1 cup

½ cup currant jelly   2 ounces apricot brandy
⅓ cup orange juice concentrate

Heat currant jelly and orange juice concentrate and mix until blended; add apricot brandy and stir. Baste only after 30 minutes baking time; lower heat to 350° F and baste every 10 minutes. Serve remaining sauce with Rock Cornish Game Hens at the table.

WILD RICE STUFFING

This scrumptious dressing is good with any poultry, domestic or wild. Simple to make.

Yield: Approximately 4
cups—enough for 4 Cornish
hens

⅓ cup wild rice
1 tablespoon beef bouillon granules
¼ cup butter
¼ pound mushrooms, sliced
1½ cups finely chopped celery
½ cup frozen chopped onions

1½ teaspoons salt
Dash pepper
Pinch sage
Pinch thyme
⅓ cup chopped pecans

Wash and rinse wild rice thoroughly. Cook rice in 2½ cups water, to which bouillon granules have been added. Bring to a boil, lower heat, and continue cooking uncovered for 1 hour, or until rice is tender and soft. If the rice is not fully soft, allow it to stand for an additional 10 minutes. Drain.

While rice is cooking, sauté mushrooms, celery, and onions in butter until onions are limp and clear. Add seasonings and continue to cook for an additional 2 minutes. Add cooked rice to sautéed vegetables and cook together until mixture is heated through. Add pecans and mix well. If more convenient, wild rice stuffing may be prepared in advance and refrigerated and just heated through in the oven before serving.

LONG ISLAND DUCKLING WITH ORANGE SAUCE

If you haven't tried one of these delicious birds found fresh or frozen in your supermarket, you have been missing a taste treat. Found as an entrée in most better restaurants, this elegant dish is simple to prepare at home.

NOTE TO THE OUTDOOR CHEF. Don't be afraid to try one of these delicious birds on your outdoor barbecue rotisserie for adventuresome cooking.

If duckling is frozen, thaw in refrigerator overnight in original wrapping. Remove neck, heart, and gizzard from the inside; clean thoroughly, making sure that all pinfeathers have been removed. Stuff or not, as you wish. Put in a shallow baking dish and bake in a 325° F preheated oven for 2 to 2½ hours for a 5½ to 6 pound stuffed duckling, at which time it should be tender and nicely browned. If duckling is not stuffed, decrease baking time 30 to 40 minutes.

Orange Sauce

2 tablespoons drippings from duckling
1 tablespoon flour
1 cup water
Grated rind of 1 orange
Juice of 1 orange
1 tablespoon frozen orange
    concentrate, thawed
2 drops bitters (to taste)
1 teaspoon sugar (adjust to taste)

Remove the duckling from pan and skim off most of the fat, leaving 2 tablespoons. Blend 1 tablespoon of flour into the drippings and add 1 cup of water, stirring constantly over medium heat. Now add the grated orange rind, orange juice, and concentrate, stirring constantly. When mixture comes to a boil, add bitters and sugar. Simmer for 5 minutes. Strain and serve with duckling.

Vegetables

✳✳✳✳✳✳✳✳✳✳✳✳✳✳✳✳✳✳✳✳✳✳✳✳✳✳✳✳✳✳✳

Luckily for the American homemaker, frozen vegetables abound at local supermarkets in every size, shape, and form; they're a convenience that everyone now takes for granted. These frozen vegetables duplicate the taste of fresh, garden-grown vegetables more closely than those preserved by canning or any other method. Buy in quantity when they're on sale. Frozen vegetables are the greatest timesavers of all foods.

Many people assume that fresh vegetables are more nutritious than frozen. Actually, there is minimal nutrient loss in modern commercial processing methods. Vegetables are packed at the peak of ripeness when they have the best nutritive value, as well as flavor, and are immediately frozen in a nearby plant. Oftentimes, quick-freezing plants on mobile units are brought right to the field where the fresh produce is processed within minutes of being picked. The nutrient content of frozen vegetables may indeed be greater than that of so-called "fresh" vegetables which may have been picked green or unripened and have taken five or more days to reach the market. Storing and handling of these fresh vegetables is also difficult to control.

The recipes in this chapter are mainly for dishes that use frozen vegetables and for vegetable dishes that can be frozen.

BLANCHING, STEAMING, AND FREEZING FRESH VEGETABLES

Only the highest grade of produce should be used for freezing and all vegetables should be processed as quickly after harvest as possible.

Take corn as an example: one day can make an amazing difference in quality. The best way to freeze corn is to pick it and freeze it the same morning.

All vegetables should be washed thoroughly, with the exception of lima beans, green peas, and other vegetables protected by pods. Vegetables like spinach and broccoli need to be very carefully washed to remove all sand and grit. Swish them vigorously through the water and then lift them out, leaving the sand in the bottom of the sink. Empty and repeat until water is free of residue.

Blanching vegetables before freezing kills the enzymes that cause loss of flavor and color. If the vegetables are not blanched or aren't blanched sufficiently, enzymes continue to be active, even in the freezer. Your vegetables may discolor, toughen, or develop off-flavors, which will cause them to be unappetizing.

Blanching

CONVENTIONAL METHOD. The easiest way to blanch vegetables is in boiling water. If you intend to do a lot of vegetable blanching, a large vegetable blancher is a convenience. Ordinarily, however, a large pot with a capacity of at least 5 or 6 quarts will suffice. Use a basket from your French fryer, or some other such container, to lower the vegetables into the boiling water. Put lid on blancher or kettle and start timing immediately, keeping heat high for the entire cooking time. The water may not boil again while the vegetables are being blanched, but make sure that it reaches a full boil before you start on a second batch. Blanching water may be used over again so long as it's clean and not too discolored. Be sure to keep adding enough water each time to bring the total amount to full measure. If blanching kettle is large enough, a double batch of vegetables (2 pounds) may be processed at once, but then use twice the amount of boiling water indicated on the chart.

VEGETABLE BLANCHING CHART: STOVE-TOP METHOD

Wash all vegetables thoroughly, discarding any with imperfections; then follow directions given below.

	Quantity of Vegetables	Maximum Amount of Boiling Water	Time in Water
ASPARAGUS. Select tender young stalks with compact tips. Sort according to thickness of stalk. Wash well, swishing through water to remove all soil. Break or cut off tough ends of stalks. Stalks may be cut in uniform lengths to fit package or in 2-inch lengths.	1 pound	6 quarts	Small stalks—2 minutes Medium stalks—3 minutes Large stalks—4 minutes
BEANS—GREEN STRINGLESS, SNAP, AND WAX. Select only young, tender stringless beans that snap when broken. Cut off ends and cut into 1-inch pieces or French-cut lengthwise.	1 pound	4 quarts	3 minutes
BEANS, LIMA. Select only tender, young, well-filled pods. Avoid beans with yellow or dried pods. Sort beans according to size. You may shell limas before or after blanching, whichever you prefer. Pack into containers, leaving ½ inch of head space.	1 quart	4 quarts	Small beans or pods—2 minutes Medium beans or pods—3 minutes Large beans or pods—4 minutes
BEETS. Select tender young beets, no more than 3 inches in diameter. Trim tops, leaving ½ inch of stems. Cook in boiling water until tender; peel; cut into slices or cubes.	Cook instead of blanching		25 to 30 minutes for small 45 to 50 minutes for medium
BROCCOLI. Select tight, dark-green heads that are compact with tender stalks, free of woodiness. Split lengthwise so that flowerets are not more than 1½ inches across. Blanch or steam.	1½ pounds	5 quarts	3 to 4 minutes 5 minutes (for steaming)
BRUSSELS SPROUTS. Select firm, green, compact heads. Remove coarse outer leaves and sort according to size.	1 pound	4 quarts	Small heads—3 minutes Medium heads—4 minutes Large heads—5 minutes

	Quantity of Vegetables	Maximum Amount of Boiling Water	Time in Water
CARROTS. Select young, tender, mild, or sweet-flavored carrots. Cut off tops, peel, or scrape. Small carrots may be frozen whole; larger carrots may be split lengthwise, diced, or sliced.	1 pound	4 quarts	Whole, small—5 minutes Diced or sliced—2 minutes Sliced lengthwise—2 minutes
CAULIFLOWER. Choose firm, tender, snow-white heads. Break or cut into 1-inch pieces, removing any leaves.	1 pound	6 quarts	4 minutes
CHARD. Same as spinach.	—	—	—
CHILIES. Same as peppers.	—	—	—
CORN. Use only sweet or supersweet corn for freezing. Freeze shortly after picking it, while it is still in the milky stage. Ears should be fully developed, with plump tender kernels. For cut corn, cut kernels from cob after blanching and cooling.* Although you may have heard of people freezing corn in the husk, don't attempt it. It certainly is an easy way to ruin good corn. I have tested several varieties of corn and it simply doesn't work.	8 medium-sized ears	5 quarts	On the cob, small ears—7 minutes On the cob, medium ears—9 minutes On the cob, large ears—11 minutes
MUSHROOMS. Wash thoroughly and trim stems. Slice no more than ½ inch thick, thinner if you like. I have had great success in freezing mushrooms without any blanching or further ado. However, if you wish to blanch them, the timing is given here.	1 pound	4 quarts	Whole—5 minutes Buttons or quarters—3½ minutes Slices—3 minutes
PEAS, GREEN. Choose bright-green, plump pods with sweet tender peas. Shell; then blanch.	1 pound	4 quarts	1 minute
PEPPERS—GREEN AND HOT. Peppers may be frozen without blanching, to be used uncooked. Unblanched peppers should not be kept for more than a month. If they're to be used in cooked dishes, blanch them first for more compact packaging, either halved, quartered, or julienne-sliced. Select firm, crisp, thick-walled peppers.	1 quart (about 6 peppers)	5 quarts	Halves—3 minutes Quarters—2½ minutes Slices—2 minutes

Vegetable	Preparation	Amount	Water	Time
PUMPKINS.	Prepared in the same manner as Winter Squash.	—	—	—
SPINACH.	Select crisp, tender green leaves and stalks. Wash very thoroughly to remove all sand. Discard any yellow or ragged leaves. Leave whole or shred coarsely.	1 pound	5 quarts	1 minute
SQUASH, SUMMER.	Select young squash with small seeds and tender rind. Wash, trim, and cut in ½-inch slices. Do not peel. Leave ½ inch of head space when packing.	1¼ pounds	4 quarts	3 minutes
SQUASH, WINTER.	Select fully mature, yet firm, squash. Halve; remove inner pulp or seeds. Cook until soft in boiling water, steam, or bake. Remove cooked squash from shell and mash or press through a sieve. Pack into containers, leaving ½ inch head space.	Cook instead of blanching	—	—
SWEET POTATOES.	Prepared in the same manner as Winter Squash.	—	—	—
TOMATOES.	Pour boiling water over tomatoes and let set for a minute or two; then peel. Pack tightly in freezer containers, leaving ½ inch of head space. These tomatoes can be used in place of stewed tomatoes in sauces, gravies, casseroles, et cetera.	No blanching	—	—
TOMATO JUICE.	Wash tomatoes, quarter, and simmer for 10 minutes. Strain off juices (a jelly bag is good for this). Add ½ teaspoon salt for each pint. Be sure to leave ½ inch of head space.	No blanching	—	—

* An easy way to cut corn from cob is to stick narrow end of cob into center of a large tube cake pan. Not only will it hold the ear of corn, the pan will catch all the corn. Use an electric knife if available to cut kernels from the ear.

MICROWAVE METHOD. While blanching vegetables in a microwave oven takes almost the same amount of time as conventional stove-top blanching, there are several advantages to this method. It isn't necessary to bring large quantities of water to a boil, which not only saves time, but also leaves your kitchen cooler and less steamy. Microwave blanching also uses less energy, not a minor consideration.

Prepare vegetables as you normally would and measure into 1-pound or 1-quart quantity, as recommended in conventional manner (see page 361). Put prepared vegetables in proper-sized, covered casserole. Add water as given in chart. Cook for the recommended amount of time on high or cook setting. Set timer to half the time recommended. Stir, continue cooking, and stir again. Check vegetables at minimum time on cooking chart; if vegetables are not evenly bright in color, stir well and continue cooking to maximum time. Be careful not to overcook.

Timing is very important. Overcooking causes the vegetable to become mushy and undercooking will not adequately destroy enzymes. These enzymes continue to be active in the freezer, making the vegetables less sweet and more starchy, which results in an over-mature taste. It is also important that the microwave heat the vegetables evenly; for this reason, it is necessary to stir them halfway through the recommended cooking time.

Most vegetables require heating to 190° F prior to freezing in order to destroy the enzymes that change the sugars to starches. There are many types of vegetables other than those listed on the chart. Should you wish to experiment, keep this in mind. Use the small microwave thermometer and check the vegetables for proper temperature and timing. Plunge vegetables immediately into ice water to prevent further cooking. Continue as in conventional method.

VEGETABLE BLANCHING CHART: IN MICROWAVE OVEN AT HIGH POWER LEVEL*

Vegetable	Amount	Casserole Size	Water	Minutes
Asparagus	1 pound, cut into 1 to 2-inch pieces	2 quart	¼ cup	3 to 4
Beans—Green or Wax	1 pound	1½ quart	½ cup	4 to 6
Broccoli (1-inch cuts)	1 bunch—1¼ to 1½ pounds	2 quart	½ cup	4 to 5½
Carrots	1 pound, sliced	1½ quart	¼ cup	4 to 6
Cauliflower	1 head, cut into flowerets	2 quart	½ cup	4 to 5½
Corn on the Cob†	—	—	—	—
Onions	4 medium, quartered	1 quart	½ cup	3 to 4½
Parsnips	1 pound, cubed	1½ quart	¼ cup	2½ to 4
Peas	2 pounds, shelled	1 quart	¼ cup	3½ to 5
Spinach	1 pound, washed	2 quart	None	2½ to 3½
Squash—Summer or Yellow	1 pound, sliced or cubed	1½ quart	¼ cup	3 to 4½
Turnips	1 pound, cubed	1½ quart	¼ cup	3 to 4½
Zucchini	1 pound, sliced or cubed	1½ quart	¼ cup	3 to 4½

* The Microwave Guide and Cookbook, General Electric Co.
† For most even blanching, cut corn off the cob beforehand. Blanch corn cut from 4 ears at a time. Place cut corn in 1-quart casserole. Add ¼ cup water. Cover. Cook 4 to 5 minutes, stirring after 2 minutes. Cool by setting casserole in ice water, stirring occasionally until cool.

Steaming

Steaming is a satisfactory method of blanching some vegetables, such as broccoli, pumpkin, sweet potatoes, and winter squash. To steam, use a kettle with a rack that holds a steaming basket, usually about 2 to 3 inches above the bottom of the kettle. (Hamilton-Beach makes a marvelous electric steamer cooker. Can be used for many things, but is particularly great for blanching vegetables.) It's very important that your steaming kettle have a tight-fitting lid. Put 1 or 2 inches of water in the kettle and bring it to a full boil. Vegetables in the basket should be arranged in a single layer so that the steam will reach all parts quickly. Cover kettle and keep heat high. Start counting steaming time as soon as the lid goes on the kettle. (Use blanching chart for timing.) Steam vegetables one minute longer than indicated on chart in areas with an elevation of 5,000 feet or more above sea level.

Cooling

A very important step, cooling should be done properly. When the vegetables have been blanched the proper amount of time, lift them out and plunge them into a container of cold water. Keep running additional cold water from the faucet or add ice cubes. When you are using ice, it will take about 1 pound of ice for each pound of vegetables. Cooled vegetables may then be drained thoroughly and packed. Be sure to get your food into the freezer without delay.

APPROXIMATE YIELD OF FROZEN VEGETABLES FROM FRESH

Vegetable	Fresh, as Purchased or Picked	Frozen
Asparagus	1 crate (twelve 2-pound bunches)	15 to 22 pints
	1 to 1½ pounds	1 pint
Beans, Lima (in pods)	1 bushel (32 pounds)	12 to 16 pints
	2 to 2½ pounds	1 pint
Beans—Snap, Green, and Wax	1 bushel (30 pounds)	30 to 45 pints
	⅔ to 1 pound	1 pint
Beet Greens	15 pounds	10 to 15 pints
	1 to 1½ pounds	1 pint
Beets (without tops)	1 bushel (52 pounds)	35 to 42 pints
	1¼ to 1½ pounds	1 pint
Broccoli	1 crate (25 pounds)	24 pints
	1 pound	1 pint
Brussels Sprouts	4 quart boxes	6 pints
	1 pound	1 pint
Carrots (without tops)	1 bushel (50 pounds)	32 to 40 pints
	1¼ to 1½ pounds	1 pint
Cauliflower	2 medium heads	3 pints
	1⅓ pounds	1 pint
Chard	1 bushel (12 pounds)	8 to 12 pints
	1 to 1½ pounds	1 pint
Collard Greens	1 bushel (12 pounds)	8 to 12 pints
	1 to 1½ pounds	1 pint
Corn, Sweet (in husks)	1 bushel (35 pounds)	14 to 17 pints
	2 to 2½ pounds	1 pint
Eggplant	1 pound	1 pint
Kale	1 bushel (18 pounds)	12 to 18 pints
	1 to 1½ pounds	1 pint
Mustard Greens	1 bushel (12 pounds)	8 to 12 pints
	1 to 1½ pounds	1 pint
Peas	1 bushel (30 pounds)	12 to 15 pints
	2 to 2½ pounds	1 pint
Peppers, Green	⅔ pound (3 peppers)	1 pint
Pumpkin	3 pounds	2 pints
Spinach	1 bushel (18 pounds)	12 to 18 pints
	1 to 1½ pounds	1 pint
Squash, Summer	1 bushel (40 pounds)	32 to 40 pints
	1 to 1¼ pounds	1 pint
Squash, Winter	3 pounds	2 pints
Sweet Potatoes	⅔ pound	1 pint
Tomatoes	5 pounds	4 to 4½ pints

Freezing Casseroles

The vegetable dishes that can be frozen are frequently of the casserole variety. You won't want all your casserole dishes in the freezer, so line the dish with foil, letting the foil extend above top edge on all sides. Put in or arrange casserole according to directions in the recipe, and freeze. When food is solidly frozen, pull on foil to remove the frozen, foil-nested block. Freezer-wrap and return immediately to the freezer, making sure to label and date all dishes.

TO COOK WHEN FROZEN. Recommended procedure is to peel all the foil from bottom and sides of frozen casserole and place into proper size baking or casserole dish. Cover top (with lid, foil, or plastic wrap) and place in refrigerator for thawing. Overnight thawing in refrigerator is recommended. When completely thawed, bake according to directions in recipe. *Always put baking dish in a preheated oven.*

Microwave ovens have added a new dimension to thawing and cooking frozen dishes. If your microwave unit has a defrost cycle, completely thaw dish according to manufacturer's directions. Keep casserole covered with plastic wrap.

Although a completely frozen casserole may be placed in the oven and cooked until done, the results usually are not as satisfactory as when done in two stages. The outside of the casserole tends to be dry and overcooked, while the center of it is still icy.

COOKING FROZEN VEGETABLES

Do not thaw vegetables before cooking; all vegetables, with the exception of corn on the cob, are best cooked in their frozen state. Corn on the cob should be allowed to thaw slightly so that the cob itself will be completely thawed when the corn has finished cooking. Half a cup of boiling water is usually sufficient for a pint of frozen vegetables. Bring water to a full boil in saucepan, add vegetables, cover, and bring back to a full boil. Some vegetables, such as chopped spinach, will need to be turned and broken up as they begin to thaw. Start timing cooking period after the water has reached a full boil again; lower heat and continue cooking as directed in chart. Make sure the pot lid is on securely. Add seasoning as desired, and serve immediately.

Frozen vegetables are often used in casserole dishes. Partially defrost vegetable to separate pieces. Put vegetable in greased casserole dish and combine with remaining ingredients according to your recipe. Cover and bake until just tender.

To bake corn on the cob, partially thaw the ears first. Brush liberally with melted butter or margarine, season with salt and pepper to taste, and wrap in foil. Bake in a hot 400° F oven for 20 minutes. Serve immediately; the corn tends to get mushy if allowed to stand for any length of time.

The secret of cooking good vegetables, both frozen and fresh, is to cook them in a minimum amount of water and only until they are just tender, but still a bit crisp. Not only do they taste better, but they look better and are more nutritious, since all the vitamins haven't been cooked out. Following is a timetable for cooking frozen vegetables, both in the conventional stove-top manner and in a microwave unit. Remember, cooking frozen vegetables in the microwave oven does not require additional water. Turn microwave unit on cook or high (see below) and cook right in the package. Sauces or melted butter may also be prepared in your microwave unit. Prepare in serving dish, add vegetables, and serve. No extra pots or pans to wash.

TIMETABLE FOR COOKING FROZEN VEGETABLES

VEGETABLE	AMOUNT	Conventional Cooking (use ¼ cup water) TIME IN MINUTES AFTER WATER RETURNS TO BOIL	Microwave Cooking at High Power Level* TIME IN MINUTES
Asparagus	10 ounces	5 to 10	8 to 10
Beans, Lima			
Large type	10 ounces	6 to 10	7 to 8
Baby type		15 to 20	
Beans—Snap,			
Green or Wax	10 ounces		
1-inch pieces		7 to 10	10 to 12
Julienne		5 to 7	
Beets, fresh,			
sliced or diced	10 ounces	3 to 5	22 to 25
Broccoli	10 ounces	5 to 8	8 to 10
Brussels Sprouts	10 ounces	4 to 9	8 to 10
Carrots	10 ounces	5 to 6	8 to 10
Cauliflower	10 ounces	5 to 8	8 to 9
Corn			
Whole kernel	10 ounces	3 to 5	5 to 7
On the cob	1 ear	3 to 4	5 to 6
frozen	over 1 ear	3 to 4	3 to 4 minutes additional for each ear
Peas, Green	10 ounces	5 to 8	5 to 6
Spinach	10 ounces	4 to 6	7 to 8
Squash, Summer	10 ounces	10 to 12	5 to 7

* *The Microwave Guide and Cookbook*, General Electric Co.

STEAMING. Partially thawed vegetables that have been separated may be steamed over actively boiling water. Cover and start timing immediately, using the preceding chart. Add seasoning as desired and serve immediately.

ARTICHOKES TO ZUCCHINI

ARTICHOKES

You'll find fresh whole artichokes readily available at your market during March and April and again in October and November. A limited amount is available throughout most of the year, but at premium prices. When purchasing artichokes for the freezer, select compact heads that yield slightly when squeezed. Avoid those with opened or turned-out leaves. A few of the outside leaves may be a bit discolored. However, the artichoke, on the whole, should have a healthy green color.

The size of an artichoke is determined by the place it grows on the plant, the largest coming from the top, medium-sized ones from the center of the plant, and the baby artichokes from around the bottom. These baby ones are used for canned and frozen artichoke hearts. They are very tender; hence the entire "choke" can be eaten.

To prepare artichokes for the freezer, don't blanch them; cook them fully before freezing. When fully cooked, they need only to be thawed and may be served cold or steamed for a few minutes to heat them through.

If you wish to cook your artichokes fully before freezing, wash them well and, with a sharp knife, slice about 1 to 1½ inches from the top of the artichoke. Cut stem very flat and flush with the bottom. Baby artichokes, if you're lucky enough to find them, are eaten whole and do not need to be trimmed. Place artichokes in a large kettle, preferably upright. Pour boiling water into kettle to a depth of about 2 inches; add about 3 tablespoons of olive oil, and 2 minched cloves of garlic. For each artichoke add ½ teaspoon of lemon juice. Sprinkle each artichoke with ¼ teaspoon salt. Cover pan tightly and cook over moderately high heat for 20 to 45 minutes, depending on size, or until stem end can easily be pierced with a fork. Don't overcook or they will fall apart after cooking. When they are done, remove and drain upside down. Cool, remove the center "flower," and then freeze.

FROZEN ARTICHOKE HEARTS

Artichoke hearts are a wonderful addition to any tossed salad, particularly with Caesar or vinegar-and-oil dressing. Cook artichoke hearts according to directions on package. Drain and cool. Toss enough olive oil on the hearts to cover lightly; add a dash of vinegar, and salt and pepper to taste. Chill. Serve plain or use in a tossed salad.

VARIATION. Here's another interesting way to use frozen artichoke hearts: cook in ¼ cup of olive oil instead of water, adding 1 clove of garlic and ¼ teaspoon salt. Cook, covered, until tender. Remove garlic and add a dash of vinegar and pepper to taste. Serve warm or cold.

ANCHOVY SAUCE FOR ARTICHOKES

This is good with either cold or hot artichokes.

Yield: Enough sauce for about 5 artichokes

3 ounces softened cream cheese
One 2-ounce can flat anchovies, oil and all

2 tablespoons lemon juice
2 tablespoons mayonnaise
1 teaspoon instant minced onion

Put all ingredients into the blender and whirl for a few seconds, making sure that everything is well blended. If you don't have a blender, chop the anchovies finely and mix all the ingredients with a mixer.

Artichokes are delicious served with Hollandaise Sauce (page 372), as well as with plain melted butter with lemon and salt added.

ARTICHOKE HEARTS PROVENÇALE

So easy to make—so elegant to serve.

Yield: Serves 6 to 8
Time: 10 minutes

Two 10-ounce packages frozen artichoke hearts
½ cup grated Swiss cheese

¼ cup dry bread crumbs or seasoned Italian bread crumbs
2 tablespoons butter

Cook artichoke hearts according to package directions. Arrange in a shallow baking dish. Combine Swiss cheese with bread crumbs. Cover artichoke hearts with cheese mixture. Toss lightly and dot with butter. Bake in a preheated 325° F oven until heated through. For faster cooking, set under broiler for a few minutes. Watch closely.

ASPARAGUS

Follow cooking directions on package of frozen asparagus or use directions given in chart on page 369. Drain and serve with Quick 'n Easy Hollandaise Sauce (see page 372).

BUTTERED ASPARAGUS

Follow cooking directions on package of frozen asparagus or use directions given in cooking chart on page 369. Drain asparagus and arrange on cooking platter. Meanwhile, brown butter lightly in pan and pour it over asparagus. Or add dry bread crumbs to butter, browning the crumbs lightly, and spread this mixture over asparagus.

QUICK 'N EASY HOLLANDAISE SAUCE

This tastes every bit as good as authentic Hollandaise sauce; it has fewer calories, is less expensive, and is much simpler to make. When served over green vegetables, this yellow sauce makes an attractive vegetable platter. It is especially delicious served with broccoli, artichoke hearts, asparagus, cauliflower, or as a dip for regular artichokes.

Yield: Enough sauce for 1 or 2
  packages of frozen vegetables

4 tablespoons mayonnaise
1 tablespoon lemon juice
2 tablespoons butter or margarine

1 egg yolk (for using egg whites, see
  page 47)
Dash cayenne pepper
Dash salt

Cook your vegetables in the bottom of a double boiler. Five minutes before they're done, put top on double boiler. Combine mayonnaise and lemon juice in top and stir until well blended. Let cook about 3 minutes, until fairly warm; then add shortening and egg yolk, stirring constantly. When mixture is thick, add seasonings; stir and remove from heat. Drain vegetables, arrange on serving plate, and cover with sauce. Sauce may also be cooked over low direct heat.

ASPARAGUS AND HAM ROLLS

When served on toast rounds, this makes a quick luncheon dish or an easy late-evening snack.

Time: 10 minutes
Yield: 4 to 5 servings

One 10-ounce package frozen
  asparagus tips
5 not-too-thin slices of boiled ham
2 tablespoons butter
2 tablespoons flour

1 cup milk
½ pound sharp Cheddar cheese,
  sliced
1 tablespoon prepared mustard
1 tablespoon Worcestershire sauce

Cook asparagus tips according to directions on package or follow directions in chart on page 369. While asparagus tips are cooking, melt butter in skillet and add flour, making a paste. Add milk. Continue cooking, stirring constantly, until sauce thickens. Add sliced cheese to sauce, lower heat, and stir until cheese melts. Then add mustard and Worcestershire sauce. Drain asparagus and arrange an equal number of the tips on the center of each piece of ham. Roll ham around the asparagus tips and place on top of toast or Holland rusk. Spoon cheese sauce over the top and serve immediately. Plates or serving platter may be garnished with quartered hard-boiled eggs or olives.

GREEN BEANS WITH ALMONDS

Follow cooking directions on package of frozen French-cut green beans or follow directions in chart on page 369. While the beans are cooking, place ⅛ cup of blanched slivered almonds on a baking sheet or pie tin and roast at 350° F until nicely browned (about 3 to 5 minutes). See Broiler-Toaster (p. 12). Watch closely so they don't burn. Drain beans when they're done. Melt 2 or 3 tablespoons of butter, add beans and nuts, and toss gently. Place in serving bowl; serve immediately.

SOUR CREAM BEAN SOUP

Quick and easy, this can be made into a full meal. Nice for a Sunday-night supper. Serve with hot rolls or Italian bread.

Time: 5 minutes
Yield: 4 generous servings

1 pound lean ground beef
One 10-ounce package frozen
  French-cut green beans
½ cup frozen chopped onions
2 cups frozen hash-browned potatoes
4 cups water

6 teaspoons bouillon granules
¼ teaspoon pepper
1 pint commercial sour cream
Salt and pepper to taste

Put all ingredients, except the sour cream, in a large saucepan. Slowly heat to a boil; turn heat down and simmer for about 15 minutes or until beans and potatoes are tender. Remove from heat, add sour cream and salt and pepper to taste. Serve immediately. (It is not necessary to brown meat; it may even be added while frozen.)

GREEN BEANS WITH MUSTARD SAUCE

French-cut green beans, cooked according to directions on package or those given in the chart on page 369, are delicious served with this sauce.

SINGLE RECIPE
Time: 2 minutes
Yield: Enough sauce for 1 package
of frozen beans

¼ cup commercial sour cream
1 tablespoon prepared mustard
1 tablespoon butter
1 teaspoon Worcestershire sauce
Salt and pepper to taste

DOUBLE RECIPE
Time: 2 minutes
Yield: Enough sauce for 2
packages of frozen beans

½ cup commercial sour cream
2 tablespoons prepared mustard
2 tablespoons butter
2 teaspoons Worcestershire sauce
Salt and pepper to taste

In a small saucepan, combine all ingredients and cook over low heat until all the butter is melted. Pour immediately over cooked beans and serve. Sauce may be warmed in top of double boiler while beans are cooking in the bottom.

GREEN BEAN CASSEROLE

Quick and easy and, oh, so good!

Time: 5 minutes
Yield: 1 quart

One 10-ounce package frozen
  French-cut green beans
1 can undiluted mushroom soup

1 can French-fried onion rings
Slivered almonds (optional)
Salt and pepper to taste

Cook beans until completely thawed and water is boiling. (Follow directions on package or in chart on page 369.) Mix beans with mushroom soup and almonds, if desired. Place onion rings on the top. Bake at 350° F for 40 minutes. If beans are fully cooked, you may reduce baking time to 30 minutes.

BROILED TOMATOES WITH GREEN BEANS

This is especially good during the summer months, when tomatoes are abundant.

Time: 15 minutes
Yield: 6 servings

3 large tomatoes
Salt and pepper to taste
1 clove garlic
1 tablespoon butter
One 10-ounce package frozen
   French-cut green beans

Sauce:
1½ tablespoons butter
1½ tablespoons flour
½ teaspoon salt
1 cup milk
½ cup sliced or shredded sharp
   Cheddar cheese
½ teaspoon prepared mustard

Cut tomatoes into halves. Season with salt and pepper and broil for about 10 minutes or until hot and browned on top. Meanwhile, cook beans according to directions on package or in chart on page 369. In small saucepan, melt butter and sauté garlic for a few minutes. When beans are cooked, drain and mix with butter from which garlic clove has been removed.

While the beans and tomatoes are cooking, prepare the sauce. Melt butter and add flour, mixing well. Add salt. Slowly add milk, stirring constantly. Then add cheese and cook over moderate heat until all the cheese is melted. Add mustard.

Remove tomatoes when they are browned and pile buttered beans on top of each tomato half. Now spoon cheese sauce over the top and serve immediately. You may wish to garnish with broiled bacon bits (see page 41) or parsley.

MOTHER'S BEAN SALAD

This is a nice salad to serve during the winter, especially when lettuce is expensive.

Time: 4 minutes
Yield: Approximately 2 cups

Two 10-ounce packages frozen
   French-cut green beans, cooked
   and drained
1 tablespoon commercial sour cream
2 tablespoons mayonnaise
1 tablespoon salad oil

3 teaspoons sugar
2 teaspoons vinegar
½ teaspoon salt or more
4 snipped green onions, stems and all
Finely cut parsley

While the beans are cooking according to directions on package or in the chart on page 369, combine all the other ingredients in mixing bowl. Remove beans from stove when they're crisply tender and drain. Add hot beans to the sour cream and mayonnaise mixture, tossing gently. Cool at room temperature and then refrigerate. Serve chilled. Keeps well in the refrigerator for several days.

GREEN BEANS ROMANO

Here's an easy and "cheesy" bean dish.

One 10-ounce package frozen
French-cut green beans
2 large or 3 medium-sized sliced
tomatoes
2 tablespoons melted butter

1 tablespoon instant minced onion
¼ teaspoon salt
¼ teaspoon oregano
Pinch thyme
¼ pound sliced mozzarella cheese

Cook beans according to directions on package or follow those in chart on page 369. Drain and arrange on the bottom of a buttered casserole dish. Slice tomatoes over top. Drizzle butter over the tomatoes and sprinkle with seasonings. Top with cheese slices and bake in a preheated 350° F oven for about 30 minutes.

BUTTERED BEETS

Cooked beets freeze very well. You may want to prepare a large batch of buttered beets or Harvard beets and freeze them in family-sized portions.

Wash beets, cut off leaves, leaving a 1½-inch stem and root (otherwise, they will bleed). Put beets in kettle and cover about halfway with boiling water. Cook over moderate heat until tender, usually between 35 and 55 minutes. Drain and cool; then peel, slice, dice, or cut into julienne strips. Serve hot with butter; salt and pepper to taste.

TO FREEZE. Pack buttered beets into family-sized freezing cartons, label, date, and freeze.

TO SERVE WHEN FROZEN. Thaw and warm in pan, adding more butter if needed.

HARVARD BEETS

SINGLE RECIPE
2 cups sliced boiled beets
2 tablespoons butter
1 tablespoon flour
½ cup sugar
½ teaspoon salt
¼ cup vinegar
¼ cup water

DOUBLE RECIPE
4 cups sliced boiled beets
¼ cup butter
2 tablespoons flour
1 cup sugar
1 teaspoon salt
½ cup vinegar
½ cup water

Cook and prepare beets as in recipe for Buttered Beets. Melt butter in pan, add flour, and mix well. Then add sugar and salt. Combine water with vinegar and add gradually to the butter and flour mixture, stirring constantly. When thick and smooth, add beets. Simmer for a few minutes and serve.

TO FREEZE. Pack Harvard Beets into meal-sized containers, date, label, and freeze.

TO SERVE WHEN FROZEN. These beets are good cold; simply thaw and serve. Or, if you prefer, they may be heated.

FROZEN COLESLAW

This recipe is great, not only when you have an excess amount of cabbage from your own or your neighbor's garden, but also when you just want to serve a small amount at a time, as when packing lunches.

Yield: 6 cups
1 medium head of cabbage, grated
½ cup green pepper, diced
½ cup carrots, shredded
1 small onion, minced
1 teaspoon salt
Dressing

1 cup sugar	Pepper to taste
1 cup vinegar	½ teaspoon celery seed
¼ cup water	½ teaspoon mustard seed
1 teaspoon salt	

Mix cabbage, green pepper, carrots, and onion together. Add one teaspoon salt. Toss and let set together for one hour. Drain cabbage as much as possible.

While the cabbage is standing, combine the ingredients for the dressing and bring to a boil. Simmer 3 to 4 minutes and cool. Toss over well-drained coleslaw and spoon into freezer cartons. Label, date, seal, and freeze.

SWEET-SOUR RED CABBAGE

It's easy to make this in large quantities and freeze some for future meals.

MEDIUM RECIPE
Time: 15 minutes
Yield: 1½ quarts

1 medium (3½ to 4 pounds) head red cabbage
1 cup boiling water
4 tablespoons butter
2 shredded or chopped apples
½ cup port
2 cloves
¼ cup brown sugar
2 tablespoons vinegar
Salt and pepper to taste

LARGE RECIPE
Time: 17 minutes
Yield: 2 quarts

1 large (5 pounds) head red cabbage
1¼ cups boiling water
6 tablespoons butter
3 shredded or chopped apples
¾ cup port
3 cloves
¼ cup plus 2 tablespoons brown sugar
3 tablespoons vinegar
Salt and pepper to taste

Shred cabbage and put into a large skillet or kettle. Add boiling water, apples, and butter, and steam for about 20 minutes at fairly high heat, covered. Stir occasionally. Then lower heat and add wine, cloves, brown sugar, vinegar, salt, and pepper. Stir well; cover and simmer for a half hour. Taste; adjust the sweet-sour flavor, if needed, by adding more sugar or more vinegar. Serve hot. This is particularly good served with goose, duck, game, or pork.

TO FREEZE. Spoon prepared red cabbage into freezer containers, leaving ½ inch of head space. Seal, date, label, and freeze.

TO SERVE WHEN FROZEN. Remove from freezer containers, add ¼ cup port for additional liquid and cook over moderate heat. Serve piping hot.

PARSLEYED CARROTS

My favorite way to serve carrots is probably the simplest—with butter and parsley.

One 10-ounce package frozen carrots
2 tablespoons melted butter

¼ cup finely cut parsley
1 teaspoon sugar (optional)

Cook carrots according to directions on package or follow directions in chart on page 369. Drain carrots and add to melted butter. Add sugar if you wish. Put into serving dish and cover with parsley; toss once or twice and serve.

BUTTERED CARROTS

You may wish to cook carrots in quantity and then freeze some. They freeze especially well. Cook them until done; then drain, cover with butter, and pack into freezing cartons or bags.

TO SERVE WHEN FROZEN. Remove frozen carrots from freezing cartons. Cook in top of double boiler over boiling water for 15 to 20 minutes, or until carrots are heated through. Sprinkle with fresh parsley and serve immediately.

BRANDIED CARROTS

This simple dish turns the lowly carrot into a gourmet dish.

Time: 10 minutes
Yield: 4 to 5 servings

4 cups of diagonally sliced carrots	2 tablespoons water
2 tablespoons butter or margarine	Pinch salt
2 tablespoons brown sugar	2 tablespoons brandy or bourbon

Clean and scrape carrots. Slice diagonally with a fluted knife, if you have one. Combine sugar, water, butter, and brown sugar, and cook until sugar is completely dissolved. Add carrots; cover and cook over moderate heat until carrots are tender. Watch closely to prevent scorching, adding another tablespoon of water if needed. Pour the brandy over the carrots and continue cooking for another minute or two. Serve immediately. Sprinkle with snipped parsley, if you wish.

CAULIFLOWER WITH BUTTERED BREAD CRUMBS

Cook package of frozen cauliflower according to directions on package or follow chart on page 369. In another pan, melt 3 tablespoons of butter; add 2 tablespoons of bread crumbs and mix well. Cook gently until bread crumbs turn golden brown; promptly remove from heat. Pour over cooked and drained cauliflower and serve immediately.

Cooked cauliflower is also good served with butter, cream sauce, or cream sauce with cheese added.

CAULIFLOWER AU GRATIN

This casserole may be assembled early in the day, refrigerated, then baked just before you wish to serve it.

SINGLE RECIPE
Time: 10 minutes
Yield: 1 quart

One 10-ounce package frozen cauliflower
½ pound ripe tomatoes, cut into ½-inch wedges
Pinch salt
Dash pepper
¼ cup melted butter
⅓ cup bread crumbs
¼ cup grated Parmesan cheese
¼ cup grated or shredded Swiss cheese
¼ cup grated or shredded Cheddar cheese

DOUBLE RECIPE
Time: 15 minutes
Yield: 2 quarts

Two 10-ounce packages frozen cauliflower
1 pound ripe tomatoes, cut into ½-inch wedges
¼ teaspoon salt
Pepper to taste
½ cup melted butter
⅔ cup bread crumbs
½ cup grated Parmesan cheese
½ cup grated or shredded Swiss cheese
½ cup grated or shredded Cheddar cheese

Arrange cauliflower and tomato wedges in a shallow buttered baking dish in an attractive manner. (I like the tomato wedges around the outer edges of the baking dish.) A 9-inch pie plate is perfect for a single recipe; use a 2-quart-sized baking dish for the double recipe. Sprinkle cauliflower and tomato wedges with salt and pepper and drizzle half of the melted butter over the cauliflower. Combine cheeses and crumbs, and sprinkle over the top. Then drizzle the remaining butter over all. Bake at 375° F for 30 minutes. (If casserole has been refrigerated, add another 10 minutes to baking time.)

CURRIED BAKED CAULIFLOWER

One of the best cauliflower recipes I have ever tasted.

Yield: Serves 6 to 8

1 large head of cauliflower
or
Two 10-ounce packages of frozen cauliflower
½ teaspoon salt
One 10½-ounce can cream of mushroom soup

One 4-ounce package shredded Cheddar cheese (1 cup)
⅓ cup mayonnaise
½ teaspoon curry powder
¼ cup dried bread crumbs
2 tablespoons melted margarine or butter

Preheat oven to 350° F. Break cauliflower into flowerets, cook in 1 inch of boiling salted water until just crunchy tender, or use thawed uncooked frozen cauliflower. Drain well. In 2-quart casserole, stir together soup, cheese, mayonnaise, and curry powder; add cauliflowerets and mix well. Toss bread crumbs in melted butter or margarine; sprinkle on top. Bake uncovered for 30 minutes at 350° F in preheated oven.

TO FREEZE. Use a freezer-to-oven casserole. When using frozen cauliflower, do not thaw, just separate flowerets and mix with other ingredients and return to freezer promptly.

TO SERVE UNFROZEN. Thaw overnight in refrigerator and bake about 40 minutes in a preheated 350° F oven.

CREAMED CELERY AND CHESTNUTS

The crisp water chestnuts add a nice texture contrast to the celery in this casserole.

SINGLE RECIPE
Time: 10 minutes
Yield: 1½ quarts

2 cups sliced celery
1½ cups water
½ cup cream
½ teaspoon salt
¼ cup butter
2 tablespoons flour
One 6-ounce can drained mushrooms
1 can drained whole water chestnuts
1 cup seasoned poultry stuffing
Pepper and cayenne to taste

DOUBLE RECIPE
Time: 15 minutes
Yield: 3 quarts

4 cups sliced celery
3 cups water
1 cup cream
1 teaspoon salt
½ cup butter
¼ cup flour
Two 6-ounce cans drained mushrooms
2 cans drained whole water chestnuts
2 cups seasoned poultry stuffing
Pepper and cayenne to taste

Cook celery in covered saucepan until tender-crisp. Drain, reserving ½ cup liquid (for single recipe). In another pan, melt 2 tablespoons butter (for single recipe) and add flour, mixing well. Then add celery liquid and cream, stirring constantly. Add salt. Cook mixture over moderate heat until thick and creamy. Add celery, mushrooms, and whole water chestnuts. Season with pepper and caynne. Pour mixture into an oven-to-table dish. Top with poultry stuffing and dot with remaining butter. Bake at 350° F for about 30 minutes. Casserole may be made early in the day and stored in the refrigerator until just before serving time. Add 10 minutes to baking time if it is taken from the refrigerator.

TO FREEZE. When making more than one-meal portions, either spoon into foil-lined baking dish or directly into casserole. (See page 367). Freeze, then freezer-wrap, label, date, and return to the freezer.

TO SERVE WHEN FROZEN. Preheat oven to 350° F. Place frozen casserole directly into preheated oven. Bake 1½-quart casseroles, uncovered, for 50 to 60 minutes, or until hot and bubbly. Smaller dishes will require less time.

CELERY CASSEROLE

This tasty casserole may easily be prepared in quantity and frozen for future meals.

SINGLE RECIPE
Time: 10 minutes
Yield: About 6 servings

4 cups sliced celery
1 teaspoon instant minced onion
½ cup water
½ teaspoon salt
One 10½-ounce can condensed cream of celery soup
¼ cup crisp crumbled bacon (see page 41)
½ cup chopped pecans or toasted blanched almonds
Cracker crumbs

DOUBLE RECIPE
Time: 15 minutes
Yield: About 12 servings

8 cups sliced celery
2 teaspoons instant minced onion
1 cup water
1 teaspoon salt
Two 10½-ounce cans condensed cream of celery soup
½ cup crisp crumbled bacon (see page 41)
1 cup chopped pecans or toasted blanched almonds
Cracker crumbs

Boil celery, onion, and salt in water for about 10 minutes, covered. Drain. Add undiluted soup, toasted nuts, and bacon, and mix. Put into a greased 1½-quart casserole. Top with cracker crumbs. (Crumbs made from bacon-flavored crackers are especially good.) Dot with butter and bake in a 350° F oven for about 20 minutes or until heated all the way through. Or freezer-wrap, date, label, and freeze for future meals.

TO SERVE WHEN FROZEN. Remove from freezer and bake in a 350° F preheated oven for about 45 to 50 minutes. Serve immediately. Top of casserole may be garnished with a sprig of parsley.

CHESTNUTS

Chestnuts are a seasonal item, but good to have on hand all year long, especially during the winter months. To freeze, simply put them in plastic bags, store in freezer, and take them out as you need them.

To peel chestnuts, cut a cross through shell at pointed end and bake on a cookie sheet in a preheated oven at 400° F for 20 to 25 minutes. The chestnuts should start cracking open before you remove them from the oven.

Chestnuts are good simply roasted, puréed, or added to vegetable dishes and dressings for poultry.

ROASTED CHESTNUTS

After the chesnuts are peeled, put them in a single layer in a shallow pan with butter, and salt them generously. Roast in a 400° F oven for 15 to 20 minutes, turning occasionally. For more crunchy chestnuts, cut into quarters and leave in the oven a few extra minutes. Watch closely so that they won't burn. Cool slightly before serving.

MARINATED CORN RELISH

This keeps well in the refrigerator and is nice to have on hand for everyday use. It also makes an attractive addition to the menu when you are entertaining and it doesn't require any last-minte attention.

Time: 10 minutes
Yield: About 1 quart

One 10-ounce package frozen corn	½ cup sugar
5 finely cut green onions, tops and all	⅔ cup vinegar
1 cup chopped celery	½ cup oil
1 chopped green pepper	1 teaspoon salt
One 4-ounce jar cut-up pimento	1 rounded teaspoon pickling spices

Combine sugar, salt, oil, vinegar, and pickling spices; bring to a boil. Simmer for 10 to 15 minutes. Meanwhile, combine uncooked frozen corn, onions, green pepper, and pimento in a bowl. Pour boiling sauce through strainer (to remove pickling spices) over the vegetables and refrigerate at least overnight, or longer. This relish improves with age.

CORN PATTIES

Here is another way of serving frozen corn.

In New England and in some other areas of the United States, these are called Corn Oysters. Quick and easy to prepare, the patties taste like corn fritters and are much easier to make.

Time: 10 minutes
Yield: 4 to 5 servings

One 10-ounce package frozen corn
   kernels
2 separated eggs
½ cup sifted flour

1 teaspoon salt
Pinch pepper
⅓ cup vegetable oil

Combine egg yolks with corn; add salt, pepper, and flour. Beat egg whites until stiff and fold into the corn mixture. Pour oil into skillet and heat. Drop corn mixture by tablespoonfuls into hot grease. Turn when lightly browned. Total cooking time about 4 to 5 minutes. Serve immediately.

VARIATION. Since these taste like corn fritters, they may be served with maple syrup.

MEXICALI CORN

A colorful dish to serve with informal dinners and barbecues.

Time: 7 minutes
Yield: 4 to 6 servings

⅓ cup butter
¼ cup snipped green onions
One 2-ounce jar pimiento
1 chopped sweet red pepper
1 chopped small green pepper

Salt and pepper to taste
½ teaspoon chili powder
Dash cayenne (optional)
2 cups frozen corn
1 tablespoon water

Combine all ingredients and simmer until corn is tender. Serve.

HARRIET'S FROZEN PICKLES

Because cucumbers are usually eaten uncooked, it's best not to freeze them except for freezer pickles. You'll be amazed at how crisp and crunchy these pickles are. A real time saver—no sterilizing of bottles or steam baths.

Yields: 2 quarts plus 3 cups

3 large cucumbers, sliced thin
1 medium onion, sliced thin
1 teaspoon salt
¾ cup sugar

¼ cup white vinegar
1 tablespoon pickling spice
¼ teaspoon turmeric
¼ teaspoon celery seed

Combine sliced cucumbers and onions, mix well, sprinkle with salt, and place in refrigerator for two hours. Drain thoroughly but do not rinse.

In the meantime, mix sugar, vinegar, and pickling spices (should be put into cheesecloth or tea strainer), along with turmeric and celery seed. Heat but do not boil. Continue cooking until all the sugar is dissolved. Let stand 5 minutes to cool and pour over well-drained cucumbers. Let stand 10 minutes before packing into freezer cartons, then date, label, and freeze.

MUSHROOM SAUCE

An especially good sauce to serve with meat loaf, beef patties, and Chicken Croquettes (page 349). You'll find many other uses for it too.

Time: 8 minutes
Yield: About ¾ cup sauce

1 cup sliced fresh mushrooms	⅛ teaspoon salt
2 tablespoons butter	Dash cayenne
1 teaspoon bouillon granules	1½ teaspoons flour
1 teaspoon lemon juice	½ cup milk

Sauté mushrooms in butter until tender. Sprinkle with lemon juice, salt, pepper, and flour. Blend well. Add milk and bouillon granule, stirring until thickened. Continue cooking for another minute.

This sauce can be made in large quantities and frozen. It has good freezing qualities.

MUSHROOM SOUP

This mushroom soup is akin to the canned variety in about the same way hamburger is related to tenderloin. I don't mean to downgrade canned mushroom soup; I use it, but this is simply delicious. What's really neat is how quickly it is put together.

SINGLE RECIPE
Time: 15 minutes
Yield: About 2 quarts

1 pound mushrooms
¼ pound butter
¼ cup flour
6 cups chicken broth to which no salt has been added
2 tablespoons bouillon granules
1 cup commercial sour cream

DOUBLE RECIPE
Time: 20 minutes
Yield: About 4 quarts

2 pounds mushrooms
¼ pound butter, more if needed
½ cup flour
3 quarts chicken broth to which no salt has been added
4 tablespoons bouillon granules
1 pint commercial sour cream

Slice mushrooms and sauté in butter. If you like whole mushrooms in your soup, set aside about one-third of the mushrooms. Now add flour, mixing well until all the flour is blended with the butter. When making a double recipe, you may need to add more butter at this point; the flour and butter should combine into a creamy paste. Add 1 cup of chicken broth and sour cream (for a single recipe) and put this mixture, together with the bouillon granules, in your blender. Give it a whirl for a few seconds and return to pan on the stove. Add remaining chicken broth and heat through. The bouillon granules should add sufficient salt, but if more is needed, add it now; also pepper to taste. Then add the reserved mushrooms and serve. Freeze any that isn't used for the first serving.

TO FREEZE. Cool; pour soup into freezing containers, leaving ½ inch of head space. Seal, label, date, and freeze.

TO SERVE WHEN FROZEN. Allow soup to thaw slightly. Cook over moderate heat until warm enough to serve.

CREAMED ONIONS

For something a bit less common, try these.

Yield: 3 cups

One 20-ounce package small whole onions
2 tablespoons butter
1½ tablespoons flour
⅛ teaspoon white pepper
1½ cups milk
2 teaspoons bouillon granules
parsley

Cook onions according to directions on package and drain. Meanwhile, melt butter in a saucepan; blend in flour and pepper. Gradually add milk, cooking and stirring until smooth. Add bouillon granules and continue cooking over low heat until granules are dissolved. Add drained onions. Garnish with parsley and serve.

PEAS AND MUSHROOMS

For something different, try this.

Time: 10 minutes
Yield: 4 or 5 servings

One 10-ounce package frozen peas
2 cups sliced mushrooms
3 tablespoons butter
1 tablespoon flour
⅛ teaspoon garlic salt
¼ teaspoon paprika
⅓ cup cream
⅓ cup liquid from peas
1 tablespoon commercial sour cream

Pour ½ cup boiling water over peas and bring to boiling point. Meanwhile, sauté sliced mushrooms in butter, adding garlic salt and paprika. Then add flour and cream. Drain vegetables. Reserve ⅓ cup liquid and add to the mushrooms. Then add sour cream and the peas. Cook together for another minute. Serve immediately.

PEAS AND ONIONS

This vegetable dish has as much taste appeal as it does eye appeal.

1 cup frozen small whole onions	One 10-ounce package frozen peas
or	Salt and pepper to taste
1 cup small white boiling onions	2 tablespoons butter

Pour boiling water over the unpeeled onions and let stand for 5 to 10 minutes. Drain. Trim root and top ends with a sharp paring knife. The onion skins will now slip off easily. Put peeled onions back in pan and add ½ cup boiling water. Cover and continue cooking for 5 to 10 minutes, depending on size of onions. Then add peas. When the water returns to boiling, cook for another 5 to 6 minutes. Drain; add salt, pepper, and melted butter. Serve immediately.

FRENCH-FRIED ONION RINGS

Serving my family one package of prepared frozen onion rings would be like offering an elephant one peanut. We eat them in such quantity that it would be almost prohibitively expensive to buy the commercially prepared variety. Try making your own, as I do, and while you're at it, make enough to freeze and serve at another time.

SINGLE RECIPE
Yield: A single recipe makes quite a batch—about a single layer on a cookie sheet
1 cup sifted flour
1 egg
1 cup milk
1 teaspoon baking powder
1½ teaspoons salt
2 very large Spanish onions

DOUBLE RECIPE
Yield: Same cookie sheet, twice as full
2 cups sifted flour
2 eggs
2 cups milk
2 teaspoons baking powder
3 teaspoons salt
4 very large Spanish onions

Combine all ingredients except the onions in a mixing bowl. Beat until smooth, either with hand or electric mixer. Cover and let stand for at least 15 minutes before using. (Standing longer doesn't hurt it.) In the meantime, heat vegetable oil to 375° F in deep-fryer. Slice onions crosswise into ⅓-inch slices. Separate the rings. Dip into batter with tongs and deep-fry a few at a time until they are brown and crisp. Let onions drain for a minute and turn out on a large cookie sheet that has been lined with paper towels. Keep the onions warm and crisp in a 200° F oven until ready to serve.

TO FREEZE. Onion rings you want to freeze should be allowed to cool slightly. Pack them into freezer bags and freeze immediately.

TO SERVE WHEN FROZEN. Preheat oven to 425° F. Take onions directly from the freezer and put them on a baking sheet or pan large enough to spread them out in a single layer. Bake for 5 to 7 minutes, or until crisp. *Serve immediately.*

TWICE-BAKED POTATOES

These twice-baked potatoes are so delicious that they're worth every bit of the time it takes to prepare them. It really pays to make a large quantity to have on hand. They seem to turn any meal into a state occasion.

SINGLE RECIPE	DOUBLE RECIPE
Time: 16 minutes	*Time: 21 minutes*
Yield: 12 stuffed potatoes	*Yield: 24 stuffed potatoes*
12 large Idaho potatoes	24 large Idaho potatoes
1 to 1½ cups scalded milk (more if necessary)	2 to 3 cups scaled milk (more if necessary)
½ pound sliced Cheddar cheese	1 pound sliced Cheddar cheese
½ cup butter	1 cup butter
2 teaspoons salt	1 tablespoon plus 1 teaspoon salt
¼ teaspoon pepper	½ teaspoon pepper
2 green onions, tops and all, cut fine with scissors	4 green onions, tops and all, cut fine with scissors
1 egg	2 eggs
One 2-ounce jar drained and chopped pimiento	Two 2-ounce jars drained and chopped pimiento

Scrub, grease, and bake potatoes until done—about 1 hour at 425° F for large potatoes, less time for smaller ones. To save time, put the green onions and the milk in the blender or food processor; give them a whirl for just a second or two at high speed.

Scald milk and add cheese. Stir until all the cheese has been melted. Cut a lengthwise slit in each potato; scoop out all the potato pulp with a spoon, leaving shells intact. Mash potato pulp, using electric mixer. When it is smooth, gradually add milk mixture, butter, and seasonings, being careful not to add too much milk. Add egg and whip until fluffy. Fold in pimientos. Fill potato shells with mixture, using a pastry tube. (This really isn't necessary, but they're so much more attractive that way.) Set on a cookie sheet or platter, and freeze. Wrap individually in foil and return to the freezer. Here again, it's a good idea to put all the foil-wrapped potatoes in a large plastic bag so that you won't lose them in the dark corners of your freezer.

Put any potatoes you're going to serve the same day into the refrigerator until half an hour before serving. Preheat oven to 350° F and bake potatoes for 30 to 40 minutes. These don't need to be wrapped in foil, and the tops will be just delicately browned.

TO COOK WHEN FROZEN. Preheat oven to 350° F. Allow 1¼ hours for frozen foil-wrapped potatoes. Remove foil, arrange on a serving platter, and garnish each potato with a sprig of parsley.

HASH-BROWN POTATOES AU GRATIN

Always a favorite—crispy browned and buttered hash browns topped with melted cheese. These potatoes are handy to have on hand frozen and may be used in many ways.

Time: Less than 3 minutes
Yield: 6 servings

3 cups frozen hash-brown potatoes   ¼ pound shredded or grated sharp
3 tablespoons butter   Cheddar cheese

Pour frozen potatoes into a buttered shallow baking dish. Dot with butter and bake in a 350° F preheated oven for 10 minutes. Gently stir the potatoes so that they're all covered with the melted butter. Continue baking for another 10 minutes, adding more butter if needed. Now put the potatoes under the broiler until they begin to brown lightly. Add cheese and broil another 10 to 15 minutes, keeping the potatoes as far away from the heat as possible. Potatoes will be cheesy and crusted when done.

VARIATION. These potatoes may be served in individual ramekins. After the potatoes have been baked in the melted butter, spoon them into ramekins or even seashells, add the cheese, and continue baking and broiling as above.

PERCY'S POTATO CASSEROLE

A single recipe makes quite a lot; divide into smaller casseroles and freeze. They are nice to have on hand for those times when you want something different and just don't know what to serve. Fine for entertaining or for potluck suppers.

SINGLE RECIPE
Time: 25 minutes
Yield: 3 quarts

4 pounds new potatoes
¼ pound butter
8 ounces cream cheese, at room temperature
1 chopped green pepper
1 bunch (4 or 5) snipped scallions, tops and all
One 2-ounce jar minced pimiento with juice
½ cup grated Cheddar cheese
½ cup Parmesan cheese
¼ teaspoon saffron (optional)
¼ cup milk
Salt and pepper to taste

DOUBLE RECIPE*
Time: 35 minutes
Yield: 6 quarts

8 pounds new potatoes
½ pound butter
16 ounces cream cheese, at room temperature
2 chopped green peppers
2 bunches (8 or 10) snipped scallions, tops and all
Two 2-ounce jars minced pimiento with juice
1 cup grated Cheddar cheese
1 cup Parmesan cheese
½ teaspoon saffron (optional)
½ cup milk
Salt and pepper to taste

Cook potatoes until done. Drain and cool only slightly. Peel. While the potatoes are cooking, melt butter; add milk, cheese, and all the remaining ingredients. Mash peeled potatoes and add cheese liquid, beating until nice and fluffy. (This mixture may seem a bit "soupy.") Pour into casserole dishes and bake, uncovered, at 350° F for about 30 minutes. Mixture should be nicely browned on top and slightly bubbly.

TO FREEZE. Simply pour potato mixture into casserole dishes; freezer-wrap or see page 367 and freeze. Bake, uncovered, at 350° F for about 1 hour.

HILDY'S SAVOYARD POTATOES

Using frozen cottage-fried potatoes in this scrumptious recipe is a real time saver. No peeling, no slicing, no waste.

* To simplify things when you are making a double recipe, combine milk, saffron, Parmesan cheese, butter, and cream cheese. Warm over low heat until butter and cheese are melted. Add onions, pimiento, and green peppers. Meanwhile, whip potatoes with mixer and transfer to a large bowl. Now stir in liquid until it is completely incorporated.

Yield: 10 servings

One 2-pound bag frozen cottage-fried potatoes
6 tablespoons butter or margarine
1 teaspoon salt
⅛ teaspoon black pepper
¼ pound (1 cup) shredded Swiss cheese
1¼ cups bouillon beef broth or
One 10-ounce can beef broth

Preheat oven to 425° F. Grease a shallow 2-quart baking dish with 2 tablespoons butter. Layer half of the frozen potatoes on the bottom of the baking dish and dot with 2 tablespoons butter. Combine parsley, salt, pepper, and cheese. Sprinkle half of this mixture over the potatoes, and dot again with 2 tablespoons butter. Layer the remaining half of the potatoes and cover with the remaining cheese mixture. Cover with bouillon beef broth. Bake in a 425° F oven for 55 to 60 minutes. When done broth should be absorbed and the potatoes should be brown and tender.

QUICK POTATO AND BACON SOUP

This soup can be made at a minute's notice. Very nourishing, with a full-bodied flavor. Make in large quantities, since it freezes well.

SINGLE RECIPE
Time: 10 minutes
Yield: 6 servings
6 medium-sized red potatoes
1 cup boiling water
1 cup milk
1 cup commercial sour cream
Pepper to taste (be generous)
1 tablespoon beef stock concentrate
4 teaspoons chicken bouillon granules
6 slices bacon, or ⅓ cup crisp bacon (see page 41)
Chopped chives

DOUBLE RECIPE
Time: 15 minutes
Yield: 12 servings
12 medium-sized red potatoes
2 cups boiling water
2 cups milk
1 pint commercial sour cream
Pepper to taste (be generous)
2 tablespoons beef stock concentrate
8 teaspoons chicken bouillon granules
12 slices bacon, or ⅔ cup crisp bacon (see page 41)
Chopped chives

Peel and cut potatoes into ¼-inch slices. Add water and cook, covered, over moderately high heat until potatoes are tender. Drain and measure liquid; add enough milk to make 1 cup. While the potatoes are cooking, assemble all the other ingredients, except chives and bacon, and put into the blender or food processor. Add cooked potatoes with liquid to ingredients in appliance and turn on high speed for 30 seconds or until smooth. Return to pan. Heat and add bacon bits. Garnish each bowl with scissor-snipped or freeze-dried chives, and serve.

CANDIED SWEET POTATOES

Sweet potatoes can be prepared with many variations. Here's a basic recipe that may be served in several ways. Sweet potatoes freeze well; so make enough for several meals at once.

Time: 5 minutes
Yield: 8 servings

4 large sweet potatoes or yams (2 to 3 pounds)	2 tablespoons butter
	⅓ cup fruit juice
½ cup maple-flavored syrup	¼ cup brown sugar

Cook sweet potatoes or yams in boiling water until just tender. Cool and peel. Sweet potatoes may be sliced, halved, or quartered. However, they have a more candied flavor if they're cut into the smaller pieces. Put the potatoes into a deep casserole dish and cover with a syrup made from the maple-flavored syrup, butter, fruit juice, and brown sugar. Combine all these ingredients in a small pan and bring to a boil. Simmer for 2 minutes and pour over potatoes. Bake in a preheated oven at 350° F for 30 minutes, basting several times to insure a good candied glaze on the sweet potatoes.

TO FREEZE. Pour the prepared syrup over the cooked sweet potatoes, freezer-wrap, date, label, and freeze.

TO SERVE WHEN FROZEN. Add about 30 minutes to the baking time. Put frozen casserole into preheated oven at 350° F.

VARIATIONS. Use concentrated frozen orange juice instead of the fruit juice for delicious "orangy" candied sweet potatoes.

Miniature marshmallows may be sprinkled over the top of sweet potatoes, and they may be put under the broiler just before serving.

PINEAPPLE AND SWEET POTATOES. Simply add a small 8-ounce can of crushed pineapple to the sweet potatoes. Especially good with ham.

RITA'S SWEET POTATO CASSEROLE

A holiday favorite to make ahead.

Yield: 1½ quarts

3 large sweet potatoes (2½ to 3 pounds)	1 tablespoon cornstarch
	½ teaspoon salt
½ cup brown sugar	1 cup orange juice

¼ cup butter
3 tablespoons sherry
2 tablespoons nuts, broken

½ teaspoon shredded orange peel
½ cup seedless raisins or canned
grapes, drained

Bake sweet potatoes in a moderate oven until done. Cut each potato in half crosswise and scoop or squeeze out the pulp into a large mixing bowl. Beat until light and fluffy. In a saucepan, combine brown sugar, cornstarch, salt, and orange juice. Stir well and bring to a quick boil. Cook until clear and slightly thickened. Add butter and sherry and continue stirring until melted. Add to whipped sweet potatoes. Now add orange rind and raisins or grapes; continue mixing until well blended. Pour into a well-greased 1½-quart casserole. Cover top with nuts. Bake at 350° F about 20 minutes.

TO FREEZE. After the nuts have been arranged on top of the casserole, cover tightly with freezer wrap and freeze immediately.

TO SERVE WHEN FROZEN. It is best to thaw dish completely. Then follow baking directions above.

BAKED SPINACH WITH ARTICHOKE HEARTS

This is a colorful and unique vegetable dish that takes only minutes to prepare.

One 10-ounce package frozen
creamed spinach
1 beaten egg

One 9-ounce package of frozen
artichoke hearts, thawed or 1 can of
artichoke hearts
Butter

Thaw spinach and mix with beaten egg. Generously butter a 1-quart casserole. Arrange artichoke hearts in the bottom of dish. Pour creamed spinach mixed with egg over the artichoke hearts. Bake in a 375° F oven for 45 minutes, or until an inserted knife comes out clean. Generously spoon Hollandaise Sauce over the top (see page 372).

CREAM OF SPINACH SOUP

You can make this soup in 10 minutes—less time than it takes for dehydrated soups. Particularly good when served on a wintry evening or as a first course.

SINGLE RECIPE
  Time: 10 minutes
  Yield: About 3 cups

6 slices crumbled bacon
2 tablespoons flour
2 tablespoons bacon drippings
1½ cups milk
One 10-ounce package frozen
  chopped spinach
3 teaspoons bouillon granules
½ teaspoon salt
Pepper to taste
½ cup sour cream

DOUBLE RECIPE
  Time: 15 minutes
  Yield: About 6 cups

12 slices crumbled bacon
¼ cup flour
¼ cup bacon drippings
3 cups milk
Two 10 ounce packages frozen
  chopped spinach
6 teaspoons bouillon granules
1 teaspoon salt
Pepper to taste
1 cup sour cream

Broil bacon until crisp; cool and crumble. (See Bacon, page 41.) Meanwhile, put bacon drippings in a 1-quart pan or larger and add flour; mix well and add milk. Add frozen chopped spinach and continue heating, stirring occasionally. Add seasonings and bacon and simmer for a few minutes. Add sour cream just before serving. Top with croutons or additional bacon crumbs.

GREEK SPINACH AND CHEESE PIE

This spectacular, yet easy, vegetable dish will be a hit at any meal. A luscious cheese, egg, and spinach filling between layers of buttery phylo dough, available in 1-pound packages in frozen food section of supermarket or in specialty stores. The dough is already prepared, so all you have to do is whip together the filling. Make ahead and freeze for easy entertaining.

*Yield: One 9 x 13-inch baking
  dish; serves 9 to 12*

6 slices bacon
1 cup frozen chopped onions
2 tablespoons butter
Two 10-ounce packages frozen
  chopped spinach, cooked
1 cup large or small-curd cottage
  cheese
One 8-ounce package cream cheese

¼ pound feta cheese
4 eggs
2 teaspoons farina or cream of wheat
Salt and pepper to taste
½ teaspoon nutmeg
16 phylo pastry sheets
½ pound melted butter

Preheat oven to 350° F. Cut bacon into small pieces and fry until crisp. Drain on absorbent towels and set aside. Sauté onions in butter until soft and clear. Add cooked spinach, which has been well drained. Now add bacon, blend well, and sauté for 5 minutes.

In a large mixing bowl, cream the cream cheese; add cottage cheese and feta cheese. When well blended, add eggs one at a time, beating well after each addition. Add farina and spices. Now fold in the spinach mixture.

Line a 9 x 13-inch baking dish with 8 phylo pastry sheets, buttering each sheet generously with a large pastry brush before adding the next. The phylo dough I get is best used extending up the sides of baking dish. Extend every other sheet up one side and then the other, alternating. After layering 8 thicknesses of pastry dough, pour in the filling and spread evenly. Then cover with an additional 8 layers of buttered phylo pastry. With a sharp knife, score through the fist three layers into serving-size pieces, either squares or triangles. Bake at 350° F for 45 minutes. Cool at last 10 minutes before serving; otherwise, the filling will be scalding and spinach mixture not set.

NOTE. Handle the phylo sheets only a few at a time, as they dry out quickly. Keep the remainder covered with a sheet of waxed paper, then lay a damp towel over that. *Do not let the damp towel touch the pastry sheets.*

TO FREEZE. After assembling pie, cover with heavy-duty foil and freeze.

TO SERVE WHEN FROZEN. Thaw covered casserole in refrigerator overnight or on counter for several hours. Bake as directed above, allowing more time if casserole is still quite cold and not at room temperature when placed into oven.

STEWED TOMATOES

It's either feast or famine with regard to tomatoes, at least in the Midwest. The feast comes at the end of summer and in early fall, when everyone is trying to figure out what to do with the over-abundant crop. Making stewed tomatoes and freezing them is one prudent way of preserving these marvelous fruits. Most recipes ask that you peel and seed your tomatoes. I don't know of any easy way to seed them, so just avoid this step. A few tomato seeds will add roughage to your diet!

SINGLE RECIPE
Yield: Approximately 8 cups

5 pounds ripe tomatoes
¼ cup vegetable oil
1 large onion, finely chopped
   or
1 cup frozen chopped onions
½ cup celery, finely chopped
½ cup green pepper, chopped

½ cup parsley, snipped
½ teaspoon dried basil
1 teaspoon Worcestershire sauce
Salt and pepper to taste
½ teaspoon sugar
3 tablespoons butter, optional

DOUBLE RECIPE
Yield: Approximately 16 cups

10 pounds ripe tomatoes
½ cup vegetable oil
2 large onions, finely chopped
or
2 cups frozen chopped onions
1 cup celery, finely chopped
1 cup green pepper, chopped

1 cup parsley, snipped
1 teaspoon dried basil
2 teaspoons Worcestershire sauce
Salt and pepper to taste
1 teaspoon sugar
6 tablespoons butter, optional

Drop tomatoes into gently boiling water for one minute to loosen skins. After tomatoes have been peeled, chop coarsely or cut into wedges and set aside. In large skillet or heavy pot, sauté onions in vegetable oil until clear and slightly brown (about 10 minutes). Add celery, green pepper, and continue cooking for about 5 minutes, adding more oil if necessary. Add prepared tomatoes, parsley, basil, Worcestershire sauce, salt and pepper, and sugar. Bring to a gentle boil. Lower heat and simmer until much of the excess moisture has evaporated. Cool thoroughly and pour into freezer container, seal, date, label, and freeze.

VARIATION. For a single recipe, add 1 or 2 cloves of minced or pressed garlic and sauté with the onions; also add a teaspoon of oregano to tomatoes.

CHEESE SAUCE

This sauce is especially good served with cauliflower, broccoli, zucchini, or any vegetables that go well with cheese.

Time: 5 minutes
Yield: About 2 cups of sauce

¼ cup butter
¼ cup flour
2 cups milk
1 teaspoon prepared mustard, or
more if desired

1 teaspoon salt
Pepper to taste
¼ pound sliced or diced Cheddar
cheese

Melt butter and add flour, making a paste. Add milk, stirring constantly. Continue cooking over moderate heat until sauce is thick and smooth. Add salt, pepper, and mustard, mixing well. Now add cheese. Lower heat and simmer gently until cheese is completely melted, stirring occasionally. Serve immediately.

BUTTERED ZUCCHINI AND CARAWAY SEEDS

Although all the books and charts will tell you to blanch zucchini squash, I've had more success and better-tasting squash by cooking them before freezing. Blanched zucchini tends to become rubbery after freezing.

Select small, tender young zucchini, in which the seeds have not yet formed. Wash and cut ends off 1 pound of squash. Cut ½-inch slices into cooking pan. Add about ¼ inch of water to the bottom of pan and steam zucchini, covered, until soft. Stir occasionally, making sure the squash doesn't stick or burn. As the zucchini cooks, a lot of juice forms in the bottom of the pan. Remove lid and let juices cook down. Add 2 tablespoons of butter and sprinkle with 1 tablespoon of caraway seeds. Simmer for 5 additional minutes, and serve.

ZUCCHINI AU GRATIN

Follow the instructions for zucchini with caraway seeds and to 1 pound of zucchini add about ¼ pound thinly sliced Cheddar cheese. Continue cooking only until the cheese is melted. Serve immediately.

TO FREEZE. If you're cooking zucchini to freeze, don't add the cheese until after freezing and just before serving. Simply warm the frozen squash over low heat until bubbly. Then add cheese. Continue cooking until cheese is melted, and serve.

COMBINATION DISHES

VEGETABLE MEDLEY

This is one of my favorite vegetable dishes, because it's so low in calories, yet extremely tasty. The easy preparation will make it a hit with many a cook. When summer produce is abundant, you may wish to make this up in large quantities and freeze. All the ingredients can be prepared and combined early in the day, thus eliminating any last-minute "kitchen duties" for the hostess.

SINGLE RECIPE
Yield: Approximately 2 quarts

2 medium-sized zucchini squash, sliced
1 small eggplant, peeled and sliced
2 medium or 1 large potato, peeled and sliced
2 green peppers, cored and sliced into julienne strips
1 large Spanish onion, peeled and sliced
2 large cloves garlic, pressed
1 tablespoon oregano
1 teaspoon basil
1 teaspoon thyme
Two 1-pound cans seasoned stewed tomatoes or equivalent fresh tomatoes, peeled

DOUBLE RECIPE
Yield: Approximately 4 quarts

4 medium-size zucchini squash, sliced
2 small eggplants, peeled and sliced
4 medium or 2 large potatoes, peeled and sliced
4 green peppers, cored and sliced into julienne strips
2 large Spanish onions, peeled and sliced
4 large cloves garlic, pressed
2 tablespoons oregano
2 teaspoons basil
2 teaspoons thyme
Four 1-pound cans seasoned stewed tomatoes or equivalent fresh tomatoes, peeled

Prepare all the above ingredients and put in a large saucepan. Add seasonings; stir mixture and bring to a boil. Lower heat and continue cooking until the potatoes are done (usually about 15 or 20 minutes). Serve with Parmesan cheese if you wish.

TO FREEZE. When preparing this recipe for the freezer, omit potatoes, as they tend to get mushy when reheated. Add when you are reheating; because the potatoes are sliced, they only require a short cooking time.

AILEEN'S HERBED PEAS AND MUSHROOMS

Try this for a different and delectable way to serve peas. Takes only a very short while to prepare. Easy when you are entertaining a crowd.

SINGLE RECIPE
Time: 3 minutes
Yield: 4 to 5 servings

2 tablespoons butter
8 ounces fresh mushrooms
or
One 4½-ounce jar sliced mushrooms
One 10-ounce package frozen peas
1 healthy pinch marjoram leaves
1 healthy pinch thyme leaves
Salt and pepper to taste

TRIPLE RECIPE
Time: 4 minutes
Yield: 12 servings

⅓ pound butter
1½ pounds fresh mushrooms
or
Three 4½-ounce jars sliced mushrooms
30 ounces frozen peas
½ teaspoon marjoram leaves
½ teaspoon thyme leaves
Salt and pepper to taste

Melt butter and sauté mushrooms, covered, for about 5 minutes (for fresh mushrooms) or 1 minute (for canned). Add all the remaining ingredients and cook, covered, over moderate heat for 15 minutes. Serve immediately.

PEAS AND ARTICHOKE HEARTS

Quick and easy and a little bit different.

One 9-ounce package frozen artichoke hearts
One 10-ounce package frozen peas

4 tablespoons melted butter
Finely chopped parsley
Salt and pepper to taste

Cook peas and artichoke hearts according to directions on package. Drain; add melted butter and chopped parsley. Salt and pepper to taste. Toss lightly and serve.

LUCY'S CASSEROLE WITH MORNAY SAUCE

For something different, try this mixed vegetable casserole. Make several at a time and freeze some for future use.

SINGLE RECIPE
  Time: 15 minutes
  Yield: One 1½-quart casserole or
  2 small 1-quart dishes
One 20-ounce bag frozen mixed vegetables
¼ cup hot water
1 teaspoon salt
¼ teaspoon garlic salt
2 tablespoons butter
Mornay Sauce
¼ cup butter
¼ cup flour
2 cups liquid (cooking liquid plus canned milk to make 2 cups)
2 tablespoons white wine (optional)
1 teaspoon salt
¼ cup grated cheese
Pinch nutmeg
Pinch thyme
⅛ teaspoon garlic salt
3 tablespoons melted butter
2 cups seasoned bread stuffing

DOUBLE RECIPE
  Time: 20 minutes
  Yield: 3 quarts
Two 20-ounce bags frozen mixed vegetables
½ cup hot water
2 teaspoons salt
½ teaspoon garlic salt
4 tablespoons butter
Mornay Sauce
½ cup butter
½ cup flour
4 cups liquid (cooking liquid plus canned milk to make 4 cups)
4 tablespoons white wine (optional)
2 teaspoons salt
½ cup grated cheese
⅛ teaspoon nutmeg
⅛ teaspoon thyme
¼ teaspoon garlic salt
6 tablespoons melted butter
4 cups seasoned bread stuffing

Cover vegetables with ¼ cup boiling water (½ cup for a double recipe). After vegetables start to defrost, cook an additional 5 minutes. Drain, reserving liquid. Put cooked vegetables into buttered casserole dish and season with garlic salt, salt, and butter.

While vegetables are cooking, start your sauce. Melt butter, add flour, and mix well. Drain vegetables, add canned milk to vegetable liquid, and add to butter-flour mixture, stirring well. Cook until thick, add remaining ingredients, and simmer for 5 minutes. Pour sauce over vegetables. Cover sauce thickly with seasoned bread stuffing and drizzle entire surface with melted butter. Bake 30 minutes at 350° F. Brown under broiler if necessary before serving. Single recipe serves 8.

TO FREEZE. Cool prepared casserole, freezer-wrap, label, date and freeze (or see page 367).

TO SERVE WHEN FROZEN. Bake frozen casserole in 350° F preheated oven for 55 to 60 minutes, depending on size of dish. Vegetable dish should be hot and bubbly. Brown bread stuffing under broiler if necessary before serving.

LEEK AND HAM SOUP

This is a very hearty soup. Along with a salad and rolls, it makes a complete meal. Also a good way to use up your ham bone and leftover meat.

SINGLE RECIPE
  Time: 6 minutes
  Yield: 2½ to 3 quarts
. 1 ham bone with a fair amount of meat on it (approximately ½ pound)
2 quarts of water
1 large carrot, cut into 1-inch pieces
¼ cup parsley, well packed
2 bay leaves
3 medium-sized potatoes
Leaves cut from the tops of 3 celery ribs
2 large or 3 medium-sized leek
3 peppercorns
7 bouillon cubes or 2 slightly rounded tablespoons of bouillon granules
1 cup commercial sour cream
Milk

DOUBLE RECIPE
  Time: 8 minutes
  Yield: 5 to 6 quarts
1 ham bone with approximately 1 pound meat on it
4 quarts of water
2 large carrots, cut into 1-inch pieces
½ cup parsley, well packed
4 bay leaves
6 medium-sized potatoes
Leaves cut from the tops of 6 celery ribs
4 large or 6 medium-sized leek
6 peppercorns
14 bouillon cubes or 4 tablespoons plus 2 teaspoons bouillon granules
2 cups commercial sour cream
Milk

Bring water to a boil; then add ham bone, carrot, parsley, bay leaves, peppercorns, potatoes, leek, and celery leaves. Bring water almost to a boil; then lower heat and simmer for several hours. Remove bone and meat from soup; cut meat into small pieces, discarding any fat, and reserve the meat. (Discard bone, bay leaves and peppercorns.) Put remaining vegetables and stock into blender, food processor, or through food mill, and return to a large kettle. Add bouillon cubes or granules and sour cream. (This is a perfect example of salting with bouillon cubes. See page 41.) It's best to blend sour cream with some broth in blender or whip with a French wire whisk before adding it to soup. Add milk until the soup is the desired consistency. Then add cut-up meat and heat for serving.

If you have a blender or food processor, follow these very simple directions: Remove bone and meat, bay leaves, and peppercorns, and pour the rest of the mixture, a few cups at a time, into your blender or food processor. Run at high speed for a few seconds. Then pour into a large kettle. Continue until all the ingredients have been processed in this manner, including bouillon cubes and sour cream. If you prefer a really smooth soup, remove meat from bone and put it into the blender with the broth. However, the texture of little pieces of meat in the soup is rather nice. This recipe yields quite a lot of soup, but it goes quickly. Freeze whatever isn't used for the first serving.

TO FREEZE. Cool; pour soup into freezing containers, leaving ½ inch of head space. Seal, label, date, and freeze.

TO SERVE WHEN FROZEN. Allow soup to thaw slightly; then cook in pan over moderate heat until warm enough to serve.

MIXED VEGETABLE SALAD

Make this early in the day, or even the day before. It stores well in the refrigerator.

Time: 10 minutes
Yield: Approximately 4 cups

One 10-ounce package frozen mixed
    vegetables
½ cup snipped green onions and tops
½ cup chopped celery
1 small chopped green pepper
One 1-pound can drained kidney
    beans

½ cup sugar
½ cup vinegar
1 tablespoon flour
½ teaspoon salt
1 tablespoon prepared mustard

Pour boiling water over the frozen vegetables and cook until the water returns to boiling. Remove from heat and let stand for 5 minutes. Meanwhile, combine and prepare all the other vegetables.

In a small saucepan, combine sugar with flour, mixing well. Add vinegar, salt, and mustard and cook until thick and clear. Drain frozen vegetables and add to the other vegetables. Pour sauce over this and mix well. Chill in refrigerator for several hours.

HEARTY VEGETABLE BEEF SOUP

I always have the ingredients on hand for this delicious soup. It's a great standby when time is short or the cupboards are bare. I particularly like the mixed vegetable combination with okra, even though okra is not one of my favorite vegetables. It adds a certain texture and flavor to this soup.

Yield: About 4 quarts

1½ to 2 pounds lean ground beef
1 to 2 tablespoons cooking oil
1 tablespoon instant granulated beef bouillon
½ teaspoon pepper
Salt to taste
½ teaspoon garlic powder
⅓ teaspoon basil
2 cans chicken broth

1 can beef bouillon
1 cup frozen chopped onions
¼ cup raw rice
One 20-ounce package frozen mixed vegetables
One 16-ounce can tomato sauce with tomato bits
One 1-pound can stewed seasoned tomatoes

Brown beef in large Dutch oven or skillet. If you are in a hurry, start cooking broth and rice in a separate kettle. While it is heating, you can brown meat and sauté onions. Drain off excess fat. Add seasonings and broth, along with an equal amount of water. Add onions and rice and bring mixture to a boil. Cover, lower heat, and simmer gently for 1 hour. Add frozen vegetables, tomatoes, and tomato sauce. Bring to a boil, then lower heat and simmer for 10 minutes. Serve.

RICE AND PASTAS

Rice and pastas (spaghetti, macaroni, manicotti, lasagne, et cetera) are all good potato substitutes and freeze well. However, care must be taken in cooking rice and pastas; they should be slightly underdone to avoid sogginess when they are reheated after freezing.

Pastas should be cooked in a large kettle with an ample amount of boiling water—about 3 quarts of water for every 8 ounces of pasta. Each piece or strand should be separated, which will allow the water to flow freely. This keeps the pasta from becoming starchy and gummy. A teaspoon of salt for each quart of water will further help to prevent pieces from sticking together. Then also add a teaspoon of olive oil to the water. Not only does it improve the flavor and quality of pastas, but it also prevents the water from boiling over.

Before adding any kind of pasta, let the water and salt boil briskly for a few minutes. When cooking spaghetti, lasagne, and other pastas that are very large in size, don't break into pieces. Put the large pieces into the boiling water; as the pasta softens, curl it around in the pan until the entire length is submerged. With a large wooden spoon, give it a good stir. Keep the water boiling vigorously during the entire cooking time. Don't cover.

Pasta that's going to be frozen in a casserole dish should be removed from the boiling water before it is completely done—when it is just soft. For immediate use, continue cooking until tender, or *al dente*, as the Italians say. Butter and serve immediately.

Rice that's to be frozen should be fluffy and not overcooked. Rice is usually frozen in meat, poultry, or fish dishes, as well as in a variety of desserts. Rice can be frozen for 6 to 8 months, so usually the freezing time should be limited by the holding quality of the other ingredients in the rice dish. For suggestions on using leftover rice and noodles, see page 407.

MACARONI, CHEESE, AND TOMATO CASSEROLE

Always a favorite; make this in large quantities to have on hand in the freezer. Some cooks may prefer to omit the tomatoes.

SINGLE RECIPE
> *Time: 20 minutes*
> *Yield: Approximately 3 quarts*

One 8-ounce package macaroni, cooked
3 tablespoons shortening
3 tablespoons flour
1 to 1½ cups milk
1 teaspoon salt
Freshly ground pepper to taste
1 tablespoon prepared mustard
1 tablespoon Worcestershire sauce

2 dashes Tabasco sauce
1 pound sharp Cheddar cheese
  or
½ pound sharp Cheddar cheese and
  ½ pound American cheese
One 1-pound can stewed tomatoes
Bread crumbs
Butter

DOUBLE RECIPE
Time: 25 minutes
Yield: Approximately 6 quarts

One 16-ounce package macaroni, cooked
¼ cup plus 2 tablespoons shortening
¼ cup plus 2 tablespoons flour
2 to 3 cups milk
2 teaspoons salt
Freshly ground pepper to taste
2 tablespoons prepared mustard
2 tablespoons Worcestershire sauce
4 dashes Tabasco sauce
2 pounds sharp Cheddar cheese
  or
1 pound sharp Cheddar cheese and 1 pound American cheese
Two 1-pound cans stewed tomatoes
Bread crumbs
Butter

Cook macaroni several minutes less than the directions call for on the package. In a large skillet, melt shortening and add flour; stir until you have a smooth paste. Add all the milk and seasonings, stirring constantly, until sauce is smooth and thick. Now lower heat and slice ½ pound of the cheese (for single recipe) into the sauce. Continue cooking over low heat, until cheese is completely melted. Meanwhile, butter casseroles. Put 1 layer of macaroni on bottom and cover with slices of cheese and then some tomatoes. Spoon cheese sauce generously over the macaroni and repeat layering until all the ingredients have been used. Top each casserole generously with bread crumbs and dot with butter. Bake in a preheated oven at 375° F for 30 minutes. Bread-crumb crust should be nicely browned and the macaroni and cheese should be bubbly. Serve immediately.

TO FREEZE. Freezer-wrap casseroles before baking, label, date, and freeze (see page 367).

 TO SERVE WHEN FROZEN. Bake frozen casserole in a preheated 375° F oven for 45 to 60 minutes, depending on the size of casserole. Bread-crumb crust should be nicely browned and cheese sauce bubbly underneath.

VARIATION. For a single recipe, 1 to 1½ pounds of ground beef, browned, may be added.

TWO-LAYER ITALIAN MACARONI

This is an interesting variation on the usual macaroni and cheese casseroles.

SINGLE RECIPE
Time: 20 minutes
Yield: 8 servings

DOUBLE RECIPE
Time: 25 minutes
Yield: 16 servings

¼ cup butter	½ cup butter
½ cup chopped onions	1 cup chopped onions
½ cup chopped celery	1 cup chopped celery
1 minced clove garlic	2 minced cloves garlic
3½ cups water	7 cups water
One 6-ounce can tomato paste	Two 6-ounce cans tomato paste
½ pound macaroni	1 pound macaroni
2 teaspoons salt	1 tablespoon plus 1 teaspoon salt
1 teaspoon sugar	2 teaspoons sugar
¼ teaspoon savory	½ teaspoon savory
⅛ teaspoon marjoram	¼ teaspoon marjoram
½ cup chopped parsley	1 cup chopped parsley
2 cups cream-style cottage cheese	4 cups cream-style cottage cheese
½ cup grated Parmesan cheese	1 cup grated Parmesan cheese

In a large skillet, melt butter; sauté onion, celery, and garlic until onion is transparent. Stir in water, tomato paste, macaroni, salt, sugar, savory, and marjoram. Cover and simmer for about 25 minutes, stirring occasionally. Stir in parsley. Turn half this mixture into a buttered 1½-quart casserole or baking dish. Top with half of the cottage cheese and sprinkle on half of the Parmesan cheese. Repeat this process, ending with the Parmesan cheese. Bake for 20 minutes in a preheated 350° F oven, or until bubbly.

TO FREEZE. Freezer-wrap baking dish or casserole before baking (see page 367). Date, label, and freeze.

TO SERVE WHEN FROZEN. Put frozen casserole in preheated oven at 350° F for about 45 minutes, depending on size of dish. Serve when hot and bubbly.

RITA'S NOODLE RING

For a change of pace, try this delicious noodle ring. Make several at a time, because they freeze well. If you don't have a ring mold (or several, when you are making this in quantity for freezing), other molds may be used, provided the capacity is about 6 to 8 cups. An 8-cup mold will hold a whole pound of noodles.

SINGLE RECIPE
Time: 15 minutes
Yield: One 6 to 8-cup mold

4 tablespoons butter
½ pound brown sugar (1 cup plus 2 tablespoons firmly packed)
½ pound whole pecans
¾ to 1 pound cooked egg noodles
2 eggs
⅔ cup melted butter
⅓ cup sugar, or less if desired
¼ teaspoon cinnamon

DOUBLE RECIPE
Time: 17 minutes
Yield: 12 to 16 cups

¼ pound butter
1 pound brown sugar
1 pound (2 cups) whole pecans
1½ to 2 pounds cooked egg noodles
4 eggs
1⅓ cups melted butter
⅔ cup sugar, or less if desired
½ teaspoon cinnamon

Melt butter in bottom of a 6 or 8-cup ring mold. Add brown sugar and mix evenly in bottom of mold. Add pecans and arrange generously. Use just enough pecans to make an attractive arrangement. Drain cooked noodles and combine with beaten eggs and butter, until butter is melted. Add sugar and cinnamon. Pour into mold and bake at 350° F for 50 to 60 minutes. Unmold on serving platter and serve immediately.

TO FREEZE. Freezer-wrap unbaked mold, label, date, and freeze.

TO SERVE WHEN FROZEN. Bake frozen mold at 350° F for 1 hour and 20 minutes (less time if partially thawed). Unmold and serve.

NOODLE NESTS

This is an excellent way to use egg whites. Make these nests in quantity to have on hand for creamed foods, such as Chicken à La King, (page 352), creamed chipped beef, and Chicken à La Briar (page 348).

SINGLE RECIPE
Time: 10 minutes
Yield: 6 nests

¾ cup egg whites
½ teaspoon salt
½ teaspoon cream of tartar
Two 3-ounce cans Chinese noodles

DOUBLE RECIPE
Time: 15 minutes
Yield: 12 nests

1½ cups egg whites
1 teaspoon salt
1 teaspoon cream of tartar
Four 3-ounce cans Chinese noodles

Preheat oven to 425° F. Thaw egg whites until they reach room temperature. Beat until frothy and then add cream of tartar. Continue beating at high speed until soft peaks form when the beater is raised. Add salt and beat a little more. Then gently fold in Chinese noodles. On a well-greased baking sheet, drop noodle mixture, using about ⅔ cup for each nest. With back of spoon, shape into nests. Bake 10 to 12 minutes, or until nicely browned.

TO FREEZE. Leave nests on baking sheets and set in freezer. When they are frozen, pack into freezer bags or other containers and return to freezer, labeled and dated.

TO SERVE WHEN FROZEN. Bake in a preheated oven at 350° F for about 5 minutes, or until nicely warmed.

RICE

Because rice is so simple to prepare, there's no need to freeze it as a timesaving device. However, leftover rice freezes very well and can be used for such dishes as stuffing, Rice Pudding (page 247), Marie's Rice Pancakes (page 125), Cantonese Fried Rice (page 407), and Marie's Crispy Crunchy Rice (page 408).

Plain cooked rice is best reserved for the recipes mentioned above. Seasoned rice is good for any number of dishes and, once you get into the habit of cooking rice in chicken stock, beef broth, tomato soup, et cetera, you'll wonder why you've been cooking it in plain salted water all these years. The flavor is incomparable. You may find it advantageous to cook this type of rice in large quantities for future use.

TO FREEZE. Freeze rice in meal-sized portions. It's easiest when spooned into freezing cartons. However, you may prefer to freeze it in an aluminum-lined casserole dish (see page 367). Seal, date, label, and freeze. If you're freezing flavored rice or rice that has been cooked in broth, be sure to indicate the flavor on the label. Rice keeps well for 6 to 8 months at 0° F.

TO SERVE WHEN FROZEN. Thaw. Spread in a single layer on shallow pan or cookie sheet. Heat in preheated 375° F oven for about 5 minutes, or until rice is warmed through. Serve immediately.

CANTONESE FRIED RICE

Delicious anytime, but especially when served with the traditional Oriental Sweet-Sour Pork (see page 296). You may want to add chicken, shrimp, and/or lobster to the fried rice and make it a one-dish meal. Good no matter how you serve it. In fact, this is a perfect leftover meal; simply add anything you have—chicken, beef, pork, and so on.

Time: About 12 minutes
Yield: 8 servings

3 tablespoons bacon drippings or
    other shortening
¼ cup snipped green onions
¼ cup coarsely snipped parsley
1 cup diced celery
One 4½-ounce jar or can sliced
    mushrooms

3 cups rice cooked in chicken broth
2 tablespoons toasted sesame seeds
2 tablespoons soy sauce
2 slightly beaten eggs
⅔ cup crumbled bacon (see page 41)
    or
12 slices crisp bacon, crumbled

If you don't have any chicken broth in your freezer (see page 341), you may use bouillon or beef broth. If your chicken broth hasn't been seasoned, add 3 beef bouillon cubes or 3 teaspoons granules for fuller flavor and for salt. (See page 41 for salting foods with bouillon cubes or granules.)

To toast sesame seeds, bake in a shallow pan at 425° F for about 4 to 5 minutes. If you wish, you may substitute toasted blanched slivered almonds that have been chopped.

In a large skillet, heat shortening and add onions and celery. Cook rapidly for about 3 minutes, stirring constantly. Add mushrooms and parsley and continue cooking for another minute. Add rice and sesame seeds and mix well. Continue cooking for another minute or two, until rice is heated through. Meanwhile, combine eggs and soy sauce, beating slightly. Add to rice mixture and cook until the eggs are set. Add crumbled bacon and serve immediately with additional soy sauce, if desired.

MARIE'S CRISPY CRUNCHY RICE

This is a marvelous dish to serve as a potato substitute. Because of all the vegetables in it, you won't need much else—perhaps just a salad. Don't be surprised if it disappears in a wink; it's so good you'll need to make an ample amount. A fine way to use leftover and frozen rice.

SINGLE RECIPE
Time: 7 minutes
Yield: About 2 cups

⅓ cup rice
⅔ cup seasoned broth
    or
1 cup rice that has been cooked in
    broth
¼ cup finely chopped carrots
¼ cup chopped celery

DOUBLE RECIPE
Time: 10 minutes
Yield: About 4 cups

⅔ cup rice
1⅓ cups seasoned broth
    or
2 cups rice that has been cooked in
    broth
½ cup finely chopped carrots
½ cup chopped celery

¼ cup snipped parsley	½ cup snipped parsley
⅓ cup snipped green onion	⅔ cup snipped green onion
¼ cup chopped blanched almonds	½ cup chopped blanched almonds

When you are using chicken broth that has not been salted, add 1 beef bouillon cube or 1 teaspoon granules for each cup of broth. This gives the rice a deep brown color and a rich flavor.

Cook rice in broth until it's light and fluffy. If you are using frozen rice, heat through (see page 407). Add all the other ingredients at one time and mix well. Continue cooking over very low heat for about 5 minutes. Serve immediately. Vegetables should only be heated, not cooked. This gives the rice a fine crunchy texture.

Index

✳✳✳✳✳✳✳✳✳✳✳✳✳✳✳✳✳✳✳✳✳✳✳✳✳✳✳✳✳✳